Free, Prior, and Informed Consent: A Critical Analysis through the Eyes of Courts

International Studies in Human Rights

VOLUME 153

The titles published in this series are listed at *brill.com/ishr*

Free, Prior, and Informed Consent: A Critical Analysis through the Eyes of Courts

By

Bertus de Villiers

BRILL | NIJHOFF

ISSN 0924-4751
ISBN 978-90-04-72478-5
ISBN 978-90-04-72479-2 (PDF)
DOI https://doi.org/10.1163/9789004724792

Library of Congress Control Number: 2026948466

Brill Nijhoff and Koninklijke Brill BV are part of De Gruyter Brill.
www.degruyterbrill.com

Questions about General Product Safety Regulation: productsafety@degruyterbrill.com

Contents

Dedication

I have negotiated with and represented Indigenous Peoples as a legal advisor, witnessing the inherent power imbalances they experience first-hand. I have also seen the goodwill that exists yet often goes unacknowledged and unreported where indigenous and non-indigenous interests reach agreement. As a legal advisor to South African National Parks, I negotiated on behalf of the state with tribal and indigenous communities, particularly in matters relating to land claims in national parks and commercialisation opportunities and use of natural resources within national parks. These negotiations necessitated striking a balance between preserving South Africa's conservation estate and recognising that many national parks lie on the ancestral lands of indigenous communities. One especially significant case involved the Kgalagadi Peace Park, where negotiations were held with the Khoisan people, who regard themselves as the true and only Indigenous People of southern Africa (De Villiers, 1998). Having had many of their traditional lands usurped by other interests, the Kalahari Desert remains one of the few places the Khoisan can still claim part of their ancestral territory (De Villiers, 2008). Seeing them return to a part of the Kgalagadi Peace Park filled me with jubilation. Another highlight of my experience was my involvement in negotiating the Makuleke agreement – between the Makuleke community, the South African government, and South African National Parks – which returned ownership of the northern part of the Kruger National Park to the Makuleke community while allowing the land to continue being used for conservation and eco- and cultural tourism. At the time, the Makuleke agreement was described as groundbreaking, demonstrating that a win-win outcome is possible even in very challenging and adversarial circumstances (De Villiers, 1999). The Makuleke agreement has become a practical embodiment of what is nowadays referred to as the effort to achieve free, prior and informed consent, resulting in one of the most extensively cited and widely studied community-conservation-tourism partnerships in Africa (De Villiers, 2023c).

Later, as a legal advisor to Aboriginal communities in the Goldfields of Western Australia, I witnessed the challenges traditional landowners face when dealing with adversarial governments and aggressive mining companies. Although the statutory framework, called the Native Title Act, promoted 'good faith' negotiations at law, in practice the odds were (and remain) heavily stacked against the traditional landowners. Small breakthroughs and concessions were celebrated with delight by people who had resided on these lands for countless generations, but now had to fight for every protective measure.

I also observed first-hand how non-indigenous interests sometimes sought to use indigenous communities for their own benefit, leading to a form of neo-colonialism in which indigenous voices were seemingly co-opted to advance the agendas of others. The notion of free, prior, and informed consent (FPIC) felt light-years removed from the practical realities of the Australian bush.

In the arid outback of Kalgoorlie and its surrounds, negotiations were harsh – on a playing field that was anything but level. As a legal representative, it was difficult to explain to hopeful Elders the realities of a legal system that appeared biased, negotiation processes that were far from ideal, the elasticity of the term 'good faith' that allowed for broad discretion, the frequent prioritisation of public over indigenous interests, and the hard truth that some form of agreement may sometimes be better than none. Perhaps most disheartening was the risk that an indigenous community's participation in negotiations could confer legitimacy and credibility on a system that often offered them few or no tangible results. I often envied – but also viewed with some cynicism – those in academic and policy circles who espoused lofty ideals, positions, and assurances about the meaning of FPIC as though it were a truly justiciable right or a veto power. That kind of lecture-room assurances rarely carries weight at real-world negotiation tables or in litigation in courts.

Yet, despite this harsh negotiation environment, the highlight for me in the Goldfields was witnessing the evolution of native title – from its portrayal in the 1990s as a threat to the state, to mining interests, and to farmers – to its current standing as sound public policy, good business practice, and a legitimate reflection of public interest. Many mining companies and indigenous interests now rush to the media to share another story of cooperation and partnership. Native title, once the subject of front-page controversy in the mid-1990s, has largely receded from the headlines. In this respect, Australia deserves more credit for the progress made since 1992 than it receives.

I dedicate this book to the Makuleke and Khoisan people of South Africa, and the Aboriginal people of the Goldfields of Australia. It was an honour to share a small part of their journey. The generation of Aboriginal Elders with whom I worked is now passing on, which fills me with deep sadness. I spent only a brief moment in time with them – gaining a glimpse into their dreams and aspirations, assisting in their efforts to secure a better deal, and witnessing their determination to protect their traditional lands. I listened to their ancestral stories and helped convey those stories to courts and policy-makers (De Villiers, 2004). I had the privilege of spending time in the bush with them, writing down their witness statements, and seeing how they come alive on their ancestral land. I sat beneath the night sky while camping and heard stories that, until recently, had never reached white ears. I listened as they sang the songs of an ancient waterhole, or tell in reverence the story of how a hill or a rocky outcrop was created.

In this book, I am critical of the assurances given by advocates to Indigenous Peoples that FPIC requires their actual consent before their ancestral lands can be accessed. While the advocates' intentions are mostly sincere, legally baseless promises of a veto or co-decision-making often leave Indigenous Peoples despondent and disillusioned. Presenting FPIC as a justiciable right of veto creates expectations that cannot be fulfilled under domestic laws. In my profession and experience, I have learned that the most valuable service I as lawyer can offer a client is honesty, not advocacy. Understanding one's true legal position is the first step toward knowing where improvements can be sought, what can be meaningfully advocated for, and when a deal should be clinched. Blurring the line between advice and advocacy often leads to disappointment, disillusionment, and resentment.

In my view, FPIC is not a justiciable legal norm in either international law or customary international law. It is neither adequately practiced nor legislated for the term to have a co-decision-making, legal bearing on the conduct of negotiations or judicial findings under municipal law. FPIC as an aspirational norm does not grant indigenous communities a legal veto over what happens on their lands under municipal law. To suggest otherwise risks doing a disservice to such communities by creating expectations that cannot be legally sustained.

Nonetheless, I propose that FPIC can serve as a normative instrument to improve policies, interpret statutes, expand rights, modernise practices, and bring about greater social justice. The concept of FPIC and the debates arising from it have contributed immeasurably to better understandings of the practical requirements for good faith consultation. FPIC has become a *grundnorm* that reflects the aspirations of self-determination and co-decision-making of indigenous people.

FPIC is more than a purported right – it represents a new philosophy for indigenous engagement. As such, it may ultimately prove even stronger, broader in scope, and more enduring than a legal entitlement.

I hope readers of this book will find my assessments plausible, my criticisms credible, and my proposals thought-provoking. I will be criticised by some for the honest assessment I give of the weak legal status of FPIC, but hopefully critics will also credit me for proposing that FPIC can become a norm with wider inspirational and philosophical value as a mere legal principle.

A book is the product of a team, with many people working behind the scenes to bring it to life. However, only the author is credited (and criticised). I would therefore like to express my deepest appreciation to Brill as the publisher; to the Alexander von Humboldt Foundation, for their support of my research endeavours for more than 35 years; and to the library staff at the universities of Johannesburg and Curtin, as well as the Max Planck Institute for Comparative International Law in Heidelberg, and finally to the editing team. The value of dedicated and enthusiastic library staff, especially in this era of self-service, cannot be overstated. I thank them all.

My wife, Corrien, has shared my research and advisory journey, enduring my enthusiasm, successes, frustrations, and disappointments – the latter perhaps more than the former. Yet, her support has never wavered. Without her, none of what is written here would have been possible, as she is the one who inspires and encourages me. Together, we had the privilege of camping with Elder Rita Elliott, learning much from her and her family. How sweet were the honey ants they dug up from metres underground in the hot desert sun, and how delicious was the damper baked in the fire under the starry night. How inspirational to sing Christian hymns with them, while at the same time listening to their Dreamtime stories. Never have I felt so close to eternity with its complexity and simplicity as when hearing them sing mission-hymns, while at the same time respecting their ancestral creator-beings.

Dankie vir jou Corrien. Jy was, en is, en sal vir altyd my alles wees.

Bertus de Villiers
June 2026

Abbreviations

ACHR	American Convention on Human Rights
ACMC	Aboriginal Cultural Materials Committee
African Charter	African Charter on Human and Peoples' Rights
AIATSIS	Australian Institute of Aboriginal and Torres Strait Islander Studies
CERD	Committee on the Elimination of Racial Discrimination
CIL	Customary International Law
CRC	Committee on the Rights of the Child
Declaration on Minorities	United Nations Declaration on the Rights of Persons Belonging to National, Ethnic, Religious and Linguistic Minorities
ECtHR	European Court of Human Rights
ECOSOC	UN Economic and Social Council
FCNM	Framework Convention for the Protection of National Minorities
FPIC	Free, Prior, and Informed Consent
FAO	Food and Agriculture Organization of the United Nations
IACHR	Inter-American Commission on Human Rights
IACrtHR	Inter-American Court of Human Rights
ICESCR	International Covenant on Economic, Social and Cultural Rights
ICCPR	International Covenant on Civil and Political Rights
ICJ	International Court of Justice
ILO	International Labour Organization
ILO 169	Indigenous and Tribal Peoples Convention, 1989 (No 169)
ITPC	Indigenous and Tribal Populations Convention 107 of 1957
ILO MNE Declaration	Tripartite Declaration of Principles concerning Multinational Enterprises and Social Policy
NNTT	National Native Title Tribunal
NCP	National Contact Point
OECD	Organisation for Economic Co-operation and Development
OECD Guidelines	OECD Guidelines for Multinational Enterprises
PKKP	Puutu Kunti Kurrama and Pinikura Peoples
RSPO	Roundtable on Sustainable Palm Oil
UNDRIP	United Nations Declaration of the Rights of Indigenous Peoples
UNGPs	UN Guiding Principles on Business and Human Rights
UNPFII	United Nations Permanent Forum on Indigenous Issues
VCLT	UN Guiding Principles on Business and Human Rights
WGIP	Working Group on Indigenous Rights

Outline

The term free, prior, and informed consent (FPIC) has become a call to action for Indigenous People – an anthem, a vision, an aspiration, an inspiration, even a quasi-ideology. At law, the concept of 'informed consent' is not new, but 'free, prior and informed consent' is arguably the most frequently invoked expression in the pursuit of the recognition and protection of indigenous rights in general and their right to self-determination in particular.

FPIC is not intended to be limited to obtaining approval for access to indigenous customary lands; it is also sought by advocates to be applied more broadly in relation to legislation, policies, and administrative acts that may directly affect indigenous communities. These include environment-related and socio-economic polices concerning housing, education, health, and criminal justice. Note in this respect legislative amendments in Finland in 2025 according to which the obligation to negotiate with the Sámi Parliament about measures affecting the Sámi homeland or if measures 'particularly impact' the Sámi language or culture, the status of the Sámi as indigenous people in respect of areas such as land use, conservation, mining, climate change, childhood education, health and social services (Sámi Parliament as amended, 2025, sec. 9). However in the Pabai case, the Australian Federal Court declared firstly that the government did not have a duty of care towards Indigenous People in respect of their lands being impacted by climate change, the manner how global warming is impacting on their lands, and that emissions reductions in response to climate change were part of the 'policy' options of government that was not subject to judicial review based on a lack of consultation (Pabai case, 2025). The Court acknowledged that it may not be easy to distinguish between policy and operational decisions:

> Courts continue to recognise that it is or may be inappropriate to recognise or impose a duty of care on the government or public authorities in respect of some categories of government conduct which involves policy or politics. The vexing question is how to delineate or identify those categories of conduct. (Pabai case, 2025, para. 112)

In short, FPIC embodies the demand of Indigenous Peoples for special consultation and co-governance rights regarding policies and actions in the widest sense that affect them collectively as a people as well as their traditional lands. But governments and courts have been reluctant to expand FPIC outside the domain of traditional lands.

FPIC reflects the philosophy of accommodating the collective rights of Indigenous Peoples to self-determination by recognising their distinct status as a community, rather than by assimilating them solely through individual rights that seek to integrate their interests into those of the general population. Other claimed collective rights naturally follow from FPIC, such as autonomy, power-sharing, self-government, treaty, truth-telling, and reconciliation.

The obvious question for purposes of this book is: what does mean FPIC at law?

This is where the discussions, disagreements, and disappointments, begin. This book seeks to investigate, analyse, and comment on these ongoing developments in courts. There are many claims, propositions, and assertions in literature, policy materials and public statements about the purported meaning of FPIC, but ultimately it remains a term undefined in international law, characterised and shaped by advocacy and disagreement, without legal clarity or certainty at either the international or domestic level.

This book examines how courts interpret FPIC, how they give content to the principles of good faith consultation, and the practical standards required by courts to effective and meaningful indigenous participation. I am keenly aware of the constraints to compare judgements from different jurisdictions, but I am equally aware of the utility to identify common trends in judicial reasoning.

Some advocates argue that FPIC implies a legal entitlement in international law to a veto that can be exercised by an indigenous group. Others reject this interpretation of FPIC, asserting that the term is aspirational, to be approached as a social directive, a value-based principle, an ideal, or a promissory statement, rather than a justiciable right. They contend that FPIC is about striving for consent, not mandating a legal obligation to obtain it. They also stress that the ultimate authority over land access policies and broader socio-economic decisions rests with the state and its regulatory and consultation processes.

FPIC does not imply that the state has delegated or abdicated its decision-making authority to an indigenous community. While the state may take indigenous and public interests into consideration in its decision-making, the state retains ultimate authority for policy, administrative, and regulatory processes and approvals. An indigenous community can only exercise a veto if and when domestic legislation explicitly grants it such a right. Otherwise, FPIC, as outlined in international instruments such as the United Nations Declaration of the Rights of Indigenous Peoples (UNDRIP) and Indigenous and Tribal Peoples Convention, 1989 (No 169) (ILO 169), is not legally enforceable in domestic law and does not grant an indigenous community a right of veto in domestic settings.

It is furthermore suggested that FPIC arises from the right of Indigenous Peoples to self-determination. While this may be the case in a philosophical sense, self-determination itself remains legally undefined and is invoked in various contexts, including individual rights, collective cultural rights, minority rights, sovereign state rights, and the rights of colonies and settler communities. Self-determination is not a term of law to be applied solely to indigenous rights.

An undefined term such as self-determination giving rise to another undefined term like FPIC to be exercised by an undefined entity called Indigenous People, does little to enhance legal certainty in domestic law. From a legal perspective, this means the legal subject, legal object, and legal remedy remain undefined.

Literature is saturated with scholarly works exploring the meaning, scope, and application of FPIC. Many scientific publications take a normative social sciences approach, offering descriptive accounts of reasonable steps of what ought to comply with FPIC. However, from a legal sciences viewpoint, the normative standards suggested for FPIC as it appears in international law and municipal law remains largely unclear and undefined. The term 'consent' in particular creates an expectation of veto if taken in its ordinary meaning, but this is not supported by jurisprudence in international expert bodies or domestic courts.

As a legal practitioner and member of a judiciary, I am particularly curious about how courts interpret FPIC, particularly in respect of its normative effect and practical benchmarks in domestic settings. Having served as a legal advisor to indigenous communities, I know that for them, a single authoritative court judgement in a domestic setting ultimately carries more weight than a raft of scientific opinions or advocacy efforts in international fora. Courts can provide clarity, shift boundaries even if only slightly, imply rights, and set precedents. My interest, therefore, is to gain insight into how courts in different jurisdictions – in international and domestic law – approach FPIC. When courts make reference to FPIC, it is often in the context of parties striving towards an agreed outcome, and it is frequently used interchangeably with good faith consultation.

Good faith consultation is a well-established principle across various legal fields such as medical law, administrative law, and contract law. However, few judgements explicitly dissect FPIC as a distinct embodiment of indigenous rights, and even fewer suggest FPIC implies a legal veto under common law, civil law, or international law. Courts typically focus on process of consultation, reasonable steps to accommodate and involve, and material opportunities for Indigenous People to be heard and to effectively participate, as opposed to a right of veto where the indigenous community rather than the state is the final decision-maker.

There is a particular focus in the book on whether courts rely on the term FPIC to resolve disputes, or whether courts cite FPIC in passing as part of a broader process of good faith consultation and recognition of aspirational rights, without implying a right of veto. Where judgements do refer to FPIC, I attempt to determine the meaning ascribed to the term – in particular whether it is seen as a veto or used to describe good faith consultation in substance.

Comparative jurisprudence on FPIC presents its own complexities, as its application depends substantially on municipal legal provisions, political culture, other policy arrangements relating to Indigenous People, a country's recognition of international instruments, and the extent to which international law is codified into domestic law. Any claim about the 'universality' of FPIC as a legal norm should, therefore, be approached with caution, until or unless the specific domestic legal contexts in which it is used are considered and any definitional challenges are addressed.

Despite its legal limitations, FPIC has been a game-changing and transformative concept. It embodies the aspirations of Indigenous People in respect of self-determination, autonomy, co-decision-making, and consultation. Its influence has spread from international organisations such as the UN and ILO to civil society, including the World Bank, OECD, auditing standards, shareholder meetings, insurance standards, and funding conditions imposed by banks. It appears in multiple declarations, protocols, policy statements, and objectives. FPIC has set the stage for indigenous involvement, introducing a philosophy that acknowledges Indigenous Peoples, practical steps that involve them in decision-making, recognition of their individual and collective rights, and promotion of their fair treatment.

In this book, I attempt to dissect FPIC principally by jurisprudential analysis. Chapter 1 examines the context in which FPIC is used. Chapter 2 explores the distinction between indigenous and minority rights, questioning whether the differing approaches stem from principle or effective advocacy. Chapter 3 delves into the conception and emergence of FPIC, the circumstances that have given rise to its prominence, and the ongoing definitional challenges that limit its application as a legal term. Chapter 4 analyses jurisprudence in international law to assess the assertion that FPIC has become – or is on its way to becoming – a justiciable right in customary international law. Chapter 5 takes a broader perspective, discussing FPIC in the context of being more akin to a directive principle of state policy rather than a legally enforceable right. Chapter 6 reflects on the domestic application of good faith negotiations and the legally endorsed practical measures that satisfy the requirements of good faith consultation. Chapter 7 takes a bird's-eye view of international case law in which FPIC has been referenced, aiming to distil its legal significance. Chapter 8 investigates how the private sector, through self-regulation and cooperation with states, has sought to better address indigenous rights, with a specific focus on and discussion of the OECD's National Contact Points. Chapter 9 revisits the Juukan Gorge debacle in Australia, discussing how, at a practical level, failures in approval processes can occur despite commitments to FPIC, and proposing practical measures to prevent similar incidents. Finally, Chapter 10 consolidates international jurisprudence to identify legal benchmarks of universal relevance concerning FPIC and good faith consultation.

CHAPTER 1

The Context of Free, Prior, and Informed Consent

1 Introduction

The term 'free, prior, and informed consent' (FPIC) has emerged as a rallying cry representing the collective desire of Indigenous Peoples to be effectively consulted and involved in decision-making about matters affecting them. FPIC is a practical embodiment of the right to self-determination of Indigenous People (Martin, 2025). Many indigenous groups invoke FPIC in pursuit of joint decision-making, power-sharing, autonomy, as well as a form of veto. However, the term lacks the clarity of legal definition (De Villiers, 2023d, p. 101). Instead, it embodies simultaneously a desire, an objective, a legal demand, a purported right, a doctrine, a philosophy, a code of conduct, and sometimes even a quasi-ideology.[1] In the Community Garifuna of San Juan case arising from the Honduras, the Court described the object of FPIC as follows:

> This entails the obligation of States to ensure that indigenous and tribal peoples participate in measures that may affect their rights, especially their right to communal property, in accordance with their values, customs and forms of organization. (Community Garifuna of San Juan case, 2023, para. 119)

The meaning often attributed to FPIC by international bodies, social scientists and advocates – implying a right of veto – does not align with judicial interpretation. Courts, both international and domestic, do not typically distinguish between 'consultation' and FPIC unless domestic law explicitly refers to FPIC, and even then, its substance mirrors the principles of good faith consultation. There is an advocacy element of FPIC, suggested to imply a right of veto, that has not (yet) been widely adopted as a legal entitlement by municipal jurisprudence. The normative advances in international forums in respect of operationalising FPIC have not had the follow through in domes-

1 Mathiba refers to those who do not support an actual veto in the context of FPIC as the 'anti-FPIC movement' (Mathiba, 2024, p. 332). Mathiba is of the opinion that consent as used in FPIC should be taken at its ordinary, plain meaning, namely that approval is required. However, in the same breath, Mathiba speaks about the requirement that FPIC give Indigenous communities 'the power to participate in and influence decisions' (Mathiba, 2024, p. 335) – a standard that falls short of a controlling veto or co-decision-making role.

HTTPS://DOI.ORG/10.1163/9789004724792-002

tic systems (Yakovleva, Gavrilyeva and Makarov, 2023). For example, in the case of ASEAN countries it has been found that FPIC 'remains a regime of unfulfilled promises' (Hassan, Nordin and Wook, 2025).

The discourse surrounding FPIC has, however, contributed to greater judicial, policy, administrative, and practitioner awareness, shaping the development of good faith consultation requirements. Nevertheless, its application remains complicated by unresolved questions: Who qualifies as 'Indigenous People'? What are the jurisdictional areas to which FPIC applies? And does 'consent' legally imply a veto, or something less? Notably, FPIC is sometimes also invoked when referring to the consultation rights of local communities more broadly, such as in planning processes, rather than being exclusive to the domain of indigenous rights. FPIC has therefore become a phrase that signifies public involvement in the process of decision-making.

There is no agreed definition of Indigenous People in international law, and I do not propose to develop to develop a definition in this book. It is left to self-definition and for states to determine whether a community in its population is regarded as 'indigenous'. The African Commission on Human and Peoples' Rights through its Working Group on Indigenous Populations/Communities suggested three criteria for identification of indigenous people: self-identification based on community values and tradition; special association with ancestral lands; and some form of marginalisation (African Advisory Opinion, 2007). Importantly, there is no 'minority' test by reference to the numerical size of a community.

The following useful working definition of Indigenous People was proposed by José R. Martínez Cobo, Special Rapporteur of the Sub-Commission on Prevention of Discrimination and Protection of Minorities:

> Indigenous communities, peoples and nations are those which, having a historical continuity with pre-invasion and pre-colonial societies that developed on their territories, consider themselves distinct from other sectors of the societies now prevailing on those territories, or parts of them. They form at present non-dominant sectors of society and are determined to preserve, develop and transmit to future generations their ancestral territories, and their ethnic identity, as a basis of their continued existence as peoples, in accordance with their own cultural patterns, social institutions and legal system. (Cobo, 1986, p. 12)

It is not surprising that the protection of indigenous rights has been described as 'problematic' since so many aspects of international indigenous rights instruments require clarification (Toki and Raman, 2024, p. 2). Although it is said that FPIC originated from the self-determination provisions of articles 1 of the ICCPR and the ICESC, the right of self-determination is also claimed by sovereign nations, ethnocultural minorities, subjugated peoples, and individuals. The meaning of self-determination is therefore determined in the context of its use. In particular, the implementation of FPIC has been described as an 'implementation paradox' due to the 'highly ambiguous' interpretation of the protections it entails and the contrast between aspiration and practice (Flemmer, 2022). It is acknowledged that an 'implementation gap' often exists between international norms, particularly in soft law, and municipal practice (Wright and Tomaselli, 2019). The implementation gap is exacerbated by a lack of consensus on the meaning of FPIC, whether it constitutes a justiciable right distinct from consultation, its scope of application, the mechanisms for its implementation, and the sanctions for non-compliance (Lizarazo-Rodriguez and De Lombaerde, 2025).

Notably, FPIC can overlap with other land-access approval processes, such as environmental impact assessments and indigenous heritage protection arrangements, and this may add – rather than reduce – complexity in considering and assessing development proposals (Giupponi, 2018, p. 487). For example, should an FPIC process involving Indigenous People be separate from other community consultation, or can it be part of general community consultation? Note, in this respect, the Sipakapense case in which Guatemala argued that it had fulfilled its consultation obligations with the indigenous community within the context of environmental impact assessment processes (Communities of the Sipakapense case 2014). In the Community Garifuna of San Juan case the Court emphasised the importance of consultation with Indigenous People in respect of their traditional lands by stating that FPIC is required '(w)ith specific regard to the right to collective property, States must guarantee the rights to consultation and to participation in any project or measure that may affect the *territory* of an indigenous or tribal community or other rights that are essential for their survival as a people' (emphasis added) (Community Garifuna of San Juan case, 2023, para. 144).

FPIC reflects an awareness that indigenous communities warrant special consideration when governments or private entities contemplate measures that could adversely affect their interests.[2] FPIC has been called the 'gold

2 A question arises as to who the party is expected to comply with the obligations of FPIC – the state, the entity seeking access to land, or both? (Tomlinson, 2019) The answer is arguably nuanced since the state, as the regulatory authority that issues approvals, is required to ensure that obligations under international and municipal law are satisfied. However, the proponent of a development must also, as a condition for approval, satisfy the statutory and administrative conditions of FPIC to the extent this is required by domestic regulations. Domestic law is the principal source to ascertain the scope of consultation obligations. A

standard' for engagement with indigenous communities (Zillmann and Moffatt, 2025). This elevated status of Indigenous People as a special group requiring consultation arises from their ongoing adherence to and practice of customary legal systems, principally in relation to traditionally held lands and associated activities such as hunting, fishing, and resource management (Mahuika case, 2000, para. 8.2).

In a broader context, FPIC reflects the recognition that modern liberal democratic states must respond more effectively to the plurality of their populations, particularly in their interactions with Indigenous Peoples. FPIC coincides with the growing focus on legal pluralism and respect for population diversity, which seek to preserve non-state legal systems (De Villiers, 2025e, p. 267).

This book cites numerous examples where courts and other expert bodies have intervened in the approvals processes of projects on the basis of insufficient consultation with Indigenous People. The obligations associated with FPIC extend beyond state institutions to include non-state entities whose activities may affect the rights and interests of Indigenous Peoples. There is, however, a lack of consistency in the application of FPIC in international law or municipal law, such as whether it applies solely to major developments affecting traditional lands or also to other socio-economic measures impacting Indigenous Peoples. In the African Commission on Human Rights and Peoples' Rights case the African Court on Human and Peoples' Rights emphasised the connection of an indigenous community to traditional lands prior to other settlers (African Commission on Human Rights and Peoples' Rights case, 2017, para. 107). This emphasises the traditional-land connection of FPIC.

FPIC is in many respects a rallying call, the specifics of which are determined by the statutory framework, policies, and administrative arrangements of each state (Tomaselli, 2016). The UNDRIP, in effect, distinguishes between two types of duties: the first relates to provisions that prohibit states from carrying out specific acts without indigenous consent, while the second concerns provisions requiring states to consult Indigenous Peoples with the view to obtain their consent before implementing measures. But account must be taken that both categories of duties do not contain any legal force but is rather regarded as soft law or, as I propose later in this book, directive principles of policy.

---

government that approves a measure for which proper authorisation has not been obtained risks facing a compensation claim (Timber Creek High Court appeal, 2019). Should the state override the indigenous interests, it must be satisfied about the 'necessity and proportionality' of the approved measure (Mahuika case, 2000, para. 8.1).

International soft (non-binding) law, in which reference is made to FPIC, may influence the way courts and expert bodies interpret and expand individual rights, even if FPIC is not in itself justiciable (Tiina Sanila-Aikio case, 2018). FPIC holds some level of 'legal significance' although it does not at law entail co-decision-making or a veto (Ravna, 2020). In the Canadian Kebaowek case the court emphasised that FPIC, even if enshrined in legislation as the case is with Canada, does not grant a veto power to Indigenous People (Kebaowek First Nation case, 2025, para. 131). FPIC is also not a binding legal norm of customary international law or international treaty law.[3] The nature, scope, and remedies associated with FPIC as a purported norm of international law remain unsettled, particularly in light of Article 38 of the Statute of the International Court of Justice, which defines the sources of international law. Giupponi characterises FPIC as a 'second-order right' (Giupponi, 2018, p. 525), which may be just another way to describe a legally unenforceable aspirational concept.

FPIC is regarded as a guiding standard of soft international law, meaning that while it may not be justiciable, it serves as a tool for policy development, human rights advancement, statutory interpretation, and advocacy. Its enforceability depends largely on a combination of state-based measures, public and shareholder pressure, industry self-regulation, social standards, and judicial declarations. Nevertheless, the philosophy underpinning FPIC has influenced how many states engage with Indigenous Peoples. This is exemplified by the South African Baleni case, in which Justice Basson cited international jurisprudence and literature to demonstrate contemporary international law requirements for consulting Indigenous Peoples when their traditional lands are accessed (Baleni case 2019, paras 78–82). Similarly, in the Fosen case, a Norwegian court linked the protection of indigenous rights to the individual right to culture under international law (Fosen case, 2021). In Australia a review has been conducted to ascertain compliance of the native title regime of the country with the principle of FPIC (Australia Inquiry into UNDRIP, 2023). The reliance on human rights treaties and soft law to assist in the interpretation of domestic rights was endorsed in the Kichwa case, when the court observed that those are 'living instruments' and that their interpretation must 'evolve over time and reflect current living conditions' (Kichwa case, 2012, para. 161).

---

3 Kusniati proposes that 'even though FPIC is an international customary *law*', the right is often breached (emphasis added) (Kusniati, 2024, p. 171). As elaborated on in Chapter 4, I do not agree with the proposition that FPIC is a justiciable right in customary international law.

The universal individualism of international human rights instruments is in some respects challenged by the communalism of FPIC, which recognises that Indigenous Peoples – having collectively endured various historical and ongoing injustices – are entitled to both individual and collective direct participation in matters affecting their interests, in addition to their participation in ordinary election and parliamentary processes (Newman, 2020). In this regard, the Preamble of UNDRIP states:

> Concerned that Indigenous Peoples have suffered from historic injustices as a result of, inter alia, their colonization and dispossession of their lands, territories and resources, thus preventing them from exercising, in particular, their right to development in accordance with their own needs and interests. (UNDRIP, 2007 Preamble)

There is often disagreement over the scope of FPIC's application: Indigenous Peoples generally seek a wider obligation for consultation that is not limited to their traditional lands, while governments aim to narrow the reach of consultation to solely or principally traditional lands. The UN Human Rights Council has observed that 'a number of countries and stakeholders have endorsed a policy not to proceed if Indigenous Peoples withhold consent' (Human Rights Council-FPIC, 2018, para. 28), but this is an unsubstantiated generalisation. Few, if any, countries have in fact enacted in legislation a general veto right for Indigenous Peoples and evidence is abound of projects proceeding regardless of opposition by Indigenous People.

Indigenous Peoples generally cite their political, social and economic marginalisation, as well as protection of their individual rights, such as the rights to property and culture, as rationales for advocating that a broader range of policy measures should fall within the ambit of FPIC. Decision-makers, meanwhile, tend to focus principally on the traditional lands of Indigenous Peoples when determining FPIC obligations.[4] This dichotomy was, for example, highlighted in the 2023 Voice referendum debate in Australia, where deep divisions arose in the lead-up to the referendum over the range of issues the pro-

4 Note, for example, the Tsilhqot'in Nation case, in which the Supreme Court of Canada held that once it has been established that land traditionally belonged to Indigenous People, their consent is required for developments on the land (Tsilhqot'in Nation case, 2014). This seems to highlight the land ownership element of consultation. In the same case, the Court did acknowledge, however, that consent is not an absolute entitlement and may be overridden if the state can demonstrate that it has fulfilled its consultation duties properly and that the objective pursued serves the broader public interest.

posed Voice would address (De Villiers, 2024b).[5] There were concerns by critics that the Voice may demand a broader consultative scope, posing potential risks of racial division in public policy, exploitation of Indigenous Peoples by special interest groups, and the undermining of the sovereign legislative and executive powers of Cabinet and Parliament. Advocates for the Voice argued, however, that the interests of Aboriginal people cannot be reduced solely to their traditional lands, but that their rights to self-determination, to a treaty, and to social justice should be widely interpreted as falling within the scope of the proposed Voice.

The rights arising from FPIC are both restorative and empowering in nature – restorative in addressing past injustices, and empowering in granting enforceable participatory rights in the contemporary environment (Human Rights Council-FPIC, 2018, para. 11).[6] FPIC does not seek to replace general civil, political, economic, and social rights but rather complements them, redressing historical harm and marginalisation and ensuring the recognition of Indigenous Peoples' individual and collective rights in matters that uniquely affect them.

Nonetheless, care must be taken to ensure that recognising the uniqueness of indigenous rights does not lead to a form of administrative *apartheid*, whereby separateness fosters inequality (Brown case, 1954). History shows that what may be seen as collective rights can easily slip into collective discrimination. Note in this respect Mukaddam's concern that legal pluralism, including the recognition of customary law, could become a vehicle for separateness, the erosion of fundamental rights, and endorsement of inequality (Mukaddam, 2024, p. 143). The following, perhaps harsh, example can be used to illustrate this dilemma: in South Africa several young men die yearly as part of initiation practices. For example, in the summer of 2024 around 30 young men died in the Eastern Cape province while undergoing initiation rituals (Dorfling 2024b). If such deaths were to occur as part of a sporting event, a political demonstration, or recreational activities, it would cause a public outcry, but because those young men die pursuant to a customary practice, it becomes a seemingly accepted norm. Such indifference to individual rights cannot be defended under the veil of indigenous or tribal custom.

5 Uncertainty about the powers and functions of indigenous advisory bodies often causes conflict between governments and advisory bodies due to unfulfilled expectations on the part of indigenous bodies (De Villiers, 2023b).

6 The Human Rights Council states that the objectives of FPIC are threefold: to restore control over land; to restore cultural integrity; and to redress power imbalances (Human Rights Council-FPIC, 2018, para. 11).

FPIC relates specifically to interests tied to the identity of Indigenous Peoples, their historical sovereignty within the context of indigenous laws and customs, and their traditional lands (FPIC & Rights Forum, 2020). It is therefore incumbent under international law (ILO 169, 1989, art. 14.2) for states to clearly demarcate the traditional territories of Indigenous Peoples, as this defines the principal areas where FPIC should be sought (Demarcation of territories case, 2022). The demarcation of territories not only assists with consultation, but also facilitates the protection of Indigenous Peoples against encroachment into their traditional lands (Protection against invasion case, 2021).

Notably, the right to consultation is not necessarily exclusive to Indigenous Peoples. In administrative law, it is an established principle that individuals affected by administrative decisions may have a right to be consulted prior to a decision and to seek judicial review of a decision. For example, the Promotion of Administrative Justice Act in South Africa sets out the following indicia for determining a fair administrative process: (Promotion of Administrative Justice, 2000, sec. 3(2)(b)) adequate notice of the nature and purpose of the proposed administrative action; a reasonable opportunity to make representations; a clear statement of the intended administrative action; adequate notice of the right to review; and adequate reasons for the decision.

FPIC often, but not exclusively, relates to the interests of Indigenous Peoples in respect of their traditional lands. In the Milirrpum case, Justice Blackburn stated the following about the link between Indigenous Peoples and their ancestral land:

> the fundamental truth about the aboriginals' relationship to the land is that whatever else it is, it is a religious relationship. … There is an unquestioned scheme of things in which the spirit ancestors, the people of the clan, particular land and everything that exists on and in it, are organic parts of one indissoluble whole. (Milirrpum case, 1971, para. 167)

Courts generally do not rush to extend consultation obligations with Indigenous People to socio-economic policies that also affect them as part of the broader population. Hence, FPIC implies that Indigenous Peoples are entitled to be consulted on specific measures affecting their collective interests, particularly concerning traditional lands under their custodianship (Iseli, 2020). Gaspardus also emphasises the 'overriding obligation to safeguard' the rights of Indigenous People in respect of their traditional lands (Gaspardus, 2025, p. 215).

The scope of FPIC consultation obligations becomes ambiguous when addressing broader socio-economic issues such as housing backlogs, high unemployment, disproportionate incarceration rates, shorter life expectancy, and delays in educational progress. Indigenous Peoples are often 'disproportionally' represented in key socio-economic indicators of marginalisation (Toki and Raman, 2024, p. 3). Petkar argues that FPIC ought to apply 'to all facets of indigenous life', implying a scope far broader than territorially delineated consultation obligations (Petkar, 2017, p. 10). Which, if any, socio-economic measures affecting Indigenous People should be subject to FPIC remains an unresolved question.

For example, is the executive required to seek FPIC from Indigenous Peoples when socio-economic policies are enacted aimed at addressing marginalisation, poverty, and discrimination? The answer is arguably no, but the debate continues.[7] It is important that governments generally consult with communities affected by policies, but such general consultation and the hearing of submissions about the appropriateness of policies should not be mistaken for FPIC, which according to advocates represents a stronger form of co-participation and may even involve co-decision-making.

The complexities surrounding the application of FPIC have become particularly observable beyond Indigenous Peoples' traditional lands, as urbanised indigenous communities may demand separate consultation in respect of policy measures impacting them in urban areas, for example in respect of housing, health, and education. Added thereto, rural indigenous and other rural communities with whom they share land may not share the same interests.[8]

---

7 The question arises as to whether executive policies (e.g. entering into international treaties, foreign affairs, budget allocations and spending priorities, economic growth policies, response to climate change, defence policies), which are distinct from administrative actions and legislative measures, can also be the subject of judicial review. In the South African Law Society case, Mogoeng CJ rejected the proposition that the executive is subject to the same public participatory and consultation obligations as the legislatures. He explained his reasoning as follows: 'Public participation in the law-making process is a requirement, specifically provided for in our Constitution, that must be met by our law-making institutions. But, participatory democracy is not provided in similar terms in relation to the exercise of presidential or executive power…And there is no legal provision or principle that *even remotely* imposes an obligation on the Executive to invite the public to participate in its decision-making processes as proposed' (emphasis added) (Law Society case 2019, paras 86–88).

8 It has been suggested that one of the reasons why the referendum in Chile to grant greater recognition to indigenous self-determination had failed, was that rural communities, other than indigenous, were concerned that their interests would be become subservient to those of Indigenous People (Morales and Pérez-Cosgaya, 2025, p. 13).

Generally, decision-makers prefer to limit FPIC to activities directly associated with traditional lands and Indigenous Peoples with a close connection to those lands. For example, this is exemplified by the persistent demands of urbanised Sámi in Finland to be included in consultations concerning matters impacting their people both within and beyond their homeland. Additionally, it raises the question of who, ultimately, is responsible for determining Sámi membership – the Supreme Administrative Court or the Sámi Parliament? (Tiina Sanila-Aikio case 2018; UN Human Rights Committee 2019).[9] A similar discourse prevails in Australia between urban and rural Aboriginal interests (De Villiers, 2021, p. 72).

The context within which FPIC takes place is informed by rectification and restoration, rather than mere consultation about contemporary views and opinions. This distinguishes FPIC with Indigenous People from general consultation with the broader community. In this respect, the Awas Tingni case affirmed that Indigenous Peoples hold both individual and collective rights over their traditional lands and this is the pre-settlement right-holding that mandates FPIC rather than mere consultation (Awas Tingni case, 2001, para. 148). In the Taromenane case the Court upheld the choice of the indigenous community to live in isolation and held that they had not given free, prior, and informed consent for their lands to be encroached (Taromenane case, 2024). That said, compliance with FPIC obligations is not determined in the abstract, but in the facts, legal regime, administrative arrangements, policies, and circumstances surrounding a proposed measure in a particular country.

2 Implication of the Word 'Consent' in FPIC

FPIC, by incorporating the word 'consent', attempts to position itself as a stronger right with more stringent legal obligations than mere consultation. FPIC seeks to enhance indigenous participatory and joint decision-making rights, distinguishing itself from consultation which may simply entail an invitation to express an opinion. However, it is not only the inclusion of the word 'consent' that seeks to elevate FPIC to a new norm. The words 'free', 'prior', and

9 In 2025 major reforms took place in respect of registering on the Sámi electoral roll for the Sámi Parliament. The rights to register requires that a person who regards themselves as Sámi, and who meets the following requirements, the person or one of their parents, grandparents or great-grandparents must have learned the Sámi language as first language, may register (Sámi Parliament as amended, 2025, sect. 3). An Appeals Board, appointed on the recommendation of the Sámi Parliament, may hear disputes about Sámi registration on the electoral roll (Sámi Parliament as amended, 2025, sect. 41(b)).

'informed' each represent a distinct normative standard aimed at strengthening the effective participation rights of Indigenous Peoples, both collectively and individually, from the earliest stages of a measure's consideration.

While free, prior, and informed may already be imbedded or implied in the term consultation, FPIC seeks to formally raise those standards to a distinct normative level that can more effectively inform and guide decision-makers and courts. Although FPIC has become widely adopted as a guidance norm, municipal jurisprudence has not (yet) drawn such a fine distinction between consultation and FPIC, thereby underlining the aspirational nature of FPIC. It is worth noting, for example, the conclusion reached by the Court in the Kichwa case: 'the *obligation to consult*, in addition to being a treaty-based provision, is also a general principle of international law' (emphasis added) (Kichwa case, 2012, para. 164). Notably, the Court did not differentiate between consultation and FPIC, nor did it cite FPIC as a distinct principle of customary international law.[10] The Kalina case is similarly significant in this context, as the Court made reference to free, prior, and informed *consultation* rather than consent (Kalina and Lokono case, 2015). In the Baleni case the court referred to FPIC, but the legal effect in that case arose from a veto to certain communities due to their historic occupation of land in the domestic legislation, not from the international use of FPIC (Baleni case, 2019).

As demonstrated by case law in this book, while FPIC is principally associated with indigenous rights, courts have generally interpreted FPIC in a way similar to good faith consultation. The meaning attached to consultation and the requirements for good faith consultation are always evolving to cater for new circumstances. It seems problematic for courts to draw a legally defendable distinction between FPIC and good faith consultations. In this respect, the South African Wild Coast appeal case is instructive, as it highlights practical measures for fulfilling the duty to consult with a local community (not necessarily defined as 'indigenous') without invoking FPIC (Wild Coast appeal case, 2024). However, even if consultation does not entail a right of veto, Indigenous Peoples must be given a meaningful opportunity to influence the decision-making process (Saugeen First Nation case 2017, paras 10–29). It has been suggested that FPIC includes the obligation for the engagement to be 'effect-

10 The Court did observe as follows: In other words, nowadays the obligation of States to carry out special and differentiated *consultation processes* when certain interests of Indigenous Peoples and communities are about to be affected is an obligation that has been clearly recognised. Such processes must respect the particular *consultation* system of each people or community, so that it can be understood as an appropriate and *effective* interaction with State authorities, political and social actors and interested third parties' (emphasis added) (Kichwa case, 2012, para. 165).

ive' (Poma Poma case, 2002, para. 7.6), but without suggesting that the use of the word 'effective' implies a right of veto.

'Meaningful', 'effective', and 'having regard' are essential normative aspects of good faith consultation and FPIC, with their practical meaning determined in the context of negotiations (Osman case, 2025). The regulatory authority may consider as fact the withholding of consent by an indigenous community when a decision is made about a measure, but unless a veto power exists in domestic law (e.g. Baleni case), the international understanding of FPIC does not constitute a final veto. For example, in the Saramaka case it was emphasised that Indigenous Peoples should be involved in consultation from the earliest stages of consideration of a measure, but without suggesting that they become the sovereign decision-maker, or that they have a veto to the exclusion of the state (Saramaka case, 2007).

The principal difference between consultation and FPIC appears to lie more in the latter's political, policy, and advocacy origins and objectives, than in its legal substance. In municipal legislation, the term 'consult' is generally the normative standard found in statutes, rather than FPIC. ILO 169, the only legally enforceable treaty on indigenous rights, also refers to consultation, while mentioning FPIC only in a very limited context. In contrast, UNDRIP, which is not legally enforceable, uses both FPIC and consultation without clarifying the distinction between the two terms. Although the UN Human Rights Council proposes that FPIC embodies a stronger right based on co-decision-making rather than mere consultation, municipal law has not embraced this interpretation. In the Kichwa case, it was suggested that even states not party to ILO 169 'need to carry out prior *consultations* with indigenous, autochthonous or tribal communities regarding any administrative or legislative measure that directly affects them, as well as with regard to the exploitation of natural resources on their territory' (emphasis added) (Kichwa case, 2012, para. 164). Furthermore, the limitations faced by ILO 169 are such that Jiménez cautions that one should 'think twice before getting too enthusiastic' about its possible reach (Jiménez, 2022, p. 183).

Even if the term 'FPIC' does not appear in municipal legislation, courts often impose consultation standards with indigenous communities based on the following indicia which are arguably influenced by the rise of FPIC in international law: voluntary participation from an early stage; representation through chosen or nominated representatives; provision of timely and complete information about a measure and its rehabilitation; openness from all parties to adjust their position without a legal obligation to actually do so; meaningful participation and engagement; regular communication; and a genuine desire to reach an agreement (De Villiers, 2025e, p. 325).

The converse also applies: objections raised by an indigenous community to a proposal must be reasonable and credible. An objection ought to arise from traditional law and culture or a custodial relationship to land. The decision to withhold consent must be rational and informed. Failure to negotiate, or raising unreasonable or unsubstantiated objections, may be deemed a lack of good faith on the part of the indigenous community and even result in cost orders. Note, for example, the Munkara case in Australia where the Court found that evidence being relied upon by a sub-group of an indigenous community to object to the laying of an undersea pipeline was not credible, that expert evidence supporting the objection was unreliable, and that coaching of witnesses may have occurred (Munkara case, 2024).[11] This underscores that the obligation of good faith applies to both parties.

Essentially, it is apparent that FPIC has become a term of soft law and a norm for policy standards of conduct, embodying the aspiration for agreement as much as it does a fair and reasonable consultation process.

3 FPIC versus Consultation

The obligation for decision-makers to consult community groups and individuals on measures that may affect their interests, is neither unique nor limited to the rights of Indigenous Peoples. In many facets of public policy, administrative law, employment law, planning law, environmental law, and commercial activity, to name a few, a decision-maker or development proponent may be obligated to consult with interested and affected parties. As a general principle, consultation requires that an indigenous community be given a "reasonable opportunity to participate in decision-making" (Tipakalippa case 2022, para. 104). This does not imply an abdication of decision-making to the indigenous community, but rather an opportunity for them to be heard and their interests to be accommodated as far as possible in the context of overall considerations of a proposed measure.

11 The presiding judge described the expert evidence as 'so lacking integrity that no weight can be placed on them'. The Court ultimately awarded A$9 million in legal costs against the Environmental Defenders Office (a tax-funded body) which had supported and financed the proceeding of the indigenous community (Rauso 2024; Munkara consent orders cost 2024). Rolf raises the concern, in the context of objections against proposed developments in Australia by Aboriginal people, that it would appear the objections are more likely to be lodged against resource extraction proposals than against renewable proposals, hence opening the risk of ideologically based objections (Rolfe, 2024).

In the Australian case of Communications Services Union, the following was stated about the inherent meaning of the obligation to consult:

> A key element of that content is that the party to be consulted be given *notice* of the subject upon which that party's views are being sought before any final decision is made or course of action embarked upon. Another is that while the word always carries with it a consequential requirement for the affording of a *meaningful opportunity* to that party to present those views. What will constitute such an opportunity will vary according to the nature and circumstances of the case. In other words, what will amount to "consultation" has about it an inherent *flexibility*. Finally, a right to be consulted, though a valuable right, is *not a right* of veto.... (emphasis added) (Communications Services Union, 2010, para. 44)

In the McJannet case, the practical burden imposed by consultation was explained as follows:

> Consultation *is not* an exercise in collaborative decision-making. All that is necessary is that a *genuine opportunity* to be heard about the nominated subjects be extended to those required to be consulted *before* any final decision is made...It does not mean that one cannot approach consultation with a particular outcome in mind, only that one's mind *not be unduly fixed.* (emphasis added) (McJannet case, 2016, para. 60)

From these judgements, essential standards for consultation can be identified: giving adequate notice; seeking input before a final decision is made; providing a meaningful or reasonable opportunity to influence the decision; maintaining flexibility; not requiring collaborative decision-making; keeping an open mind; considering opposing views; having regard to the indigenous interests, but not granting a right to veto.[12]

FPIC, as used in UNDRIP, seeks to address perceived shortcomings in the common understanding of consultation. Consultation is generally seen by Indigenous Peoples as a weak right that places an emphasis on hierarchy and on the supremacy of the non-indigenous decision-maker. The UN Human Rights Council views consultation as the starting point of FPIC, which engage-

12 Ironically, if a right of veto had been intended in FPIC, then it would be unnecessary to develop such extensive procedural guidelines for compliance with FPIC. An indigenous community could simply exercise their right of veto, but it is clearly not the case – hence the focus on procedural requirements.

ment must then lead to 'effective' participation, signifying a stronger entitlement than consultation (Human Rights Council-FPIC, 2018, para. 17). The Council proposes the use of the word 'effective' to signify a form of co-decision-making, considered a defining element of FPIC. UNDRIP reinforces the idea of joint decision-making by using the word 'consent' and recognising, as a point of departure, the historical sovereignty of Indigenous Peoples. For example, UNDRIP states:

> Indigenous Peoples have the right to maintain and strengthen their distinct political, legal, economic, social and cultural institutions, while retaining their right to participate fully, if they so choose, in the political, economic, social and cultural life of the State. (UNDRIP, 2007, art. 5)

In this respect, a divergence exists between the rights of Indigenous Peoples and those of ethnocultural minorities, with the former grounding their right to FPIC in their pre-settlement sovereignty and previous or existing customary legal systems.[13] Ethnocultural minorities often assert collective and individual rights primarily based on political marginalisation, self-government in historically inhabited areas, or protection against discrimination, without relying on pre-settlement sovereignty or a distinct legal system as a separate society (De Villiers, 2025d, p. 41).

In ordinary consultation processes, an implied hierarchy exists between parties, whereas FPIC seeks to establish greater legal equality or parity between parties. FPIC aims to create a level playing field, though such equality is not necessarily supported by domestic law or jurisprudence. In the Indigenous Federations case it was emphasised that contracts entered into with indigenous communities must be fair and reasonable (Indigenous Federations from Peru case, 2025, p. 20). FPIC emphasises the traditional rights

---

13 Note, for example, Article 231 of the Constitution of Brazil, which stipulates the following about the rights of Indigenous Peoples: 'Indians shall have their social organization, customs, languages, creeds and traditions recognized, as well as their original rights to the lands they *traditionally* occupy, it being incumbent upon the Union to demarcate them, protect and ensure respect for all of their property. Paragraph 1. *Lands traditionally* occupied by Indians are those on which they live on a permanent basis, those used for their productive activities, those indispensable to the preservation of the environmental resources necessary for their well-being and for their physical and cultural reproduction, according to their uses, customs and traditions. Paragraph 2. The lands *traditionally occupied* by Indians are intended for their permanent possession and they shall have the exclusive usufruct of the riches of the soil, the rivers and the lakes existing therein' (emphasis added) (Constitution of Brazil, 2010, art. 231). Decree No 48.893 of 11 September 2024 provides that in defined circumstances FPIC must be complied with.

and interests of Indigenous Peoples, their societal existence, and their ongoing desire to protect their collective traditional rights and interests in accordance with their traditional laws and customs. As illustrated in the Mabo and Alexkor cases in Australia and South Africa respectively, indigenous rights and interests must be understood within the context of their own customary legal systems rather than through the lens of an external legal system assessing or judging them (Mabo case (2) 1992; Alexkor case 2003).

The proposition of co-existence of indigenous legal systems with contemporary legal systems may be more aspirational than actual, as in many instances, traditional legal systems have been eroded or are no longer widely observed within indigenous communities. What was once a distinct customary *legal* system may have diminished into ordinary culture, habits, practices, or memories not dissimilar to ethnocultural communities. The Australian case of Ward foreshadows the possibility of an indigenous community's bundle of rights being diminished if they no longer use their land or maintain adherence to their traditional customs (Ward case, 2002, para. 32).

In South Africa, for example, customary legal systems are placed on an equal footing with the civil legal system pursuant to section 211 of the Constitution, provided those customary systems do not conflict with the norms set out in the Bill of Rights (Bhe case, 2005). Customary systems are regarded as legal systems in their own right (Alexkor case 2003, para. 54; Shilubana case 2008).

Nonetheless, the equality between parties said to underpin FPIC is, in both practice and law, more notional than real – unless explicit co-decision and veto rights are granted to an indigenous community by way of municipal statute or policy. This is confirmed by James Anaya, Special Rapporteur of the United Nations, who clarifies that 'consent' in FPIC should not be construed as a means of blocking a proposal or a right to co-decision-making (S. J. Anaya, 2009, p. 16).[14]

By seeking to establish a higher normative standard, FPIC implies greater control by Indigenous Peoples over activities that may be prejudicial to their interests, particularly those related to their traditional lands. The UN Human Rights Council suggests that 'matters of broad societal application' may affect Indigenous Peoples 'in ways not felt by others in society' and, hence, that consultation should include these broader elements (Human Rights Council-FPIC, 2018, para. 33). This is a broad yet vague and aspirational statement,

---

14 Mathiba finds this statement by Anaya 'confusing and somewhat contradictory', but he acknowledges that there is 'still a lack of consensus on what consent should mean and imply in practice' (Mathiba, 2024, p. 339).

likely to result in disagreements in its practical application in municipal law. MacKay expresses the view that 'consultation processes are often deeply flawed' and, thus, FPIC gives rise to a stronger right (Mackay, 2018). Municipal courts have been reluctant to extend consultation obligations to policy areas or measures unrelated to the traditional lands, customs, or cultures of Indigenous Peoples. As a general guideline, a sliding scale can be applied: the greater the direct impact of a measure on indigenous traditional lands, the more intensive the required consultation (Poma Poma case 2002; CSF case 2016).

The question remains: is there a substantive difference under municipal or international law, between the *legal effect* of consultation versus the *legal effect* of *FPIC*?

Although some in literature suggests that FPIC constitutes a stronger right than consultation, and potentially grants Indigenous Peoples a veto, neither municipal case law nor international law supports such a proposition. While the consultation obligations of FPIC resemble those of consultation, the legal meaning of 'consent' in FPIC depends on state-based statutory, policy, and administrative measures. Generally, FPIC as understood in international law, does not confer an absolute veto on an indigenous community. An indigenous community's refusal to grant consent for a proposed measure may be a significant factor for the government or regulatory authority to consider as the ultimate decision-maker, but the final decision-maker must usually also consider broader societal interests before reaching a final decision (Forrest appeal case, 2024).

Consent as used in FPIC cannot be interpreted in isolation from the legal and policy context of the country in which it operates. For example, the use of the phrase 'in order' in UNDRIP concerning FPIC (e.g. in Articles 19 and 32) signifies an effort to obtain consent rather than a legal obligation to achieve it. In this respect, it is worth paying attention to the different outcomes of the Baleni and Bengwenyama Minerals cases in South Africa which were decided pursuant to different statutes, the one using consent and the other consultation. In the Bengwenyama Minerals case, it was held that the statutory standard pursuant to the Mineral and Petroleum Resources Development Act 28 of 2002 does not mandate consent or a veto. It does, however, require timely information-sharing and consultation in an attempt to reach agreement (Bengwenyama Minerals case, 2011). Meanwhile, in the Baleni case, the Court found that the indigenous community did indeed have a right of veto according to the Interim Protection of Informal Land Rights Act 31 of 1996 (Baleni case, 2019). In this case, the veto arose from the community's status under specific South African legislation rather than from an international customary law norm or UNDRIP.[15] Similarly, in 2013, the Supreme Court of India found that consultation with the Dongria Kondh people regarding proposed mining operations on their lands had not been adequate under municipal legislation. In the Orissa Mining case, the Court ruled that a precondition for mining to proceed was the approval of the indigenous community, as their collective rights and interests were directly affected by the proposal (Orissa Mining case, 2013, para. 51).

An illustration of how a right can be given effect by cross-references to other rights, is where the Inter-American Court of Human Rights (IACrtHR) has invoked the right to culture to demonstrate its interlinkage with the rights to health and the environment (Lhaka Honhat Association case, 2020, para. 370). While that case did not involve consultation obligations, it highlights the interrelatedness of rights, in particular how civil and political rights can be contextualised by reference to the property and cultural rights of Indigenous Peoples. This is echoed by the Fosen case in Norway, where the individual right to culture was linked to inadequate consultation with Indigenous Peoples (Fosen case, 2021). Similarly, in South Africa, a proposal to open a coal-fired power station was rejected because of insufficient consideration of its long-term impact on the rights of children (African Climate Alliance case, 2024, para. 25). In Finland the Committee on the Rights of the Child (CRC) found that the grant of a lease for mining activity impacted upon the rights of children to learn and benefits from their culture (M.E.V., S.E.V., and B.I.V. case, 2024). Meanwhile, in Australia, the Gomeroi case established that the potential effect of climate change on traditional lands is a relevant factor to raise in good faith negotiations (Gomeroi People case, 2024).

While at law FPIC and consultation may not differ significantly – since neither grants a veto – FPIC, through the term 'consent', seeks to emphasise a higher degree of self-determination and autonomous decision-making for Indigenous Peoples. FPIC endeavours to affirm indigenous ownership and control over land, positioning the parties as equals, akin to scenarios involving the owners of freehold land.

15 The Interim Protection of Informal Land Rights Act 31 of 1996 provides that land may not be acquired without consent and, if held communally, only in compliance with the custom and usage of the community (s2(1) and (2)). This grants a right of co-decision to the community and thereby a veto, but the right is statutory based, rather than a common law or international law understanding of consultation or FPIC.

4 FPIC as a Collective Right

Although FPIC is viewed as a collective right benefitting an entire community, individual rights also underpin consultation with Indigenous Peoples, particularly in relation to their right to self-determination – both as a community and as individuals – and their associated cultural and property rights (Endorois Welfare Council case, 2003). The collective right of an indigenous community within the context of consultation and FPIC reflects the dynamic interpretation of individual rights – such as the right to culture, property, and self-determination – as found in international legal instruments like the ICESCR and the ICCPR. The Fosen case is noteworthy in this regard. The Court emphasised that Article 27 ICCPR 'must be viewed in context with Article 108 of the Constitution of Norway, which imposes a duty on the state authorities "to create conditions enabling the Sámi people to preserve and develop its language, culture and way of life"' (Fosen case, 2021, para. 99).

In Kenya, in the matter involving the Endorios Welfare Council, a dispute arose about the purported lack of consultation that preceded the removal of a community from their traditional lands to create a game reserve. The Endorios community claimed that their traditional rights had been affected and they should have been consulted (Endorois Welfare Council case, 2003). Those traditional rights found their origin in indigenous property rights, even though they are not recognised in Kenyan common law (Barrie, 2011). It was argued that Article 14 of the African Charter (African Charter, 1981) protects property rights, permitting encroachment only in the public interest and in accordance with relevant laws. The community contended that their collective indigenous rights fell within the scope of property rights, entitling them to the same protections and procedures as ordinary landowners. The African Commission on Human and Peoples' Rights found in favour of the community. After extensive reference to the Mabo and Richtersveld judgements, the Commission observed:

> 150. The African Commission also notes that the African Charter, in Articles 20 through 24, provides for peoples to retain rights as peoples, that is, as collectives....154 The African Commission notes that there is a common thread that runs through all the various criteria that attempts to describe Indigenous Peoples – that Indigenous Peoples have an unambiguous relationship to a distinct territory and that all attempts to define the concept recognise the linkages between people, their land, and culture... 156 the African Commission is of the view that Endorois culture, religion, and traditional way of life are intimately intertwined with their ancestral lands – Lake Bogoria and the surrounding area.

> It agrees that Lake Bogoria and the Monchongoi Forest are central to the Endorois' way of life and without access to their ancestral land, the Endorois are unable to fully exercise their cultural and religious rights, and feel disconnected from their land and ancestors….157 The African Commission, therefore, accepts that self-identification for Endorois as *indigenous individuals* and *acceptance* as such by the group is an essential component of their sense of identity…. 199. (emphasis added) (Endorois Welfare Council case, 2003)

In the Awas Tingni case, a dispute arose concerning the interpretation of the Inter-American Convention's protection of property rights in a manner that includes the rights of indigenous community members within the framework of communal property. The Court declared that indigenous communities' possession of land should be sufficient for official recognition of their ownership, even in the absence of formal title. It found that the community's evidence regarding their collective occupation, land use, subsistence, and stewardship was adequate to establish traditional title (Awas Tingni case 2001). The Court determined that, in accordance with the community's traditional laws and customs, they held collective rights to the land, which must be respected by contemporary legal norms. While stopping short of declaring a right of veto, the Court mandated the state to enact measures to demarcate the traditional lands:

> 128. Due to the lack of specific and effective legislation for indigenous communities to exercise their rights and to the fact that the State has disposed of lands occupied by indigenous communities by granting a concession… 138. The Court believes it necessary to make the rights recognized by the Nicaraguan Constitution and legislation effective, in accordance with the American Convention. Therefore, pursuant to article 2 of the American Convention, *the State must adopt* in its domestic law the necessary legislative, administrative, or other measures to create an effective mechanism for *delimitation and titling* of the property of the members of the Awas Tingni Mayagna Community, in accordance with the customary law, values, customs and mores of that Community. (Awas Tingni case, 2001)

Likewise, in the Lhaka Honhat Association case, the meaning of the right to culture was expanded to include the rights to health and a clean environment (Lhaka Honhat Association case, 2020). These judgements demonstrate how, as explained in the Aikio case, the gap between individual and collective rights can be bridged by recognising that the substance of an individual right may gain value when exercised collectively within the community (Tiina Sanila-Aikio case, 2018, para. 6.9).

The traditional ownership of land by an indigenous community, tied to their historic sovereignty and customary legal and governance systems, form the foundation of FPIC. However, regardless of the historical and collective uniqueness of FPIC, it does not legally imply joint decision-making or power-sharing. FPIC is not a legal norm that establishes a treaty between equal partners, though it is viewed as originating from the 'historic treaty-making process that characterized indigenous-State relations for several hundred years in many regions of the world' (Human Rights Council-FPIC, 2018, para. 4). FPIC may encapsulate and reflect the desire for a treaty, but it does not propose or represent any treaty-powers, or a legal status of equality in decision-making.

5 Origin of FPIC

The term FPIC evolved from the concept of consultation, which appears in the Indigenous and Tribal Peoples Convention, 1989 (No 169) (ILO 169).[16] The Committee on the Elimination of Racial Discrimination (CERD) was the first international human rights body to formally adopt the benchmark that free, prior, and informed consent must be obtained from Indigenous Peoples when their rights and interests are affected (CERD General Recommendation, 1997). The General Recommendation by the UN High Commissioner for Human Rights stated the following about the obligations on states:

> Ensure that members of Indigenous Peoples have equal rights in respect of *effective participation* in public life and that no decisions *directly* relating to their rights and interests are taken without their informed consent...
> The Committee especially calls upon States parties to recognize and protect the rights of Indigenous Peoples to own, develop, control and use their communal lands, territories and resources and, where they have been deprived of their lands and territories traditionally owned or otherwise inhabited or used without their *free and informed consent*, to take steps to return those lands and territories. (emphasis added) (CERD General Recommendation, 1997, para. 4(d), 5)

16 For example, Article 6(1) of ILO 169 states: 'In applying the provisions of this Convention, governments shall: (a) consult the peoples concerned, through appropriate procedures and in particular through their representative institutions, whenever consideration is being given to legislative or administrative measures which may affect them directly.'

The real impetus for FPIC in indigenous advocacy comes from its use in UNDRIP where its objective is stated as follows in various parts of the Declaration:

> Indigenous Peoples shall not be forcibly removed from their lands or territories. No relocation shall take place *without the free, prior and informed consent* of the Indigenous Peoples concerned and after agreement on just and fair compensation and, where possible, with the option of return (UNDRIP, 2007, art. 10).
>
> States shall provide redress through effective mechanisms, which may include restitution, developed in conjunction with Indigenous Peoples, with respect to their cultural, intellectual, religious and spiritual property taken without their *free, prior and informed consent* or in violation of their laws, traditions and customs (UNDRIP, 2007, art. 11(2)).
>
> States shall consult and cooperate in good faith with the Indigenous Peoples concerned through their own representative institutions in order to obtain their *free, prior and informed consent* before adopting and implementing legislative or administrative measures that may affect them (UNDRIP, 2007, art. 19). Indigenous Peoples have the right to determine and develop priorities and strategies for the development or use of their lands or territories and other resources. 2. States shall consult and cooperate in good faith with the Indigenous Peoples concerned through their own representative institutions *in order to* obtain their *free and informed consent* prior to the approval of any project affecting their lands or territories and other resources, particularly in connection with the development, utilization or exploitation of mineral, water or other resources. (UNDRIP, 2007, art. 32(1))

Much has been written since the adoption of UNDRIP about how 'consent' is to be defined and obtained, but while the sentiment and objectives of FPIC are widely shared, translating the duties associated into enforceable rights within municipal law has been difficult, inconsistent and slow. Although international expert bodies have continuously endeavoured to develop FPIC and the obligations arising from it, Strydom observes that states are often slow to act, reluctant to engage, and even dismissive of the findings and recommendations made by bodies such as the UN Human Rights Committee (Strydom, 2021, p. 237). Citations to UNDRIP, which is not a treaty, carry little, if any, weight in domestic courts. The ILO summarises the obligation to consult in an effort to reach consent as follows:

> In keeping with paragraph 2 of Article 6, consultation must take place in accordance with procedures that are appropriate to the circumstances, through the Indigenous Peoples' representative institutions, in good faith and with the objective of achieving agreement or consent to the proposed measures... There is *no single model of appropriate procedures*, which should take into account national circumstances, the circumstances of the Indigenous Peoples concerned and the nature of the measures which are the object of the consultation process. (emphasis added) (ILO Brazil 2009, para. 142)

The reality is that the answers to many questions about the operationalisation of UNDRIP remain vague, particularly concerning who should be regarded as Indigenous Peoples, the definition of self-determination, the legal meaning of 'consent', the types of activities or policy areas to which FPIC applies, the use of consent and consult in UNDRIP, and the remedies if FPIC is not obtained.

UNDRIP does not define the legal subject as the beneficiary of its protections, leaving it to sovereign states to determine which, if any, of their ethnocultural communities qualify as 'indigenous'. In some instances, particularly in Africa, there has been a reluctance to recognise any sub-groups as indigenous, with the emphasis kept solely on customary, traditional, or tribal communities within historically tribal areas. A similar debate continues in Europe over who should be considered indigenous. This is similar to the question who is a national minority. Notably, France has refused to recognise minorities within its population (Cardoret and Le Bihan case, 1991, para. 4.9).[17] The challenge to define indigenous and minority highlight the limited ability of the law to ascribed rights to an entity that is sociological in nature.

In the Quera Aboriginal Community case in Argentina, the court considered the legal status of an indigenous community to determine its standing to initiate proceedings. It concluded that formal recognition of the community's legal personality is an act that simply acknowledges its pre-existence at the time of the request. Once the community demonstrates characteristics such as a shared language, religion, preservation of customs, group identifica-

17 '4.9 With respect to the alleged violation of Article 27, the State party recalled that, upon ratification of the Covenant, the French Government had made the following statement: "In the light of Article 2 of the Constitution of the French Republic, the French Government declares that Article 27 is not applicable as far as the Republic is concerned." Thus, the State party argued that "the idea of membership of an 'ethnic, religious or linguistic minority' which the applicant invokes is irrelevant in the case in point, and is not opposable to the French Government which does not recognize the existence of 'minorities in the Republic', defined, in Article 2 of the Constitution, as 'indivisible, secular, democratic and social ...' (indivisible, laïque démocratique et sociale)".

tion, intention to possess land collectively, and free choice of representatives, the court must acknowledge its existence as a community and give effect to it. The court's role is to affirm a collective identity that already exists. The court declared:

> the National Constitution recognizes not only the ethnic and cultural pre-existence of the Indigenous Peoples in Argentina, but also guarantees the right to legal personality for their communities and the community possession and property over the lands they traditionally occupy (Article 75, Subsection 17). The intention of the constitutional principles is that by granting legal personality, this will serve to make an already existing right functional; in other words, this basic principle does not establish the right but rather declares its pre-existence and makes it effective, guaranteeing among others, the right to community property and land. Thus, there is recognition that the aboriginal communities were pre-existing before the State (…) and the preventative measures adopted include the allocation of "traditionally occupied" lands, which necessarily *guarantees the right to property over the lands historically exercised by these communities and is not based on their coming into being as legal persons*. (emphasis added) (Quera Aboriginal Community case, 2001)

The difficulty to define indigenous is, for example, notable in respect of the Khoisan in South Africa, who assert they are the sole Indigenous People of the subcontinent (Pieterse-Robertson 2019). However, the Traditional and Khoi-San Leadership Act, 2019 failed to define terms such as 'traditional', 'tribal', or 'indigenous' and created the impression that these terms could be used interchangeably (Khoisan Act 2019).[18] Also note how the UN Committee on the Elimination of Racial Discrimination attempted to sidestep the issue of who is indigenous in Botswana by referring to 'ethnic' communities rather than Indigenous Peoples in a complaint involving the Khoisan. For example, when the CERD made recommendations to allow indigenous Khoisan people from a certain area to return to their ancestral lands, the Committee stated the following:

> The Committee urges the State party to fully implement the High Court's decision in Roy Sesana and others v. Attorney General, by allowing *all ethnic groups originating from the Central Kalahari Game Reserve* to return and settle

18 This Act was declared unconstitutional due to shortcomings in the public consultation process giving rise to it (Khoisan Act appeal, 2023). At the time of publication, a new act had yet to be promulgated.

> there unconditionally. The Committee also recommends that the State party provide them with effective access to basic social services and enable them to resume their traditional activities without hindrance. (emphasis added) (Mackay, 2022, p. 29)

This expert opinion highlights the terminological vagueness and inconsistency of terms such as 'minority', 'Indigenous Peoples', 'tribal', and 'ethnic'.

6 Conceptual Confusion

The terms 'consent' and 'consultation' are often misunderstood and used interchangeably in discussions about FPIC. While 'consent' in its ordinary sense implies agreement, within the context of UNDRIP, it is the process of seeking consent that is established as the norm, rather than consent as the required norm. As for 'consultation', notably as an example the South African Parliament has distinguished between the terms 'in consultation' and 'after consultation', with the former implying consent and the latter aligning with the conventional understanding of consultation as process to take into account views, opinions, and preferences. For example, Section 233 of the Interim Constitution explicitly defined these terms as follows:

> (3) Where in this Constitution any functionary is required to take a decision *in consultation* with another functionary, such decision shall require the concurrence of such other functionary: Provided that if such other functionary is a body of persons it shall express its concurrence in accordance with its own decision-making procedures.
>
> (4) Where in this Constitution any functionary is required to take a decision *after consultation* with another functionary, such decision shall be taken in *good faith* after consulting and giving *serious consideration* to the views of such other functionary. (emphasis added)

While the term 'free, prior, and informed consent' seems to imply a veto by using the word 'consent', the proper interpretation of UNDRIP does not support joint decision-making, power-sharing, or an actual veto. Although UNDRIP seeks to clarify and enhance the rights of Indigenous Peoples, in fact 'the lack of conceptual clarity surrounding the notion of Indigenous consent is rightly considered an obstacle to its institutionalisation' (Papillon, Leclair and Leydet, 2020, p. 224).

The divergent opinions expressed in literature about the meaning of FPIC are illustrated by the following expert opinions:

Doyle suggests that the right to FPIC implies 'that Indigenous Peoples have a *right to determine* if any projects that directly impact on them may, or may not, proceed and under what conditions' (Doyle, 2014, p. 146). While this interpretation seems to support a legal veto, Doyle acknowledges that 'political will' rather than judicial imposition is required to effectively operationalise FPIC (Doyle, 2014, p. 246). She concludes that 'experience [with FPIC] in contexts where consent is mandated by law, or commitments have been made to obtain it under voluntary standards, *points to the limitations of the concept in practice* and the challenges associated with operationalising it' (emphasis added) (Doyle, 2014, p. 250).

Rombouts, meanwhile, argues that the use of the word 'consent' in FPIC signifies that a bona fide effort must be made to reach agreement, rather than an enforceable requirement that mandates agreement (Rombouts 2018, 7). It is therefore the attempt made by parties to reach agreement that may be judicially evaluated, rather than the outcome of the consultation, the reasons for disagreement, or the merits of the respective proposals (Rombouts, 2014).

The approach recommended by Rombouts is consistent with, for example, Australian jurisprudence arising from the native title regime and its obligation on proponents to negotiate 'in good faith' with Indigenous Peoples when activities impact on their native title rights. Consultation with Aboriginal people is not limited to their areas of native title. For example, in the Murray Rivers Indigenous People case it was found that the obligation to '*have regard* to Indigenous values and Indigenous uses' had not been complied with (Murray Rivers Indigenous People case, 2025). Courts in Australia have primarily focused on the processes of negotiations rather than considering the reasonableness, merit or appropriateness of the merits of proposals or adopted positions (Strickland case 1998; De Villiers 2022, 127; Munkara case 2024).

The Human Rights Council of the United Nations expressed the decision-making power of Indigenous Peoples as follows:

> Consent is a key principle that enables Indigenous Peoples to exercise their right to self-determination, including development that involves *control* over or otherwise affects their lands, resources and territories. With such an understanding, Indigenous Peoples are considered to engage with and are entitled to *give or withhold consent* to proposals that affect them. (emphasis added) (Human Rights Council-FPIC, 2018, para. 25)

Notably, withholding consent is not necessarily construed as a veto, as the state remains the final decision-maker unless otherwise determined by municipal law. Southalan correctly observes that 'there is no universal agreement on exactly what FPIC entails' (Southalan and Fardin, 2019, p. 373). Eichler suggests the following:

> International human rights law has established a sort of middle way conciliating the two positions: consent is understood as an objective to be reached in any prior consultation process affecting Indigenous Peoples in terms of its administrative, judicial or other measures; *exceptions reserving consent to be legally binding* are limited to forced relocation, the disposal of hazardous materials and military activities to be executed on Indigenous Peoples' territories. (emphasis added) (Eichler, 2019, p. 9)

Macnab succinctly summarises the obligation arising from Article 19 of UNDRIP as follows:

> ...the emphasis is not on the consent or achieving the consent, *it's in the process of working towards achieving consent.* So, the idea is in a consultation context with Indigenous People, it should be the government's goal always to work to *try and achieve consent* with Indigenous People. But it doesn't mean that if no consent is reached, nothing can go forward. (emphasis added) (Macnab, 2020)

Alva-Arevalo states that the discourse about actual consent or veto power within the context of FPIC is 'a pointless discussion since veto power is not expressly recognised by any international instrument. The emphasis [of FPIC] is on the principle of good faith...' (Alva-Arevalo, 2021, p. 236).

Barrie's view is that, as promising as UNDRIP may be, the challenge lies in its implementation (Barrie, 2013). He also says that 'FPIC is a complex doctrine that includes a number of related aims and aspirations. It has room to evolve and its ongoing development will take time' (Barrie, 2024b, p. 224). Tomaselli, meanwhile, provides a useful overview of case studies where indigenous self-government and autonomy rights have found their way into the municipal law of states (Tomaselli, 2016). She concludes that, although some would suggest that the right to autonomy, similar to FPIC, has become an element of international customary law, such a categorisation is probably too optimistic.[19] She writes that:

19 Two important elements form the basis for international customary law: a general *practice* and its *acceptance* as law (UN International Law Commission, 2018, p. 123). Based on this standard, neither autonomy nor FPIC can be considered rights in customary international law (see Chapter 4).

> the right to autonomy or self-government of Indigenous Peoples, on the basis of Art. 4 of the UNDRIP, may be defined – at least – as an *emergent* international standard. (emphasis added) (Tomaselli, 2017, p. 420)

In short, the phrase '*in order* to obtain their free, prior and informed consent' in UNDRIP is not construed in international law or municipal law as implying a veto, a legal requirement that agreement must be reached, an abdication of sovereign decision-making by the state, or a form of co-decision-making.

7 Norm Setting by the UN Permanent Forum on Indigenous Issues

In 2005, the United Nations Permanent Forum on Indigenous Issues (UNPFII) hosted an 'International Workshop on Methodologies regarding Free, Prior and Informed Consent and Indigenous Peoples'. The aim of the workshop was to provide clarity on the meaning of FPIC and make detailed recommendations (ECOSOC: Guidelines FPIC, 2005, pp. 11–13). Useful as these recommendations are, it is notable that they do not address the meaning of consent beyond stating that it is an objective to be achieved. More significantly, they make no mention of a right of veto, co-decision-making, or the ability of FPIC to override government regulatory processes.[20] Petkar correctly observes that despite efforts to provide clarity, 'there continue to be a profusion of readings of FPIC itself, including the specifics of what constitutes consent' (Petkar, 2017, p. 24).

---

20 Note, in this respect, the Bear Creek Case in which a mining company relied on the approval of the Peruvian authorities to argue that it had met its obligations to consult with the local Indigenous People to secure their consent. The Tribunal emphasised the importance of the legal regime under which the mining company operated and that, in this case, the Peruvian authorities had approved the processes leading to the issuing of the mining permit. Therefore, according to the Tribunal, the company 'could take it for granted to have complied with all legal requirements with regard to its outreach to the local communities' (Bear Creek Mining case, 2021, para. 412). This contrasts with the Juukan Gorge outcome in Australia, where the mining company acted based on state approval but still faced major national and international backlash, along with much negative publicity for its actions and reputational damage (Parliament Juukan Gorge 2020; Final Report Juukan 2021; chapter 9).

8 Themes Explored in Jurisprudence

Expert bodies and courts in various jurisdictions have been called upon to resolve disputes by referring to standards implied by the term 'consultation'. While expert opinions in literature contribute to scientific debate, this book primarily focuses on the directions provided by courts through their judgements. Courts are ultimately responsible for interpreting international treaty obligations and municipal statutes, adjudicating disputes, giving content to rights and interests, and discerning obligations of parties. Through judicial reasoning, common inter-jurisdictional denominators can be identified, differences explored, law developed, and new areas navigated.

This book explores the following themes, highlighting trends in case law regarding the rights to consultation and FPIC:

8.1 Who Are Indigenous People?

The question who qualifies as an Indigenous People is answered by examining the history and circumstances of a particular country and its peoples, rather than through an abstract definition. Similar to the concept of 'minority', there is no universal definition of Indigenous People. Generally, the term refers to a society of people bound by common ancestry that occupied land in accordance with their system of traditional laws and customs prior to the arrival of settlers. They continue to share a common culture, customs, traditions, language, and religion and adhere to the traditional laws handed down by their ancestors. This approach is both simple and complex in its application. Many African nations do not mention the term 'Indigenous People' in their domestic legislation or policies, using instead other terms such as 'tribes', 'traditional', or 'customary'. Note also that the African Charter on Human and Peoples' Rights does not use the word 'indigenous', preferring the term 'peoples' (African Charter, 1981). There is also an ongoing debate in Europe about who is indigenous to the continent (Sarivaara, Määttä and Uusiautti, 2013).

8.2 Legal Obligations Arising from FPIC

In Shakespearian terms the question can be posed – is consent to be or not to be? What legal obligations are imposed by international instruments arising from FPIC?

International law does not impose a legally enforceable obligation for co-decision-making, nor does FPIC, as understood in international instruments, grant Indigenous Peoples a veto over proposed measures. Although FPIC under international law does not inherently confer a veto right, this does not preclude municipal legal frameworks from establishing such a right. Furthermore, when analysing international law, a distinction must be drawn between a justiciable right that can be enforced pursuant to a treaty and an aspiration that is dressed up as a right but cannot be legally enforced based on an international Declaration by the United Nations. UNDRIP suggests that a right to veto may exist in certain areas, such as protection against removal from traditional lands and the prevention of hazardous material storage on such lands (UNDRIP 2007, arts. 10 and 29). However, even in these cases, UNDRIP does not create legally enforceable rights to the exclusion of state authority.

8.3 Is FPIC a Customary Norm?

If FPIC is not a treaty-based legal norm in international law, is FPIC a legal norm arising from customary international law?

The answer to this question is no – even though consultative processes with Indigenous Peoples are widely endorsed as best practice in international law and practice, those practices have not evolved into justiciable rights and legal obligations. Ultimately, indigenous consultation rights primarily derive from domestic laws rather than international declarations or expert opinions. While international legal instruments can enrich and inform domestic laws, and may also assist and encourage greater awareness of indigenous rights in their interpretation, customary international law does not establish FPIC as a legally enforceable norm.

Two important elements form the basis for the existence of a legal norm in customary international law: a general practice by states and the acceptance of the practice as law (UN International Law Commission, 2018, p. 123). The collective rights of Indigenous People – particularly the requirements of 'consent' as envisaged by UNDRIP – remain aspirational in nature. Since customary international law emerges from widespread and consistent state practice accepted by states as law, the 'consent' element in FPIC cannot be regarded as a widely or universally acknowledged binding legal norm under customary international law since neither of those thresholds are met.

An argument can perhaps be made that international best practice requires consultation with Indigenous Peoples when their interests are affected, but this falls well short of 'consent'. While FPIC may be recognised as a best practice, its vagueness and inconsistent applications prevent it from being regarded as a binding legal norm in customary international law.

8.4 Indigenous versus Minority

The question often arises how are Indigenous Peoples are distinguished from ethnocultural minorities? Both terms suffer from definitional vagueness since they refer to a sociological state of humans rather than a clearly definable legal subject. Volumes have been written about what constitutes 'Indigenous People', 'minority', 'national minority', and 'ethnic group', including what differentiates these concepts (Castellino 2010; De Villiers 2012). Courts, however, have typically kept away from this quest for definitional clarity. While courts have acknowledged traditional lands, sometimes called native title or aboriginal title, in countries such as Australia, New Zealand, South Africa, Canada, South America, and the USA, in doing so they have not attempted to generically define 'indigenous' or to distinguish between 'indigenous' and 'minority' in the abstract. The key distinction between 'Indigenous Peoples' and 'ethnocultural minorities', as derived from jurisprudence and expert commentary by international organisations, is that the former are generally recognised as pre-settlement societies with a shared ancestry, governed by their own laws and customs, having exercised sovereignty over their traditional lands, and continuing to exhibit these characteristics as a community in contemporary society (Yorta Yorta (HCA) case 2002; Alexkor case 2003; Delgamuukw case 1997). In contrast, ethnocultural minorities, despite a long presence in a country, do not constitute a pre-settlement traditional society and their rules are generally regarded as customs and practices rather than rights of self-government and sovereignty. This distinction is, however, open to challenge.

8.5 Indigenous Rights: Collective or Individual?

A pertinent question is whether the rights of Indigenous Peoples are exercised individually or collectively? The rights of Indigenous Peoples can be exercised through individual rights or collectively as a community. While international law principally recognises cultural, language, religious and other identity rights as being individual in nature, the presence of a society with its own legal system and customs that are collectively adhered to means that Indigenous Peoples can also exercise their rights collectively as community (Tiina Sanila-Aikio case, 2018, para. 6.9). It is important, however, for indigenous legal systems to be understood in their own terms rather than from the perspective of a different legal system (Forrest case, 2023).

8.6 Meaning of Consult

What is the meaning of consult? The term 'consult' is not a term of art with a settled meaning. Nonetheless, courts and expert bodies have developed indicia of practical steps to take in an attempt to meet the obligation to consent. Those indicia, while open to expansion, include the following: voluntary participation by the community in the consultation process; representation by their own chosen or nominated representatives;[21] provision of timely and complete information about the proposed measure; openness from all parties to adjust their positions, but without a legal obligation to do so; meaningful participation and engagement; regular communication; and a genuine desire to reach an agreement.

8.7 Meaning of 'Good Faith'

What is the meaning of 'good faith'? While international law does not offer a justiciable definition of FPIC, courts in the Americas have referenced it, and the concept of 'good faith consultation' with Indigenous Peoples is also known in several foreign jurisdictions, including Canada, New Zealand, Botswana, Kenya, South Africa, and Australia.

Importantly, good faith is an obligation that applies to all parties in the consultation process. However, even in jurisdictions where good faith consultation with Indigenous Peoples is a normative legal requirement, its legal and practical application depends on the specific circumstances of each case. There is no universal normative standard or checklist to conclusively determine whether good faith consultation has occurred. Instead, it depends on the facts of each dispute and a value-judgement of the conduct of the parties (Sesana case 2006). For example, in Australian native title proceedings, the test for 'good faith' is applied to the conduct of the parties rather than the merits of their respective positions or the reasons for their disagreement (WMC case 1999). A similar approach was adopted in the Murray Rivers case in which it as found that the obligation to 'have regard' to the interests of Aboriginal People had not been satisfied (Murray Rivers Indigenous People case, 2025). Meanwhile, in the South African Observatory Civic Association case, while the Court did not cite FPIC explicitly, it nevertheless reflected the spirit of good faith consultation in reaching the following conclusion:

---

21 In the Richman case the Tribunal found that a party seeking access to land had not negotiated in good faith by opting to negotiate with a person outside the authorised representatives of the indigenous community (Richman case, 2025).

> The fact that the applicants may have unduly delayed instituting urgent review proceedings did not detract from the relevant decisionmakers' *duty to properly consult* with the First Nations peoples,[22] and the duty of the courts to ensure that the rights of vulnerable indigenous groups were protected... There was no reason why an urgent review should not be heard after *proper consultation* with the affected First Nations peoples. (emphasis added) (Observatory Civic Association case, 2023, p. 585)

General good practice guidelines on how to comply with FPIC have been developed internationally. However, these do not constitute binding legal norms, as adhering to good faith consultation for compliance with FPIC ultimately depends on specific circumstances and the prevailing municipal law (World Bank, 2016).[23]

There is, however, an element of uncertainty that underlies good faith consultation because parties may not have any certainty that their conduct, if assessed retrospectively, would meet the thresholds for good faith. For example, in the Bear Creek case the court accepted that a private entity can rely on the state's approval process to demonstrate that the process of consultation with Indigenous People had met legal and social license obligations (Bear Creek Mining case, 2021). In contrast, the Juukan Gorge incident demonstrates the risk of a company acting solely on government approval, only to face public backlash and reputational damage for its actions (Chapter 9).

8.8 What Information to Share?

What information should be shared with Indigenous Peoples in order to comply with the good faith requirements of FPIC? A threshold requirement for meeting consultation obligations is that the decision-maker or the proponent of a measure, shares all relevant information with the indigenous community as soon as possible in the consultation process. It is a value judgement based on the facts of a situation to ascertain if this standard has been met. However,

22 Notably, the Court did not use the term 'First Nations' to denote the legal status of the party but merely as a term of self-description, as used by the party itself.

23 Mathiba criticises the World Bank for prioritising consultation over consent, arguing that it endorses free, prior, and informed consultation rather than free, prior, and informed consent (Mathiba 2024, 331). In my view, the World Bank's position – that FPIC implies an effort to achieve consent rather than an obligation to obtain it – is sound and reflective of international law. A similar approach was taken by the insurer AXIS in 2022, when it announced it would not underwrite energy, mining, or other projects affecting indigenous communities without their support (Hussain and Jessop 2022).

this duty allows for certain policy-sensitive, commercially confidential, or culturally secret details to be withheld or access to specific information to be restricted.

The nature and extent of information shared must be reasonable and sufficient to enable the indigenous community to make an informed decision (Human Rights Council-FPIC, 2018, para. 22). Furthermore, if an indigenous community opposes land access, it is obligated to explain the reason(s) for its opposition to enable the proponent of a measure to propose steps in mitigation or to consider another location or other mitigatory or remedial measures. Importantly, information sharing must form part of attempts to reach a mutually acceptable outcome. If a decision-maker uses consultation merely as a pretence to inform an indigenous community of a decision that has already been made, or if an indigenous community opposes a measure without merit, the requirements for conducting good faith consultation, such as keeping an open mind and proper sharing of information, have not been met (Barngarla case 2023). Sharing of information is a mutual obligation, for example, if an indigenous community procrastinates in consultation, fails to participate or engage in FPIC-processes, opposes a measure without giving reasons, or commences litigation without the necessary evidence, a court may find that the community did not act in good faith (FMG case, 2009, para. 29) or may even award costs against it (Munkara consent orders cost, 2024).

8.9 When Is FPIC Applied?

A critically unanswered question in the development of normative standards for FPIC is in which areas should FPIC be sought? International law does not provide a definitive list of topics or governance matters that require FPIC. Unless otherwise specified, consultation as a normative standard is required, inter alia, in respect of administrative, environmental, developmental, and legislative measures that may affect Indigenous Peoples directly or disproportionately. While FPIC is particularly relevant when indigenous land interests are at stake, its application is not limited to such cases. Article 18 of UNDRIP states:

> Indigenous Peoples have the right to participate in decision-making in matters which would affect their rights, through representatives chosen by themselves in accordance with their own procedures, as well as to maintain and develop their own indigenous decision-making institutions.

Consultation is, however, not mandated for general socio-economic matters, public policies or legislation that also affect broader communities and individuals. Ultimately, the duty to consult arises principally from domestic law in respect to the traditional lands of Indigenous People. This explains why there is such an emphasis in UNDRIP for traditional lands to be clearly demarcated. In the Milirrpum case, Justice Blackburn stated the following about the link between Indigenous Peoples and their ancestral land:

> the fundamental truth about the aboriginals' relationship to the land is that whatever else it is, it is a religious relationship. ... There is an unquestioned scheme of things in which the spirit ancestors, the people of the clan, particular land and everything that exists on and in it, are organic parts of one indissoluble whole. (Milirrpum case, 1971, para. 167)

8.10 Who Should Be Consulted With?

A challenge that may arise in the process of FPIC is who should be consulted within an indigenous community? An indigenous community is entitled to determine how it wishes to be represented by its leaders or elders in the consultation process. However, the community must ensure that its internal processes are transparent, representative, and fair to all its various segments. It cannot be assumed that an indigenous community will reach internal consensus on every issue it addresses. The ability of community members to express dissent is a crucial element of the consultation process, but a proponent must be able to rely on the outcome of consultation as reflecting the overall view of the indigenous community.

The potential dilemma for Indigenous Peoples is that their participation in consultation may confer legitimacy on both the process and its outcome, even if they ultimately disagree with it.[24] The final decision-maker is the regulating authority. On the other hand, if Indigenous Peoples refuse to participate in consultation, they may be regarded as not acting in good faith. The UN Human Rights Council has stated the following in this respect:

---

24 Dunlap cautions that FPIC can become a 'bureaucratic trap' which potentially undermines the interests of Indigenous Peoples (Dunlap, 2018). Consequently, FPIC has served to entrench state power and reinforce existing political and economic asymmetry between different actors' (emphasis added) (Dunlap, 2018, p. 105). Also noteworthy is the observation by Cambou that the Norwegian case of Fosen (Fosen case, 2021) highlights that 'in the context of the green transition, consultation is assuredly considered a necessary instrument for guaranteeing human rights, but as the Fosen case illustrates, it is a *double-edged sword* that can either support Indigenous self-determination or legitimise green colonialism when it perpetuates decisions that deprive Indigenous communities of the benefits of their lands and livelihoods' (Cambou, 2024, p. 65).

> It is a concern if participation is used as support for State decisions where consent is not achieved, as this could discourage Indigenous Peoples from participating in decision-making processes. (Human Rights Council-FPIC, 2018, para. 22(c))[25]

8.11 Dealing with Intra-indigenous Dissent

Regardless of efforts to secure unanimity in an indigenous community, disagreements about the merit of a proposed measure may arise. The question is how dissent among Indigenous Peoples is addressed?

It is essential that third parties have confidence in the preferred negotiating mechanism of an indigenous community, including in the way the community deals with dissenting opinions in its midst and how it makes decisions. Dealing with various sub-groups or factions may complicate FPIC, but a proponent should at least attempt to create a reasonable opportunity for community sub-groups to participate in the consultation process (Tipakalippa case, 2022). That said, neither international law nor municipal law mandates consultation with or agreement by all sub-groups or individuals (Munkara case, 2024). If an indigenous community fails to participate in consultation as a cohesive unit, or is splintered into feuding groups, it may fall short of its obligation to engage in good faith consultation. Caution must also be displayed to ascertain whether those claiming to represent the community are genuinely authorised by the community to act on their behalf. For example, it was found in the Khoi case that the individual ostensibly acting on behalf of the community did so fraudulently and without authorisation of the community (Khoi case, 2022, para. 28).

8.12 Meaningful

Reference is often made that FPIC requires 'meaningful' involvement of Indigenous People in the process of consultation. What is meant by 'meaningful'? 'Meaningful' is a broad phrase of which the meaning is determined by the specific context and findings of fact by a court. It is reflected in the conduct, interactions, responses, behaviour, communication, and mannerisms of the proponent, which collectively indicate whether consultation has been mean-

25 Note, for example, the Norwegian Sara case in which the Sámi's participation in deliberations was construed as if they endorsed the outcome, which was clearly not the case (Sara case, 2017). The HRC found as follows: 'Although the Sámi Parliament has not succeeded with its view on all points, the rules implement a substantial degree of self-determination. Against this background, I have concluded that Sara's rights under ICCPR Article 27 have not been violated' (Sara case, 2017, para. 94).

ingful. However, it is important to note that 'meaningful' does not legally equate to a veto. For example, in the Maledu case, the respondent sought an eviction order against an indigenous community (Maledu case 2018). As the holder of mining rights over certain land areas, the respondent applied for an interdict to prevent the applicants from entering the land, bringing livestock onto it, or erecting structures thereon. The applicants asserted ownership of the land, emphasised the lack of consultation pursuant to the relevant legislation, and highlighted the absence of their consent for mining operations on the land to proceed. The applicants relied on the provisions of the Interim Protection of Informal Land Rights Act (Maledu case 2018, para. 16). While the Court did not directly refer to international developments regarding FPIC, it acknowledged the essential principles underlying FPIC by stating the following: the legislature expressed 'serious concerns' about the rights and interests of landowners and lawful occupiers of land; (par 78) some 'accommodation' needs to be sought between parties; (para 79); adequate information is essential to enable landowners, including informal landowners and occupants, to make informed decisions; (para 80, 97) communities have a right to determine what happens on their land; (para 95) and the impact of a mining lease would deprive the community of their rights (para 102). The Court concluded that the mining lease could not be granted since the applicant community had refused its terms (para 109).

The reasoning of the Court in the Malesu case highlights the importance of the statutory regime under which a dispute emerges. The Court found no reason to cite or consider international or foreign law, because the rights of the community to be consulted and to give consent arose from the relevant statute in South African municipal law. In the Osman case it was found that the local indigenous community had not been consulted in a way that enabled them to meaningfully express an opinion about the establishment of a wildlife conservancy (Osman case, 2025).

8.13 Lack of Agreement

The questions arising from FPIC is, what are the consequences of a lack of agreement? Failure to consult in good faith can lead to litigation, potentially resulting in the annulment of legislation, revocation of an administrative measure, or setting aside of an approval. Additionally, compensation may be awarded if an act had occurred or damage to customary land had been caused without good faith consultation having taken place (Timber Creek High Court appeal 2019; Yunupingu appeal case 2025).

In the Kichwa case, the Court emphasised the State's duty to ensure 'that the rights of Indigenous Peoples are not ignored in any other activity or agreement reached with private individuals, or in the context of decisions of the public authorities that would affect their rights and interests. Therefore, as applicable, the State must also carry out the tasks of inspection and supervision of their application and, when pertinent, deploy effective means to safeguard those rights through the corresponding judicial organs' (Kichwa case 2012, paras. 167, 219). In practice, however, compensation is rarely awarded for a lack of consultation.

The converse may also apply: an indigenous community which does not engage in good faith consultation, prolongs negotiations, engages in litigation without good reason, of gives evidence that is found wanting or lacks credibility, thereby causing an unreasonable delay to a project, may be held liable for compensation or legal costs (Munkara case 2024; Munkara consent orders cost 2024).

8.14 Differences in Legal Obligations

Finally, is there a difference in legal obligations between consultation and FPIC? There is arguably no substantive difference arising from international law in the legal obligations pursuant to consultation and the obligations arising from FPIC.

FPIC is a term specifically intended to enhance the consultation rights of Indigenous Peoples, but it does not legally imply an actual veto or co-decision-making authority – rather, it emphasises the effort to reach an agreement.

Legally, FPIC aligns with the concept of consultation, which entails providing a reasonable opportunity to influence a decision or to participate meaningfully in the decision-making process before a final determination is made. The normative framework within which FPIC must take place can generally be described in relation to the following: (a) material information about an intended event, measure, or action must be provided to those affected or with an interest; (b) the information must be provided promptly and as soon as possible; (c) the information must be detailed enough, for the entire project as well as rehabilitation, to enable those affected to obtain advice, including expert advice, and to formulate a position intra-community; (d) consultation must be aimed at reaching some form of agreement, without any legal obligation to do so, before a final decision is made; (e) the position adopted by the community must be developed freely, without undue pressure or influence; and (f) both sides are under an obligation to conduct consultation in good faith.

CHAPTER 2

Indigenous and Minority Rights: The Same and Yet Different?

1 Introduction

The recognition and protection of the rights of ethnocultural minorities and Indigenous Peoples have followed similar, yet distinct, paths. While the protection of minority rights has been on the agenda of international law and state municipal law for many decades or even centuries, the separate recognition of indigenous rights is of more recent origin (Anaya, 1996). The decolonisation processes following the establishment of the United Nations, along with the plight of ethnocultural minorities and Indigenous Peoples within those new (and existing) sovereign states, brought greater attention to constitutional and policy responses to population pluralism in general, and more specifically to the potential impacts of pluralism on the design of institutions in the modern liberal democratic state. These processes resulted in the separate treatment of the rights of ethnocultural minorities and Indigenous Peoples (Makonen, 2000).

Broadly speaking, the contemporary proposition is that the rights of ethnocultural minorities are principally protected through the individual rights of their members, whilst indigenous communities can exercise individual and collective rights. This proposition is, however, not without controversy. The extent to which collective rights accrue to ethnocultural or indigenous communities as separate legal entities from their individual members remains evolving.

One of the principal questions affecting constitutional design especially since the establishment of the United Nations and the democratisation process that had commenced in so many countries has been whether and to what extent population diversity should influence constitutional drafting and institutional design (e.g. Lijphart 1969; Capotorti 1979; Horowitz 1993; McGarry, O'Leary, and Simeon 2008; Kymlicka 2012). The appropriate institutional response to population diversity remains a thorny issue to many established as well as young and emerging democracies.

In the immediate aftermath of the Second World War, any suggestion to deal with ethnocultural minorities explicitly in institutional design, such as through collective rights, was frowned upon. However, over time, population

HTTPS://DOI.ORG/10.1163/9789004724792-003

plurality re-emerged as a relevant consideration in the design of democratic constitutions. The European Court of Human Rights (ECtHR) has acknowledged the broad discretion of states to determine how, if at all, provision should be made for minorities in institutional design. Thus, a 'wide margin of appreciation' is granted to states, recognising their sovereign right to respond to population plurality when designing institutions (Bakirdzi case, 2022, para. 44). The ECtHR has also described pluralism as 'indissociable from a democratic society' (Kokkinakis case 1993, para. 31).[1] By acknowledging the relevance of pluralism, the ECtHR has not, however, mandated that institutional design should be based or reflect population diversity. The decision of institutions is a matter for sovereign states. As aptly summarised by Kymlicka: 'Minority rights, like all rights, are not self-enacting: they only emerge if there are political forces within society to claim them, and political forces within the state to enforce them' (278).

It came as no surprise when Francesco Capotorti, Special Rapporteur of the Sub-Commission on the Prevention of Discrimination and Protection of Minorities of the United Nations, made the following observation in his groundbreaking report on the protection of minorities in 1979:

> For quite a long time after the end of the Second World War, it was thought – and stated in writing – that the question of the international protection of minorities was no longer topical. During the past few years however, *that view has proved to be mistaken.* (emphasis added) (Capotorti, 1979, p. iii)

At the time of the Capotorti report, the constitutional status of Indigenous Peoples as separate rights-bearing groups also began to gain greater traction and recognition in international law. Indigenous Peoples positioned themselves as a special category, distinct from ethnocultural minorities, asserting that their unique status derives from historic sovereignty over and enduring ties to their traditional lands. This distinction is said to entitle indigenous communities to specific recognition and tailored institutional arrangements, particularly regarding their traditional lands. In 1989, ILO 169 became the first international legally binding instrument to address indigenous rights, stating the following in its Preamble:

1 In the case of Fedotova, the ECtHR emphasised that 'according to the Court's case law, this pluralism has to be accepted as a hallmark of democratic societies and the existing diversity of views among both Europeans and European States should be perceived not as a threat but as a source of enrichment' (Fedotova case, 2023, para. 2.3).

> Considering that the developments which have taken place in international law since 1957, as well as developments in the situation of indigenous and tribal peoples in all regions of the world, have made it appropriate to adopt new international standards on the subject with a view *to removing the assimilationist* orientation of the earlier standards... (emphasis added) (ILO 169, 1989 Preamble)

ILO 169 relies as a point of departure on the acknowledgement of the distinct interests of Indigenous Peoples, affirming their right to separate recognition and protection from the general population. While the post-UN framework largely promoted the institutional assimilation of ethnocultural minorities on the premise that their individual rights were protected, ILO 169 represented a shift from this approach. It became the first legal instrument to endorse a model of collective self-determination, recognising Indigenous Peoples collectively as distinct communities separate from the broader population and in addition to the rights of their members.

The notion of the separateness of Indigenous Peoples is not without controversy given that separateness may also be grounded in inequality or discrimination, as famously declared in the US Supreme Court *Brown* case (Brown case, 1954). Separateness may erode national unity, disrupt the social fabric, and challenge the principle of equality before the law.[2] Arguably, the very reasons put forward for not recognising collective rights of ethnocultural communities, can also be raised in response to demands of Indigenous People for collective rights.

The recognition of the collective rights of Indigenous Peoples is primarily based on their pre-settlement sovereignty, pre-existing separate legal and customary systems, traditional land ownership and control, collective experiences of discrimination, and their existence as self-governing societies with their own legal and customary systems that predate the modern state (J. Anaya, 2009, pp. 1–3).

The separate and distinct character of Indigenous Peoples as pre-settlement societies therefore serves as *the* legal and policy basis for their collective rights to self-determination, recognising their customs and traditions alongside their individual civil rights (Cobo, 1986). ILO 169 states as follows:

2 Note, for example, the proposition that one of the reasons why the referendum in Chile to recognise the rights of Indigenous People was rejected was the perception that different system of law and administrative were to be established which could undermine the principle of equality before the law (Morales and Pérez-Cosgaya, 2025, p. 18).

> This Convention applies to:
> (a) tribal peoples in independent countries whose social, cultural and economic conditions distinguish them from other sections of the national community, and whose status is regulated *wholly or partially by their own customs* or traditions or by special laws or regulations;
> (b) peoples in independent countries who are regarded as indigenous on account of their descent from the populations which inhabited the country, or a geographical region to which the country belongs, *at the time* of conquest or colonisation or the establishment of present state boundaries and who, irrespective of their legal status, *retain some or all* of their own social, economic, cultural and political institutions. (emphasis added) (ILO 169, 1989, art. 1)[3]

The rationale for indigenous rights is generally rooted in the proposition that indigenous communities have had their traditional systems of government interrupted or dismantled by settler societies without adequate treaty, agreed-upon compensation, consultation mechanisms, recognition of their collective rights, acknowledgement of their status as original inhabitants, or institutional arrangements that uphold their rights consistent with their pre-settlement society.

It is also important to note that some Indigenous Peoples, particularly in the Americas, saw the post–Second World War international minority protection regime as principally applicable to Europe and based on assimilation and integration, rather than self-determination and collective rights. They feared that assimilation based solely on individual rights may undermine the uniqueness of indigenous collective rights and diminish their right to self-determination (Lorca and Marin, 2024, p. 26). The rise of indigenous rights therefore took a distinct path to the prevailing thoughts of ethnocultural rights, with the essential distinction being the proposition that Indigenous People enjoy collective rights in addition to individual rights. But, as observed

3 Note that the non-binding Indigenous and Tribunal Convention 107 of 1957 committed the international community to developing a binding Convention to recognise and protect the rights of tribal and Indigenous Peoples. An essential objective was stated as follows: 'Governments shall have the primary responsibility for developing co-ordinated and systematic action for the protection of the populations concerned and their *progressive integration* into the life of their respective countries' (emphasis added) (Indigenous and Tribunal Convention 107, 1957, art. 2). It is worth noting in this regard the contrast between the 1957 position of 'progressive integration' with the main population and the 1989 objective to remove the 'assimilationist orientation'. Rombouts describes this as a 'significant shift' on indigenous rights (Rombouts, 2017, p. 13).

by Nut, 'confusion may arise between the rights of Indigenous Peoples and minorities because many of these features are common to both' (Nut, 2015, p. 102).

The purported rationale for separate recognition of indigenous collective rights is not without criticism, for example:

Firstly, the notion of pre-settlement sovereignty as a basis for contemporary collective rights is not settled in international law, especially not if the sovereignty of existing states may be challenged as a result of unresolved claims arising from historic sovereignty.

Secondly, pre-settlement concepts of sovereignty may have differed from contemporary understandings of the term.[4] The proposition that there was pre-settlement stability in respect of exclusivity of land occupation or governance systems may be fictional or poorly documented.

Thirdly, the exact nature and extent of pre-settlement sovereignty and legal systems are often undocumented or, when recorded, interpreted through the lens of contemporary laws and understandings, not to mention political and ideological biases.

Fourthly, the legal status of an indigenous community that no longer maintains its societal or customary ties to traditional lands, or no longer adheres to traditional customs and systems of law, remains unclear. This then raises the question: at what point, if any, does an indigenous community that no longer maintains their connection with traditional lands or no longer practice traditional laws and customs, become an ethnocultural group with only their individual rights recognised based on assimilation rather than an indigenous community entitled to separate collective and individual rights? In the Australian Ward case, it was suggested that traditional rights could be lost if not observed or practiced (Ward case, 2002, para. 32).

Fifthly, the legal status of urbanised Indigenous People that no longer maintain traditional connection to land or no longer functions as a 'traditional society' remains unclear since the collective rights they often seek to exercise relate to contemporary socio-economic policies and not to traditional lands.

Sixthly, the emphasis placed by international jurisprudence on some form of association by Indigenous People with their customary and traditional lands, is regarded by advocates of indigenous rights as too narrow to reflect the contemporary needs of Indigenous People. This debate was evidenced in

4 Note, for example, Wiessner who talks about 'authentic indigenous sovereignty' being a 'safe space' for Indigenous Peoples. This is some distance removed from the concept of sovereignty understood in international law concerning states (Wiessner, 2008).

the Voice referendum in Australia where proponents of the advisory Voice sought to expand the subject matters on which it could give advice beyond the scope of traditional lands (De Villiers, 2024b).

These issues remain unresolved, with courts avoiding becoming entangled in such normative issues. For example, in the Yanner, Yorta Yorta, and Moriarty cases in Australia, courts had to consider whether Indigenous Peoples continue to exercise their rights as a society and whether traditional rights could be modernised for exercise within a contemporary context (Yanner case 1999; Yorta Yorta (HCA) case 2002; Moriarty case 2024).[5] Meanwhile, in the South African Bhe case, a traditional custom was declared incompatible with the Constitution because it was deemed to discriminate against women (Bhe case, 2005). Notably, concerns have been raised in South Africa (and other parts of Africa) that despite the constitutional recognition of customary systems, the requirement for customary laws to comply with the Bill of Rights may ultimately lead to the supersession of such traditional laws by national laws, reducing them over time to the status of mere non-legal customs and traditions (Rautenbach, 2024). Diala, for example, is critical of the notion that customary law, despite its ancient roots, is simultaneously recognised as equal to other legal systems while being treated as subservient to the Constitution. The South African Constitution, he states, makes a 'mockery of indigenous law's parity with the common law' and perpetuates the repugnancy clause (a term often used by colonial authorities to dismiss indigenous customs) in a different way (Diala, 2019, p. 16). Sachs observes, however, that customary law is not frozen in the past and can adjust to retain its relevance as a living system of law (Sachs, 2024), emphasising the following:

> Customary law is not being singled out for therapeutic constitutional treatment as though it were some junior, immature system of law in need of vitamin injections. The exact same developmental injunction applies to the common law. And similarly, all legislation must be interpreted with the purpose of promoting the spirit of the Bill of Rights. (Sachs, 2024, p. 477)

---

5 In the Moriarty case, the Court had to consider whether an indigenous person's harvesting of abalone and selling it for commercial gain to someone outside the indigenous community was consistent with the exercise of traditional rights. The Court concluded that, pursuant to Section 211 of the Native Title Act 1993 (Cth), traditional fishing without a permit is allowed for the purposes of a household or the benefit of the indigenous community; the catching of fish for the purpose of commercial selling to an external person is not protected by traditional fishing as intended in s211; and the proof rests on the prosecutor to establish that a defence pursuant to s211 is not applicable (Moriarty case, 2024, para. 180).

Indigenous and ethnocultural communities share the common denominator of being 'minorities' in the general sense of being non-dominant groups that maintain a shared identity through culture, language, religion, customs, or traditions. However, they differ in the source of their rights, their historic sovereignty, their relationship to traditional land, their institutions of self-government, and the nature and scope of the recognition and protections they seek.[6]

The distinction that is said to exist between ethnocultural minority rights and indigenous rights is rather weak in principle and not endorsed in jurisprudence. Eide and Daes, for example, explain the distinction as follows:

> Bearing the conceptual problem [of distinguishing Indigenous Peoples from minorities] in mind, I should like to suggest that the ideal type of an "Indigenous People" is a group that is aboriginal (autochthonous) to the territory *where it resides* today and chooses to perpetuate a *distinct* cultural identity and *distinct* collective social and political organization within the territory. The ideal type of a "minority" is a group that has experienced *exclusion* or *discrimination* by the State or its citizens because of its ethnic, national, racial, religious or linguistic characteristics or ancestry. ... From a purposive perspective, then, the ideal type of [a] "minority" focuses on the group's experience of discrimination because the intent of existing international standards has been to *combat discrimination*, against the group as a whole as well as its individual members, and to provide for them the opportunity to integrate themselves freely into national life to the degree they choose. Likewise, the ideal type of "Indigenous Peoples" focuses on aboriginality, territoriality, and the desire to remain collectively distinct, all elements which are tied logically to the exercise of the right to *internal self-determination, self-government,* or *autonomy.* (emphasis added) (Eide and Daes, 2000, paras. 48–49)

This purported distinction between the rights of ethnocultural minorities and those of Indigenous Peoples is by no means watertight or legally secure. On

6 Castellino states that indigenous rights are a subset of the international 'minority rights regime' (Castellino, 2010, p. 415). One of the pertinent characteristics of the minority rights regime is that the sovereignty of the state is respected in the sense that international law does not impose positive legal obligations on it to promote the interests of minorities or Indigenous Peoples (Castellino, 2010, p. 416). He explains that while the protection of individual rights has a universal norm-setting value and hence seeks to limit the sovereignty of the modern state, minority, and indigenous protection arrangements lack legal norm-setting value and are subjugated to the sovereignty of the state (Castellino, 2010, p. 422).

proper analysis the distinction is informed by political expediency rather than by legal principle.

It remains unexplained, except perhaps due to effective advocacy, why ethnocultural minorities are expected to integrate institutionally with the majority, while Indigenous Peoples are regarded as entitled to separate collective institutional recognition. Kymlicka is particularly blunt in criticising the purported distinction between minority and indigenous rights in international law, stating: 'The UN approach has the virtue of simplicity; however, it is arguably inadequate to the real-world challenges of ethnic diversity' (Kymlicka, 2008, p. 6).

Kymlicka goes on to pose the question of why international law seemingly affords stronger protection of collective rights to Indigenous Peoples than to ethnocultural minorities. He then offers the following response, drawing on the general justifications found in the literature:

> There are two familiar justifications for according Indigenous Peoples stronger rights of self-determination than stateless nations. The first claims that Indigenous Peoples exercised historical sovereignty, which was wrongfully taken from them, and so self-determination is simply restoring their inherent sovereignty.... A second familiar line of argument says that Indigenous Peoples need self-determination to preserve their pre-modern way of life. On this view, stateless nations typically share a common civilization with the majority, and so do not need self-determination in the same way as Indigenous Peoples, whose way of life is incompatible with modern state structures (Kymlicka, 1999, pp. 286–287)[7]

In contemporary society, there is growing awareness of the relevance of ethnocultural and indigenous pluralism in the design of institutions of governance and the protection of rights. Arguably the most pertinent reason for the failure of democratisation is the underlying dissatisfaction of ethnocultural minorities and Indigenous Peoples within existing institutional and policy arrangements. Bloch puts it succinctly: 'Most conflicts in the world today

---

7 Kymlicka points out, by reference to the work of Anaya, that both these propositions are rejected on the basis, firstly, that the historical sovereignty-principle is not accepted in international law and it ignores pre-settlement overlaps and competing claims by indigenous communities and, secondly, that cultural isolation is not the objective of the recognition of indigenous rights and all minorities have equal claim to self-determination (Kymlicka 1999, 287; Anaya 1996). Kymlicka argues that attempts in international law to address the 'indigenous versus minority dichotomy' have 'proven to be inadequate', thereby raising 'deep questions' about the 'capacity of international law to articulate and protect minority rights' (Kymlicka, 2008, p. 2).

are ethnic conflicts within states, arising from internal power struggles' (Bloch, 2001, p. 373).

International law supports individual rights to self-determination and freedom of association, thereby providing the foundation for communities to collectively preserve their cultural, linguistic, religious, and customary rights (ICCPR 1966, arts. 1, 27; Tiina Sanila-Aikio case 2018, para. 6.9). In this regard, the Fosen case in Norway is illustrative of how the individual right to self-determination and the right to culture interlink to form a collective right for Indigenous Peoples to protect their traditional lands (Fosen case, 2021). In the Community Garifuna of San Juan case the court also linked the individual right to property to the rights of the indigenous community to collectively own, manage and enjoy their traditional lands (Community Garifuna of San Juan case, 2023).[8] This is similar to the Moriarty case in Australia, in which the Court held that natural resources taken by an indigenous person from their traditional land are presumed to be lawfully taken as part of the community's entitlement through traditional ownership, unless proven otherwise (Moriarty case, 2024).

Noteworthy, however, is the South African Constitutional Court's observation that the recognition of the diversity of Indigenous People (and ethnocultural minorities) does not have 'governmental consequences', implying that diversity cannot be relied on to justify separate political institutional arrangements for ethnocultural communities and Indigenous Peoples (Certification case, 1996, para. 195).[9] The Court drew a distinction between acknowledging population pluralism as a societal reality and respecting customary legal systems, while emphasising that these should not be construed as a basis for separate political collective rights.

This chapter briefly examines how indigenous rights and ethnocultural minority rights have gained recognition in international law. It starts by considering the concept legal plurality, emphasising how modern states increas-

---

8 The Court observed as follows: 'The culture of the members of indigenous communities directly relates to a specific way of being, seeing and acting in the world, developed on the basis of their close relationship with their traditional lands and the resources therein, not only because these are their main means of subsistence, but also because they are an integral element of their worldview, their religiosity and, therefore, their cultural identity' (Community Garifuna of San Juan case, 2023, para. 91).

9 In its Certification judgement of the new Constitution in 1996, the South African Constitutional Court referred to the 'diversity' of cultural, religious, customary, and language communities, but did not suggest that those communities function within the context of legal pluralism whereby they exhibit separate collective legal systems and procedures that ought to be separately accommodated in the constitutional design (Certification case, 1996, paras. 179, 205, 210).

ingly recognise, legally or pragmatically, the existence of non-state customary laws, traditions, customs, and practices. Against this backdrop, the chapter explores selected jurisprudence affirming the individual rights of persons that associate with ethnocultural communities, contrasting these with the recognition of collective indigenous rights. The aim is to highlight both the similarities and differences in the legal recognition and protection of the respective communities. This discussion underscores why this book specifically focuses on the consultation rights of indigenous communities, as ethnocultural communities generally do not assert equivalent consultation rights, such as FPIC in respect of their traditional areas, under international law.

2 Legal Pluralism: An Old and New Phenomenon

In social sciences, pluralism describes population diversity based on factors such as ethnocultural, religious, and indigenous composition. Legal pluralism, on the other hand, refers to the coexistence of multiple systems of law, customs, traditions, and rules with the force of law that apply within the same territorial space (Woodman, 1999). Pluralism as a sociological concept should not be conflated with legal pluralism; not all plural societies exhibit legal pluralism. In a social sense, pluralism implies diversity in population, practices, customs, and opinions. The ECtHR has described societal pluralism as 'indissociable from a democratic society' (Kokkinakis case 1993, para. 31). The same Court cautioned, however, that pluralism in a legal sense, whereby different legal systems compete in the same territorial space, introduces greater complexity, as courts may need to determine which legal norm applies and whether the religious or cultural 'law' invoked by a community is consistent with national law (Refah Partisi case, 2003).[10]

Legal pluralism predates the modern state. It is as much an idea as an ideology, a norm, a historical fact, and a social occurrence (Neo, 2020, p. 899). Despite the uniformity of laws that the modern state seek to impose on all inhabitants based on state sovereignty, universality, and uniformity, legal pluralism – as an expression of cultural, religious, and customary iden-

10 In this case, the ECtHR found that the banning of a political party that sought to propagate and rely on Sharia law within the context of Europe was a lawful restriction since the legal system on which Sharia is based is inconsistent with the provisions of the European Convention on Human Rights. A similar approach was adopted by the Constitutional Court of South Africa when, without engaging in the teachings of a religious group, it declared that the refusal to marry same sex couples was in breach of the Constitution, regardless of the doctrinal teachings of the church (Gaum case, 2019).

tity – has persisted in many countries (Rautenbach, 2021). In particular, sub-national legal systems such as customary law and religious law may, in some jurisdictions, compete with state legal norms.

In the context of this book, legal pluralism is particularly associated with indigenous rights and interests, given that indigenous customary systems often incorporate legal elements alongside customs and traditions (De Villiers, 2025d, p. 32). This raises a potential challenge for courts: how to ascertain whether a specific practice sought to be relied on is a custom (with no legal force) or a legal norm (with legal force).[11]

Legal pluralism in the context of indigenous customary law is, according to the South African Constitutional Court, a reality and must be taken seriously by courts (Alexkor case, 2003, paras. 45–51). It is worth noting, however, that this constitutional acknowledgement of the status of customary law as a distinct legal system is not commonly shared by countries with indigenous or tribal communities. The South African courts have emphasised that tolerance of and respect for pluralism and diversity are fundamental values of a democratic society (Prince case, 2002, para. 150). The ECtHR has also accepted that even within the uniformity of the modern European state, in this case Greece, elements of legal pluralism may exist (Kokkinakis case, 1993). Nonetheless, the same Court has also been cautious not to endorse legal pluralism as general norm within European states, especially when the norms espoused by a non-state religious legal system may be inconsistent with European liberal democratic norms and standards (Refah Partisi case, 2003).

Since the 1970s, the term 'legal pluralism' has been increasingly used in both its scientific application and advocacy (Teubner and Bukovina 1997; Teubner 2012). Interest in legal pluralism has grown in parallel to the increased attention paid to the rights of ethnocultural communities and Indigenous Peoples in international and domestic laws. Legal pluralism may find general expression easily, but 'there is no chance of defining it' (Seinecke, 2018, p. 21). Tamanaha describes the term as a 'folly' that exhibits the appearance of a well-established theory of law but whose basic tenets remain unclear (Tamanaha, 1993). Praet states that the popularity of legal pluralism is an indication of the 'perceived failure of legal grand narratives such as the nation-state' (Praet,

11 Note, for example, the Sengadi case in which the court had to decide whether the handover of a bride was a necessary customary legal requirement for a valid marriage or whether it was only a custom or practice. The Court ruled that is was not a legal requirement, much to the dissatisfaction of critics (Sengadi case, 2019, para. 42). Sibisi, for instance, argues that culturally, marriage is incomplete without this ceremony and that empirical evidence does not support the notion that this important step can be waived (Sibisi, 2024, p. 935).

2018, p. 31). According to Griffiths, legal pluralism is an attribute of a pluralistic society, where various legal systems within the same social field have different origins (Griffiths 1986, 39). Sani, meanwhile, criticises the literature on legal pluralism as 'muddled in confusion' (Sani 2020, 83), with Neo arguing that legal pluralism can be framed as a 'normative good' because it reflects societal diversity and reality (Neo 2020, 899).

Despite its lack of definition, legal pluralism refers generally to 'the presence in a social field of more than one legal order' (Griffiths, 1986, p. 1). This proposition can hardly be regarded as controversial since there are so many examples where indigenous, customary, religious, and tribal communities exist within the context of their own legal systems regardless of the state legal system. In their judgements, courts often respond to legal pluralism, particularly religious and indigenous plurality (e.g. Mabo case (2) 1992; Mahuika case 2000; Alexkor case 2003; Kashela case 2018), but courts do not create legal pluralism.

Legal pluralism is considered one of the 'most important challenges' facing contemporary constitutionalism (Pavel, 2021, p. 143).[12] Indeed, in some respects, legal pluralism is the very antithesis of the uniformity and universality sought to be provided by international human rights norms and municipal normative laws and rights. In literature, use of the expression legal pluralism is diverse, and its meaning depends on the circumstances in which it is applied. The term is widely cited without being restricted to a precise legal definition.[13] Importantly, according to Pirie, from a historical perspective 'different forms of law have existed through history and in different parts of the world, not all

---

12 Pavel points to the inconsistencies that prevail between the uniformity sought by international law and constitutionalism – whereby uniform liberal democratic norms are promoted – and legal pluralism which supports a multiplicity of norms originating from communities (Pavel, 2021, pp. 148–149). This is a typical top-down and bottom-up dichotomy, with universal norms seeking to standardise rights, while legal pluralism seeks to distinguish between different legal systems based on grassroots identities. Tusseau, meanwhile, notes the perspective that legal pluralism implies autonomy of a nature that 'excludes constitutionalism' (Tusseau, 2020, p. 12).

13 Griffiths refers to the 'ideology of legal centralism' which implies that 'law is and should be the law of the state, uniform for all persons, exclusive of any other law, and administered by a single set of state institutions' (Griffiths, 1986, p. 3). Consistent with this, Griffiths describes the state as the sole source of laws, while other cultural, religious, or indigenous customs and rules are not regarded as state laws, even if members of the respective communities may regard such community customs as 'laws'. This is, however, a rather one-dimensional approach to law, contrasting with the acknowledgement by South African, Australian, South American, and Canadian courts of the plural and multidimensional nature of their respective legal systems (Delgamuukw case 1997; Yanner case 1999; Alexkor case 2003; Bhe case 2005; Kokkinakis case 1993; Moriarty case 2024).

connected with a state or even a centralized government' (Pirie, 2023, p. 20). At its most extreme, legal pluralism – especially in the context of religious radicalism – can even be invoked to justify the creation of a new state through secession.

Legal pluralism does not necessarily imply two competing legal systems of equal status in every aspect of social, customary, or religious life. Legal pluralism may instead relate to specific rules, customs, or laws that affect only a subset of a community's social life.[14] Buchler attempts to describe, rather than define, the complexity of legal pluralism as follows:

> Legal pluralism refers to a plurality or multiplicity of norms within one legal order and to norms which coincide in the same social sphere and overlap in their approach to the same issues, people and territory. It is thus both an analytical framework and the cypher determining the simultaneous fragmentation, pluralisation, superposition and fusion of legal systems. (Büchler, 2016, p. 80)

Legal pluralism can create a dilemma for legal subjects in them having to choose which of the competing legal norms to follow (Teubner and Bukovina 1997). For courts, the challenge is to determine when, if at all, to recognise or give effect to non-state laws of Indigenous People. The complexity of interactions between state law and indigenous non-state law is reflected in Diala's assertion that 'modern states have lost absolute claims to normative sovereignty' (Diala 2019, 3).

While scientists struggle to define with any precision the nature and character of legal pluralism, for the purposes of this book I adopt a rather simple approach: laws, regulations, directives, judgements, and administrative actions that arise from state agencies (principally legislative, executive, and judicial institutions) are referred to as 'state law'. In contrast, rules, customs, traditions, and practices that arise from non-state entities, such as customary or tribal institutions, or cultural and religious customs and practices and traditional courts, are referred to as 'non-state law', provided the relevant community to whom those rules apply regards them as binding law (De Villiers, 2025g, p. 542). Perspectives within a community may vary on how a

14 Note, for example, the case of Prince in the USA, where members of a Jehovah's Witness Church denied their child an essential blood transfusion. The Court had to consider the religious beliefs of the parents and concluded as follows: 'Parents may be free to become martyrs themselves, but it does not follow that they are free, in identical circumstances, to make martyrs of their children before they have reached the age of full and legal discretion when they can make that choice for themselves' (Prince case, 1944).

particular custom should be regarded – as a law or as a voluntary, cultural, or religious practice.

Returning to the interaction and distinctiveness of indigenous and ethno-cultural minority rights: in relation to legal pluralism it is notable that these realms overlap and intersect. Legal pluralism as it relates to customary land generally emphasises the existence of a distinct legal system as typically found in the customary laws of indigenous communities, while minority protection focuses on institutional design to facilitate political participatory rights and protection against discrimination, even if the community does not have a separate legal system.

The linkage between an indigenous community and their ancestral legal system was summarised as follows in the Australian Yorta Yorta case in which it was established that, to qualify for native title land rights, Aboriginal people must meet the following criteria to prove their ongoing connection to traditional land: (a) they must continue to function as a 'society' of traditional owners that are linked to ancestral land and the occupiers thereof, (b) the functioning must be in accordance with their ancestral laws and culture, and (c) their culture and cultural practices are not be frozen in time, allowing for adaptations to contemporary circumstances (Yorta Yorta (HCA) case 2002). This approach is also reflected in the Community Garifuna of San Juan case of Honduras in which the Court declared as follows about the linkage between Indigenous People and their ancestral land:

> The Court has taken into account that indigenous and tribal peoples, by the fact of their very existence, have the right to live freely in their own territory; the close ties that they have with the land must be recognized and understood as the *fundamental basis of their cultures*, their spiritual life, their integrity and their economic survival. For indigenous communities, the relationship to the land is not merely a matter of possession and production but a material and spiritual element that they should be able to enjoy fully, especially in order to preserve their cultural legacy and to transmit it to future generations. (emphasis added) (Community Garifuna of San Juan case, 2023, para. 91)

Ahren also observes that for Indigenous Peoples to fall within the scope of protection by UNDRIP, they must demonstrate having '*established societies* in their traditional lands with at least *key institutions* intact' (Ahren, 2023, p. 175). In the Awas Tingni and Sawhoyamaxa cases, the links between customary institutions and traditional lands were also highlighted (Awas Tingni case 2001; Sawhoyamaxa Community case 2006, para. 118). In the Poma Poma case, the relationship between the right to culture and the right to (indigenous) property was invoked to grant relief for the indigenous community to be consulted (Poma Poma case, 2002, para. 7.2). In the Taromenane case the Court upheld the choice of the indigenous community to live in isolation and held that they had not given free, prior, and informed consent for their lands to be encroached (Taromenane case, 2024).

Although cultural and linguistic minorities do not necessarily rely on pre-settlement societal legal systems to justify their demands for special protection and collective political rights, they may nevertheless feel threatened, persecuted, discriminated, or marginalised because of their unique culture, language, or traditions. As a result, ethnocultural communities may advocate for specific constitutional or statutory design measures in order to safeguard their identity, language, and culture – even without them having a separate legal system (UN Declaration on Minorities 1992; European Framework Convention 1998; Lund Recommendations 1999; Ljubljana Guidelines 2012). The proposed distinction at law between indigenous and ethnocultural rights is blurred and not supported by in-depth scrutiny.

Kymlicka correctly cautions against the simplification of the distinction between indigenous and minority rights, observing as follows:

> In the practice of Western democracies, national minorities belong with Indigenous Peoples on the *accommodation* side of the ledger; according to UN norms, they would belong, with the new minorities, on the *integration* side. (emphasis added) (Kymlicka, 2008, p. 10)

I note the following in respect of the purported distinction between ethnocultural and indigenous rights:

(a) The legal distinction between ethnocultural minorities and Indigenous Peoples, as if it were universally accepted and legally incontestable, is open to challenge;
(b) The concept of indigenous sovereignty is not without controversy, as contemporary legal notions of sovereignty may not align with traditional approaches to land rights;
(c) The lack of definitional clarity surrounding the terms 'indigenous' and 'minority' limits the application of the rights associated with them and the remedies that arise from their breach;
(d) As far as rights of consultation and FPIC are concerned, these generally accrue to Indigenous Peoples in respect of their traditional lands and

matters associated therewith. In contrast, ethnocultural minorities rarely benefit from formal consultative mechanisms akin to FPIC;[15]

(e) FPIC and consultation cannot be legally construed as granting a form of political power-sharing, co-decision-making, or veto, since FPIC is at best a procedural right rather than a co-governance right;

(f) The uniqueness of customs and practices of ethnocultural communities and Indigenous People does not mean those practices amount to non-state law;

(g) The reliance on historic sovereignty is arguably *the* essential consideration said to distinguish the rights of Indigenous Peoples from those of ethnocultural minorities. Nonetheless, the proposition is tenuous, and its relevance dubious, when traditional ties to land diminish or traditional practices are no longer observed; and

(h) Broadly, the origin of consultation with Indigenous Peoples is causally linked to their traditional lands, laws, and customs. Were this not the case, an indigenous community would arguably be not entitlement to any different treatment than any other ethnocultural community.

While jurisprudence has acknowledged the collective nature of certain indigenous communities (De Villiers 2023e, 33–41), it is essential to note that an ethnocultural community typically lacks the attributes of a 'society' with its own legal norms associated with pre-settlement land, as is commonly observed in the case of Indigenous Peoples. This is consistent with the approach adopted by Anaya who emphasises that a characterising element of Indigenous Peoples is that their 'ancestral roots are embedded in the lands on which they live' (J. Anaya, 2009, p. 1).

In summary, legal pluralism is a relatively recent scientific concept with varied applications, yet its definition remains vague and ambiguous. A threshold question arising from the term is what constitutes 'law'. All customs or cultural practices cannot be regarded as law. Legal pluralism aims to describe an existing social condition whereby more than one legal system operates within the same territorial jurisdiction. Legal pluralism can deepen democracy, enhance individual rights and freedoms, and promote the principles of subsidiarity and self-determination. Nonetheless, if taken to its extreme,

---

15 It is worth noting, however, the South African example where the Constitution (s 33) and the Promotion of Administrative Justice Act recognise fair and reasonable administrative processes for all individuals, thereby including ethnocultural and indigenous communities who may feel their individual rights are infringed by an administrative measure. This right to consultation in South Arica is thus available to any individual or community whose interests are directly affected by an act of government (Wild Coast appeal case, 2024).

legal pluralism may undermine national unity, erode social integration, weaken community cohesion, challenge the legitimacy of state-law, encroach on individual rights, and even cause violence or the breakup of the state. Courts do not create legal pluralism – instead, different legal systems may inherently exist within the social fabric as a fact. However, courts may determine whether a non-state, indigenous legal system is recognised, identify its legal norms, assess their relevance to a proceeding, evaluate their role in dispute resolution, and consider their enforcement or implementation, as well as their consistency with the constitution.

For the purposes of this book, indigenous customary systems serve as the most prominent example of a potential non-state legal system.

3 Background to the Protection of Ethnocultural Minorities and Indigenous Peoples

International law has experienced fluctuations over decades, and perhaps centuries, regarding the recognition and protection of ethnocultural minority rights. In contrast, the protection of indigenous rights has only recently become a focal area for international law. Prior to the establishment of the United Nations, responding to the demands and claims of Indigenous Peoples was seen as a domestic issue that fell outside the ambit of international relations (J. Anaya 2009, 9–38).

Some of the earliest treaties between European states focused on the protection of specific vulnerable minorities, particularly in relation to their religious rights. Outside the European sphere, the recognition and protection of the rights of ethnocultural communities and Indigenous Peoples first gained acceptance in the 1960s and has only built-up real momentum since the 1990s. The consideration given to the rights of Indigenous Peoples is reflected in several post-1990s judgements from courts and international expert bodies, with Mabo, Richtersveld, Endorois Welfare Council, Delgamuukw, Poma Poma, Saramaka, Sesana, Orissa Mining, Baleni, Kashela, Fosen, Community of Garifuna of San Juan, and Kebaowek Fist Nations cases leading the way.[16]

The recognition and protection of minority rights was a major concern, principally within the European context, of the League of Nations (Thorn-

16 (Mabo case (2) 1992; Delgamuukw case 1997; Poma Poma case 2002; Alexkor case 2003; Endorois Welfare Council case 2003; Sesana case 2006; Saramaka case 2007; Orissa Mining case 2013; Kashela case 2018; Baleni case 2019; Fosen case 2021; (Community Garifuna of San Juan case, 2023, para. 119) Kebaowek First Nation case 2025).

berry, 1991). After the Second World War, the United Nations initially sought to shift the debate away from collective minority 'rights' to focus solely on the protection of individual rights (Capotorti, 1979). Practical realities, however, necessitated a re-evaluation of the individualised approach, and since the 1960s, various initiatives have been undertaken in international law under the auspices of the United Nations, as well as other international and regional agencies, to protect and promote the rights of ethnocultural minorities and Indigenous Peoples, individually and collectively.

Since there is no agreed definition in international law of the concepts of minority, indigenous or tribal peoples, it is left to states to determine whether any community within their jurisdiction satisfies those descriptions and if so, the collective rights if any that attach to the community. This complicates efforts to develop universal norms for the protection of those communities as distinct legal entities. The distinction between Indigenous Peoples and ethnocultural minorities often becomes 'blurred' (Toki and Raman, 2024, p. 9).[17] A further complicating factor is that members of communities potentially considered indigenous or tribal may have moved away from their traditional lands and integrated into urban communities. Some may have lost connection to their traditional lands or no longer observe traditional customs, yet still feel marginalised as a racial or ethnocultural community.

It is left to individual states to determine whether ethnocultural or indigenous communities exist within their state and, if so, to adopt measures relevant to them that align with international law.[18] The effectiveness of international instruments aimed at protecting the rights of ethnocultural minorities and Indigenous Peoples is limited, as they rely not on legal enforcement – other than through individual rights – but rather on goodwill, advocacy, and appropriate domestic policy settings.

---

17 Toki and Raman caution that grouping together Indigenous Peoples with local communities in a generic sense has the potential to 'undermine the effectiveness and impact of indigenous advocacy' (Toki and Raman, 2024, p. 9). Note, in this respect, South African case law such as Baleni and Wild Coast, in which the Courts emphasise the rights of local communities *without* seeking to distinguish whether rights to consultation are limited specifically to 'Indigenous People' (Baleni case 2019; Observatory Civic Association case 2023; Wild Coast appeal case 2024).

18 The ECtHR has referred to the wide discretion given to states to determine how, if at all, provision should be made for minorities in the design of institutions, as a 'wide margin of appreciation'. This implies recognition of state sovereignty in designing institutions in accordance with the priorities of the specific state (Bakirdzi case, 2022, para. 44).

3.1 Characteristics of Minorities and Indigenous Peoples

As a general proposition, ethnocultural minorities and Indigenous Peoples can be said to share the following characteristics: a community of individuals formed through free association in pursuit of a common identity based on cultural, linguistic, customary, and religious beliefs and practices; usually constituting a numerical minority; and being non-dominant, with a shared desire to maintain and promote their identity both individually and collectively. I have referred to the individual rights associated with these characteristics as 'identity rights' (De Villiers, 2025a, p. 13). In addition to the identity rights shared by individuals belonging to ethnocultural minorities and indigenous groups, Indigenous Peoples also demonstrate a physical, emotional, and spiritual connection to their traditional ancestral lands, often continuing to function as a society with distinct customary rules, laws, and traditions.[19] Importantly, those rights are exercised not only individually but also collectively (Community Garifuna of San Juan case, 2023, para. 119).

Notably, international soft law has only since the 1970s seriously sought to recognise the separate legal status of ethnocultural minorities and Indigenous Peoples. This purported distinction is reflected in the UNDRIP and the Declaration on Minorities. Neither of these declarations is legally binding.

Significantly, the point of departure for international law concerning the rights of ethnocultural minorities and Indigenous Peoples is found in a shared principle, namely the protection of the individual rights of persons who associate with such communities as well as their protection against discrimination pursuant to the right to self-determination (ICCPR 1966; ICESCR 1966; Taylor 2020). Both the ICCPR and ICESCR are legally binding treaties.

International treaty law does not support collective rights for ethnocultural minorities or Indigenous Peoples as if they are distinct legal entities. International hard and soft law envisage that individuals associating in a community with each other may promote their interests through class actions, which may appear as if the community is exercising a collective right; however, a class action does not give the community a legal identity separate from the

19 Toki and Raman add to the element of ancestral land a unique 'worldview' that is held by Indigenous Peoples (Toki and Raman, 2024, p. 11). They argue that a principal element of indigenous advocacy is the desire for self-determination and that this is not shared by ethnocultural minorities (Toki and Raman, 2024, p. 16). This is, however, a debatable proposition, as many ethnocultural minorities also seek self-determination of various kinds, be it on a territorial or non-territorial basis. Furthermore, to suggest that a community can be characterised by its 'worldview' is at best dubious, as it proposes a standard of unity within a community that may be fictional.

legal identity of its members. Furthermore, international soft law anticipates that Indigenous Peoples exhibit collective rights by virtue of the societies within which they function (Tiina Sanila-Aikio case 2018; Lhaka Honhat Association case 2020; Fosen case 2021; Community Garifuna of San Juan case, 2023). In the Community Garifuna of San Juan the Court said: 'Indigenous communities are considered collective subjects of international law that exercise certain rights, such as the collective ownership of the land' (Community Garifuna of San Juan case, 2023, para. 99).

In essence: It is due to their connection with traditional lands and traditional systems of governance that the collective status of Indigenous Peoples is approached with greater vigour that the case is with ethnocultural minorities.

3.2 The Individual as a Legal Entity

The legal entity under international treaty law that bears identity rights is the individual. However, awareness of identity rights must be understood within the context of bills of rights, which recognise the right of individuals to practice their culture, adhere to their customs, and speak their language in association with other members of the same minority. In this respect, courts may consider that when an individual exercises their rights in association with others, it also serves to protect the broader community's interests (Fosen case, 2021; Endorois Welfare Council case, 2003). Courts may also accept the corporate status of indigenous communities to commence proceedings on behalf of their entire community (Harrington-Smith case 2007; Quera Aboriginal Community case 2001; Alexkor case 2003; Sawhoyamaxa Community case 2006). Noteworthy is the Lhaka Honhat Association case, in which the Inter-American Court of Human Rights emphasised the 'interrelated' nature of individual rights, declaring that the 'State is responsible for the violation of the right to take part in cultural life as this relates to cultural identity, a healthy environment, adequate food, and water' (Lhaka Honhat Association case 2020, para. 202, 207, 289, 370). The individual right to culture was used as a basis for a broader interpretation of rights (Lhaka Honhat Association case, 2020, para. 337). In a 2021 judgement, the IACrtHR held that the rights of the Maya people to protect and promote their culture were improperly constrained by restrictions placed on their members' freedom of communication through the unfair regulation of radio stations (Maya Peoples case 2021).

To the extent that specific political participatory rights are granted to an ethnocultural minority or an Indigenous People within a state's institutional design – for example through quotas, guaranteed seats in the legislature, vetoes over certain policy areas, participation in a government of national unity, advisory bodies, or cultural self-government on a territorial or non-territorial basis – these arrangements do derive from municipal measures designed to address the specific circumstances of a particular state (Hannum, 2023).[20] This explains why the Constitutional Court of South Africa was careful to recognise the diversity of the population as a societal fact, but emphasised that this diversity could not be relied on to seek separate political rights for the respective communities (Certification case, 1996, para. 195).

The protection of the rights of ethnocultural minorities and Indigenous Peoples, though often vague and unenforceable under international treaty law, remains central to global democratisation and conflict-resolution efforts. Despite attempts to individualise these rights, political realities, collective discrimination, persecution, and other challenges arising from democratisation processes and conflict resolution have kept the collective protection of ethnocultural minority and Indigenous Peoples' rights on the agenda of international organisations. The importance of accommodating population pluralism in constitutional design was echoed by the Venice Commission, which in 1994, while major constitutional transitions were underway in many parts of the world, observed that since the 1970s, the recognition and protection of minority rights had become a priority within the European sphere:

> It was an urgent choice: violent ethnic conflicts were beginning to rise up in several places on the new European map. (Venice Commission, 1994, p. 2)

3.3 Development of Minority Protections

The recognition and protection of the rights of ethnocultural minorities have been a subject of attention for centuries, gaining prominence, particularly in the European sphere, since the early twentieth century as democratisation and constitutionalism spread globally.

One of the most notable earlier arrangements for minority self-government was enacted during the Ottoman Empire (c. 13–1923) when the millet system

---

20 See, for example, the non-binding guidelines that have been developed in Europe to encourage institutional arrangements that better accommodate political participation by ethnocultural minorities (Lund Recommendations 1999; Ljubljana Guidelines 2012). Although international law emphasises the rights of the individual as the cornerstone in the protection of minorities, these rights should be considered a minimum threshold. States are encouraged to go beyond this threshold and establish expanded institutional and policy arrangements for the protection of ethnocultural minorities and Indigenous Peoples (Dinstein and Tabory, 2023).

was used to grant to communities, principally religious (Greek Orthodox, Armenian, and Jews) but also ethnic (the Kurds also had a Millet (Tas, 2013, p. 168)), a form of local community self-government which enabled them, within the highly centralised empire, to arrange their community affairs in line with their traditions, customs and beliefs (Barkey and Gavrilis, 2017; Malloy, 2020).

Another noteworthy example of an early minority protection instrument was the Edict of Nantes, signed on April 30, 1598, which recognised the rights of the Protestant minority in Catholic-dominated France (Sutherland, 1987). Meanwhile, the 1648 Peace of Westphalia, comprising the Treaty of Münster (24/10/1648) and the Treaty of Osnabrück (15/5/1648), which brought an end to the Thirty Years' War, sought in particular to protect religious (Christian) minorities (Reus-Smit, 2013).

One of the first international instruments to formally recognise the rights of minorities was the Polish Minority Treaty (1919).[21] This provided in article 8 that minorities, most notably Jewish communities residing in Poland, had the right to establish, manage and control, at their own expense, charitable, religious and social institutions, schools and other educational establishments, including the right to use their own language and exercise their religion freely therein.

3.4 The League of Nations

The League of Nations was established in 1919 with the objective of maintaining and promoting international peace.[22] The organisation oversaw the establishment of new territorial arrangements, particularly in Europe and parts of

21 June 28, 1919 (Fink, 1998). Fourteen countries (Albania, Austria, Bulgaria, Czechoslovakia, Estonia, Greece, Hungary, Iraq, Latvia, Lithuania, Poland, Romania, Turkey, and Yugoslavia) adopted similar treaties aimed at protecting minorities within their national boundaries. These were ad hoc arrangements, primarily due to concerns about the disruptive potential of minority demands not being accommodated, and arising from the insistence of kin-states whose citizens were residing in other countries. The role of kin-states in promoting the interests of their community members residing in other countries remains relevant in contemporary society (Hofmann, Malloy and Rein, 2018a, p. 21).

22 Article 22 of the Covenant of the League of Nations made reference to religious and other communities within certain parts of the world, but there was no universal commitment to protecting the rights of ethnocultural minorities and Indigenous Peoples. The so-called Minority Treaties that arose from the Treaty of Versailles sought to address the situation of minorities in particular countries, but did not establish binding international norms.

the Middle East where many states had diverse populations in terms of language, religion, and culture. Many ethnocultural communities had been split into two or more national territories, finding themselves within newly created states or on the 'wrong' side of newly drawn international borders. Extensive practical measures were undertaken to create arrangements recognising population diversity, driven by concerns that overlooking plurality might lead to new instability within the broader European context (Roucek, 1929; Ermacora, 1983). At that time, international law showed little concern for minorities (or Indigenous Peoples) in other parts of the world (except in certain parts of the Middle East, such as Iraq and Turkey).

The challenge of defining the concept of 'minority' had already emerged at this stage. Key questions included who qualifies as a minority, how a community is collectively defined, does community have a legal identity and rights separate from its individual members, and who represents such a group without formal legal incorporation. The Permanent Court of International Justice, created by the League of Nations in 1922, attempted to give content to the concept of minority rights by describing a minority as a group of persons residing in a particular country or locality, distinguished by their race, religion, language, and traditions. These individuals are united by this identity and share a sense of solidarity aimed at preserving their traditions, maintaining their religious practices, bringing up and educating their children in accordance with the spirit and traditions of their race, and offering mutual assistance[23] (PCIJ-Greco-Bulgarian case 1930, para. 17).

The point of departure was that the individual, not the community to whom they belonged, was the legal entity and the rights bearer, whilst the community was a sociological rather than a legal concept.

3.5 The United Nations

Following the Second World War and its associated atrocities, where the identification of individuals belonging to certain minorities was exploited for persecution and genocide rather than protection, the international focus shifted away from minority rights. The attention turned to safeguarding individual rights and protection of individuals against discrimination as the sole means to protect the rights of individuals belonging to minorities. Institutionally, the

23 In the Albania case, the Court found that the right to establish and manage their own schools is 'indispensable in enabling the minority to enjoy the same treatment as the majority, not only in law but also in fact' (Albania case 1935 par 67). The Court did not, however, mandate state funding for such community schools (Albania case 1935 par. 79).

most effective way to protect minority rights was seen to be assimilation, informal coalition forming, and decentralisation to localities where minorities reside in sizeable numbers. Any formal recognition of collective rights on a non-territorial basis was resisted. This approach left those minorities without a territory in a weak legal and practical position.

For the first time in international law, the rights of Indigenous Peoples became depicted as separate from those of other minorities. But, the recognition of indigenous rights was also based on the principle of individuality and assimilation. This explains why the non-binding Indigenous and Tribal Populations Convention 107 of 1957 committed the international community to developing a binding Convention to recognise and protect the rights of indigenous and tribal peoples by facilitating their integration with the dominant society. An essential objective of the Convention was stated as follows: 'Governments shall have the primary responsibility for developing coordinated and systematic action for the protection of the populations concerned and their *progressive integration* into the life of their respective countries' (emphasis added) (Indigenous and Tribal Populations Convention 107 1957, art. 2).

Assimilation, within the context of protecting individual rights, was viewed as the path to recognising the rights of individuals belonging to ethnocultural minorities and indigenous groups. Anaya summarised the prevailing approach to indigenous rights at the time as follows:

> The universe of values that promoted the emancipation of colonial territories during the middle part of this century simultaneously promoted the assimilation of members of culturally distinctive indigenous groups into dominant political and social orders that engulfed them. Assimilation and rights of full citizenship were used to bring within the fold of self-government the indigenous groups living in independent and newly independent states. (emphasis added) (Anaya, 1996, p. 44)

It was thought, overly optimistically in hindsight, that the rights of all individuals, including those belonging to minority and indigenous groups, could best be protected through a bill of rights focusing on the rights of individuals to equality, non-discrimination, freedom of association, religion, and so forth (Capotorti, 1979).

Activists in the Americas were, however, persistent in their view that minority rights should not be conflated with indigenous rights, as the latter are based on historic customs, traditional lands, self-government, and pre-settlement sovereignty. Therefore, they felt, Indigenous Peoples should not be regarded or treated as 'minorities' (Cristescu, 1981). Given this, the 'assimilationist' approach adopted concerning minorities was seen as inconsistent with the recognition of the separate nature of indigenous rights (Lorca and Marin, 2024, p. 28). It was argued that Indigenous Peoples were entitled to recognition of both individual and collective rights, particularly in regard to their ancestral lands, customs, laws, and traditions.

The United Nations did not at the time envisage special mechanisms or measures for protecting ethnocultural minority rights or indigenous rights in the context of institutional design in the immediate post–Second World War period. In 1954, Kunz described the accepted approach in this period as follows:

> Today the well-dressed international lawyer wears "human rights" as the new fashion, while prior to World War II the fashion was "minority rights". (Kunz, 1954, p. 282)

Since the 1960s, international opinion on the recognition and protection of ethnocultural minority rights and indigenous rights has evolved. In contemporary international and constitutional law, a greater awareness exists of the importance of protecting the rights of minority and indigenous groups and, where applicable, of the merits of developing institutional arrangements and political processes that facilitate their effective participation in public affairs. The United Nations recognises that the outcome and stability of democratisation efforts and conflict resolution often hinge on the effective accommodation of ethnocultural minority and indigenous rights (UNHRC 2022; UNHRC 2010). The adoption of the ICCPR and the ICESCR in 1966, and their entry into force in 1976, represented a major step towards the recognition of identity rights that relate to culture, language, religion, customs, and self-determination.[24] The same can be said of the enactment of ILO 169 which recognises the rights of individuals associating with indigenous groups, but also opens the door to recognising the collective rights of Indigenous Peoples, such as their right to '*retain some or all* of their own social, economic, cultural and political institutions' (emphasis added) (ILO 169, 1989, art. 1). Meanwhile, the adoption of the term 'self-determination' to apply not only to new sovereign states in the context of decolonisation, but also to the rights of peoples

24 Article 27 is said to have marked a 'new era' for the protection of minorities (Taylor, 2020, p. 787), and 'the promotion and protection of the rights of persons belonging to national or ethnic, religious and linguistic minorities contribute to political and social stability and peace, and enrich the cultural diversity and heritage of society as a whole in the States in which such persons live' (UN Resolution, 2004).

within those nations, as well as the rights of individuals, further enhanced the framework of identity rights under international law (Cassese, 1995).

3.6 International Instruments

Several international instruments have been adopted to facilitate the protection of ethnocultural minority and indigenous rights. This section briefly highlights the most relevant ones for purposes of this book: ILO Convention 169, the Declaration on Minorities, and UNDRIP.

ILO 169 is the only legally binding treaty in international law dealing specifically with the rights of Indigenous Peoples.[25] It applies a 'holistic' approach to a wide range of policy issues affecting Indigenous Peoples, including their consultative rights (Handbook ILO, 2013, p. xi). It establishes a minimum threshold for the protection of Indigenous Peoples in general, and for the recognition of their consultative and participatory rights in particular (Yupsanis, 2011). The underlying rationale for ILO 169 is that Indigenous Peoples retain their inherent historical sovereignty, which entitles them to be consulted, in accordance with their traditional laws and customs, on matters that affect them, particularly those concerning their traditional lands, customs, and culture (Kryazhkov and Garipov, 2021, p. 1009).

The ILO 169 Handbook emphasises, however, that the Convention does not create any 'special' rights for Indigenous Peoples. It explains:

> Indigenous Peoples' rights are not "special" rights, but are articulations of universal human rights, as they apply to Indigenous Peoples. This means contextualizing rights to the situation of Indigenous Peoples and taking the collective aspects of these rights into account. (Handbook ILO, 2013, p. 3)

In the absence of an agreed definition of who constitutes a minority or an Indigenous People, what is the meaning of self-determination, or what collect-

---

25 ILO 169 is an international treaty that becomes legally binding upon states through ratification. Beyond the ratifying countries, ILO 169 also serves as a frequently cited international reference point. It is also used as a norm-setting standard by UN and regional human rights bodies, in literature and training materials, and occasionally by national courts (Handbook ILO, 2013, p. 5). The binding nature of the treaty's provisions is likely the reason why so few countries have ratified ILO 169 (at the time of writing, only 23 had done so, with notable abstentions of countries with indigenous populations being Australia, New Zealand, Canada, Indonesia, India, Malaysia, South Africa, and the USA). Larsen argues that 'despite relatively low ratification numbers, the relevance and global reach of the Convention has grown significantly not least through its incorporation in a wide range of complementary standards and jurisprudence' (Larsen, 2020, p. 94).

ive rights these communities possess beyond the individual rights of their members, remains challenging (Magazzini, 2024, p. 1829). Courts and expert bodies can use international soft law to inform their interpretations of domestic rights, explain the interrelatedness of rights, and expand traditional understandings of fundamental rights (Tiina Sanila-Aikio case, 2018, para. 6.9). In Canada, where UNDRIP has been incorporated into legislation, it has been found that a proponent ought to have taken into account the consultation obligations in UNDRIP in the discharge of its responsibilities (Kebaowek First Nation case, 2025, para. 183). The Court reiterated, however, the consultative nature of FPIC.[26] In Finland, where the negotiation rights of the Sámi were expanded in 2025, an obligation is placed on 'authorities and other parties handling public administrative tasks' to 'negotiate' with the Sámi Parliament about 'legislation, administrative decisions or other measures that may carry particular importance for the Sámi are under preparation'. The aim of the negotiation is 'a *view to* reaching a consensus…or obtain consent prior to decision-making' (emphasis added) (Sámi Parliament as amended, 2025, sec. 9).[27]

The Declaration on Minorities seeks to expand the intended operation of Article 27 of the ICCPR, by requiring that states take positive action to assist ethnocultural minorities (Phillips, 2015).[28] While not legally enforceable, the adoption of the Declaration underscores how the notion of protecting minorities has gained credibility, relevance, and prominence since the UN's establishment. The Declaration attempts to set new practical, not legal, standards for the protection of minorities, including by how it recognises the right of minorities to 'participation' (Barten, 2015).[29] Notably, when the Declaration

26 Note in this respect the use of the word 'consultation' rather than 'consent' by the Court in the Community of Garifuna of San Juan case: 'the *right to consultation* of indigenous and tribal peoples, in addition to being treaty-based, is also a general principle of international law' (emphasis added) (Community Garifuna of San Juan case, 2023, para. 138).

27 The obligation to negotiate concerns measures affecting the Sámi homeland or if it 'particularly impact' the Sámi language or culture, the status of the Sámi as indigenous people in respect of areas such as land use, conservation, mining, climate change, childhood education, health and social services (Sámi Parliament as amended, 2025, sec. 9).

28 It is notable that, in general, Article 27 of the ICCPR does not place a positive obligation on the state to assist individuals in maintaining their identity, but rather that the state must create circumstances within which individuals can freely exercise their rights and self-organise. However, the suggestion arises from UNDRIP that in respect to the rights of Indigenous Peoples, states are under a 'positive obligation to adopt 'special measures' to 'ensure' that members of indigenous and tribal groups 'enjoy the full and equal exercise' of their rights (Kichwa case, 2012, para. 171).

29 (UN Declaration on Minorities, 1993, art. 2(3)): Participation: 'Persons belonging to minorities have the right to participate freely in decisions on the national and, where

on Minorities is compared to UNDRIP, the former does not contain any references to FPIC, underlining the importance placed by the international community on the special consultative rights of Indigenous Peoples.

UNDRIP is the most advanced and widely endorsed international instrument seeking to protect and promote the rights and interests of Indigenous Peoples.[30] Although UNDRIP is non-binding at law – in contrast to ILO 169 – countries are nevertheless expected to develop, promote, and adjust domestic policies in a manner consistent with its terms.

UNDRIP was drafted through the standard-setting processes of the United Nations, with Indigenous Peoples participating in the lengthy (more than two decades) process (McCreery, 2012, p. 16). The extent to which countries enact policies and practical measures to give effect to UNDRIP remains a sovereign decision, reflecting the unique circumstances and approaches each country adopts regarding its Indigenous Peoples (Macnab, 2020).

3.7 Regional Instruments

Several other international and regional instruments seek to protect and promote ethnocultural minority and indigenous rights. These include the Framework Convention for the Protection of National Minorities (FCNM) and the American Convention on Human Rights (ACHR), which are briefly elucidated in this section.

The most important contemporary regional instrument intended to protect national minorities is the European-wide FCNM (European Framework Convention, 1998; Hofmann, Malloy and Rein, 2018b) The FCNM is, to date, the first and only legally binding charter designed solely for the protection of ethnocultural minority rights within international law, although its scope is limited to the European region[31] (Weller, 2005). It is exclusively dedicated to

---

appropriate, regional level, concerning the minority to which they belong or the regions in which they live, and in a manner not incompatible with national legislation.'

30 UNDRIP was adopted by the General Assembly of the United Nations on September 13, 2007, with 143 countries voting in favour, 11 abstaining and 4 voting against. The countries that voted against UNDRIP, referred to as the CANZUS Alliance, are Canada, New Zealand, Australia, and the USA. Nonetheless, these four countries have since endorsed UNDRIP.

31 At the time of publication, 40 countries (including Kosovo with special arrangements) had ratified the FCNM. Note that the European Union and its member states are not bound to the FCNM pursuant to the EU's founding treaties. The FCNM is a separate treaty to which individual states in the European Union may choose to become signatories. As a distinct treaty, it has also been signed by states that are not members of the European Union.

the rights of 'national' minorities, acknowledging in its Preamble that within the context of Europe 'the protection of national minorities is essential to stability, democratic security and peace' (Hofmann, Malloy and Rein, 2018a). The FCNM sets out general principles which must be given practical effect by member states through their constitutional, political, and policy arrangements (Explanatory Report on FCNM, 1995, para. 11). The FCNM does not define what constitutes a national minority, instead leaving it to the states to determine which communities within their population ought to be treated as one for the purposes of the FCNM (Explanatory Report on FCNM, 1995, para. 12). The FCNM prescribes general principles but is silent on the specific methods for implementing these principles within states.[32] The FCNM does not seek to recognise collective rights, but rather to enhance the recognition of individual rights of members of ethnocultural minorities and to encourage states to adopt measures, legal, policy, and practical, to give effect to those rights. The enforceability of the FCNM is based on consensual political processes and advocacy, rather than litigation.[33]

Meanwhile, the Inter-American system for the protection of human rights was created with the adoption of the American Declaration of the Rights and Duties of Man in 1948 (American Declaration), followed by the American Convention on Human Rights (American Convention) in 1969. Established under the auspices of the Organization of American States (OAS), the system comprises 35 member states from North, Central and South America as well as the Caribbean. However, not all OAS members states have accepted the American Convention. Member states are required to comply with the rights set out in the American Declaration and, where applicable, the American Convention. The American Declaration defines the human rights that ratifying states have committed to respect and uphold. It also establishes the Inter-American Court of Human Rights (IACrtHR) and the Inter-American Commission on Human Rights (IACHR). Both the American Declaration and American Convention safeguard individual rights and freedoms, including, of particular relevance to indigenous rights, the protection of property rights (American Convention, 1969, art. 21). Only states and the Commission may refer a dispute to the IACrtHR. The IACrtHR has handed down various judgements in which

32 The FCNM is not enforceable through litigation, but rather through political mechanisms, reporting, and advocacy. The Committee of Ministers of the Council of Europe and the Advisory Committee (ACFC) are involved in monitoring the implementation of and adherence to the FCNM. The ACFC has contributed considerably to the forming of a normative 'force' concerning protection of minorities (T. H. Malloy and Caruso 2013, 12).

33 The lack of consistency in minority protection among states within the European context has been critically referred to as 'double standards' (Henrard, 2010).

the rights of Indigenous Peoples to property, consultation, and protection of their traditional lands have been recognised (Awas Tingni case 2001; Saramaka case 2007; Kalina and Lokono case 2015; Community Garifuna of San Juan case, 2023). Furthermore, courts across the Americas have been relatively active in recognising indigenous rights pursuant to municipal constitutions and statutes. In Latin America, while extensive lip-service has been paid to indigenous rights and the importance of FPIC when indigenous land interests are affected, courts have generally been slow to adopt normative consultation standards that require actual 'consent' from Indigenous Peoples. As a result, FPIC is seen as a consultative process rather than a right of veto, leaving Indigenous Peoples to 'continue to face significant power imbalances' (Tomaselli and Cittadino, 2021, p. 175). Note in this respect the use of the word 'consultation' rather than 'consent' by the Court in the Community of Garifuna of San Juan case: 'the *right to consultation* of indigenous and tribal peoples, in addition to being treaty-based, is also a general principle of international law' (emphasis added) (Community Garifuna of San Juan case, 2023, para. 138).

Several judgements and expert opinions, discussed later in greater detail, emphasise the right of Indigenous Peoples to consultation on measures that may impact their traditional lands. Importantly, while international law relies on individual rights as a point of departure for protecting ethnocultural minorities and Indigenous Peoples, it is acknowledged that, depending on the rules of interpretation in a specific country, the interpretation given to identity rights can be informed by both hard and soft international law. Consequently, the Declaration on Minorities and UNDRIP can provide context for integrating Article 27 of the ICCPR with the non-justiciable objectives imbedded in those Declarations (Strydom, 2021, p. 234). In this respect, the opinion expressed by the UN Human Rights Committee in the Sanila-Aikio case is instructive:

> Moreover, although the rights protected under article 27 are individual rights, *they depend in turn on the ability of the group to maintain* its culture, language or religion. The Committee further recalls that the preamble of the United Nations Declaration on the Rights of Indigenous Peoples establishes that Indigenous Peoples possess collective rights which are indispensable for their existence, well-being and integral development as peoples. In view thereof, the Committee considers that in the context of Indigenous Peoples' rights, articles 25 and 27 of the Covenant (ICCPR) have a *collective dimension* and some of those rights can *only* be enjoyed in community with others. (emphasis added) (Tiina Sanila-Aikio case, 2018, para. 6.9)

4 Summary

A dichotomy persists between universal standards that safeguard ethnocultural minority and indigenous rights through individual rights, and the demands of marginalised and threatened minorities – both indigenous and ethnocultural – seeking more effective collective protection of their rights to meaningful political participation and consultation in matters affecting them as individuals and as a community. This demand is consistent with social reality whereby individuals belonging to Indigenous People and ethnocultural communities are often the target of discrimination, unequal treatment, repression, or persecution because of their collective identity and association.

The emphasis in international law on the protection of ethnocultural minorities and Indigenous Peoples by way of individual rights may be legally sound and valuable as a minimum norm, but in practice this sole focus on the rights of the individual is often simplistic, inadequate, and Since identity rights reach their full expression (only) when exercised within a community of others who share the same culture, language, religion, traditions.

The unresolved predicament of the lack of a clear threshold for granting some form of collective participatory rights to ethnocultural minorities or indigenous communities was highlighted in a report by a group of UN expert advisors, which notes that 'many United Nations member states lack effective and genuinely comprehensive legal frameworks for the prevention of discrimination and promotion of equality' (UN Experts 2022). Despite this critique, there appears to be little appetite in the international community for adopting a treaty that establishes universal legal standards for the collective protection of ethnocultural minority or indigenous rights.

The only justiciable universal norm that can be agreed on is that the individual rights – and not collective rights – of persons belonging to minorities and Indigenous People should be protected. The 'homogeneity' approach adopted by international law emphasises a bill of rights as the sole instrument for the protection of ethnocultural minorities and Indigenous Peoples. This stands in contrast to the 'pluralism' approach which encourages additional mechanisms, most notably collective political participatory rights, for the protection of such groups (Ahmed, 2011, p. 3). While special collective political rights for ethnocultural minorities and Indigenous Peoples are not uncommon in municipal law, those measures remain confined to the specific states that implement such arrangements and have not been elevated to a universal standard in international law. Similarly, courts – particularly in the Americas – have expanded the interpretation of fundamental rights, particularly the right to property, by referencing ILO 169 and UNDRIP, but these do not constitute broadly accepted international norms or widely adopted state approaches to the interrelatedness of rights.

The development of the rights of ethnocultural minorities and Indigenous Peoples has followed similar, yet distinct, paths in both theory and practice. Until the mid-1970s, international law focused primarily, if not completely, on individual rights as the sole basis for protecting these communities. However, with the adoption of ILO 169 and later UNDRIP, recognition of indigenous rights has grown significantly to become a distinct area of scholarly, political, and judicial attention, particularly in respect of the collective exercise of indigenous rights. Ethnocultural minorities and Indigenous Peoples share some characteristics such as being non-dominant communities with common cultural, linguistic, customary, religious, and traditional ties. However, they are also distinct, as the rights of Indigenous Peoples are often linked to their pre-settlement self-governing status, their special connection to traditional lands, and their ongoing adherence as a society to their own traditional laws and customs.

CHAPTER 3

The Conception and Emergence of Free, Prior, and Informed Consent

1 Introduction

The term 'free, prior, and informed consent' (FPIC) has, since the enactment of UNDRIP in 2007, become synonymous with the rights of Indigenous Peoples. FPIC has no settled meaning. FPIC is simultaneously an ambit claim, a rallying cry, a desire, a slogan, an objective, an ideological statement, and a directive principle for indigenous engagement – but not a justiciable right. It is a macro norm that tolerates and welcomes many interpretations and aspirations. FPIC 'has come to symbolically and substantively represent the crux of the international struggle to uphold Indigenous rights' (Petkar, 2017, p. 10). It represents more than a right – it reflects a philosophy.

As discussed in Chapter 1, the efficacy of FPIC as used in UNDRIP is affected by the lack of clarity about its meaning, legal effect, and remedy, particularly concerning the use of the word 'consent' and the implications thereof. While general principles of interpretation would suggest that the word 'consent' should be understood in its ordinary meaning, those same principles of interpretation also require that the meaning of a word or phrase be determined in the context of its use, rather than as a stand-alone term divorced from its contextual framework.[1] Context is important. 'Consent', as used in FPIC as it appears in UNDRIP, does not carry its ordinary literal meaning.[2] This is because of the preceding words 'in order to obtain' in UNDRIP suggest that it is the effort to reach consent rather than consent itself being the subject of recognition. As observed by Pulver:

> Over the years since the Declaration's adoption, the pertinent bodies referred to above have maintained that the principle of FPIC *should not* be interpreted as vesting Indigenous Peoples with a general veto right; rather, the scope of FPIC

1 The Vienna Convention on the Law of Treaties (VCLT) serves as the starting point for interpreting international law (Vienna Convention, 1969, arts. 31–33). Article 31(1) states: 'A treaty shall be interpreted in good faith in accordance with the ordinary meaning to be given to the terms of the treaty in their context and in the light of its object and purpose.'

2 The Law Reform Commission on Australia succinctly defined consent as 'free and voluntary agreement' (Australian Law Reform Commission, 2010).

 | HTTPS://DOI.ORG/10.1163/9789004724792-004

> depends on the circumstances and the interests of the Indigenous Peoples involved. (emphasis added) (Pulver, 2022, p. 115)

Some scholars and advocates contend that the word 'consent' in FPIC should be interpreted, according to its ordinary and literal meaning, as implying a legal veto. However, its use in UNDRIP is ambivalent, as the Declaration is a non-legally binding instrument and FPIC is formulated in a qualified manner. Domestic courts, meanwhile, have been reluctant to attribute greater rights to FPIC than to consultation,[3] given that UNDRIP is a non-binding declaration, it lacks a definition of FPIC, and it frames the concept in terms of efforts to achieve consent rather than conferring an absolute right of veto or co-decision-making. Even the protection under Article 10 of UNDRIP against forcible removal of Indigenous People from traditional land is not absolute and is qualified by the requirement of just and fair compensation. To complicate matters further, UNDRIP employs other terms that may overlap and compete with FPIC in meaning and function, such as 'consultation' (Articles 15.2, 17.2, 19, 30.2, 32, 36 and 38), 'cooperation' (Articles 19, 32), and 'good faith' (Articles 19, 32.2, 46.3), without defining them or clarifying their legal or substantive differences with FPIC. This reflects the programmatic and aspirational nature of UNDRIP.

1.1 Chapter Content

This chapter examines the origins of FPIC and explores why and how international norms addressing indigenous claims have evolved from using the term 'consultation' to 'free, prior, and informed consent'. It considers state responses to ILO 169 and UNDRIP, as well as how courts and expert human rights bodies have applied these instruments to develop domestic law and jurisprudence. The chapter then reflects on FPIC in the context of medical science to ascertain potential guidelines for its meaning as used in UNDRIP. Lastly, it reviews the development of FPIC both before and under UNDRIP.

The term FPIC appears in 6 articles of UNDRIP, with Articles 19 and 32 illustrating the programmatic nature of the Declaration:

> 19 States shall consult and cooperate in good faith with the Indigenous Peoples concerned through their own representative institutions *in order to* obtain their

3 Note in this respect the use of the word 'consultation' rather than 'consent' by the Court in the Community of Garifuna of San Juan case: 'the *right to consultation* of indigenous and tribal peoples, in addition to being treaty-based, is also a general principle of international law' (emphasis added) (Community Garifuna of San Juan case, 2023, para. 138).

> free, prior and informed consent before adopting and implementing legislative or administrative measures that may affect them.
>
> ....
>
> 32.2 States shall consult and cooperate in good faith with the Indigenous Peoples concerned through their own representative institutions *in order to* obtain their free and informed consent prior to the approval of any project affecting their lands or territories and other resources, particularly in connection with the development, utilization or exploitation of mineral, water or other resources. (emphasis added)

1.2 FPIC as an Advocacy Tool

FPIC is generally relied on for the purposes of advocacy, education, non-legal standard setting, and mobilising public opinion. Importantly, consistent with the focus of this book, FPIC also serves as a reference point for interpreting indigenous rights to good faith consultation.

FPIC is said to originate from the right to self-determination as found in article 1 of the ICCRP. Special Rapporteur Rodolfo Stavenhagen endorsed the proposition of the Working Group on Indigenous Populations (WGIP) that the right to self-determination serves as the 'bedrock' of all human rights, and that Indigenous Peoples have an 'intrinsic right' to decision-making over their lands, natural resources, cultural identity, language, and education (Stavenhagen Report, 2003, para. 12). He further noted that the right to free, prior, and informed consent is of 'crucial concern' to Indigenous Peoples, as so many 'large-scale developments' take place on their traditional lands without their consent (Stavenhagen Report 2003, para. 13).

The WGIP was effectively the first forum under the auspices of the UN dedicated exclusively to the rights and interests of Indigenous Peoples. Stavenhagen underscored the importance of FPIC in the context of large-scale projects, making the following recommendations:

> Free, prior, informed consent is essential for the human rights of Indigenous Peoples in relation to *major development projects*, and this should involve ensuring mutually acceptable benefit sharing, and mutually acceptable independent mechanisms for resolving disputes between the parties involved, including the private sector....*To the extent* that major development projects impinge upon traditional indigenous territories or ancestral domains, indigenous land and property rights must be considered as human rights at all times, whether they are so recognized legally or not. (emphasis added) (Stavenhagen Report 2003, para. 66, 75)

In reality, and despite some initial fears and hopes, FPIC has neither emerged as the wolf in sheep's clothing it had been made out to be,[4] nor as *the* effective legal standard for indigenous empowerment, sovereignty restoration, and co-decision-making that many had hoped for. FPIC has, however, deeply impacted on the discourse about indigenous rights and it has become a reference point to assess conduct.

At its core, FPIC is aspirational. It represents a philosophy, an attitude, and a framework for responsible social policy. Although UNDRIP is not legally enforceable, it seeks to encapsulate and reflect fundamental rights and aspirations enshrined in international human rights treaties. It also reflects developing international opinion, though not as a legally enforceable or justiciable right. Notably, caution was expressed in UNDRIP concerning the right to self-determination and its potential implications for state sovereignty, as clarified in Article 46(1):

> Nothing in this Declaration may be interpreted as implying for any State, people, group or person any right to engage in any activity or to perform any act contrary to the Charter of the United Nations or construed as authorizing or encouraging any action which would dismember or impair, totally or in part, the territorial integrity or political unity of sovereign and independent States.

FPIC influences policy formulation rather than serving as a substantive legal principle for litigation. It functions as a legally rightful process, than a justiciable right. There is no case law citing FPIC as a separate, stand-alone source of rights derived from international law that implies an absolute veto within domestic law. The same case law referencing FPIC is frequently cited in literature, but with little further expansion or clarification beyond the term being an objective or having good faith consultation at its core. When cited, FPIC is often framed in the context of good faith. Note in this respect the use of the word 'consultation' rather than 'consent' by the Court in the Community of Garifuna of San Juan case: 'the *right to consultation* of indigenous and tribal peoples, in addition to being treaty-based, is also a general principle of international law' (emphasis added) (Community Garifuna of San Juan case, 2023, para. 138).

States are left to respond to FPIC at their discretion. Several states have enacted various forms of consultation-legislation, but FPIC has not been

4 At the UN Permanent Forum on Indigenous Issues, Canadian Minister of Crown–Indigenous Relations Carolyn Bennett declared: 'Let's be honest, implementing UNDRIP should not be scary' (Wohlberg, 2016).

adopted by any state as a comprehensive domestic veto-mechanism for Indigenous People. McGlade notes that she cannot 'point to any country that is doing a great job of implementing the Declaration' (Australia's Inquiry into UNDRIP 2023, para. 2.3). Tomaselli adds that even in the Americas courts have been slow to expand the meaning of FPIC, leaving Indigenous Peoples vulnerable to power imbalances (Tomaselli and Cittadino, 2021, p. 175). In the Kebaowek First Nation case, the Canadian Supreme Court emphasised the consultative aspect of FPIC (Kebaowek First Nation case, 2025, para. 183).

Tomaselli rightly observes that the definitional challenges underlying UNDRIP remain a 'thorny issue' (Tomaselli 2016, 510). Various key terms in the Declaration – such as Indigenous Peoples, self-determination, free, prior, and informed consent, collective right, and autonomy – remain vague and undefined. Put simply, if, for example, a 'right' to FPIC is recognised in international law, but the legal subject (entity) entitled to the right – whether a natural or legal person – or the content of the right is not clearly defined, what is its potential legal or practical effect, or the remedy for its violation? In my view, Barrie correctly critiques this lack of definitional clarity as undermining the 'normative value' of the terms in question (Barrie, 2013).

Nevertheless, the lack of definitional clarity and specificity should not diminish FPIC's role in increasing awareness of indigenous rights and interests. FPIC has provided content, direction, advocacy, and momentum to ongoing efforts aimed at the fair and just protection of indigenous rights.

1.3 FPIC in Judgements

Judgements that refer to FPIC typically do so by reference to a relevant municipal law or fundamental rights, citing, for example, the municipal right to property, environment, or culture (Kichwa case 2012; Baleni case 2019, paras 78–82). Courts are reluctant to draw a distinction between a general requirement for good faith consultation and FPIC as a purported veto under UNDRIP. For example, in the Australian Yunupingu case, the Federal Court, in its consideration of a compensation claim by an Aboriginal community, made no reference to international instruments such as UNDRIP, ILO 169, or FPIC (Yunupingu case, 2023; Yunupingu appeal case, 2025). In the South African case of Baleni, UNDRIP is referenced, but the right of veto recognised by the Court derives from domestic legislation. In judgements across the Americas, declarations are usually grounded in domestic law, with ILO 169 and UNDRIP cited for context and interpretation rather than as independent sources as a right of veto.

FPIC primarily serves to inspire, inform, and guide, rather than representing a substantive co-decision-making right. Much like the term Ubuntu has influenced South African law as a source of inspiration and direction (De Villiers, 2022a; De Villiers, 2025c, p. 259),[5] FPIC has shaped indigenous consultation standards. It assists courts in interpreting and explaining the requirements for consultation, without being a right in itself. Even in cases like Baleni, where FPIC was cited to recognise an indigenous community's right of veto, it was applied within the context of a particular South African statute (Interim Protection of Informal Land Rights Act 31 of 1996) which grants local communities the right of veto over matters affecting their land. The Baleni judgement did not imply, as some literature suggests,[6] that the community's veto arose from FPIC as if it were a legal norm of international law (Baleni case 2019, paras 78–82).

1.4 State Responses to FPIC

States have responded to UNDRIP in various ways, from denying the existence of Indigenous Peoples within their populations, to formally enacting legislation to implement its principles. Others have remained silent or have used UNDRIP as a source of inspiration to improve policies dealing with indigenous rights, without enacting UNDRIP or its provisions by way of legislation. Courts have generally been cautious about using UNDRIP as a stand-alone guide for statutory interpretation or as a source of rights. Canada is one of a few countries that have taken legislative action, by enacting the United Nations Declaration on the Rights of Indigenous Peoples Act, the preamble of which refers to UNDRIP as a 'source of law' (Canada UNDRIP Act, 2021 Preamble). UNDRIP is recognised in Canada as a 'universal international human rights instrument' applicable to Canadian law and intended to 'provide a framework' for its implementation (Canada UNDRIP Act, 2021, art. 4). However, a restrictive approach has been evident in the Supreme Court's interpretation of this recognition, particularly regarding resource harvesting rights such as fishing rights, Aboriginal title to land, Métis rights, treaty rights, and governance rights. McNeil argues that while the inclusion of Section 35 in the Constitu-

5 The Constitutional Court has referred to Ubuntu due to its inherent characteristics of 'humaneness, social justice and fairness' (Makwanyane case 1995, para. 236).

6 To suggest, as Mukwevho does, that the Baleni case 'cemented' the application of the FPIC principle within South African law (Mukwevho, 2022, p. 160) is, with respect, an overreach. While the relevant statute under which the proceeding took place granted the right of veto to the local occupiers of land, it is a right that – according to the statute – only applies to some communities whose land tenure is threatened – not to all tribal communities.

tion's Bill of Rights[7] has had a significant impact on indigenous rights recognition, the Supreme Court's interpretation of it still 'falls short' of UNDRIP's requirements (McNeil, 2021, p. 82). Canadian courts approach FPIC as a process of consultation (Kebaowek First Nation case, 2025, para. 183).

Other countries that have enacted legislation to give effect to ILO 169 and UNDRIP include Argentina, Bolivia, the Philippines, Colombia, the USA, Vietnam, and Mexico. Vietnam, for example, has enacted FPIC concerning the United Nations Collaborative Program on Reducing Emissions from Deforestation and Forest Degradation in Developing Countries. However, in defining 'consent', the legislation in Vietnam stops short of granting a veto. While it does state that Indigenous Peoples may withhold consent, this does not necessarily imply that the regulatory authority forfeits its ability to grant approval regardless of Indigenous People withholding their consent:

> Consent: consultation and participation are crucial components of a consent process. Consultation should be undertaken in good faith, requires time and an effective system for communicating among interest holders. Indigenous Peoples should be able to participate through their own freely chosen representatives and customary or other institutions. The inclusion of a gender perspective is essential. This process may include the option of withholding consent. (Tan, Truong and Van K'Tip, 2010, p. 2)

Australia, New Zealand, South Africa, Norway, and Denmark are among the countries with indigenous populations that have not enacted UNDRIP in legislation. The Parliament of Australia has, by way of a parliamentary committee, investigated the country's compliance with UNDRIP, but it has not recommended legislation to specifically enact the Declaration or FPIC (Australia Inquiry into UNDRIP, 2023). In a submission to the Inquiry, the Australian Human Rights Commission explained that FPIC 'is much stronger' than consultation since it implies 'ongoing discussion and engagement with Indigenous Peoples', rather than a one-off consultation. The Commission acknowledged, however, that the process of FPIC 'must therefore be managed on a case-by-case basis and not through a 'one-size-fits-all' model of consultation' (Human Rights Commission, 2009, para. 5.19). In the Murray Rivers case the obligation was to 'have regard' to the interests of Aboriginal People had not been satisfied (Murray Rivers Indigenous People case, 2025). Meanwhile, in

7 35 (1) The existing aboriginal and treaty rights of the aboriginal peoples of Canada are hereby recognised and affirmed.

2023 New Zealand announced that it does not regard UNDRIP as binding international law (Hall, 2023).

Denmark, in a response to the UN Expert Mechanism about the implementation of UNDRIP, emphasised that 'one of the most fundamental ways' to comply with FPIC is through 'consulting and cooperating in good faith with Indigenous Peoples' with the objective of achieving their consent (Denmark: UNDRIP, 2018). Denmark has not yet enacted the provisions of UNDRIP in domestic law. In the Girjas case in Sweden, the Court ruled that indigenous rights as recognised in international law, including ILO 169, should be considered when interpreting national statutes, despite the country not having ratified ILO 169 (Girjas case, 2020). Norway, in contrast, is a signatory to ILO 169 and has endorsed UNDRIP without enacting it into law. In the Nesseby case, the country's Supreme Court declared that UNDRIP 'must be regarded as a central document within indigenous law, as it reflects international law principles in the field and has gained support from a large number of states' (Nesseby case, 2018, para. 97). Nonetheless, the Court stopped short of elevating FPIC to a binding legal norm separate from good faith consultation.

Several other countries acknowledge indigenous lands and customs, though this cannot necessarily be construed as an endorsement of FPIC. Kusniati, for example, suggests that Indonesia's recognition of customary law in Article 18B(2) of its Constitution implies an endorsement of FPIC (Kusniati, 2024, p. 173). However, this proposition is open to challenge, since the recognition of customary law as a general principle does not automatically imply acceptance of FPIC as a legal norm of veto. This is further exemplified by many African countries, including South Africa, which recognise customary law as a legal system without accepting UNDRIP as a legal instrument or FPIC as a legal norm.[8]

In short, the responses of countries to UNDRIP have been 'uneven' (UN: UNDRIP after 14 years, 2021), sporadic, aspirational, and for the most part UNDRIP in general and FPIC specifically remain unlegislated in municipal jurisdictions. This notwithstanding, FPIC is considered an important norm-

8 The Democratic Republic of the Congo (2006), Ecuador (2008), Kenya (2010), Mexico (2011 and 2016), Morocco (2011), Sweden (2011), Costa Rica (2014), El Salvador (2014), Nicaragua (2014) and Chile (2016) are examples of countries that have amended their constitutions to advance Indigenous Peoples' rights in line with UNDRIP (United Nations Implementing UNDRIP, 2019, pp. 9–11). In Canada, there have been positive efforts to implement UNDRIP not only at the federal level, but also by the respective provinces and even at some local levels. While these provincial and local initiatives are aimed at increasing indigenous consultation, their 'adequacy are the subject of ongoing debate and litigation' (Boirin-Farguess and Theriault, 2024, p. 28).

setting instrument for the purposes of advocacy, social policy standard setting and, to a lesser extent, the interpretation of domestic statutes.

1.5 FPIC and Consultation

While FPIC is regarded as an advancement in the consultative rights of Indigenous Peoples, courts have not rushed to draw a clear distinction between the right to good faith consultation and the right to FPIC. Instead, they have used FPIC to develop the meaning of consultation by considering the unique interests of indigenous communities, but without treating FPIC as a separate legal standard. Even in judgements and expert opinions that reference FPIC, the focus lies on the consultation process rather than a veto or equal decision-making authority.

In 2014, in the Communities of the Sipakapense case, the Inter-American Commission on Human Rights (IACHR) provided some useful insights into the meaning of FPIC,[9] such as: public participation should not necessarily be equated with consultation with a specific indigenous community; the state has a positive duty to make available effective mechanisms to seek FPIC; FPIC must be sought before a final decision is made; (par 35) material must be produced in a language understandable to the indigenous community; (par 36) a lack of economic resources may impact negatively on the community in expressing their opinions; (par 36); and domestic regulations ought to be made consistent with international norms such as ILO 169; (par 37) (Communities of the Sipakapense case 2014). Furthermore, in the Kichwa case, it was found that encroachment on the property rights of the indigenous community also affected their cultural identity and personal integrity (Kichwa case, 2012, para. 341). Various individual rights have therefore been given effect by cross-reference to other rights. In the Awas Tingni case, meanwhile, the Court acknowledged the spiritual connection of indigenous groups to their lands (Awas Tingni case, 2001, para. 159). In the Community Garifuna of San Juan case the following was said about PFIC: 'As to its characteristics, the Court has established that the consultation must be carried out in advance, in good faith, with the aim of reaching an adequate, accessible and informed agreement' (Community Garifuna of San Juan case, 2023, para. 138).

None of these cases attempt to distinguish at law between consultation and FPIC as if they constitute different sources of rights. Instead, the respective courts and expert bodies focus on ensuring fair, just, transparent, and reason-

9 On proper analysis, these practical indicia of FPIC may arguably also apply to good faith consultation.

able consultation processes when indigenous rights and interests are concerned, with an emphasis, as has been expressed in South Africa and Australia, on effective and meaningful participation or to 'have regard' to Aboriginal interests (Maledu case 2018, Tipakalippa case 2022, para. 94; Murray Rivers Indigenous People case, 2025).

One could argue that much like the evolution of legal terms such as procedural fairness, equity, and rules of natural justice, the understanding of consultation is also continuously developing. An essential element arising from case law is that indigenous customary property rights should be recognised as real property in the context of domestic law and respected accordingly, including through the payment of compensation when such rights are infringed (Timber Creek High Court appeal 2019; Yunupingu case 2023; Yunupingu appeal case 2025). Moreover, as indigenous culture is tied to property, a broader interpretation could be given to the right to property, encompassing the spiritual connection to land held by Indigenous Peoples for cultural and traditional purposes. In essence, traditional law, traditional customs, traditional land rights, rights to culture, identity and self-determination are closely interwoven (Community Garifuna of San Juan case, 2023, para. 138).

The unique status of indigenous property law was described as follows by the Australian Federal Court in the Fortescue case:

> it is to misunderstand the concept of native title rights and interests to require them to fit into non-Aboriginal concepts of property, the exercise of proprietary rights and the enforcement of property rights. That is why what occurs is *recognition* of native title; not conferral, and not transformation into non-Aboriginal property rights. Whether or not others outside Aboriginal society believe the sanctions for transgression of the law will eventuate or not is beside the point. The *very foundation* of traditional Aboriginal law and customs, or "customary law" as Dr Palmer prefers to describe it, is in the *spiritual,* and the intermingling of the spiritual with the physical, with people and with land. That is how Aboriginal law works. (emphasis added) (Fortescue Metals case, 2019, paras. 287–288)

While it is often asserted that FPIC is rooted in the right to self-determination, this proposition is largely conjectural, as self-determination is also recognised as an individual right under the ICCPR and ICESCR, benefitting all individuals, not just Indigenous Peoples. If the right to FPIC were derived from these covenants, it would be equally available to other ethnocultural communities and individuals.

FPIC, as it arises from the right to self-determination, is not absolute. Public interest remains a relevant consideration within the state's regulatory authority. FPIC, therefore, does not create a legal enclave beyond the state's reach; even if consent is withheld pursuant to FPIC, the state may still grant approval for a measure to proceed. The withholding of consent is therefore a relevant fact for the decision-maker to consider, but the withholding is not determinative (Munkara case, 2024). Conversely, indigenous consent does not guarantee state approval, as decisions may be based on other considerations, for example public interest or environmental considerations. FPIC is thus part of a complex network of government decision-making. This principle is reflected in the Forrest appeal, where the original tribunal decision was set aside and remitted for reconsideration because the panel, in seeking to protect Aboriginal heritage, had not adequately considered the broader impact, societal interests, and potential benefits of the proposed agricultural development to the public (Forrest appeal case 2024; Forrest case 2023).

In legal theory and practice, the right to self-determination, as set out in the ICCPR, ICESCR, and UNDRIP among others, remains complex to define or be given practical effect. Even the legally binding ILO 169 does not use the terms self-determination or FPIC in a generic sense. ILO 169 refers to FPIC in the context of protection against relocation, but even then it does not confer an absolute right of veto (ILO 169, 1989, art. 16.2). Moreover, the rights associated with FPIC under ILO 169 and UNDRIP cannot be directly enforced by Indigenous Peoples against their governments (Handbook ILO, 2013).

The inclusion of FPIC in UNDRIP was seen as a major advancement in indigenous rights recognition, addressing perceived shortcomings associated with the term 'consultation'. FPIC is said to be grounded on the premise of equality arising from sovereignty, self-determination, ownership, and co-decision-making, whereas consultation implies a hierarchical relationship.

The use of 'informed consent' as a requirement for lawful action is well established in various areas of law. The next section specifically examines its development in medical science, where consent is applied in its ordinary meaning. The concept of FPIC is closely linked to patient treatment and rights, particularly the right to be informed and to make free-willed decisions.

2 Medical Science: Basic Elements of Free, Prior, and Informed Consent

The term 'free, prior, and informed consent' is particularly associated with medical treatment in the context of the doctor–patient relationship. It encompasses the obligation of the medical practitioner to disclose all pertinent material information to a patient, explain the patient's condition and implications of treatment, set out the rationale for a procedure or proposed treatment along with alternatives, provide an opportunity for the patient to seek other opinions, and ensure that the patient's consent is freely given based on all relevant and material information (Becher, 1988).

The standard of FPIC is a relatively recent development in the medical profession.[10] According to Murray, it was only around the start of the 20th century that tort law concerning assault and negligence evolved into a duty for medical professionals to disclose and explain, alongside a patient's right to give informed consent for medical treatments and procedures (Murray, 1990, p. 104). The contemporary standard of FPIC in medicine is summarised by Nandini:

> The pre-requisites of informed consent are that the patient or research participant should be competent and the disclosed facts should be comprehended before giving consent freely. (Nandini, 2013, p. 23)

The adequacy of information is assessed from the patient's perspective, not what the medical practitioner deems sufficient, because it is the patient who must give or withhold consent based on free will.

Sarela notes that in some circumstances, it may be challenging to obtain patient consent. In such cases, the medical practitioner is required to take 'reasonable steps' to secure consent – though the specific standards or steps are not prescribed or defined (Sarela, 2024). What constitutes reasonable steps and what material information must be disclosed to a patient depend on the facts of each case. While this may create some uncertainty for medical practitioners, it is unavoidable, as the adequacy of the information provided can only be assessed in light of the factual circumstances to determine whether the patient was sufficiently informed to make a decision (Sarela, 2024, p. 60).

The way courts have, over time, given content to the duties of medical practitioners arising from FPIC may assist to develop and advocate practical approaches to FPIC concerning Indigenous Peoples within the framework of UNDRIP. Even if FPIC is not a justiciable right, it is conceivable that rules of natural justice, procedural fairness, principles of administrative review, and

---

10 Mazur suggests that the concept is much older and refers to the case of *Slater v. Baker and Stapleton* in 1767, in which the Court declared that the amputation of a patient's leg had been contrary to their will (Mazur, 2012, p. 1). However, he adds that the legal principle of patient consent as a general principle in medical sciences is of more recent origin, possibly from around the mid-1960s.

good faith consultation could be developed to reflect the essential principles of FPIC. Notably, FPIC in medical science is principally derived though the development of case law, much like the way FPIC in indigenous rights is being developed through jurisprudence.

The following examples of medical case law are intended to provide practical insights into the meaning of 'free, prior, and informed consent' and how the concept can be applied to indigenous rights pursuant to FPIC as understood in UNDRIP:

2.1 Point of Departure for Consent: Individual Self-Determination

The point of departure for consent in the context of medical treatment is the principle that 'a man is the master of his own body…' (Natanson case, 1960). The right to self-determination entitles an adult to consent to or to refuse medical treatment. This implies that to the extent an adult is capable of making reasonable decisions regarding their own body, they can decide to accept or decline medical treatment. Consequently, all material information relevant to a procedure – viewed from the perspective of the patient – must be disclosed to them to ensure an informed decision. One of the earliest US rulings to establish the right to FPIC in medical treatment stated:

> every human being of adult years in sound mind has a right to determine what shall be done with his own body; and a surgeon who performs an operation without his patient's consent commits a battery for which he is liable in damages. (Schoendorff case, 1914)

The principle underlying FPIC in the context of UNDRIP is that Indigenous Peoples, based on their pre-settlement rights and contemporary right to self-determination, are entitled to decide what happens on their customary lands in general, and to participate in decisions affecting them solely as a people. The right to self-determination, as exercised both individually and collectively, entitles an indigenous community to be fully informed of all material aspects of a proposed measure that may impact on their traditional lands. This includes sufficient time for consideration and consultation, the opportunity to seek advice, the ability to consider alternatives, the liberty to propose mitigation measures, the right to negotiate or receive compensation, and ultimately the right to make an informed decision. However, unlike a competent adult's right to refuse a medical procedure – which constitutes a fundamental legal entitlement – FPIC, as set out in UNDRIP, does not grant a comparable right of veto to indigenous communities. Furthermore, indigenous interests are not entitled to absolute protection as the case is with an individual's decision about medical treatment. Usually, indigenous interests and must be weighed against other public interests, for example economic development, development of infrastructure, and residential development (Forrest appeal case, 2024). International law is also not specific about when FPIC applies to a proposed measure, for example does it apply to any measure that affects customary land even if it is minimal or does it only apply with large scale developments on land? FPIC broadly appears to concern access to traditional land, but this is not unequivocal, as UNDRIP also refers to other issues affecting Indigenous Peoples such as spiritual connection to land, cultural identity, as well as environmental and property rights (Fosen case 2021, Endorois Welfare Council case 2003). UNDRIP's vague scope is highlighted in case law.

2.2 Providing All Relevant Information at the Earliest Opportunity

The necessity of explaining a medical procedure or treatment to a patient before obtaining their consent and ensuring they fully understand its nature and implications are fundamental legal principles and requirements in the doctor–patient relationship. This principle was highlighted in the Corn case, where a patient was assured by the medical practitioner that her breast would not be removed. However, when admitted to hospital, she signed a form allowing a mastectomy to be performed, later explaining that she had been unaware of the form's inscription or its meaning. The Court found that the procedure was unauthorised, as it, along with its implications, had not been adequately explained to the patient before she consented (Corn case, 1955).

In the Sidaway case, meanwhile, the Court emphasised that a patient must be advised of all the 'material risks' involved in treatment. The test for determining what information should be disclosed to a patient is based on what a reasonable person in the patient's position would require to make a free-willed decision (Sidaway case, 1985). The essence of informed consent was also affirmed in the Australian case of Rogers, where the Court explained that the test to ascertain what risks are material to medical treatment is based on what a reasonable person in the position of the patient (not the medical practitioner) would need to know to make an informed decision (Rogers case, 1993).

The crux of informed consent in medical practice is, therefore, that the adequacy of information provided by the medical practitioner is assessed from the patient's perspective to ascertain whether all information of material importance was disclosed and discussed before the patient made their informed decision (McCormack, Gulati and Mangwani, 2018, p. 690).

In the context of FPIC as it appears in UNDRIP, it is required that all relevant information about an intended measure be provided to the indigenous community at the earliest opportunity, in a manner they can understand the nature and scope, before their response is sought. The adequacy of the material information provided ought to be evaluated from the indigenous community's perspective, as they are the ones whose response is being sought based on all the available information and how their interests may be impacted (Mahuika case, 2000). The information must be provided early in the decision-making process, enabling the indigenous community to seek expert advice, consider alternatives, develop a response, propose mitigation, ask questions, negotiate compensation, and fully comprehend the measure's scope in its entirety, including its long-term implications such as how the land will be rehabilitated or restored. Furthermore, the information must be presented in a manner that facilitates understanding by the indigenous community, whether through their language, the media they use, specially designed presentations, or village meetings (Paradise Park case, 2023). A presentation suited to a boardroom or public gathering may not be appropriate for conveying information at a village meeting of Indigenous People.

2.3 Providing Information about Options and Conditions for Approval

A patient must give consent for *each* invasive diagnostic test or procedure to be performed. General consent upon admission, given through the signing of a standardised form, does not necessarily indicate that all material information about the specific procedure or procedures had been provided to the patient and that they consented to each procedure (Darrah case, 1969). The patient must not only be informed about the general consequences of a procedure or treatment, but also about all the steps with potentially adverse implications that it involves. However, while disclosure of all material information is a prerequisite for valid consent, this does not imply that all potential eventualities, including very unlikely ones, need to be discussed with the patient or approved by the patient (Canterbury case, 1972). Ultimately, the test is whether a reasonable person in the patient's position would consider the information provided to be material and adequate for making an informed decision.

In the context of FPIC as it arises from UNDRIP, this standard suggests that Indigenous Peoples should be informed of all reasonably likely risks and impacts associated with a proposed measure. The measure's details across its phases should be explained to the indigenous community, including affected areas, their ongoing involvement, required infrastructure, potential destruction of or damage to historical sites, environmental impacts, and proposed mitigation steps. They must be given time to seek expert advice, make counter proposals about the proposed measure and possible mitigations, negotiate compensation, and suggest alternatives or conditions for approval (Daniel case, 2002).

2.4 Avoiding a Fait Accompli, Ensuring Genuine Participation

The information provided to a patient should be material and informative while respecting the patient's autonomy to make a final decision. It should not be presented in an intimidating manner or pressure the patient into consenting to a procedure. Honesty or transparency should not take the form of a threat. The importance of voluntary consent was highlighted in the Melideo case, where the patient had agreed to a medical procedure, but it was later held that her decision-making had been impaired due to mental duress. The medical practitioner concerned had failed to discuss reasonable treatment alternatives, leading the court to conclude that her consent had been given under the perception that she had no real choice in the matter (Melideo case 1976).

The essence of free choice implies that a decision is made freely and without undue influence. This requires that alternatives be discussed, other opinions considered, and input from family members and friends sought if desired. Even when a diagnosis leaves no viable alternatives, the medical practitioner remains obligated to present the information in a manner that does not amount to duress.

In medical science, undue influence may arise from various circumstances, but the underlying question remains substantively the same as in other areas of law when considering whether undue influence has been exerted (Barclays Bank case, 1994). Ultimately, the court must ascertain whether the person, when the decision was made, acted of their own free will, based on all relevant information and without duress. While a patient may seek advice and choose to act on it, such advice must be intended to assist the patient in making a decision, not to override their self-determination or substitute their independence with the decision of the advisor (Re T case, 1992, para. 662). In practice, of course, a patient may simply trust a medical practitioner without seeking further opinions or challenging the information or advice provided, or by acting solely based on their underlying confidence in the patient–doctor relationship (Steward and Lynch, 2003, p. 601). Ultimately, courts must consider all the surrounding factors to ascertain whether consent was freely given, rather than merely relying on a 'signature [on] a piece of paper' (Cocanour, 2017).

In the context of FPIC under UNDRIP, this principle suggests that Indigenous Peoples must be allowed the opportunity to influence the outcome of a proposed measure from its earliest stages and, if necessary, be involved on an ongoing basis – perhaps throughout the project's lifespan. Meaningful involvement is essential and, in some cases, FPIC may also extend to the right to withdraw approval, depending on the nature of the project. This is where the concept of co-decision-making vis-à-vis advices arises. Indigenous Peoples must not be presented with a fait accompli, whereby they are merely informed of a measure under the guise of consultation, without any real opportunity to influence the outcome (Barngarla case 2023).[11] FPIC is not just about sharing information or presenting a predetermined reality to a community. It requires a genuine opportunity for substantial participation in decision-making, meaningful influence over the outcome, internal community discussions, access to expert advice, and consideration of all material information before a decision is made. Ultimately, courts consider the fairness of the process followed, rather than the merits of the proposal or response (Strickland case, 1998).

2.5 Sliding Scale of Consent

A patient's capacity to give consent may depend on the nature of the proposed medical procedure and their mental state at the time consent is sought. Procedures with significant consequences may require a deeper comprehension of the details as well as the time to consider options and alternatives. In the Large case, the Court held that while the patient, despite limited cognitive capacity, could consent to hip surgery, she lacked the testamentary capacity to consent to the execution of her will. The surgery involved relatively straightforward information, whereas executing a will required a legal capacity to grasp its implications, which the patient did not possess (Large case, 1986). Ascertaining capacity is therefore not a static one-dimensional test, but depends on the nature and scope of the procedure and the ability of the patient to weight up all relevant information before making a decision.

---

11 In Australia, a 2023 judgement handed down by the Federal Court in the Barngarla case declared that although extensive consultation had taken place with the Aboriginal community about the location of a nuclear waste storage facility, the facts indicated 'apprehended bias' on the part of the government, as it had already made up its mind about the location of the site *before* the commencement of consultation. Thus, the process that had taken place was better described as information sharing rather than consultation. The Court in this case did not consider the merits of the site's proposed location, but rather the inadequate process that led to the identification and acquisition of the proposed site.

In the context of FPIC under UNDRIP, this implies that a sliding scale can be applied to the process of consultation, whereby the impact, scope, and longevity of a proposed measure may determine the standards for information sharing, consultation duration, consultation participants, and the consideration of alternatives, mitigation options, potential compensation, approval conditions, and possible ongoing involvement (Saramaka case 2007). For example, accessing indigenous land for low-impact tourism may require a different standard of FPIC than that for operating an open pit mine on the land.

2.6 Individual Self-Determination versus Community Self-Determination

The individual right to self-decision in medical treatment arising from FPIC shares some similarities with FPIC in the context of UNDRIP, but there are also some important differences. While medical FPIC is based on the right of a competent adult to consent to or refuse medical treatment, FPIC under UNDRIP is not a justiciable right but rather an entitlement to consultation which a community seeks to exercise. It may be difficult, or even impossible, to ascertain the opinion of an entire community – whether by majority vote or the decisions of elders. The broader public interest may also be a relevant factor in the consideration process. FPIC, as it arises from UNDRIP, aims to restore an equilibrium among parties, seeking to emphasise equality rather than hierarchy. In this sense, just as the notion of self-determination applies to individuals, it is also recognised for Indigenous Peoples, both individually and collectively, when it comes to decisions affecting them and their traditional lands. In medical science, a once-prevailing 'paternalistic attitude' has been replaced with a more 'patient-centred' approach (Murray, 1990, p. 109). In the same way, FPIC seeks to move away from a hierarchical dynamic where decisions are made about Indigenous Peoples, toward a framework of equality where decisions are instead made with and by them.

2.7 Application of Medical FPIC to Indigenous FPIC

While the principle of individual self-determination underpins FPIC in the medical field, importing this principle of consent as a legal entitlement into the decision-making process of an indigenous community is not straightforward for several reasons:

First, an indigenous community is not a legal entity, and even if it holds corporate status pursuant to traditional customs, internal opinions about the merit of a proposed measure may vary. This makes reaching a collective decision more challenging than the decision of an individual.

Second, a community's right to veto a proposal is not as firmly established at law as an individual's right to personal integrity, which allows them to refuse medical treatment. Consent in the medical treatment context functions as an effective veto, whereas in the realm of indigenous rights, FPIC is regarded as aspirational since it refers to the process of consultation rather than a veto over a decision. Even where legislation grants a community the right of veto, the process by which the community reaches its decision may still be open to legal challenge.

Third, an indigenous community is likely to encompass different opinions about a proposed measure, making bland majority rule an inappropriate approach.[12] Assuming that all indigenous individuals will share the same perspective on a proposed measure is both unrealistic and condescending. The views of dissenters cannot be ignored, yet internal disagreements may undermine efforts to achieve consent. Furthermore, a community that does not participate effectively in consultation efforts may be deemed to have failed in its good faith obligations. In the FMG case in Australia, for example, the Court held that the inability of the parties to agree on the rules of negotiation could mean that the mining party had complied with 'good faith' mediation, even if no actual negotiations had taken place (FMG case, 2009, para. 29). In the Munkara case substantial costs were awarded because a subset of an indigenous community had opposed a proposed measure on grounds that were

12 The ICCPR observed the following on how consultation negotiations took place in New Zealand with the Māori and the response to minority views within the community: 'In such circumstances, where the right of individuals to enjoy their own culture is in conflict with the exercise of parallel rights by other members of the minority group, or of the minority as a whole, the Committee may consider whether the limitation in issue is in the interests of all members of the minority and whether there is reasonable and objective justification for its application to the individuals who claim to be adversely affected... While it is a matter of concern that the settlement and its process have contributed to divisions amongst Māori, nevertheless, the Committee concludes that the State party has, by engaging itself in the process of broad consultation before proceeding to legislate, and by paying specific attention to the sustainability of Māori fishing activities, taken the necessary steps to ensure that the Fisheries Settlement and its enactment through legislation, including the Quota Management System, are compatible with article 27' (Mahuika case 2000, para. 9.6, 9.8). In this case, an agreement reached between the government and the Māori about the regulation of fishing had been disputed by some within the Māori community. They lodged a complaint claiming that New Zealand was violating their cultural rights (and its own international obligations) under the ICCPR. The Committee rejected the complaint.

found by the Court to be wanting (Munkara case 2024; Munkara consent orders cost 2024).

Fourth, public interest considerations often play a role in measures that may affect indigenous lands, such as mining, urban expansion, agriculture, or infrastructure development. The regulatory function of government cannot, as a general principle, be displaced by the requirement for FPIC (Forrest appeal case, 2024). This is consistent with the view that indigenous interests do not enjoy 'automatic prevalence' over other national interests (Tomaselli and Cittadino, 2021, p. 166). It is instructive here to compare the Ogoni case in Nigeria, where the government was found to have violated the rights of an indigenous community by granting approval to a third party to exploit natural resources on their traditional lands (Ogoni case, 2001), with Australia where many mining approvals have been granted despite the objections raised by Aboriginal communities (WMC case, 1999). Australian courts focus on the process of consultation or 'having regard' rather than the merits of the positions adopted by the parties involved (De Villiers, 2025d, p. 313; Murray Rivers Indigenous People case, 2025).

These examples illustrate an unsurprising lack of standardisation when FPIC is applied to the legal rights of Indigenous Peoples. This contrasts with the certainty provided when consenting to a medical procedure or treatment (Petkar, 2017, p. 21). While 'consent' in medical contexts signifies an unequivocal right of veto, in UNDRIP 'consent' refers to efforts to achieve a specific outcome, rather than constituting a legally enforceable right of veto. Consequently, while an indigenous community's decision to withhold consent may be noted by the relevant regulatory authority, withholding consent is generally not equated to a veto.

3 The Development of FPIC in UNDRIP

A new philosophy underlying the concept FPIC began to emerge in the 1980s. Before this shift, the non-binding Indigenous and Tribal Populations Convention 107 of 1957 (ITPC 107 1957) committed the international community to developing a binding convention to recognise and protect indigenous and tribal peoples' rights by facilitating their integration into the dominant society. The emphasis was consistent with the prevailing approach under the United Nations at the time, by which Indigenous Peoples (and ethnocultural minorities) were to be assimilated and integrated into the rest of society, with the rights of their members protected in a similar way to other individual rights, but with no collective rights. The focus was, therefore, on equality and non-discrimination rather than on positive recognition of their unique identity. One of the Convention's key objectives stated:

> Governments shall have the primary responsibility for developing coordinated and systematic action for the protection of the populations concerned and their *progressive integration* into the life of their respective countries. (emphasis added) (Indigenous and Tribunal Convention 107, 1957, art. 2)

The ITPC 107 1957 also declared in Article 12 that Indigenous Peoples shall not be removed without their 'free consent' from their 'habitual territories'. No other mention was made in the Convention about universal rights to consultation or FPIC. The ITPC 107 1957 was consistently opposed by many Indigenous Peoples due to its focus on assimilation rather than self-determination.

In 1986, a Meeting of ILO Experts concluded that a revision of the 1957 Convention was necessary because its 'integrationist language' had become 'outdated' (ILO Experts, 1988, para. 46). This view reflected the prevailing approach at the time regarding ethnocultural minority rights, which called for greater recognition and accommodation of diversity.

3.1 Rise of FPIC

From the 1980s, the concept of FPIC and indigenous right to self-determination gained prominence among scholars and expert bodies with reference to obtaining consent from Indigenous Peoples, especially when displacement from their traditional lands was at stake (Goodland, 2004, p. 67). The origins of FPIC can arguably be traced back to the Western Sahara case, which held that if a territory was inhabited at the time of occupation by a foreign power, 'the acquisition of sovereignty was not generally considered as effected unilaterally through "occupation"' of terra nullius by original title *but through agreements concluded with local leaders*' (emphasis added) (Western Sahara case, 1975, p. 39). This forms the core of the sovereignty Indigenous Peoples are said to have retained pursuant to section 1 of the ICCPR and ICESCR. While the Western Sahara case cannot be legally applied to every indigenous community, its recognition of historical sovereignty and the right to self-determination resonated with Indigenous Peoples' aspirations.

FPIC relies on that notion of undisturbed sovereignty to establish new principles for engagement by Indigenous People with contemporary society. The link between historical sovereignty and the contemporary concept of self-determination has become the basis for Indigenous Peoples to reassert their special status in relation to the modern state. According to this approach,

Indigenous People are not only a sub-set of the community, it is said that they are a nation that must be deal with as an equal to the current nation. At the centre of this assertion is the endeavour and right to protect traditional lands (Motoc, 2005, para. 34). In this context, the UN Human Rights Committee stated in 1999 that it:

> … emphasizes that the right to self-determination requires, inter alia, that all peoples must be able to freely dispose of their natural wealth and resources and that they may not be deprived of their own means of subsistence (art. 1, para. 2). … The Committee … recommends that the *practice of extinguishing inherent aboriginal rights be abandoned as incompatible* with article 1 of the Covenant. (emphasis added) (CCPR/C/79/Add.105)

The term FPIC in the context of indigenous rights arose fairly recently, becoming 'fully realised' only in UNDRIP (Yafee, 2018, p. 20). The Cobo Report of 1986 did not elaborate on the phrase 'free, prior, and informed consent' (Cobo, 1986). The principle of free and informed consent in respect of indigenous right was first raised in 1984 by the Working Group on Indigenous Populations (WGIP), which adopted the World Council of Indigenous Peoples Declaration of Principles (WGIP Principles, 1984). Regarding traditional lands, the WGIP Principles stated that the 'lands and resources' of Indigenous Peoples may not be taken from them without their free and informed consent (Principles 9, 12 and 16). However, WGIP did not propose a general right to FPIC about any policy, legislation, or administrative measure that may impact on Indigenous People.

FPIC as a term gained prominence as Indigenous Peoples began their efforts to renegotiate their relationship with the modern state concerning their traditional lands (Motoc, 2005, para. 5). In doing so, they sought to use FPIC to draw inspiration and lessons from other areas of law where informed consent serves as the foundation for interaction between parties.

ILO 169, which was adopted in 1989 and took effect in 1991, also refers to the concepts of consultation and consent in the context of an 'objective to achieving agreement' (Article 6.2). It requires that consent be obtained before Indigenous Peoples are relocated from their land, but with the proviso that if consent is not achievable, the removal should take place in accordance with 'national laws and regulations' (Article 16.2).[13] It also mandates consultation

---

13 Gaspardus observes how there are many examples where Indigenous People are relocated from their traditional lands without FPIC being adhered to (Gaspardus, 2025, pp. 210–211).

with Indigenous Peoples when measures may directly affect them (Article 6.1(a)), adding that such consultation must be conducted in 'good faith' (Article 6.2). Additionally, consultation is required regarding the use of natural resources on indigenous lands, the alienation of such lands, research involving Indigenous Peoples, and the education of indigenous children in their own institutions and facilities (Articles 15.2, 17.2, 22.3, and 28.1).

ILO 169 – an example of hard treaty law – is the only legally enforceable treaty concerning indigenous consultation rights. It offers greater security in terms of enforceability than UNDRIP, but its scope of application is limited. Only a few countries (23) have ratified ILO 169, and because only state parties may commence proceedings, its utility as a universal legal instrument – apart from being inspirational, establishing norms, and serving as an interpretative guide – has been limited. Nonetheless, ILO 169 has had a wider impact beyond the few ratifying nations. The norm-setting associated with it has influenced scientific discourse, impacted on jurisprudence, encouraged the enactment of domestic laws, and contributed to the adoption of UNDRIP. The impact of international instruments like ILO 169 on the domestic law of nations has been particularly acknowledged in the Americas, where its role has been described as follows:

> the impact of ILO 169 has not been limited to that of a model for law-making. In addition, the Convention is important *in local political processes*. It is used and invoked by indigenous communities and peoples, and by other actors, both public and private, who have defended the rights and interests of these communities. Litigation before domestic courts and where possible, before regional human rights bodies, has been an important area in this regard. (emphasis added) (ILO Case Book 2009, 7)

Anaya describes ILO 169 as a 'manifestation of the movement towards responsiveness' in the greater recognition of indigenous rights (Anaya, 1996, p. 48). Several states, particularly those in the Organization of American States, have incorporated ILO 160 into domestic law. Moreover, while not necessarily extending to consent as required by FPIC, the principle of good faith consultation has become widely applied by courts in countries that have ratified ILO 169, and beyond. This broad application of the duty to consult was summarised in the Kichwa case as follows:

> The obligation to *consult* the indigenous and tribal communities and peoples on any administrative or legislative measure that may affect their rights, as recognized under domestic and international law, as well as the obligation to

> guarantee the rights of Indigenous Peoples to *participate* in decisions on matters that concern their interests, is directly related to the general obligation to guarantee the free and full exercise of the rights recognized in the Convention (Article 1(1)). (emphasis added) (Kichwa case, 2012, para. 166)

In the Community Garifuna of San Juan case, the duty to consult was set out as follows:

> The right to consultation of indigenous and tribal peoples, in addition to being treaty-based, is also a general principle of international law. that is grounded, inter alia, on their close relationship with their land and on the respect of their rights to collective property and to cultural identity. Those rights must be especially respected in a pluralist, multicultural and democratic society. (Community Garifuna of San Juan case, 2023, para. 138)

In formally adopting the benchmark that free, prior, and informed consent must be obtained from Indigenous Peoples when their rights and interests are affected, the Committee on the Elimination of Racial Discrimination (CERD) broke new ground in its role as an international human rights body (CERD General Recommendations 1997). With regard to the obligation on states, General Recommendation 23 from the High Commissioner for Human Rights stated:

> Ensure that members of Indigenous Peoples have equal rights in respect of effective participation in public life and that no decisions *directly* relating to their rights and interests are taken without their *informed consent*…
> The Committee especially calls upon States parties to recognize and protect the rights of Indigenous Peoples to own, develop, control and use their communal lands, territories and resources and, where they have been deprived of their lands and territories traditionally owned or otherwise inhabited or used without their *free and informed consent*, to take steps to return those lands and territories. (emphasis added) (CERD General Recommendation, 1997, para. 4 (d), 5)

While the term 'consultation' is legally familiar and finds application in many aspects of law, FPIC has gained more recent prominence and popularity, particularly through its use in the UNDRIP. Motoc optimistically describes the rights arising from FPIC as 'compatible with the principle of state sovereignty' (Motoc, 2005, para. 52).

FPIC has come to be associated with the notion that indigenous involvement in a project is often a continuous process, rather than a single event. This means that Indigenous Peoples maintain a form of control over measures that affect them, they can withdraw any approval granted, they may impose conditions, and their participatory rights are recognised (Institute for Human Rights and Business, 2022). This is an aspirational statement since approval granted may not be open to be rescinded, but the point made is valid namely that indigenous involvement in a long-term project should also be for the long term. Support for FPIC as a guiding principle has increased since the 1990s, with specific references made by UN Special Rapporteurs about indigenous land rights (E/CN.4/Sub.2/2001/21), treaties between states and Indigenous Peoples (E/CN.4/Sub.2/AC.4/1998/CRP.1), and indigenous intellectual and cultural heritage (E/CN.4/Sub.2/1993/28), as well as by the Commission on Human Rights' Special Rapporteur about the human rights and fundamental freedoms of Indigenous Peoples (E/CN.4/2002/97).

These international instruments and statements are complemented by regional instruments such as the African Charter on Human and Peoples' Rights (African Charter, 1981) and the American Convention on Human Rights (American Convention, 1969), both of which recognise the right to self-determination, though not explicitly the term FPIC.

3.2 FPIC in UNDRIP

FPIC, as it is used in UNDRIP, seeks to address what were previously perceived as shortcomings in the understanding and practice of consultation. Consultation was seen as a one-event opportunity involving a hierarchical process that placed Indigenous Peoples in a subordinate position relative to the state. In contrast, FPIC is generally described as a broader and more inclusive process of ongoing engagement and shared decision-making between equal parties. The rights of Indigenous Peoples as traditional holders of property are encompassed by FPIC, recognising their cultural and other interests associated with traditional lands. However, there remains 'significant philosophical scepticism regarding the possibility of a genuinely collective form of consent' (Healey, 2019, p. 252). Some basic principles underlying FPIC are yet to be clarified, including issues surrounding 'transparency, accountability, and fairness' (Kusniati, 2024, p. 186). It is not surprising that courts have been reluctant to apply FPIC as a right of substance. Instead, they tend to use it as the equivalent of good faith consultation, or as a spiritual guide to encourage consultation rather than as a legal entitlement of veto. The Community of San Juan case the court was careful to set out the obligation to consult, not to consent, within the context of general societal interests:

> States must also ensure that the rights of Indigenous Peoples are not ignored in any activity or agreement reached with third parties or in decisions of public authorities that would affect their rights and interests. Thus, States must also inspect and supervise and, if applicable, deploy effective means to safeguard those rights through their respective judicial bodies. (Community Garifuna of San Juan case, 2023, para. 138)

The HRC views consultation as the initial step of FPIC, followed by engagement with the indigenous community that must lead to 'effective' participation, signifying a stronger and more enduring entitlement than consultation alone (Human Rights Council-FPIC, 2018, para. 17). The Council proposes the use of the word 'effective' to signify a form of co-decision-making, considered a defining element of FPIC.

UNDRIP emphasises an attempt at joint decision-making by using the word 'consent' and acknowledging, as a starting point, the historic sovereignty of Indigenous Peoples, their collective rights, their right to self-determination, and their equal standing with those seeking access to their lands. While FPIC includes consultation, FPIC has an expanded meaning by requiring an ongoing relationship, non-hierarchical engagement, equality, and informed co-decision-making. For example, UNDRIP provides as follows:

> Indigenous Peoples have the right to maintain and strengthen their distinct political, legal, economic, social and cultural institutions, while retaining their right to participate fully, if they so choose, in the political, economic, social and cultural life of the State. (UNDRIP, 2007, art. 5)

Although UNDRIP is regarded as 'soft' international law since it is not legally binding, the objectives it expresses are significant, particularly as it has received widespread endorsement by the international community through the United Nations General Assembly, and Indigenous Peoples actively contributed to its development and drafting. However, referring to UNDRIP as 'law' is a misnomer, as it does not constitute what is generally understood to be law, which includes enforceability and accompanying sanctions. Nevertheless, Fredericks argues that while the 'hard law/soft law distinction clarifies the non-binding legal status of the UNDRIP, this status does not, at a practical level, divest the UNDRIP of legal authority entirely' (Fredericks, 2016, p. 434). In my view an arguably better legal description of UNDRIP is as an international version of directive principles of state policy (see Chapter 5) aiming to influence and guide the interpretation of fundamental rights rather than constituting a justiciable right itself.

In light of the non-legal status of UNDRIP, the onus therefore remains on states to take the necessary steps to incorporate international hard and soft law into their domestic laws and practices.[14] Similarly, courts may rely on and be influenced by international soft law, much like how courts in India have drawn guidance from directive principles in municipal law. In this way, UNDRIP serves to inform, encourage, and set objectives, without being legally justiciable. In this respect, it is worth noting the Dann case where the IACHR took into account the findings of an international tribunal to argue that a determination of the land rights of Indigenous Peoples required their consent (Dann case, 1985). This is regarded as a benchmark for indigenous consent, but notably it concerned an extinguishment of title and not a right that applies to other forms of access to traditional lands. Furthermore, the IACHR declared in the Maya case that the consent required in the Dann case applied equally to FPIC (Maya IACHR case, 2004). It was also found that although various meetings had taken place in the Dann case over a substantial period, the indigenous community did not have the opportunity to effectively participate in them. In the Kichwa case, it was also emphasised that consultation must take place during 'all stages of the planning and implementation of a project' (Kichwa case, 2012, para. 167). Moreover, the consultation must be conducted in 'good faith' (Saramaka case, 2007, para. 178) and in accordance with the relevant traditions and customs of the Indigenous People (Community Garifuna of San Juan case, 2023, para. 138).

The principle of good faith negotiations is also reflected in the Native Title Act of Australia (De Villiers, 2022b, pp. 128–131). In this regard, the Consultation case of Costa Rica is also relevant. Although the Court referred to international instruments such as ILO 169 and UNDRIP, it required free, prior, and informed consultation rather than consent (Consultation case, 2023). The Court went on to explain why adequate consultation had not taken place with an indigenous community, citing shortcomings in good faith engagement, the absence of serious dialogue, inadequate consideration of the measure's impact on indigenous groups, and the recognition that land adjacent to a

14 Note the discussion in Chapter 4 about FPIC as a potential norm in customary international law. States act ambivalently by, on the one hand, endorsing UNDRIP while, on the other hand, failing to take legislative measures to give effect to FPIC as a legal entitlement in domestic law. In the sphere of policy and legal standards, several states that have enacted legislation to engage Indigenous Peoples have done so on the basis of consultation rights, rather than FPIC as a distinct source of rights.

project may still be affected by it. Notable also is that the Court in the Community of Garifuna of San Juan case repeatedly refers to free, prior, and informed 'consultation' rather than 'consent (Community Garifuna of San Juan case, 2023, para. 138).

The IACrtHR, arguably the most active court in operationalising indigenous rights, has expanded the link between individual rights of cultural identity and life and FPIC, rather than limiting consultation solely to property (Doyle, 2014, p. 130). Relatedly, Indian tribes in the USA have, pursuant to the Montana case, established their own protocols for access and FPIC within their traditional territories (Montana case 1981). Similarly, some Indigenous Peoples in Australia have adopted their own internal negotiation and consultation protocols to engage with third parties, ensure accountability among their leaders, and involve their communities in decision-making. In certain cases, courts have even considered these non-binding protocols to assess whether consultation with an indigenous community had been reasonable and adequate (Planitex case 2006). Such bottom-up processes are practical consequences of the right to self-determination, the collective rights of Indigenous People, and contribute to the resolve and unify of indigenous communities (Doyle, 2022, p. 128). Likewise, in Canada and Australia there are many examples of Indigenous Peoples establishing their own approval and negotiation processes, which may, in turn, help to 'transform existing norms and practices…' (Boirin-Farguess and Theriault, 2024, p. 29; CATSI/NTRB, 2010; De Villiers, 2024a).

3.3 Individual and Collective Rights

The rights arising from UNDRIP originate from the individual rights of members of indigenous communities, albeit in the context that these individual rights may be exercised collectively. The collective nature of the rights is evidenced in the traditional laws and customs of indigenous communities, as they traditionally exercise rights as a unified group. It is often said that UNDRIP does not create new rights,[15] yet international practice has shown that under UNDRIP greater emphasis is placed on the collective rights of Indigenous Peoples, in contrast to the scepticism shown toward the claims of collective rights by ethnocultural minorities. The societal element of Indigenous Peoples, as, for example, described in the Australian Yorta Yorta case (Yorta Yorta (HCA) case, 2002), has gained wide recognition, as it is acknow-

15 This statement is open to challenge, as some authors propose that UNDRIP does indeed create new rights. See, for example, Southalan who argues that: 'FPIC is a group right' (Southalan and Fardin, 2019, p. 373).

ledged that the identity rights of Indigenous Peoples require association and collective action to reach full fruition in pursuance of their sovereign rights and self-determination. Southalan also explores the interaction between individual and groups rights, particularly in the context of collective decision-making in indigenous communities, which may leave some individuals dissatisfied since differences of opinion may exist within the indigenous community about the merit of a measure or conditions of approval (Southalan and Fardin, 2019, p. 370).

The proposition of an individual right being exercised collectively with other persons from the same community has been summarised as follows: 'Although the rights protected under article 27 are individual rights, they depend in turn on the ability of the minority group to maintain its culture, language or religion' (ICCPR Comment Minorities, 1994, para. 6.2). Taylor summarises the individual nature of Article 27 as follows: 'Article 27 rights belong to the individual, like all rights in Part III of the Covenant, in spite of there being a collective dimension to Article 27 because they are enjoyed "in community with the other members of their group"' (Taylor, 2020, p. 789). Recognising the right of Indigenous Peoples to act collectively is, however, an essential element of their right to self-determination (Kalina and Lokono case, 2015, para. 172) and a 'necessary step' for the enjoyment of other rights (Tomaselli and Cittadino, 2021, p. 164). Additionally, the importance of a 'land base' tied to collective efforts for preserving indigenous culture and traditions was articulated by the Supreme Court of Canada in the Tsilhqot'in Nation case:

> In short, without a real and meaningful voice in the future of their core land base, Aboriginal groups face growing cultural insecurity and further dispossession of the lands and natural resources they require to sustain their distinctive societies over time. (Tsilhqot'in Nation case, 2014, para. 211)

In the Mabo case, the concept of individual and communal native title was recognised and its adjustable nature was described as follows by Justices Deane and Gaudron:

> Ordinarily, common law native title is a *communal native title* and the rights under it are *communal rights* enjoyed by a tribe or other group. It is so with Aboriginal title in the Australian States and internal Territories. Since the title preserves entitlement to use or enjoyment under the traditional law or custom of the relevant territory or locality, the contents of the rights and the identity of those entitled to enjoy them must be ascertained by reference to that trad-

> itional law or custom. The traditional law or custom is not, however, frozen as at the moment of establishment of a Colony. (emphasis added) (Mabo case (2), 1992, para. 58)

In the Community Garifuna of San Juan case the Court described as follows the intimacy between indigenous rights and land:

> The Court has taken into account that indigenous and tribal peoples, by the fact of their very existence, have the right to live freely in their own territory; the close ties that they have with the land must be recognized and understood as the fundamental basis of their cultures, their spiritual life, their integrity and their economic survival. For indigenous communities, the relationship to the land is not merely a matter of possession and production but a material and spiritual element that they should be able to enjoy fully, especially in order to preserve their cultural legacy and to transmit it to future generations. (Community Garifuna of San Juan case, 2023, para. 138)

In the Poma Poma case, the UN Human Rights Committee affirmed that while the community may be unable to exercise a collective right, an individual can pursue the matter as a member of that community, declaring: 'In the present case, it was undisputed that the author is a member of an ethnic minority and that raising llamas is an essential element of the culture of the Aymara community, since it is a form of subsistence and an ancestral tradition handed down from parent to child. The author herself is engaged in this activity' (Poma Poma case 2002, para. 7.3). The Sámi mining case judgement held that human rights treaties are 'living instruments' and their interpretation is thus influenced by evolving approaches to indigenous rights (Sámi mining case, 2024, para. 13). As such, the individual's right to practice culture under the ICCPR can be understood within the context of the community's reindeer herding practice and their right to be consulted on activities that may affect their cultural expressions (Sámi mining case 2024, para. 14.1). The individual right to culture must therefore be assessed within the context of the collective exercise of the right, in this case reindeer herding.

The entitlement of an indigenous community to collectively exercise their rights in accordance with their traditional laws and customs was also affirmed in South Africa's Richtersveld case. The judgement declared that the rights exercised by an indigenous community, as well as their organisational structure, must be evaluated, weighed, and assessed based on their communal traditional laws and customs. Once the community demonstrates cohesion and the characteristics of a community, and exercises land rights in line with their traditional laws and customs, a court is obliged to recognise their community status as a fact under contemporary law and acknowledge their collective traditional rights to the land, including the minerals it contains. The Court declared:

> we are of the view that the real character of the title that the Richtersveld Community possessed in the subject land was a *right of communal ownership* under indigenous law. The content of that right included the right to exclusive occupation and use of the subject land by members of the Community. The Community had the right to use its water, to use its land for grazing and hunting and to exploit its natural resources, above and beneath the surface. It follows therefore that prior to annexation the Richtersveld Community had a right of ownership in the subject land under indigenous law.... We are satisfied that under the indigenous law of the Richtersveld Community *communal ownership of the land* included communal ownership of the minerals and precious stones. (emphasis added) (Alexkor case, 2003, paras. 62–64)

A similar approach was adopted in the Sawhoyamaxa Indigenous Community case in Paraguay. In this case, an application was made by the indigenous community for recognition of their traditional rights as a traditional society of hunters, fishermen, and gatherers who had lived for centuries in the Paraguayan Chaco. Their ancestral lands had been divided and sold off at the end of the nineteenth century without consideration for the community or any compensation. The community claimed the land title over traditional lands that are now privately owned. It was alleged that the lack of effective action by the government of Paraguay to recognise the legal personality of the community and, in particular, its decision to grant land titles over ancestral lands had resulted in the community having to settle in an inhospitable location with extremely precarious conditions while waiting for an answer to their claim. The Court held that the rights of the community must be assessed in the context of their collective adherence to traditional laws and customs as a community of people, stating:

> 118 The culture of the members of indigenous communities reflects a particular way of life, of being, seeing and acting in the world, the starting point of which is their close relationship with their traditional lands and natural resources, not only because they are their main means of survival, but also because they form part of their worldview, of their religiousness, and consequently, of their cultural identity. (Sawhoyamaxa Community case, 2006)

In the Kashela case, the Court ruled that Namibia's independence did not extinguish the rights of communities or individuals to titles of communal land that existed prior to independence (Kashela case 2018). The applicable law effectively upheld the 'existing rights' of the community, as these communal rights existed at the time of independence, and unless explicitly extinguished, they continued to exist under customary law. The Court declared that since communal title is a *sui generis* right, the communal right to land survived independence, adding that the rights and interests granted by the community to the applicant's father were inherited by the applicant pursuant to the applicable community customs. In doing this, the Court recognised and gave effect to the community's practice of granting rights to and interests in land to its members pursuant to their traditional laws and customs. The Court was satisfied that the presumption of the legal continuity of customary land rights had not been displaced (Barrie, 2021, p. 182), concluding that

> … Ms Kashela acquired a right of exclusive possession and occupation of the land in dispute upon the passing of her father and that right survived and attached to the land even after its proclamation as town land. The right is enforceable by courts of law. (Kashela case, 2018, para. 81)

In the Isolated Indigenous People case, the Supreme Court of Brazil ordered that indigenous groups living in isolation should also be accorded the protections of municipal and international law, 'with the act of isolation considered sufficient for consultation purposes' (Isolated Indigenous People case 2023). Although the Court cited ILO 169 and UNDRIP, the legal obligation it imposed was that of 'consultation', with no reference to actual consent or veto by the indigenous community.

3.4 Bundles of Rights

Jurisprudence highlight that the nature and scope of the collective rights and interests of an indigenous community must be ascertained by the factual circumstances surrounding each community. Not all Indigenous Peoples can be grouped together with a set of standardised rights as if they possess the same traditional rights. The content of rights exercised by an indigenous community depends on the elements of its communal practice, often referred to as a bundle of rights. The content of their bundle of rights depends on the specific customs and practices of each community by reference to their traditional exercise of those rights. There is no normative standard to apply to all communities that regard themselves as indigenous. Courts are guided by evidence of the historic existence of the community, the traditional rules, and customs that regulate life within it, their ongoing adherence to those traditions and customs, and the nature of the rights and interests affected by a proposed measure. For example, some communities may exercise rights in respect of the seabed whilst others may not. Unless there has been a severance of these traditional customary rights, courts may recognise the ongoing collective character of the community. Note, for example, the Moriarty case, in which the Court had to consider whether an indigenous person's harvesting of abalone and selling it for commercial gain to someone outside the indigenous community was consistent with the exercise of traditional rights. The Court concluded that, pursuant to Section 211 of the Native Title Act 1993 (Cth), traditional fishing without a permit is allowed for the purposes of a household or the benefit of the indigenous community; the catching of fish for the purpose of commercial selling to an external person is not protected by traditional fishing as intended in s211; and the proof rests on the prosecutor to establish that a defence pursuant to s211 is not applicable (Moriarty case, 2024, para. 180).

The application of FPIC to each indigenous community thus hinges on the content of its bundle of rights. The bundle of rights of a specific community is not frozen in the past. The content of the bundle is assessed by courts in a contemporary context based on the available facts at the time of hearing. The community is required to demonstrate the ongoing exercise of its traditional rights. A court may find, for example, that a right that had existed at a particular point in time is no longer exercised by the community and, hence, no longer forms part of its bundle of rights. This principle is reflected in Australia's Ward case:

> an order in which the Federal Court makes a determination of native title has an indefinite character which distinguishes it from a declaration of legal right as ordinarily understood in such authorities as *International General Electric Co of New York Ltd v Commissioners of Customs and Excise* ([1962] Ch 784 at 789). That indefinite character reflects the requirement for the continuing acknowledgment and observance of traditional laws and customs and *continuing connection* with land implicit in the definition of "native title" in s 223(1) of the Native Title Act. (emphasis added) (Ward case, 2002, para. 32)

In many respects, the right to self-determination is 'composite' in nature, meaning the rights may differ depending on the circumstances of a specific indigenous community (Tomaselli, 2016, p. 173). A composite right is inherently collective, as it is exercised by a community consistent with its traditional customs. This parallels the application of native title rights in Australia, where the courts have held that the content of a right depends on the bundle of rights that continue to be exercised by the native title-holding community concerned according to its traditional laws and customs (Ward case, 2002).

In the Akiba case, the High Court of Australia emphasised that the content of native title rights is ascertained not by referring to the common law, but by relying on the traditional laws and customs of the particular community (Akiba case 2013, para. 20). This is consistent to the approach adopted by the Constitutional Court of South Africa in respect of the content of customary law, whereby the practiced customs are determined by evidence (Mayelane case, 2013). In cases of dispute over a claimed right, it falls to the judiciary to assess whether the community exercises that right in accordance with its customs and traditions. The court may, for example, reject the assertion of a community, for example that it had traditionally exercised rights over a portion of the sea (Munkara case 2024).

The implementation of FPIC is thus influenced by the elements within an indigenous community's bundle of rights. For instance, if indigenous rights traditionally extended to marine territories, a proposed measure in those waters may trigger consultative rights and a reasonable opportunity for input (Tipakalippa case 2022). Jimenez highlights the complexity of applying FPIC to waters beyond the territorial jurisdiction of Indigenous Peoples, ultimately concluding that the right to FPIC could extend to the ocean (Jimenez, 2024, p. 87).

Although FPIC has received attention from courts, 'the duty to consult has not yet been developed into an unconditional duty to obtain consent prior to any development planned in areas significant to Indigenous Peoples' (Ravna, 2020). While there is no binding legal instrument in international human rights law that elevates FPIC to the status of a legal norm (Giupponi, 2018, p. 495), both UNDRIP, in general, and FPIC, specifically, signify the international community's commitment to enhanced recognition of indigenous rights. Even if FPIC is not explicitly cited by courts, its underlying principles are widely acknowledged as contributing to 'emerging customary international law' (Barrie, 2024b, p. 224). I agree with Barrie that FPIC is contributing to new understandings of good faith consultation and those understandings in turn impact on domestic policy responses as is seen in chapter 8 in respect of the OECD countries.

Upon reflection, it appears that the distinction sought to be drawn in the literature between consultation and FPIC is not sound and has for the reasons explained in this chapter, not generally resonated with courts. While courts have embraced developments concerning good faith consultation and the necessary steps to uphold this obligation toward indigenous communities in relation to their property and cultural rights, courts have stopped well short of elevating FPIC – particularly the element of consent – to a term of law.

United Nations Special Rapporteur Victoria Tauli-Corpuz concludes, accurately albeit rather pessimistically, after reflection on the many arrangements created by states to accommodate the self-determination and self-government rights of Indigenous Peoples, that-

> Notwithstanding those positive practices, the Special Rapporteur considers that most of the existing autonomy or self-government arrangements do not completely fulfil the international human rights obligations of States regarding the rights of Indigenous Peoples. (Tauli-Corpuz, 2019, para. 80)

4 Summary

In summary, the following can be surmised about the origin of FPIC and its legal effect:

4.1 Essence of FPIC

FPIC represents the culmination of efforts towards better recognition of Indigenous Peoples' right to self-determination. FPIC evolved from the concept of consultation as a means of improved acknowledgment of the permanence of the interests of Indigenous Peoples, their historical status, their ongoing connection to their lands, and their aspiration to be joint decision-makers over matters that concern them, particularly in respect of their traditional lands. Rooted in the traditional customary rights and laws of Indigenous Peoples as distinct societies, with their own self-governing rules and customary institutions, FPIC, in some respects, seeks to restore rights lost during colonisation or those encroached upon or denied due to discrimination. FPIC aims, in essence, to position Indigenous Peoples as co-decision-makers on measures that directly or predominantly affect them and their traditional lands. It is proposed in literature that consultation is a first step of FPIC, but jurisprudence has not drawn such a distinction between consultation and FPIC. Rather, jurisprudence tends to enhance practical consultation obligations to ensure consultation is 'effective' and 'meaningful', but without venturing into a right of veto.

4.2 FPIC Not a Term of Law

Despite its widespread use, FPIC is not a defined term of law. Attempts to define FPIC often become descriptive, focusing on the process of compliance rather than the inherent meaning of the term. Upon analysis, the process of FPIC appears to resemble the practicalities of consultation, ranging from ad hoc engagement to ongoing involvement. While the term 'informed consent' is also used in other areas of law, such as medical treatment and law of contract, FPIC under UNDRIP is more programmatic and aspirational as opposed to a legal entitlement associated with the word 'consent'. While 'informed consent' would usually be understood according to its ordinary and obvious meaning, consent in FPIC does not imply a legal veto. In exceptional circumstances, municipal law may grant such a right to an indigenous community, but this would stem from the municipal legal framework itself rather than from UNDRIP.

4.3 Origin in Individual Rights

The rights of Indigenous Peoples are grounded in individual rights that can be exercised individually or collectively with other members of the same community. Indigenous Peoples share a desire to protect and maintain their identity rights, including rights to language, culture, customs, and traditions. UNDRIP does not grant special collective rights to indigenous communities, but, arguably more than any other international instrument, UNDRIP recognises that rights may be exercised collectively in accordance with customary laws and practices. Several municipal courts have also recognised the collective nature of indigenous rights when viewed from the perspective of the indigenous community. An indigenous community's bundle of rights determines whether a particular right, as asserted, does indeed fall within the court's sphere of competence. At a practical level, indigenous rights tend to be closely tied with traditional ancestral lands and a unique legal system distinct from the state legal framework. The term FPIC is associated with the rights of Indigenous Peoples and not with the rights of other ethnocultural communities.

4.4 FPIC and Legal Pluralism

The recognition of indigenous rights, in general, and FPIC, in particular, is closely linked to the concept of legal pluralism, where multiple legal systems operate within the same national territory. The collective nature of indigenous laws and customs must be ascertained from the indigenous perspective, not from the perspective of the dominant legal system. Although there may be a hierarchy between state law and indigenous law, UNDRIP requires the recognition of the indigenous legal system to the greatest extent possible. Since UNDRIP is not binding as treaty law, states may, through their own legislation, give legal effect to the duality of legal systems and guide the courts in resolving conflicts between the systems. Courts may also use their discretion to consider the relevance of traditional laws and customs when resolving disputes. FPIC can therefore serve as an informative, inspirational, and interpretative tool.

4.5 Relationship to Bundles of Rights

FPIC is closely tied to so-called bundle of rights that reflect the identity of a specific indigenous community. The nature and scope of an indigenous community's collective rights and interests must be determined based on the community's historical context and contemporary evidence of their ongoing adherence to traditional laws and customs. There is no normative standard for FPIC that applies to all communities identifying as 'indigenous'. The content of rights that continue to be exercised by an indigenous community depends on the elements of their communal practice – then and now (Ward case, 2002, para. 32). Courts generally rely on evidence of the community's historical existence, the traditional rules and customs that govern their way of life, continued observance of these traditions and customs, and the nature of the rights and interests impacted by a proposed measure. Consequently, the application of FPIC to each indigenous community depends on the content of its individual bundle of rights, which may evolve over time. As such, the scope of FPIC may be reduced if a community fails to show continuing adherence to a specific practice or custom.

4.6 Scope of FPIC

FPIC is ambivalent in scope. Initially, Indigenous Peoples invoked FPIC principally in response to activities impacting their traditional lands. However, efforts have since been made to expand its application to encompass socio-economic policies that affect Indigenous Peoples more broadly, not necessarily limited to their lands. In the Milirrpum case, Blackburn J commented on the link between Indigenous Peoples and their ancestral lands:

> the fundamental truth about the aboriginals' relationship to the land is that whatever else it is, it is a religious relationship. … There is an unquestioned scheme of things in which the spirit ancestors, the people of the clan, particular

> land and everything that exists on and in it, are organic parts of one indissoluble whole. (Milirrpum case, 1971, para. 167)

The causal link between indigenous rights and land is expanded by UNDRIP, which advocates for the recognition of broader interests addressing socio-economic issues, general discrimination, and political participatory rights of Indigenous People in general. Expanding FPIC to the realm of political participation while placing less emphasis on traditional lands seem to blur the distinction between indigenous rights and those of ethnocultural minorities. Not surprisingly, courts have been reluctant to extend indigenous rights to general socio-economic policies unless these involve the community's lands and customs.

The proposition that policies that may impact on Indigenous People in social policy areas such as housing, health, criminal justice, or life expectancy should be justiciable pursuant to FPIC is resisted by governments and has not been endorsed by courts.

4.7 FPIC in the Context of ILO 169 and UNDRIP

FPIC is often cited in the context of ILO 169 and UNDRIP as if both instruments are of equal legal status and as if both use the term FPIC in the same context. While courts may rely on ILO 169 and UNDRIP for inspiration as a directive principle for good policy, the two instruments are fundamentally different and should not be treated as though equal in status. ILO 169 is a legally binding treaty – but only to the countries party to it. Furthermore, the term FPIC does not appear in ILO 169 except in the context of forced removals from lands. Article 6 of the ILO 169 emphasises the 'objective of achieving consent' without thereby mandating consent. Importantly, Indigenous Peoples cannot initiate proceedings under ILO 169. UNDRIP, meanwhile, is not a legally binding treaty. It seeks to expand the use of FPIC, employs the term without defining it, and uses other terms like 'consult' without clarifying its distinction from FPIC. As with ILO 169, Indigenous Peoples cannot commence legal proceedings under UNDRIP. While the social, policy, and political effects of ILO 169 and UNDRIP have been substantial, caution is advised when attributing rights in domestic law based on these instruments.

4.8 FPIC in the Americas and Beyond

FPIC is closely associated with case law arising from the Americas. The following observations can be made in this respect: First, several countries in the Americas are signatories to ILO 169 and have enacted legislation to give effect to it in domestic law. The attention paid to FPIC in case law in the Americas is, therefore, closely linked to ILO 169 as a binding treaty. Second, ILO 169 and UNDRIP are often referred to in case law as if they share the same legal status, which is not the case. Third, FPIC is not relied on by courts as if purported to be a justiciable veto over land access measures. Generally, FPIC is subject to the regulatory power of government and does not imply an absolute veto in favour of Indigenous People. Fourth, no clear distinction is drawn in domestic jurisprudence between consult and FPIC, with the former often interpreted in a dynamic manner but without implying consent. Fifth, while selected case law arising from the Americas is repeatedly cited in literature, upon reflection jurisprudence in the rest of the world has not rushed into adopting ILO 169 or UNDRIP as a legal basis to resolve land access disputes in municipal law.

4.9 FPIC and Consultation: Is There a Difference at Law?

FPIC, as it appears in UNDRIP, is often presented as an advancement on the meaning of consultation. While consultation is considered part of FPIC, the latter is said to include aspects such as ongoing involvement, co-decision-making, a veto, and the right to withdraw approval. Some literature and advocacy frame FPIC as a form of joint decision-making between equal partners, but this is not the case unless so determined by domestic legislation. Courts have generally resisted being drawn into such subtle distinctions between consultation and FPIC, choosing not to rely on UNDRIP as a source of veto rights unless such a right is explicitly granted under municipal law. Courts have, however, adopted consultation requirements that reflect greater regard for indigenous laws and customs, using phrases such as 'meaningful' and 'effective participation', the consideration of language and communication difficulties, the distinction between consultation and mere information sharing, the meaning of good faith consultation, the importance of keeping an open mind, and the right of parties to adopt a firm stance. Despite not being considered a justiciable right by domestic courts, FPIC and the debates surrounding it are continuing to influence the understanding of consultation with Indigenous People.

CHAPTER 4

The Right to FPIC as a Customary International Legal Norm

1 Introduction

Free, prior, and informed consent is often cited as either an established legal norm in international law or an emerging legal norm in customary international law. This leads to the assertion that states are legally obliged to observe FPIC, not merely due to policy considerations. The previous chapter established that FPIC as it appears in UNDRIP is not a legal norm under international treaty law. This chapter now examines whether FPIC qualifies as a legal norm arising from customary international law.

Customary international law is an important source of public law and is based on 'unwritten law deriving from practice accepted as law' (UN International Law Commission, 2018, p. 122). The common international practice of consulting with Indigenous Peoples when their rights and interests in land are affected, along with the use of the term FPIC in UNDRIP and various other standard-setting policies, are sometimes construed as evidence of adequate state practice and adherence to establish FPIC as a justiciable obligation and right – either existing or emerging – in customary international law. For example, Kusniati proposes that 'FPIC is an international customary *law*', albeit one often breached (emphasis added) (Kusniati, 2024, p. 171). Other authors accept that FPIC has not yet attained the status of a legal norm under customary international law, suggesting instead that it is, like autonomy, an 'emerging' customary international norm (Tomaselli 2017, 420; Barrie 2024, 219). Newman observes that it is 'challenging' to determine indigenous rights by reference to international law generally and customary international law specifically (Newman, 2025, p. 466).

Although FPIC is not a justiciable treaty right under UNDRIP, the path for it to become a binding legal norm under customary international law is open, albeit uncertain. This, however, requires two conditions: consistent state practice and a belief by states that such practice is legally required. Both these conditions must be fulfilled before FPIC can be regarded as a customary international norm.

This chapter begins by looking at the requirements for a practice to be regarded as a legal norm pursuant to customary international law. It then

HTTPS://DOI.ORG/10.1163/9789004724792-005

assesses whether FPIC meets the criteria to be considered a binding legal norm of customary international law. An analysis of selected judgements from the International Court of Justice on customary international law follows. Finally, conclusions are drawn on whether FPIC constitutes an established or emerging right in customary international law.

1.1 Two Elements of Customary International Law

The substance of a norm in customary international law is traced back to the conduct of states and belief of states (Jennings and Watts, 2008, p. 25). The two 'constituent elements' of customary international law are 'a *general practice* and *acceptance* of that practice as law' (emphasis added) (UN International Law Commission, 2018, p. 125). Although total adherence by every state is not required to establish a custom in international law, Judge De Castro asserts that 'the threshold for state practice is high, with the need for substantially or practically' uniform acceptance of a norm (Icelandic Fisheries case, 1973, p. 90).

FPIC's weak legal status in UNDRIP, coupled with the absence of widespread municipal legislation endorsing it as a legal norm distinct from consultation, can perhaps be remedied through widespread state adherence to FPIC as if it were already an existing legal norm due to state practice. In other words, states would be bound by FPIC not through treaty law, but through consistent international conduct. However, relying on customary international law to establish a new legal norm is cumbersome, slow and uncertain. States may also dispute the legal status of a purported custom or simply refuse to comply with it. Furthermore, relying on customary international law to enact FPIC as a legal norm is not an ideal solution for addressing the FPIC-related gaps in international and domestic legal frameworks. The simple fact that FPIC is often described as an 'emerging right' underscores the lack of widespread adherence necessary for it to be considered a binding legal norm.

The irony cannot be ignored that the ongoing debate in literature about FPIC's status and meaning, merely serves to confirm the lack of political appetite among states to legislate FPIC into law or to develop an international treaty to give it legal effect; thereby weakening the proposition that FPIC is indeed emerging as a customary right through state custom.

1.2 Does Best Practice Imply a New Legal Norm?

While some literature suggests that FPIC is slowly evolving into a norm of customary international law, the opposite may, in fact, be more accurate. The reluctance of states to incorporate FPIC into domestic legislation and the limited number of states endorsing ILO 169 demonstrate that FPIC is not evolving into an international legal norm. At best, FPIC may serve as a guide to best practice, thus falling far short of being a legal norm.

This raises the central question of this chapter: Is FPIC a legal norm – whether actual or emerging – in customary international law?

Beham suggests that customary rules are 'mixed or smeared' until they are recognised in customary international law because states do not always act with clarity, consistency or predictability (Beham, 2022, p. 101). The conduct of states may, however, diverge from the statements they make in international forums. In fact, a state's conduct may even contradict the substance of treaties to which it is a party. Lip service by states in support of FPIC as a policy therefore cannot be construed as state adherence to FPIC in legislative and policy measures.

The conduct of states with respect to FPIC needs to be assessed by considering evidence of their actual behaviour and their subjective belief that a legal norm already exists which mandates such conduct. Mere examples of FPIC as good practice, public statements, sensible policies, one state following another's example, or opinions expressed in international forums cannot be construed to purport the existence of an international customary legal norm. While treaty law and support for non-binding declarations may be relevant to ascertain the possible existence of a customary law, they are insufficient to meet the evidentiary standard of state practice. For example, although states generally strive to promote democratic values, such endeavours do not elevate democracy or its associated institutional arrangements to the status of a customary international legal norm. It simply affirms that good governance is arguably best achieved through democratic institutions and processes, without implying a justiciable right under customary international law.

This chapter proposes that FPIC does not qualify as a legal norm in customary international law. There is inadequate evidence of state acceptance of FPIC as well as a lack of distinction in practice between FPIC and consultation, to support the proposition that FPIC is 'emerging' as a norm in customary international law. While the term FPIC is increasing in use, its substance as a potential legal norm has not progressed beyond what is generally regarded good faith consultation. A case can certainly be made that the debates arising from FPIC have contributed to new approaches to consultation with Indigenous Peoples, but this merely highlights the fact that FPIC is not, in itself, a right or an emerging right, but rather a tool of influence, direction, and advocacy. FPIC reflects a new way of thinking, a more inclusive approach, greater justice for Indigenous Peoples, increased awareness, and respect for traditional land ownership.

1.3 Consultation versus FPIC

Consultation with Indigenous Peoples is, for good reason, widely recognised by states as an essential policy measure, an objective, a moral and ethical duty, a key component of social license, and an obligation rooted in social justice. It also reflects respect for self-determination, culture, tradition, and other identity rights. However, this recognition falls short, substantially so, of FPIC being adequately clear, precise, and widely practiced to be regarded an international custom with legal effect.

Customary international law refers to international legal obligations that arise from generally accepted and established international practices by states. These practices are not set out in formal treaties or conventions but are instead unwritten norms of behaviour that states broadly observe and apply as if they (already) possess the force of law. Just as in domestic law, where a widespread practice may be regarded by the courts as a binding legal customary norm,[1] an international custom that is widely observed and respected as if it constitutes law, can attain legal status. However, the operative phrase is 'state practice', not general statements or policy positions adopted by states. Rhetoric does not amount to practice. The latter indicates an underlying belief that a legal norm already exists and hence that norm must be adhered to, whereas public statements can be made for various other reasons. In the Ure case, the Court acknowledged that departing from a rule of customary international law is treated as a breach of law, which is distinct from challenging the actual existence of the legal norm (Ure case 2016, para. 32).

Uniform state practice grants customary law both legality and legitimacy: legality through state conduct and legitimacy through deep-routed adherence by many states to the norm and belief that it constitutes law. Municipal

1 Mallonee conducts a reality check on customary use as a source of domestic law, noting that the modernisation of the state reduces reliance on conduct to establish legal norms; the state's legislative function allows for the enactment of customs that are regarded as laws; changes in traditionally held customs affect their relevance and meaning in contemporary society; and the age of individualism has weakened customary law and 'detracted from its legal force' (Mallonee, 2015, p. 4).

courts may contribute to the development of customary international law, even if only by way of subtle influence and comparative law. By considering both municipal and international practices, municipal courts can identify and reflect emerging trends. Caution, however, is warranted, as municipal courts function within a particular domestic legal framework, and judges are neither required nor trained to consider customary international law or the conduct of other states. A judge's mere assertion that a norm exists in customary international law cannot necessarily be treated as precedent or authoritative unless it falls within the court's jurisdiction and is supported by a thorough investigation by the court of state practice and the reasons behind it. Without such an investigation, the judge's assertion about a purported customary international norm should be considered as made in passing. This is exemplified by a ruling from the Supreme Court of Singapore, which observed that for customary international law to be established 'extensive and virtually uniform practice by all States' must be demonstrated (Yong Vui Kong case, 2010, paras. 96–98). It is also noteworthy that, despite the Constitution of South Africa empowering courts to consider developments in international law and the municipal jurisprudence of other states, no thorough consideration of international state conduct concerning international compliance with FPIC has yet occurred in the country.

1.4 Rules of Interpretation

Customary international law is a source of law, akin to a treaty or a convention. Importantly, courts do not create customary international law but rather may recognise what is already practiced by states and accepted as a legal norm by states. Courts must, however, refrain from using their investigative powers to 'discover' evidence of state conduct that supports a particular bias. Performing a thorough investigation and assessment of international state conduct requires substantial resources, evidence, and experience in comparative international jurisprudence, which typically falls beyond the capacity and competency of domestic judges. Added thereto, a key challenge for customary international law is the lack of agreed rules of interpretation which would give effect to it. The result is a 'mercurial process [of interpretation] whose functioning is both questioned and unregulated' (Mileva, 2022, p. 456).

This does not imply that customary international law always has worldwide application or that all states must adhere to it before a legal norm is recognised. Customary international law can also apply between two states or within a specific region. It may be easier to ascertain state conduct when the actions of only two, or a few states, are considered. For example, if FPIC is widely observed as a legal norm in the Americas, it does not mean that it is also a legal norm in the rest of the world. Ultimately, it depends on how widely a practice is adhered to and regarded as law by different states. Citations in literature to case law arising from the Americas in support of a proposition that FPIC has evolved in a customary norm in international law cannot be endorsed. A court must be satisfied of the widespread and consistent conduct of states in their observance of a custom for it to be considered a legal norm. Ad hoc or selective actions by a state or mere references by a court to the importance of FPIC would not suffice, as all actions by all organs of government must be considered. For a finding of a custom to be made, there must be adequate evidence that the norm is regarded as legally in place and binding. In a submission by the United States, the following was explained:

> customary international law develops from a *general* and *consistent practice* of States followed by them out of a *sense of legal obligation*, or opinio juris. (emphasis added) (Bellinger and Haynes, 2007, p. 444)

Silence or inaction by a state also cannot be construed as endorsing the existence of a customary norm (Baka, 2022). From this flows the obvious: not all agreements, practices, habits, policies, conduct, resolutions, or customs shared between states can be elevated to constitute binding customary international law. The International Court of Justice has generally been careful not to treat general statements, policies, and declarations without legally binding effect as evidence of customary international law.

Once international law is declared a universal norm, all states, including any that had been silent or engaged in inconsistent practices, must adhere to it. It is therefore not surprising that the importance of customary international law as a source of rights is often challenged, as states tend to prefer relying on treaties and legislative measures to which they have explicitly consented to regulate multilateral conduct. Noteworthy in this respect is the observation made in Australia that after more than a century of constitutional tradition, 'the place of customary international law as part of the domestic legal system remains without any definitive answer' (Burmester and Reye, 2000, p. 39).

Tomaselli provides a useful overview of case studies where indigenous self-government and autonomy rights have found their way through incorporation into the municipal law of states (Tomaselli, 2016). She asks whether, in light of international developments, autonomy has become a legal right in customary international law. She concludes that, despite some suggestions that the right to autonomy has become part of customary international law, such a categorisation is probably overly optimistic. In my view, the same can be said of FPIC. With regard to indigenous autonomy, Tomaselli states that –

> the right to autonomy or self-government of Indigenous Peoples, on the basis of Art. 4 of the UNDRIP, may be defined –at least– as an *emergent* international standard. (emphasis added) (Tomaselli, 2017, p. 420)

Tomaselli rightly observes that there is insufficient consensus in international law about the meaning and content of autonomy for it to be regarded as a 'right' under customary international law. The notion that FPIC is an 'emerging' norm of customary international law is also erroneous since it assumes that it is already widely practiced by states as if it were law, rather than just a sensible and commendable 'practice' or 'standard'.

The observation above is exemplified by the responses in the literature to the Baleni case in South Africa in which brief reference was made to FPIC (Baleni case 2019). There is, however, no indication in the case that Basson J undertook or relied extensively on an analysis of international state conduct to recognise the veto right of the particular local community. A proper reading of the judgement reveals that reference to international treaty law was made only in passing, as the community's veto right was derived from domestic legislation (Baleni case, 2019; De Villiers, 2025e, p. 347). Basson cited FPIC merely in passing for general comparative purposes, not to justify the outcome on an existing international customary legal norm. A mere mention of FPIC in a judgement cannot be construed as contributing to its emergence as a legal norm *unless* the context of its use justifies such a conclusion.

1.5 General Practice and Acceptance of Law

Two important elements form the basis for international customary law: a general state practice and acceptance of the state practice as law by the states (UN International Law Commission, 2018, p. 123). Sovereign states must regard the practice as law and not merely as a good practice or a sensible or responsible policy. In other words, the state follows the custom in the belief that the practice is (already) law, not because the practice is widely considered the proper thing to do.

Important to this chapter is the International Law Commission's commentary that 'where the existence of a general *practice accepted as law* cannot be established, the conclusion will be that the alleged rule of customary international law *does not exist*' (emphasis added) (UN International Law Commission, 2018, p. 125). In addition, the motivation for states to adhere to the rule is not grounded merely in general good policy, but in the belief that a rule demanding compliance already exists (Asylum case, 1950, para. 277).

This chapter concludes that FPIC meets neither of these thresholds and can therefore not be treated as a binding legal norm under customary international law.

2 When Does State Practice Become a Customary Legal Norm?

The UN Food and Agricultural Organisation (FAO) declares in its Manual for Project Practitioners the following about the nature of FPIC as being a 'good practice':

> In recognizing the unique identity of Indigenous Peoples, international law affirms that they have the right to decide their own future to ensure their cultural and physical survival. In the last two or three years, development experts have recognized that FPIC is not only important for Indigenous Peoples but it is also *good practice* to undertake with *local communities*,[2] as involving them in the decision making of any proposed development activity increases their sense of ownership and engagement and, moreover, helps guarantee their right to development as a basic human rights principle. (emphasis added) (UN Food and Agricultural Organisation, 2016, p. 4)

The Manual is not a legal document, but its illustrative value for this chapter lies in its origin from the United Nations and its practical guidance on measures to be taken when access is sought to the lands of Indigenous Peoples and other communities. FPIC seems to be evolving into a general operative concept for regulating effective consultation with all local communities, not just Indigenous Peoples.

The UN Manual highlights that while the term 'right' is widely used in the context of FPIC, its actual emphasis is on *process* rather than on a right of veto. The 'c' in FPIC is understood in substance as 'consultation' rather than co-decision-making or legal consent. If FPIC were intended to grant a veto right, there would be no need for such extensive measures to seek consent. A simple statement that FPIC entails a right of veto over land access would have

2 Note the use of the word 'communities' as a general term, rather than the more specific 'indigenous'. This highlights the importance of FPIC as a general good practice for community consultation, rather than an exclusive right for the benefit solely of Indigenous Peoples.

sufficed. The Manual (correctly) underscores that FPIC focuses on conduct, behaviour, responsiveness, involvement, and best practice. These may not be justiciable rights, but they remain important policy considerations, sound practice, best practice, and guides to conduct. Compliance with the process may be subject to judicial review, even though actual consent is not mandated. A proposed measure can be assessed based on the following questions: was adequate information provided; did the proponent demonstrate an open mind; was the consultation conducted in good faith; was engagement aligned with indigenous customs and practices; and did the parties act in good faith? In essence, was there an opportunity for meaningful and effective consultation and participation by the indigenous community in the decision-making process?

This chapter examines whether these general good policies, responsible procedures, and best practices have evolved into a justiciable right pursuant to customary international law.

2.1 Custom Reflects Reality

D'Aspremont describes customary international law as 'grounded in a particular social reality' (D'Aspremont, 2022, p. 29). The social reality is that states operate under the assumption that a legal norm already exists. There mere following of a good example or a shared value does not meet the threshold for a state acting because it believes a legal standard already exists. D'Amato notes that customary international law oscillates between 'law-formation and law interpretation' (D'Amato, 1965, p. 323).

The Vienna Convention on the Law of Treaties (VCLT) provides the foundation for interpreting international law (Vienna Convention, 1969, arts. 31–33). However, this does not necessarily assist in ascertaining and interpreting customary international law. As Arajarvi cautions: 'With CIL (customary international law) identification, one can usually find evidence to support what one is looking for…' (Arajarvi, 2022, p. 42). The biases and predispositions of the interpreter may influence the identification of an international practice and its interpretation as a law. Evidence in state conduct can easily be found somewhere in the world to support a predisposition. Mileva observes that 'international legal theory and practice presently offer little discussion and guidance on the issue of CIL interpretation, and there are no uniform guidelines for the process of CIL interpretation' (Mileva, 2022, p. 477). While the domestic rules of statutory interpretation provide guidance on issues such as handling debates leading to the enactment of a statute, the weight given to government policy and public statements, the relevance of expert papers and other materials, and what is considered the best evidence, these basic rules do not necessarily apply to customary international law.

Put simply, if interpreting a municipal statute, even with the benefit of parliamentary debates and rules about the relevance of other extraneous materials, is sometimes difficult in domestic settings, it is even more so in the case of customary international law which is unwritten, undocumented, subject to different domestic legal arrangements, and based on inferences arising from the conduct of states. While assessing state conduct in the context of a bilateral relationship may be relatively straightforward, doing so on a global scale involving many or all states, represents an overwhelming challenge. It is hardly surprising that interpretative exercises of customary international law have been described as 'methodological mayhem' resting on uncertainty (Talmon, 2005, p. 417).

In light of the availability of treaty law as a normative standard to regulate the conduct of states, customary international law's relevance in filling gaps in statutory and treaty law regarding FPIC is questionable. Put simply: if states are of the view that FPIC should be given legal status, they can enter into a treaty or enact domestic legislation, without having to wait for a legal norm to be declared pursuant to customary international law.

2.2 Reliance on Evidence Other than State Actions

The requirement to assess state practice is generally interpreted by the ICJ and municipal courts to include official documents, public statements, and treaties a state has consented to, rather than solely the actual practice and belief of states (Ryngaert and Hora Siccama, 2018). Since the state lacks a mindset that can be examined, its actions are of primary importance. Unfortunately, the scope of investigation into actual state practice can easily be reduced to focus principally, or even exclusively, on public statements, rather than to critically assess and evaluate the actual conduct of states and their subjective belief if a legal norm already exists that necessitates their conduct. Ryngaert and Hora Siccama note that by using 'shortcuts domestic courts may want to signal their impartiality and legitimacy in determining customary international law, for much the same reason as the ICJ uses such shortcuts' (Ryngaert and Hora Siccama, 2018, p. 23).

In the North Sea Continental Shelf case, the basic parameters for determining the existence of customary international law were set out as follows:

> Not only must the acts concerned amount to a *settled practice*, but they must also be such, or be carried out in such a way, as to be evidence of a *belief* that

> this practice is rendered *obligatory* by the existence of a rule of law requiring it. (emphasis added) (North Sea Continental Shelf case 1969)

When applying these two requirements to FPIC, Barrie correctly asserts that FPIC does not qualify as a legal norm in customary international law. However, he distinguishes FPIC from ordinary practices, policies, or procedures adopted by states, describing FPIC as 'moving inexorably' towards recognition as a legal norm in customary international law:

> Measured against the requirements necessary for customary international law, FPIC is moving inexorably towards meeting such demands. (Barrie, 2024b, p. 219)

Barrie's proposition that FPIC is moving towards becoming a legal norm in customary international law is open to challenge. His analysis focuses primarily on secondary materials, such as expert opinions, a few selected judgements, and non-binding documents from international organisations including the United Nations, rather than a thorough examination of the actual conduct of states in response to FPIC. While these secondary materials are no doubt influential in the policy sphere in encouraging good governance, assessing the actual conduct of states, and the belief underlying this conduct, is essential to determine whether FPIC is progressing towards a legal norm in customary international law. In this regard, my proposition is that the conduct of states and their belief of why FPIC ought to be adhered to as a good policy measure, do not support the recognition of FPIC as a legal norm in customary international law.

The UN International Law Commission has emphasised that the examination of state practice should be '*exhaustive* (having regard to its availability) and include the relevant practice of *all* the State's organs and *all* relevant practice of a particular organ'. It is only after such an in-depth examination that the 'actual position of the State can be determined' (emphasis added) (UN International Law Commission, 2018, p. 135). The suggestion that FPIC is an emerging right but without any detailed assessment having been conducted of actual state practice at a representative level is highly speculative. In the Jurisdictional Immunities case, the ICJ emphasised that isolated acts of a state do not constitute a totality of its conduct and that, in this particular case, the predominant actions of the state did not warrant a declaration that a norm exists pursuant to customary international law (Jurisdictional Immunities of the State case, 2012, p. 186).

Yafee describes the increase in citations of FPIC appearing in policy materials as follows:

> FPIC is on the rise. International actors including human rights monitoring bodies, multilateral and national lawmakers, international financial institutions, industry groups and civil society have all migrated towards the position that *either law or best practices* require obtaining the consent of Indigenous Peoples before the onset of projects on or near Indigenous land. (emphasis added) (Yafee, 2018, p. 9)

There is little doubt that FPIC is increasingly cited as a guide for interaction with Indigenous People. However, the advocacy and educational use of FPIC falls substantially short of it having evolved into a legal norm that mandates compliance.

2.3 Good Policies Do Not Equate to Embryonic Customary Rights

The growing awareness of the importance attached to consultation with Indigenous Peoples doesn't imply the emergence of a new customary legal norm. Not all commendable policies adopted by states in their dealings with their citizens give rise to embryonic rights. The challenge for FPIC to attain the status of a legal norm lies in the term's vagueness, as well as its inconsistent application and lack of observance by states. In fact, many states outright deny the existence of Indigenous Peoples within their populations.

Most of the uncertainty surrounding the concept of FPIC stems from the use of the word 'consent'. The idea that 'consent' in FPIC implies sovereign decision-making by an indigenous community to the exclusion of government approval and regulatory authority, is explicitly rejected by states worldwide. To then rely on state support for a non-binding declaration such as UNDRIP as evidence of endorsing FPIC's evolution into a binding legal norm, lacks credibility. FPIC fails to meet the following threshold determined in the Jurisdictional Immunities of the State case: 'the existence of a rule of customary international law requires that there be "a settled practice" (Jurisdictional Immunities of the State case, 2012).

McCulloch observes that: 'Fundamental issues remain with implementing the FPIC including isolation, internal participation, and overlap' (McCulloch, 2021, p. 249). A legal norm requires certainty and clarity – both of which elude FPIC. On the complex issue of the use of 'consent' in FPIC, McCulloch states: 'Finally, it remains unclear if the "consent" part of the FPIC includes veto power. Without veto power, the FPIC loses strength because projects can continue to move forward. As of now, the international community recognizes tribal consultation as the customary norm' (McCulloch 2021, 251). She rightly notes that when considering state practice, consent in FPIC does not amount to an actual veto overriding the state's regulatory power. Moreover, without 'consent' in this sense, FPIC in substance becomes largely indistinguishable from good faith consultation.

Customary law is defined as the set of rules of state practice that are consistently and uniformly followed by states out of a sense of existing legal obligation. The existence of a legal norm in custom requires adequate evidence of state adherence – as opposed to ignorance, disinterest, or mere lip service. Broad commitments to good standards and responsible policies, such as those arising from UNDRIP, do not make them equivalent to customary legal norms. It would not be overly cynical to conclude that state support for UNDRIP was specifically conditional on it not being a binding instrument. To then suggest FPIC as it appears in UNDRIP has become or is becoming a legal norm is not supported by international law.

Furthermore, the resolutions, guidelines, statements, and declarations adopted by international organisations, conferences, or expert bodies do not constitute best evidence of state conduct, even though they may influence such conduct and offer insights into the 'collective opinion' of states (UN International Law Commission, 2018, p. 147). Even if developments within international organisations are relevant to the establishment of standards for consulting with Indigenous Peoples, the non-binding nature of UNDRIP challenges the proposition that FPIC is an emerging or actual right arising from the Declaration under customary international law.

2.4 Essential Elements Underlying Customary Law

Customary international law comprises three elements: (a) state practice must be widespread and virtually uniform in conforming to the rule, or at least not strongly rejecting or ignoring it; (b) states must believe their practice is legally compelled (*opinio juris*); and (c) a significant number of states must adopt the practice, with no significant opposition from other states (Dugard, 2018, pp. 30–41). Both state practice (*usus*) and the acceptance of a custom as a legal norm entailing subsequent binding obligation (*opinio iuris sive necessitates*) are essential threshold requirements for establishing customary law.

It is important to consider actual state practice in its entirety, not just rhetoric or voting records and public statements in international organisations (Petane case, 1988). Voting in international organisations is often driven by considerations beyond the actual commitment to action by a state or without a sense of legal obligation, as evidenced by frequent discrepancies between the voting pattern of states and their actual practice. A notable example is the widespread state support for UNDRIP in the UN General Assembly, despite few states having legislated FPIC as a purportedly stronger right to consultation. UNDRIP is better regarded as a non-legal benchmark for countries to assess their own laws and policies and to inspire improvements, than as a justiciable norm.

A norm arising from customary international law does not create a 'new state of affairs' as if the court were acting as a legislature, but rather reflects the court's recognition of a belief that a legal norm already exists through 'tacit consent' (D'Aspremont, 2022, p. 29). It is not only the recognition of FPIC as a best practice and responsible social policy that is weighed, but also whether states regard FPIC as legally binding and adhere to it as if a legal norm. In both respects, FPIC arguably falls short of qualifying as a legal norm under customary international law.

Arajarvi cautions against what she calls the 'misinterpretation' of customary international law, whereby a 'self-fulfilling prophecy' leads judges to selectively identify evidence in state conduct that aligns with the outcome they intend to find (Arajarvi, 2022, p. 57). The same applies to references in literature that treat FPIC as if it were a legal standard. Citations often focus on a few selected cases where the term FPIC appears or is merely mentioned in passing, without considering the context of the reference or the scope of the purported right. This sentiment is echoed by Baka who argues that customary international law often bears elements of 'absence' and 'abstractness':

> The profound ambiguity surrounding all elements of CIL particularly as regards the subjective, psychological element of opinio juris is further accentuated by the prevailing element of absence, silence or non-action and their often-monolithic interpretation as non-objection or, even, acquiescence. (Baka, 2022, p. 62)

2.5 State Conduct as Best Evidence

The existence of a norm in customary international law can be inferred from various sources, including but not limited to general state practice, treaties, conventions, declarations, legislation, policy measures, reports of the International Law Commission, and domestic jurisprudence. These are examples of the 'external data by which the existence and efficacy of a customary norm can be recognized' (Ago, 1957, p. 723). However, the best evidence rule dictates that the primary evidence ought to be an assessment of actual state conduct.

While positive state actions may be easy to ascertain, it is not clear how international customary law responds to state silence or indifference. It is unlikely that the absence of a measure's acceptance indicates endorsement of it.

The importance of actual state conduct is simple: a state may show political support for UNDRIP, but then enact domestic policies pointing to a denial of indigenous presence in its territory or the state may adopt consultation procedures that falls short of 'consent' implied in FPIC. Therefore, support for UNDRIP cannot be viewed as the best evidence of state behaviour. Despite consistent state conduct being the best indicator of an emerging legal norm's validity, evidence of state conduct is sometimes overlooked altogether when FPIC is presented as a purported norm in international customary law. This is not unique to FPIC. Note in this respect the Kosovo case, where the ICJ, without undertaking an in-depth analysis of the practice of states and their collective opinions regarding declarations of independence, concluded that 'The practice of States in these latter cases does not point to the emergence in international law of a new rule prohibiting the making of a declaration of independence in such cases …' (Kosovo case, 2010, para. 79). Given the lack of detailed analysis of actual state practice, it would appear as if political considerations, rather than an assessment of actual state conduct, played a major part in the court's reasoning.

Similarly, the ICJ in the Pulp Mills case declared that environmental impact assessments have become so widely conducted worldwide as to warrant being considered an obligation in customary international law (Pulp Mills case 2006, para. 204). Again, the Court seemingly felt that no in-depth survey or review of international state conduct was required by law to reach this conclusion. Although it is arguably correct to observe that environmental impact studies have become a common international good practice, this does not imply that states perform such studies in the belief that a legal norm already exists. The ICJ's reasoning in this case was called 'cavalier' by Gradoni, because the evidence before the Court of consistent international state practice concerning environmental impact assessments was insufficient to justify its sweeping finding (Gradoni, 2015, p. 399).

Two sets of key observations can thus be made about FPIC in respect of its status in customary law. On the one hand, FPIC is widely cited in non-legally binding statements, policy papers, declarations, and best practices. It is included in UNDRIP, referenced in several expert reports and practice manuals from international organisations, endorsed by private enterprises as an objective, and occasionally mentioned in municipal jurisprudence and expert opinions. On the other hand, UNDRIP does not have the legal status of a binding treaty or convention, and its broad state support is based on its non-binding nature. ILO 169, which is binding, is supported by only a small number of countries. Very few countries have enacted ILO 169 and UNDRIP into domestic law. FPIC is consistently framed by states and international organisations as a process of seeking agreement rather than implying an actual veto, and FPIC is not understood to displace the regulatory authority of the state over planning decisions.

2.6 Insufficient Evidence

The principal conclusion in this chapter is that there is insufficient evidence that FPIC is endorsed by widespread international state practice as granting a right of veto, whereby the state effectively cedes its regulatory authority to an indigenous community to make final decisions on land-related and social policies affecting them. State endorsement and execution of FPIC remain, at best, vague and, at worst, inconsistent and promissory. Furthermore, the absence of explicit rejection or silence by states on the binding nature of FPIC cannot be interpreted as endorsement of its status as a legal norm. Silence can have multiple meanings. As Baka points out:

> international law does not provide any clear guidance as regards the legal effects that follow from state silence. (Baka, 2022, p. 84).

While the acknowledgment of a custom must be grounded in factual evidence of state conduct and acceptance, it is, to some extent, an exercise in fiction, as it often relies on observed behaviour rather than written records (D'Aspremont, 2022, p. 32). This means that there may be ambiguity about the extent of adherence to the custom, as well as uncertainty about the point at which it became a legal norm or, indeed, whether it has lapsed into obsolescence. Ultimately, invoking customary international law as a potential avenue to in effect 'legislate' FPIC into existence is tenuous, fraught with uncertainty, and less than adequate for Indigenous Peoples seeking clear and definitive recognition of their rights and entitlements.

Although universal acceptance is not required for a practice to be recognised as a customary norm, there must be 'widespread acceptance' for it to be held to apply generally in international law (South West Africa cases, 1966). Put differently, while strict conformity is not demanded, broad recognition of the custom is necessary for it to be considered a legal norm (Nicaragua case, 1986). In this respect, it is notable that despite the use by some states of FPIC in international forums as an objective of state policy, courts do not regard FPIC as a customary international norm to be observed within the context of municipal or regional law. Likewise, in the Americas – where the recognition of indigenous rights is arguably most advanced – case law does not establish FPIC as a distinct binding legal norm for the region (Saramaka case 2007; Kichwa case 2012). Case law in the USA, Canada, Australia and New Zealand also do not cite FPIC as an independent source of rights and obligations, though domestic laws may require meaningful consultation with Indigenous Peoples (Munkara case, 2024; Kebaowek First Nation case, 2025, para. 183).

The Statute of the International Court of Justice provides that the Courts shall apply 'international custom, as evidence of a general practice accepted as law…' (Statute of ICJ, 1945, art. 38(1)(b)). This implies that states must not only acknowledge the existence of a good practice concerning FPIC, but also regard the practice as law which is binding on the state. The conduct of states, their agreements, legislation, and policies are all therefore indicators of whether a custom is regarded as a legal norm. It is essential to recognise that while a state may act in a particular way in pursuing good policy, such as voting for UNDRIP in the General Assembly of the United Nations, its conduct does not necessarily imply that the state regards the policy as an existing legal obligation – both the conduct and the reasoning behind it must be assessed.

2.7 Dichotomy in Support for ILO 169 and UNDRIP

In the context of FPIC, state conduct is ambivalent, given that only a few states subscribe to the legally binding ILO 169, while a large number of states have supported the non-binding UNDRIP. It is reasonable to conclude that states have specifically ruled out the binding nature of FPIC by supporting UNDRIP and not ILO 169. This conclusion is enhanced by the lack of domestic legislation giving effect to UNDRIP in general and FPIC in particular. It is likely that many states have endorsed UNDRIP and not ILO 169 precisely because the former lacks legal enforceability.

Although FPIC, and UNDRIP more broadly, is sometimes described as an emerging principle of customary law, it is not legally sound to assume that statements, policies, and practices subscribed to by states regarding FPIC automatically gravitate towards its recognition as a legal norm for the purposes of meeting the requirement of Article 38(1)(b) of the Statute of the International Court of Justice.

2.8 Ambivalence in Jurisprudence

The ambivalent status of FPIC is also reflected in the jurisprudence invoking the term. For example, in the Saramaka case, the Court considered FPIC at length, but refrained from declaring that it entails a veto concerning access to indigenous lands, instead describing it as a process of engagement (Saramaka case, 2007). In the Kichwa case, the Court acknowledged the duty to consult, particularly in the case of large projects, but stopped far short of declaring FPIC as implying a legally binding veto for all access to indigenous lands (Kichwa case, 2012). In the Baleni case, reference was made in passing to FPIC but the applicable veto in the case originated from municipal law, not from UNDRIP or FPIC (Baleni case, 2019). In the Fosen case, the Court did not recognise a veto but relied on the individual right to culture to demand more meaningful consultation (Fosen case, 2021), while in the Costa Rican Consultation case, the Court cited ILO 169 and UNDRIP as if they share the same legal status – but in the context of consultation, not consent (Consultation case, 2023). In the Kebaowek First Nation case the Canadian Court reiterated the consultative element of FPIC and not as if it constitutes a right of veto. Finally, the Community of San Juan case the Court referred to consultation arising from FPIC rather than a right of veto (Community Garifuna of San Juan case, 2023, para. 138).

Case law in the Americas often relies on the rights to property as a source of consultation, rather than on FPIC as a legal norm of international law. The ECtHR, meanwhile, has not cited FPIC as a principle of customary international law in any of its judgements. The same can be said of case law in Australia, Canada, the USA, Indonesia, India, and New Zealand, where the consultative rights of Indigenous Peoples arise from municipal legislation, rather than by FPIC as if it were a legal norm in international law.

When FPIC is cited by courts, it is done so generically without clearly distinguishing it from consultation. FPIC and consultation are often used interchangeably, and jurisprudence does not interpret FPIC as implying joint decision-making or a legal veto. Mere references in case law to FPIC cannot be invoked to ostensibly reflect its acceptance as a universal norm of customary international law. McCulloch's conclusion is therefore not surprising: 'there is no indication of widespread conformance or belief that the FPIC is legally binding' (McCulloch, 2021, p. 257).

There are at least three hurdles to overcome for FPIC to be regarded as a legal norm of customary international law: the scope and content of FPIC require clarification; states must demonstrate widespread conformity with FPIC as if it were a legal norm; and adherence to FPIC as if it were a legal norm must be established.

There is a notable lack of agreement about the scope and content of FPIC. While states emphasise the non-binding nature of FPIC, in literature and policy papers FPIC is often presented as if constituting a justiciable right, which it is not. FPIC's appearance in UNDRIP does not imply its widespread acceptance by states as a legally binding norm. If anything, the opposite is true – UNDRIP enhances the non-binding nature of FPIC. The definitional issues that assail UNDRIP – such as who qualifies as indigenous, what autonomy entails, the range of FPIC's application, whether it is limited to traditional lands or extends to broader socio-economic policies concerning Indigenous Peoples, and the precise meaning of FPIC – inevitably also highlight FPIC's unsuitability as a customary norm in international law. The programmatic nature of FPIC makes it useful for guiding and encouraging certain behaviours, but it falls well short of demonstrating widespread adherence as a legal norm.

Finally, municipal courts have not adopted FPIC as a source of law deriving from customary international law. Instead, FPIC tends to be recognised as inspiring, informing, guiding, and providing a basis for good faith consultation. Yafee observes what he calls a 'normative drift' to which FPIC is exposed due to an absence of state guidance and inter-state agreement (Yafee, 2018, p. 47). On proper analysis, courts emphasise the 'meaningful' and 'effective' aspect of consultation rather than any veto right arising from it. The guidance given by courts often expands the practical requirements for good faith consultation, rather than recognising FPIC a source of a distinct category of rights.[3]

2.9 Gap-Filling by Customary Law?

The focus on FPIC as a potential customary international legal norm highlights both the fragility and uncertainty of customary international law and the weak legal basis for it to be a basis to elevate the status of FPIC into a legal norm. Customary international law develops through practice – gradually, organically, and informally. The more literature attempts to present FPIC as a customary right, the more advocates ironically emphasise the absence of state support for FPIC as a term of law.

3 The same applies to the recognition and protection of cultural heritage under the auspices of the United Nations. The United Nations Educational, Scientific and Cultural Organization (UNESCO) has five conventions that focus on preserving cultural heritage – the 1954 Hague Convention and its two protocols; the 1970 Convention on the Means of Prohibiting and Preventing the Illegal Import, Export and Transfer of Ownership of Cultural Property; the World Heritage Convention; the Underwater Cultural Heritage Convention; and the Convention for the Safeguarding of the Intangible Cultural Heritage. These instruments may also contain policy measures resembling FPIC, but not as justiciable rights.

Kammerhofer describes the shortcomings of efforts to declare FPIC as customary international law as follows:

> Instead of being able to see customary law as a primitive method of norm-creation which is severely limited in its utility and dismissing it – as their domestic colleagues are wont to do – as *entirely unsuitable* for modern legal orders which tend to be complex and technocratic, an important sub-group of international lawyers wish to see and/or create international law as such a complex legal order. To this group belong practitioners and international legal scholars with a stake in the actual functioning of the law. *They imagine customary law to be capable of performing the complex functions analogous to legislation in domestic law.* They do so not out of a sense of pride or ego, but because they genuinely believe that we cannot rely on treaties alone, that we *must* have CIL (and therefore do) in order to achieve the political goals international society or politics needs to progress (or those which they imagine do). But the question is whether that is reason enough to consciously or subconsciously change the mechanics of customary law to suit these perceived needs and whether CIL has the flexibility to react to these perceived needs. (emphasis added) (Kammerhofer, 2022, p. 3)

Kammerhofer's argument underscores the limitations of customary international law in addressing the perceived gap concerning FPIC in domestic law. First, if states wish to give FPIC legal effect as a norm, they can do so through legislation. Second, if states support FPIC as a binding legal norm under customary international law, their actions will reflect this belief. Third, if indeed there were widespread support for FPIC as an emerging norm of customary international law, states could expedite the process by endorsing an international convention or treaty explicitly recognising the legally binding nature of FPIC. Fourth, customary international law is more about recognising existing law than creating new law through judicial activism. Customary international law relies on spontaneous conduct and voluntary adherence by states, highlighting both the cumbersome nature of 'legislating' through customary international law and the tenuous nature of a justiciable right arising from it for purposes of universal application. Inconsistent statements, vague commitments, and discrepancies in actions concerning FPIC underline the gap between state practice and state rhetoric.

If FPIC is approached as an 'effort' to achieve consent, it may find greater adherence in state practice, but then nothing would remain of the distinction between good faith consultation and FPIC. Under UNDRIP, the 'consent' element of FPIC is non-negotiable, and it is precisely this notion of consent that presents the greatest obstacle to FPIC evolving into a norm of customary international law.

2.10 Summary

In summary, FPIC cannot be said to exist as a legal norm or be regarded as emerging as a legal norm under customary international law because:

(a) FPIC suffers the weight of insurmountable definitional uncertainties in respect to the legal subject, legal object, and legal remedy;
(b) there is a lack of consistent state practice regarding the content and scope of FPIC, as states generally rely on the term 'consultation' in their domestic arrangements rather than on FPIC as a distinct obligation
(c) there is inadequate evidence that states treat FPIC as an existing legal norm requiring adherence and implementation as a distinct standard separate from good faith consultation;
(d) without exception, states protect their sovereignty and deny that *the* substantial element of FPIC – the substantive meaning of 'consent' – implies an actual veto or mandates explicit approval; and
(e) If consent is removed from FPIC, little, if any, difference remains at law between FPIC and good faith consultation. The consultation measures adopted by states in domestic law cannot be construed as endorsing FPIC as a distinct legal norm.

3 Customary Legal Norms through the Eyes of the International Court of Justice

To contextualise the foregoing theoretical discourse on FPIC as a possible legal norm in customary international law, this section briefly examines selected cases to analyse the International Court of Justice's (ICJ) approach to identifying customary legal norms.[4]

Customary international law is, in effect, very 'state centric', as it is state conduct and the belief underlying the state conduct that ought to determine whether a norm can be held to exist (Baker, 2010, p. 174). It is essential for states to show trust in the ICJ – without such trust, any of the Court's findings on the existence of an international custom may ultimately be rendered inef-

4 Note that states have to declare themselves willing to be bound by the ICJ (Statute of ICJ, 1945, art. 36(2)). For example, the USA withdrew from the compulsory jurisdiction of the ICJ after the Nicaragua case and refused to give effect to the findings.

fective (Kolb, 2014, p. 404). If a customary norm is said to exist when, in fact, it does not, the credibility and legitimacy of the ICJ's judgement would suffer, as states are unlikely to adhere to a legal norm imposed through judicial creativity. Importantly, mere coinciding conduct between states is not, in itself, adequate evidence for a legal norm to exist; the conduct must stem from the belief that the legal norm already exists and mandates such behaviour. Customary law, therefore, does not create new legal standards but may acknowledge the existence of a legal standard by assessing the conduct of states (Kolb, 2013). This is why creating legal norms through customary international law is ineffective – states will be slow to follow unless the conduct is already established. Customary law remains the 'most controversial source' of international law (Petersen, 2017, p. 357).

Not surprisingly, declaring that a norm exists in customary international law is often contentious. This is partly because it involves a degree of fiction in ascertaining state conduct, discerning states' mental disposition, and concluding why certain conduct occurs. Furthermore, states do not necessarily incorporate international law into domestic law, which means adherence to international law, in general, and customary international law, in particular, is often haphazard. For example, concerns have been expressed about the ICJ expanding its role from merely declaring the law to acting as a quasi-legislature, whereby it not only determines the substance of customary law but also 'creates' it 'without reference to state practice or state consent' (Chan, 2016, p. 44). This raises questions about judicial motivation (or bias), which may become a key factor in the exercise of judicial discretion (Petersen, 2017, p. 359). Furthermore, there are risks about potential judicial bias, as judges often seem to vote in alignment with their state's interests or positions that reflect those interests (Posner and de Figueiredo, 2005, p. 624).

This section does not assess the merits of the criticism outlined above. However, it is relevant to note that for FPIC to be declared a norm in customary international law, the following conditions must be met: (a) adequate evidence is presented to the court demonstrating a general international practice by states that accepts FPIC as a norm; (b) state conduct is motivated by an assumption that adherence to FPIC is required by an already existing legal obligation; and (c) there are no substantial challenges to the assertion that requirements (a) and (b) have been met.

3.1 Two Essential Elements

Two elements must be satisfied regarding FPIC: the scope of state practice and the rationale underlying it. Just because some states believe that it is proper public policy to consult with Indigenous Peoples, or may follow each other's example in doing so, cannot be construed as meeting the evidentiary burden that those states believe they are legally bound to adhere to FPIC as a legal norm. Despite perceived efforts by the ICJ to develop customary international law through a 'moral' imperative (Petersen, 2017, p. 363), the incorporation of FPIC into international law would arguably exceed the scope of discretion open to judges. However, as noted by Petersen, contemporary approaches to customary international law may purport to rely on custom as 'an entry gate for the 'progressive' development of international law and a tool for judicial law-making' (Petersen, 2017, p. 363).

The essence of customary international law is that it recognises 'evidence of a general practice accepted as law' (Vienna Convention, 1969, art. 38(1)(b)). Naturally, this raises the question: how can an international 'general practice' by states regarding FPIC be ascertained with any degree of certainty without extensive evidence of individual states' acceptance, consistent adherence, and the rationale underpinning their actions? States disagree about even the most mundane issues, so what evidence is required to support a definitive declaration of the existence of FPIC as an international custom – especially if there is disagreement about the presence of Indigenous People, the meaning of the word 'consent', and the areas to which FPIC applies? What weight is to be given to evidence of dissent, non-adherence, or mere silence by states? And, importantly, what weight should be attached to support ostensibly expressed within international organisations for a particular standard like UNDRIP, when states do not adhere to the Declaration, lack clarity on the meaning of certain terms within it, have not taken active steps to enact it in domestic legislation, or do not consider themselves legally bound by it? Most significantly, there is a stark absence of any trend in which municipal courts treat FPIC as a binding legal norm, a source of enforceable rights, or a basis for a veto that excludes the final decision-making of the state regulatory authority.

3.2 Is State Support for UNDRIP Adequate to Signify an International Custom?

State support for UNDRIP, which is not a legally enforceable instrument, does not in itself satisfy the threshold of state conduct required to establish customary international law. In the Nuclear Weapons case, the ICJ acknowledged the support within United Nations institutions for resolutions on nuclear weapons, but noted 'continuing tensions' between voting patterns and actual state practices (Nuclear Weapons case, 1996, para. 73). The same applies to FPIC. Few of the nations that endorse UNDRIP cite FPIC in their domestic arrangements as a policy or legal standard. While states and municipal courts may refer to consultation with Indigenous Peoples, this does not equate to FPIC. In the Jurisdictional Immunities case, the ICJ emphasised that a state's isolated acts do not constitute the totality of its conduct and that, in this case, the actual conduct of the state indicated no adherence to the particular norm (Jurisdictional Immunities of the State case, 2012, p. 186).

Caution should be exercised before making a finding that FPIC constitutes a general practice of international state conduct. Furthermore, even if such a practice exists, it must be established that it arises not merely from good policy, good morals, or sound logic, but because it is accepted by the states as law. A custom can only be declared to exist after a 'systematic and rigorous analysis' of all relevant facts (UN International Law Commission, 2018, p. 127). The inherent difficulty in objectively assessing state conduct may also help explain why voting patterns of ICJ judges have been found to exhibit bias (Posner and de Figueiredo, 2005).

In the North Sea Continental Shelf cases, the ICJ established the criteria for recognising customary international law when tasked with determining the delineation of the continental shelf between Germany and Denmark, as well as between Germany and the Netherlands. The Court emphasised that two conditions must be fulfilled for a customary international norm to exist: a settled practice and a belief that the practice is rendered obligatory by the existence of a law requiring it (North Sea Continental Shelf cases, 1969, para. 77). This position confirms that the Court had to be satisfied that a norm already exists as if imposed by law, rather than to create, encourage, or develop a new norm. The ICJ should, for obvious reasons, be slow to 'discover' new legal norms in customary law, especially if those are not supported by the twin requirements of widespread state practice and a belief in their legal obligatoriness. In practice, however, the ICJ has been criticised because of its willingness to 'find' customary rules 'whenever it has deemed this necessary or convenient…' (Vicufia, 2005, p. 25).

3.3 Recognition, Not Creation, of Legal Custom

As with domestic courts, the ICJ may arguably contribute to the development of law through its interpretation of existing customary norms, but the ICJ cannot create new norms or legal standards purporting to reflect settled state practice unless there is adequate evidence to support a finding of fact (Kuc, 2022, p. 228). Nonetheless, this principle has not always restrained the ICJ from taking an active role in the development of customary law (Thirlway, 2005). For instance, in the Gulf of Maine case, the ICJ relied on the Third

United Nations Conference on the Law of the Sea (UNCLOS) to make findings based on support for an international instrument, rather than by considering broader evidence of state practice (Gulf of Maine case, 1984). Notably, this occurred when only 13 states had endorsed UNCLOS – even fewer than the number of states that have endorsed ILO 169.

Based on an analysis of 95 cases where the ICJ has found customary international law to exist, Petersen argues that the Court has often placed an emphasis on international materials rather than actual conduct of states (Petersen, 2017, p. 368). This raises the question of whether the ICJ is principally guided by the activities of international organisations instead of evidence of state practice in the conduct of their affairs, as ought to be the case.

3.4 Actual State Practice as Best Evidence

The best evidence regarding recognition of customary international law is undoubtedly actual state practice and the motivations behind it. Notably, however, the IJC has been reluctant to recognise customary international law in cases where a state has not become a signatory to a treaty (Petersen 2017, 373). This weakens the proposition that FPIC constitutes an emerging right in customary international law. First, UNDRIP is not a treaty. Second, state support for UNDRIP is clearly based on its non-binding nature. Third, ILO 169 – which is a binding treaty – has support from only a few states. Fourth, the state conduct and underlying belief in question do not meet the requirements for customary international law.

Even if state practice within international organisations is considered, adherence to FPIC in municipal law as a legal norm does not convincingly support its status as an emerging or actual right. In the United States Nationals in Morocco case, the ICJ acknowledged that the parties' efforts to find a solution and pursue an amicable outcome could not be construed as a concession of their legal position (United States Nationals in Morocco case 1952, 200). This case exemplifies the fact that a state can pursue good faith consultation with Indigenous Peoples without thereby conceding its legal position of retaining sovereignty. Consulting in good faith does not imply that states have departed from their understanding that UNDRIP is not legally binding. ILO 169, a binding treaty, has just 23 signatories, whereas the non-binding UNDRIP has received broad endorsement, but precisely *on the understanding* that it is not treaty law. Had UNDRIP contained enforceable provisions, it would be safe to argue that support for its ratification would have been much lower.

The argument that state support for UNDRIP, by some reasoning, constitutes sufficient evidence of FPIC as an emerging or established legal norm is weak at best.

Chang expresses concern that the ICJ sometimes tends to 'ignore evidence of state practice' rather than be guided by it (Chan, 2016, p. 49). Petersen similarly observes that 'detailed analyses of state practice are rare in the ICJ's jurisprudence' (Petersen, 2017, p. 375). The ICJ has also been criticised for giving greater weight to United Nations resolutions – despite their non-binding nature – than conducting thorough investigations into actual state conduct. When considering evidence from materials published by international organisations, it is important to be cautious and recognise that such organisations 'vary greatly' and that their actions must be assessed in the context of their powers, functions and, most importantly for this chapter, the limitations under which they operate (UN International Law Commission, 2018, p. 131).

An international organisation, expert body, or agency cannot declare that FPIC is legally binding if the states that have endorsed UNDRIP have made it clear that they do not regard the Declaration to be binding. While such international bodies may, to some extent, reflect state opinion, opinions and statements cannot substitute the best evidence – an assessment of state behaviour. In fact, the views, comments, or publications of international organisations, on their own, do not 'contribute to the formation, or expression, of rules of customary international law' (UN International Law Commission 2018, 132). While international organisations may assist and encourage the development of new practices, this does not amount to actual state practice.

There is a risk that the ICJ does not adequately consider actual state conduct in its inquiries. For example, in the Icelandic Fisheries case, the ICJ did not closely examine state practice concerning the purported conduct, whether in support or opposition (Icelandic Fisheries case, 1973). Likewise, in the Nicaragua case, the ICJ's consideration of state practice was observed to be at a superficial level. Nonetheless, and importantly, the Court stated:

> The mere fact that States declare their recognition of certain rules is not sufficient for the Court to consider these as being part of customary international law, and as applicable as such to those States… The Court must satisfy itself that the existence of the rule in the *opinio juris* of States is confirmed by practice. (Nicaragua case, 1986, para. 184)

3.5 Public Statements Do Not Constitute State Conduct

The fact that states do not consider themselves legally bound by FPIC or UNDRIP heightens the challenge of establishing FPIC as a norm in customary international law. Lip service cannot be regarded as actual state practice, let alone practice based on a belief in the existence of a legal norm. While there is broad political support for UNDRIP as a guide to responsible conduct, such support cannot be construed, at least without proper evidence, as state practice affirming FPIC as an existing legal norm. Not all measures of good practice can be elevated to the status of legal norms. Although customary law sometimes develops in 'mysterious ways' (Gradoni 2015, 371), the absence of state practice and the belief underlying it, coupled with the lack of international treaty law regarding FPIC, makes it unlikely that the concept will be elevated to a legal norm.

Significantly, in the Nicaragua case, the ICJ acknowledged that a norm may exist in customary international law despite a lack of state compliance. 'The Court considers that it is part and parcei of customary international law' that states do not always act consistently with international law (Nicaragua case, 1986, para. 202). Nevertheless, the Court emphasised that the *opinio juris* of states must be 'backed by established and substantial practice' (Nicaragua case, 1986, para. 202). In the Right of Passage case, the ICJ stated that both elements must be met for a norm to be declared a legally enforceable custom in international law. The Court did not accept that widespread state practice alone was sufficient, as it was not established that the custom arose from a belief in the existence of a legal norm (Right of Passage case, 1960, pp. 40–43).

Jennings is critical of the trend whereby the ICJ has declared the existence of a norm in customary international law without adequate consideration of whether the norm is supported by substantial state practice. He states that 'most of what we perversely persist in calling customary international law is not only not customary law; it does not even faintly resemble a customary law' (Jennings, 1982, p. 5). Ginsburg, meanwhile, argues that the ICJ does not consider itself constrained by state practice, and has expanded its approach to declaring law even in the absence of adequate evidence of state practice (Ginsburg, 2004, p. 639). In the Asylum case, the ICJ remarked on the existence of competing and unclear state practices:

> So much uncertainty and contradiction, so much fluctuation and discrepancy in the exercise of diplomatic asylum and in the official views expressed on various occasions, there has been so much inconsistency in the rapid succession of conventions on asylum, ratified by some States and rejected by others,

> and the practice has been so much influenced by considerations of political expediency in the various cases, that it is not possible to discern in all this any constant or uniform usage, accepted as law, with regard to the alleged rule of unilateral and definitive qualification of the offence. (Asylum case, 1950, p. 277)

The challenge of ascertaining, with any degree of certainty, what states accept as a customary legal norm is illustrated by court rulings in both South Africa and Singapore regarding the constitutionality of capital punishment. The South African Constitutional Court concluded that international norms militate against the imposition of the death penalty (Makwanyane case, 1995), while the Singaporean Court argued that 'there is a lack of extensive and virtually uniform state practice to support … [the] contention that customary law prohibits the mandatory death penalty as an inhuman punishment' (Yong Vui Kong case, 2010, paras. 95–98). The status of FPIC can hardly be described as one of uniform or predominant adherence based solely on state political support for UNDRIP.

3.6 Examples of Case Law

Although the ICJ itself has yet to reference FPIC, some domestic courts have cited it as a potential legal standard in international law. For example, in the Baleni case, the Court stated the following about FPIC:

> Lastly, granting special protection to these communities by requiring consent as opposed to mere consultation is in accordance with international law. Multiple international instruments require that communities such as the applicants have the right to grant or refuse their free, prior and informed consent to any mining development that will significantly affect them. (Baleni case, 2019, para. 78)

> In recognition of this fact, the following recommendation is made to States, with particular reference to the Indigenous Peoples' right that no decision will be taken affecting their rights without their informed consent. (Baleni case 2019, para. 79)

> Lastly, although the African Charter does not expressly provide for the concept of free, prior and informed consent, the bodies responsible for the interpretation of the Charter (the African Commission on Human and Peoples' Rights and the African Court on Human and Peoples' Rights) have held that, having

> regard to the provisions of the African Charter, no decisions may be made about people's land without their free, prior and informed consent. (Baleni case 2019, para. 82)

In the Poma Poma case, an expert committee commented as follows:

> In the Committee's view, the admissibility of measures which substantially compromise or interfere with the culturally significant economic activities of a *minority or indigenous* community depends on whether the members of the community in question have had the opportunity to participate in the decision-making process in relation to these measures and whether they will continue to benefit from their traditional economy. The Committee considers that participation in the decision-making process must be effective, which requires not mere consultation but the *free, prior and informed consent* of the members of the community. In addition, the measures must respect the principle of proportionality so as not to endanger the very survival of the community and its members. (Poma Poma case, 2002, para. 7.6)

In the Community Garifuna of San Juan case the Court observed that the 'right to consultation of indigenous and tribal peoples, in addition to being treaty-based, is also a general principle of international law' (Community Garifuna of San Juan case, 2023, para. 138), but without explaining how the conclusion was derived at. The Court went on to state as follows: 'States must guarantee the rights to consultation and to participation in any project or measure that may affect the territory of an indigenous or tribal community or other rights that are essential for their survival as a people (Community Garifuna of San Juan case, 2023, para. 138), but without explaining why it used the word 'consultation' rather than 'consent'.

The relevance of three cases for the purposes of establishing the existence of a legal norm pursuant to customary international law is limited. First, in the Baleni case, only scant reference was made to a few international instruments, but no assessment took place of state conduct. Furthermore, the right to veto applied in Baleni did not arise from international law but from specific provisions of domestic law that gave the community in question this right (Informal Land Rights Act, 1996). The same can be said of the Community of Garifuna case in which UNDRIP and ILO 169 was cited as if of the same legal status and without any reference to why UNDRIP is part of international law. Second, in Poma Poma, there was no detailed assessment of state conduct in international law, and the opinion expressed did not apply to all activities on indigenous lands. Also noteworthy was the committee's reference to indigenous and minority communities, which further complicates the question of who the beneficiaries (legal subjects) of FPIC are. Third, the ICJ's reasoning in the Fisheries case can be applied to both these judgements: that the consistency of an act implies that there must be agreement on the content of a right and its interpretation (Icelandic Fisheries case, 1973). In the absence of accepted state practice concerning FPIC and its definition, it remains, *at best*, a policy guide rather than a legal right. Although 'perfection' and absolute adherence are not requirements (Nicaragua case, 1986, para. 186), there must at least be adequate clarity about the content of a norm for it to be regarded as legally binding. Even if the threshold of conduct is met, the question remains whether the motivation behind it is adherence to good policy, or a belief that a legal norm mandates it. The former is insufficient: there must be 'evidence of a belief that this practice is rendered obligatory by the existence of a rule requiring it' (North Sea Continental Shelf cases, 1969, para. 77).

3.7 Dichotomy between State Practice and Endorsement of UNDRIP

The challenge for the ICJ, if called upon to consider international state practice regarding FPIC, lies in the dichotomy between state practice and state endorsements of UNDRIP and other policy materials. In this case actions, or the lack of actions, do speak louder than words. First, no legal treaty endorses FPIC as an ambit right for Indigenous Peoples to consent to all actions affecting their lands or socio-economic policies impacting them as a community. Second, where states engage in consultation with Indigenous Peoples, such engagements reflect the characteristics of good faith consultation rather than joint decision-making or consent. Third, state practice underscores that consultation must be conducted in good faith, but consultative rights do not grant Indigenous Peoples a veto over land access or other policies affecting them. State practice and municipal law do not treat the 'c' in FPIC as implying a binding legal veto. Fourth, unless specifically authorised by municipal legislation, FPIC cannot be legally construed in international law as limiting the scope or sovereignty of state regulatory power.[5] Fifth, the overwhelming evidence of state practice is that states do not incorporate FPIC as a municipal

5 Note, for example, the Ure case where the proposition that customary international law gives rise to the recognition of pre-settlement property rights was rejected. Before rejecting this notion, the Court argued: 'The requirement that the practice should be extensive and virtually uniform relates, of course, to acts which are opinio juris. But in a negative sense, a departure from a uniform practice may be generally treated as a breach of the rule and in such a case the disapproved departure tends to indicate the rule's existence' (Ure case, 2016, para. 32).

norm of veto into legislation or policy. Where states legislate on indigenous relations or courts recognise obligations towards Indigenous Peoples, the term *consult* rather than FPIC is generally used, and even where FPIC is used the meaning attached to it does not go beyond good faith consultation. Even where FPIC is referenced, it is rarely framed as entailing a general right of veto.

3.8 Conclusion

The conclusion drawn is that FPIC falls short on both tests for establishing a norm of customary international law. It has not been adopted as a general state practice, nor is it regarded by states as an already existing legal norm. Moreover, its meaning, scope, and application are so vague that it fails to meet the requirement of legal certainty.

4 Is FPIC an Existing Norm or an Emerging Norm of Customary International Law?

This brings us to the central question of this chapter: Is FPIC an existing legal norm or an emerging legal norm of customary international law? I propose that the answer is negative. FPIC is neither an established nor an emerging legal norm of customary international law. This conclusion is based on the following:

4.1 Absence of a Convention or Treaty

FPIC has not been declared a legal norm of customary international law by any court of competent jurisdiction. References by expert bodies and domestic courts to FPIC are usually made within the context of, and by citing, existing legal instruments, domestic laws, and policies, as well as generally accepted good and reasonable practices concerning good faith consultation. No court has, however, conducted an in-depth assessment of international state practices and adherence to FPIC to conclude that FPIC is an established or emerging legal norm of customary international law. Even in judgements and expert opinions that reference FPIC, there remains significant terminological vagueness and confusion. Uncertainties persist regarding who qualifies as indigenous, the meaning of consultation, who may give consent on behalf of a community, how dissenting views within a community are addressed, whether consent in UNDRIP constitutes an actual veto over all land access issues, the policy areas to which FPIC applies, and how good faith consultation differs in substance from 'consent' as used in UNDRIP. Furthermore, FPIC was not regarded by the drafters of UNDRIP as conferring a right of veto or establishing a requirement for joint decision-making. Where FPIC is indeed cited by courts and expert bodies, the procedural aspect of consultation is emphasised – without suggesting that FPIC constitutes an absolute veto. FPIC is consistently framed – by international instruments as well as in international and domestic jurisprudence – as an objective, sound policy, and a desirable process – but not as a justiciable right of veto. The fact that FPIC is generally understood as a process of engagement rather than entailing a justiciable right of refusal refutes the proposition that FPIC is either a new or an emerging legal norm of customary international law.

4.2 Emergence of a New Norm of Customary International Law

The precise moment when a new legal norm in customary international law emerges is ambiguous – does it arise when a court first acknowledges its existence pursuant to state conduct, or does it develop at some undefined point when a practice, inspired by a belief in its legal necessity, becomes so widespread among states that it is regarded as law – even before any court formally declares it as such?

Customary international law generally becomes formalised when a court with competent jurisdiction declares its existence, after assessing relevant state conduct and determining whether states adhere to the purported norm as if it already has legal effect. The declaration of a legal norm pursuant to customary international law implies that the norm arises from state practice based on the assumption that it already exists as a legal obligation. A court must, therefore, consider not only the conduct of states that adhere to the purported norm, but also the actions of states that remain silent or explicitly reject its legality. A state may, for example, accept FPIC as a good policy measure to guide its engagement with Indigenous People without thereby accepting it as a binding legal norm in international law. While there is no fixed numerical threshold that determines the number of states that must regard a custom as legally binding, the practice must be sufficiently widespread amongst states with indigenous populations and consistently followed to be declared an international customary norm.

4.3 FPIC as a Purported Emerging Legal Norm

Courts determine whether an international custom exists, not whether state practice is approaching the threshold of becoming a custom in international law. There is no metric by which sound state policy can be said to transform into a binding legal norm arising from custom. Customary law generally exists before it is formally declared as such. The proposition of an 'emerging' right to FPIC is, therefore, fraught with uncertainty, particularly in light of UNDRIP's non-legal status. Not all good practices, habits, or sound policies of states can be construed as 'emerging' norms of customary international law. Even if countries adopt similar approaches, learn from one another, and act in the best interests of their citizens and as responsible global actors, the mere repetition of such practices does not necessarily convert them into legal norms – an essential requirement for the recognition of customary law is the belief among states that the norm already exists as a legal obligation.

The term FPIC is imbued with so much uncertainty that it can hardly be considered a legal norm with adequate clarity – most relevantly regarding the meaning of 'consent' and the social policy areas to which it applies. The level of clarity required for state conduct to crystallise into a legal norm through custom is absent in the case of FPIC. Most notably, international state practice shies away from drawing a clear distinction between good faith consultation and FPIC.

The fact that countries, in their support for UNDRIP, expressly reject the notion of a veto or co-decision-making undermines any credibility of FPIC being considered an emerging binding norm in international law. The use of the word 'right' by expert bodies, and in policy documents and literature, does not bestow actual legal obligations under customary law – unless the thresholds of state practice, as discussed, are satisfied. Furthermore, the growing awareness among states that the rights of Indigenous Peoples and ethnocultural minorities may require special attention and unique measures in our complex world does not elevate these sensitivities and common practices to the status of emerging or actual rights in customary international law. Many international documents, not least the Declaration on Minorities, would become justiciable rights in customary international law if the logic of mere endorsement of a declaration was accepted. While countries worldwide may recognise that the plurality of their populations necessitates special policy measures, this recognition falls far short of establishing FPIC as a new right arising from customary adherence in international law.

4.4 FPIC as a Remedy to Restore Lost Indigenous Sovereignty

The proposition sometimes made in the literature that FPIC could serve as a useful legal tool or potential remedy for unlawful encroachment on pre-settlement sovereignty remains, at best, a subject of theoretical discourse, lacking adequate evidence of state practice supporting its acceptance. None of the states that have endorsed UNDRIP question the legality or legitimacy of their own state sovereignty. Furthermore, UNDRIP clearly establishes that its principles cannot be invoked to undermine or challenge state integrity, seek secession, or renegotiate a state's sovereign status (UNDRIP, 2007, art. 46(1)). On the contrary, UNDRIP in general, and FPIC in particular, uphold state sovereignty and reinforce state regulatory authority. FPIC does not, by law or conduct, create a sphere of authority beyond the regulatory power of the state. Accordingly, it cannot be said that states by way of their support for UNDRIP, endorse FPIC as a legal basis for restoring pre-settlement sovereignty, renegotiating the legal foundation of national institutions, or conceiving a general right to co-decision-making over traditional lands or social policy areas affecting Indigenous Peoples.

In short, UNDRIP more broadly, and FPIC more specifically, cannot be regarded as an emerging or established right in customary international law, as the term FPIC is too vague to be treated as a legal norm; there is inadequate evidence of state adherence to it; and the proposition that states widely consider FPIC a binding legal norm is not supported by evidence of state practice.

4.5 Customary International Law as a Substitute for State Legislation or Treaties

Customary international law is neither an effective nor efficient way to remedy shortcomings in domestic legislation or to enact non-binding declarations surreptitiously as a form of binding treaty. Customary law develops over time – often a long time – emerging spontaneously through broad international support reflected in state actions. A legal norm in customary international law already exists prior to formal judicial recognition.

Some scholars and advocates have attempted to expand FPIC into a legal norm by relying on international customary norm-making to effectively legislate in an area where states have refrained from doing so – namely, enacting FPIC as a justiciable right. This approach amounts to elevating FPIC into a legal norm by stealth. Proponents argue that state conduct implicitly acknowledges FPIC as a legal norm, even in the absence of explicit recognition in domestic legislation or international treaties. However, this argument is unsound. There is inadequate evidence to suggest widespread state practice treating FPIC as an established legal norm. On the contrary, state practice does not regard FPIC as a binding legal norm. At most, FPIC is viewed as a framework for good faith consultation, with no credible indication that states broadly endorse it as if it were a legal norm. The claim that FPIC is emerging as a norm of customary international law lacks factual support in terms of consistent and widespread state practice. The irony is that the more focus is placed on customary international law as a potential 'cure' for enforcing FPIC in a domestic setting, the more evident it becomes that international state practice rejects FPIC as a binding legal norm.

The absence of widespread state practice establishes that FPIC is neither an emerging legal norm nor an actual legal norm in customary international law. As such, customary international law cannot be relied on to fill the legislative gaps in municipal or international treaty law concerning FPIC.

4.6 Interpretation of FPIC in International Law

International treaties are interpreted in accordance with the Vienna Convention on the Law of Treaties, but no similar guide exists for interpreting customary international law. There is no authoritative legislative source or record of legislative debates that courts can reference to determine the intent of a lawmaker when an international custom emerges. The literature suggests that municipal courts may be able to assist in interpreting customary international law by applying domestic principles of statutory interpretation. However, this poses a problem, as municipal rules of statutory interpretation are not standardised, and municipal courts are not well suited to assess widely held state practices in the international arena. While treaties, like municipal statutes, are in written form – allowing the meaning of a word to be ascertained from various sources, including the debates that led to the clause – customary international law relies on unwritten rules of conduct, based on the assumption by states that a legal requirement already exists for their actions.

There is no precise text in international customary law to cite, consider, or interpret regarding FPIC. Its purported binding nature must be inferred from the conduct and mindset of states. Courts do not act as legislators; rather, they serve as scribes, documenting customary state practices that already exist. However, the recording of such practices leaves room for substantial error, as courts must often rely on the testimony of individuals who have observed the practice. This challenges the proposition that FPIC is an emerging or actual legal norm, as the term itself is not a legal one; the meaning of 'consent' in UNDRIP cannot be interpreted in its ordinary sense as implying a veto or agreement; state conduct does not even vaguely suggest an understanding that FPIC includes a veto; and the interchangeable use of terms such as good faith consultation and FPIC erodes any certainty regarding the meaning of FPIC as a distinct legal norm.

One could argue, probably with some success, that international best practice calls for consulting with Indigenous Peoples when their land interests are affected. However, this falls far short of FPIC's recognition as a distinct legal norm – whether emerging or established.

4.7 Customary International Law and Precedent

The recognition of FPIC by a particular court in a specific setting does not imply that the norm would thereby achieve a status of general legal recognition in all or most states. A court is required to make a finding of fact regarding a specific circumstance, without binding other courts or states to the same finding in different disputes over indigenous consultation rights. Article 59 of the ICJ's Statute determines as follows: 'The decision of the Court has no binding force except between the parties and in respect of *that particular case*' (emphasis added) (Statute of ICJ, 1945, art. 59). For example, a finding that FPIC constitutes a legal custom in a specific case – such as a dispute between two states in the Americas – binds only the parties involved and has no broader legal effect. This highlights the cumbersome and ineffective route for establishing FPIC as a binding legal norm through customary international law, rather than municipal law or binding treaties. This limitation does not render the judgements of the ICJ ineffective or irrelevant, as a finding that FPIC exists in a particular case may influence conduct, policies and legislative developments in other states. The Court may, for instance, initiate or acknowledge a 'general trend' in respect of FPIC (Nuclear Weapons case, 1996). Moreover, in 1950, the International Law Commission suggested that decisions of international courts could serve as a source of customary international law (International Law Commission, 1950, p. 367) H.

Notably, a court's declaration of a trend supporting FPIC as a legal norm would require substantial evidence of state practice; otherwise it would arguably only amount to a passing comment made in *obiter*, as in the Baleni case. To date, there has been no attempt to have FPIC recognised by the ICJ as a legal obligation arising from customary international law.

4.8 Domestic Courts and FPIC

Domestic courts have neither accepted nor endorsed FPIC as a distinct legal norm arising from customary international law. While the term FPIC appears in some judgements, none of these suggest that it has, in its own right, evolved into a binding legal norm in customary international law. FPIC, when referenced, is usually cited in connection with existing property or cultural rights under the ICCPR or municipal law, not as a substantial right deriving from customary international law or a source of rights that implies joint decision-making. Furthermore, the terms FPIC and good faith consultation are often used interchangeably, with an emphasis on the process of consultation rather than encompassing a legal entitlement to joint decision-making and veto. Courts are consistently respectful of state regulatory authority in ultimately deciding land-related issues, unless a right of veto or co-decision-making is explicitly established in municipal law.

In summary, there is inadequate evidence to support the proposition that FPIC constitutes either an established or emerging legal norm of customary international law. A better proposition may be to reference constitutional law, where FPIC is at best cited by courts as the equivalent of a directive principle (see Chapter 5) on how good faith consultation should be conducted. This ensures Indigenous Peoples have an opportunity for meaningful and effective participation, given their unique relationship to their customary lands, rather than establishing FPIC as a substantive right that includes a veto to the exclusion of state regulative authority.

CHAPTER 5

Free, Prior, and Informed Consent as a Directive Principle of State Policy

1 Introduction

The foregoing analysis established that FPIC is not a judicial norm, neither in international treaty law nor in customary international law. Furthermore, states have not enacted, by way of municipal legislation, FPIC as a right of veto or co-decision-making in domestic legislation. The debate over FPIC as a substantive binding legal norm is moot.

Does this mean FPIC has lost its relevance to jurisprudence and to evolving consultation standards that concern Indigenous Peoples? I would suggest emphatically the answer is 'no'.

FPIC has undoubtedly contributed to the shift in international approaches towards engagement with Indigenous Peoples. In the short time since UNDRIP's adoption, FPIC has become the operative term for indigenous recognition in the broadest sense. It serves as a catch-all term of which the intent and objectives extend beyond its narrow, literal meaning. In fact, as shown in Chapter 4, FPIC is actively encouraged by UN agencies as the standard for engagement with all local communities – not just Indigenous Peoples. FPIC has permeated expert opinions, scientific literature, international statements, policy papers, practice manuals, board agendas, banking and business standards, best practices, legislation, and more.

The shortcomings of traditional consultation with Indigenous Peoples have been exposed by the debates surrounding FPIC. The power hierarchy that once characterised such consultation has been disrupted, with FPIC contributing to a more level playing field – perhaps not quite as level as hoped, but with the contours nevertheless changed. Courts have redefined the meaning of consultation, placing greater emphasis on the importance of effective and meaningful participation by Indigenous Peoples. Courts are now far more concerned with the quality and substance of reasonable and fair consultation than with the mere assertion that consultation has taken place. The importance of meaningful consultation has become a guiding principle of which the content is determined by the specific circumstances of an indigenous community.

 | HTTPS://DOI.ORG/10.1163/9789004724792-006

In essence, FPIC has enriched the understanding of consultation with Indigenous Peoples. Though not a legal principle, FPIC has nonetheless effectively changed the content of consultation in broader legal and social contexts.

In many respects, FPIC has become the soul of indigenous consultation. What some perceive as a weakness – its lack of legal standing – I would argue is the strength of FPIC. FPIC's open-ended nature makes it dynamic, unconstrained by legal jargon, technicality, and formulaic compliance. In short, FPIC inspires.

While unlikely to evolve into an international legal norm, FPIC exerts significant influence over indigenous consultation in general, including the interpretation given to consultation obligations by arbitration bodies. Essentially, it is a dynamic term that can be adjusted to suit various situations as well as being reflective of individual indigenous communities' bundles of rights.

In the previous chapter, FPIC was briefly mentioned in reference to the Directive Principles of State Policy found in the Constitution of India. I link FPIC to India's Directive Principles because, like FPIC, those Principles are non-legal in nature yet have influenced how courts in India have given effect to fundamental rights and social policies. The Directive Principles have profoundly impacted social policy formulation in India, making it *the* leading example of a non-legal set of principles fundamentally affecting government exercise of power in general, and more specifically judicial interpretations of fundamental rights. During the Indian constitutional debates in 1937, it was said that the Directive Principles would be there –

> as a constant headline, something by which the people as a whole can judge their progress in a certain direction; something by which the representatives of the people can be judged as well as the people judge themselves as a whole. We will judge our progress in a certain direction by asking how far have we advanced in that direction. They are intended to be directive to the legislature. (Constitutional Assembly Debates, 1937, p. 69)

India's Directive Principles were intended to be non-justiciable, as their objectives were too dynamic and programmatic to be confined within the framework of fundamental rights. Essentially, they outline the state's responsibilities towards its people. Weis observes that, in general, directive principles 'appear to insert an element of political constitutionalism within the domain of legal constitutionalism' (Weis, 2017, p. 917). While fundamental rights have universal value, the Directive Principles were designed to reflect India's social circumstances as well as the political and economic imperatives for addressing inequality. Over time, however, the Supreme Court has embraced the Directive Principles, using them to interpret fundamental rights, guide government policy, and drive societal transformation (De Villiers, 2023a).

This chapter proposes that FPIC should be approached in a similar manner to India's use of its Directive Principles. Rather than expending too much energy on arguing for FPIC's justiciability, the focus should be on how it can be used to enrich Indigenous Peoples' fundamental rights, including their rights to consultation and self-determination. FPIC should be seen for what it is – a non-justiciable, directive principle of policy that has received widespread international support. The social setting of FPIC is important, as the broad endorsement of UNDRIP within the UN cannot be overlooked.

This chapter provides a succinct overview of the background to the inclusion of the Directive Principles of State Policy in the Constitution of India and their role in shaping and developing fundamental rights and conduct by government in the country. The application of these principles has had a distinctive and remarkable impact on social policy in India. FPIC could similarly influence international and municipal policy and processes, while informing and enriching Indigenous Peoples' fundamental rights. This would be a more constructive application of FPIC than becoming caught up in a sterile debate over whether FPIC constitutes a legal entitlement, an emerging right, or an actual veto.

2 Background to the Directive Principles of State Policy

The inclusion of a chapter called Directive Principles of State Policy in India's Constitution reflected the country's history, where individuals were not only entitled to fundamental rights and freedoms, but the state's historic rulers also had a duty of care towards the poor, the infirm, and the needy. The Directive Principles could be described as a social contract whereby the duties of the state towards society are captured into and reflected by the Constitution.

The Directive Principles, which are found in Part IV of the Constitution (aa 36-51), set out the essential obligations of government aimed at the betterment of society (Tripathi, 2016). The traditional *Rajadharma*, which refers to the rulers' duties towards their people, was in effect codified by including those general obligations in the Constitution as non-justiciable objectives and ideals for the state to pursue (Ready, 1980, p. 403). For the purposes of this chapter, the Directive Principles can be regarded as the moral soul of the Constitution, binding together the aspirations of the people and the government's duty to address those aspirations a non-justiciable framework

(Markandan, 1987, p. 92). Courts have embraced this philosophy, using the Directive Principles to give practical content to fundamental rights. It is my proposition that FPIC could be put to similar use.

The rationale behind the Directive Principles is that they provide constitutionally enshrined recognition of the state's obligations towards its citizens, particularly to the extremely poor and vulnerable, without converting these moral claims and aspirations into justiciable rights (De Villiers, 1992a, p. 30). The Directive Principles are supposed to ensure that a socially just 'economic democracy' is achieved *in addition* to an elected, constitutional democracy based on the rule of law, equal treatment and non-discrimination (Jain, 1978, p. 549). Along with the Bill of Rights, the Directive Principles embody the objectives of both procedural equality and substantial equality. Extensive debate and careful consideration took place to shape the wording and legal status of the Directive Principles, and though not justiciable, they were given a broader meaning in due course, influencing India's approach to the protection of fundamental rights (Constitutional Assembly, 1947).

The Directive Principles anticipate the need to ensure that the state's duty to drive socio-economic transformation is recognised in both international and constitutional law. Over time, increasing attention has been given to the possible incorporation of social and economic rights – also referred to as second – and third-generation rights – into constitutions, imposing a positive obligation on the state to facilitate the realisation of social and economic fundamental rights (Grootboom case, 2000).

In India, social justice was at the time of the drafting of the Constitution considered an objective of equal importance to the protection of fundamental rights (Sharma, 1984, p. 176). In this respect, the Constitution was ahead of its time, anticipating that transformation of India's socio-economic reality would require the state to play an active role, even if this meant placing restrictions on the scope of fundamental individual rights. The reality of the impact of poverty within the context of justiciable rights was summarised as follows:

> For those who suffer from want and hunger, the so-called fundamental rights would be meaningless and remain only paper rights. (Minerva Hills case, 1980)

The Constitution's drafters agreed to include in it both a *justiciable* chapter on fundamental rights and a *non-justiciable* chapter on Directive Principles of State Policy. The former encompassed traditional fundamental rights found in liberal democracies, enforceable against the state, whereas the latter set out the state's objectives, though not justiciable as rights. Both chapters are accorded constitutional status, implying their respective provisions must be given equal effect and interpreted harmoniously by the courts without the fundamental rights being higher in hierarchy than the Directive Principles. In this way, the scope of fundamental rights can be widened or restricted through the application of the Directive Principles.

The Constituent Assembly regarded the Directive Principles as follows:

> The principles of state policy set forth in this chapter are intended for guidance of the State. While these principles shall not be cognizable by any court, they are nevertheless *fundamental* in the governance of the country and their application in the making of law shall be the duty of the State. (emphasis added) (Constitutional Assembly, 1947, p. 406)

Although some argued against including the Directive Principles in the Constitution due to their programmatic, non-legal, non-enforceable nature, the majority of the Constituent Assembly at the time believed the Principles embodied the 'salient features of the new social and economic order' and should, therefore, be elevated to constitutional objectives. As it turns out, this was an ingenious decision, as relegating the Directive Principles to mere policy objectives outside the Constitution would have denied them equal constitutional status alongside the Bill of Rights (Chaundri, 1955, p. 221). Chaundri summarised the reasoning behind the Directive Principles as follows:

> The political, social and economic ideology expressed in the Directive Principles imparts continuity to the nation's policy and makes it comparatively free from the vicissitudes of the ideology of political parties that might come into force from time to time. (Chaundri, 1955, p. 223)

Although the Directive Principles do not provide a basis for individuals to initiate litigation to enforce rights against the state, the courts have developed the Principles into a legal and policy framework for interpreting legislative intent, defining state obligations, and clarifying the meaning of fundamental rights in the context of India's broader social objectives. Consequently, certain policies that may otherwise have been considered inconsistent with the country's Bill of Rights have, instead, been deemed valid, given their alignment with the objectives set forth in the Directive Principles. In essence, there is an implied presumption that laws ought to be interpreted in a manner consistent with the objectives of the Directive Principles; where inconsistencies arise, priority should be given to the interpretation that best resembles the intent of the Directive Principles (Balsara case, 1959).

Importantly, though, while the Directive Principles may be constructed to limit or expand the scope of a fundamental right, they cannot be relied upon to abrogate or abolish a fundamental right. The question of when a limitation on a fundamental right is 'reasonable' in light of the Directive Principles is, therefore, one of degree (Tamil Nadu case, 1984).

The Supreme Court has endorsed a general presumption that all legislation and executive actions are aimed at implementing the Directive Principles, and that the Principles can be used to resolve statutory and policy ambiguities (Tripathi, 2016, p. 209). It has further ruled that the Directive Principles can be used to ascertain the ambit of legislation as well as limit the scope of fundamental rights, provided that this serves to fulfil relevant public objectives. This means individual rights may be restricted, but not abrogated, in pursuance of policies that seek to give effect to the Directive Principles. Arising from this principle, restrictions have been allowed on fundamental rights in areas such as property (State of Bombay case, 1951), freedom of contract (Public Works case, 1959), fair labour practices (Eveready case, 1962), and access to legal aid (Hoskot case, 1978).

The transformative role of the Directive Principles did not commence immediately after the Constitution's enactment. In the initial years, the courts treated fundamental rights as sacrosanct, ruling that they could not be limited by legislation seeking to promote the Directive Principles (Madras case, 1951). At the time, the Directive Principles were clearly considered subordinate to fundamental rights. However, in later years, the courts increasingly sought greater harmony between the two, a trend that continues today. In the Chandra Bhawan case, the Court emphasised:

> While rights conferred under Part 3 [Fundamental Rights] are fundamental, the directives given under Part 4 [Directive Principles] are *fundamental to the governance of the country*. We see no conflict between the provisions contained in Part 3 and Part 4. They are *complementary and supplementary* to each other. (emphasis added) (Chandra Bhawan case, 1970)

3 Application of the Directive Principles

Over time, the Supreme Court has actively used the Directive Principles to inform and enrich its jurisprudence in a manner that may not have been anticipated by the Constitution's drafters. This places the development of jurisprudence in India, in respect of measures to address social justice and socio-economic inequality, in a unique category compared to other constitutions enacted at a similar time. For example, the Indian approach is far more adventurous than that of the Irish courts, where Directive Principles are also available to guide judicial interpretation (Article 45) but have had little practical impact (De Villiers, 1994, pp. 615–618).[1]

The following examples illustrate how some courts have relied on the Directive Principles to guide social policy and interpret fundamental rights:

In the Kerala Education case, the Directive Principles were described as a guide for the positive actions the state had to take to address social and economic challenges. This included requiring a certain percentage of children in private schools to come from underprivileged communities. The Court declared:

> The provisions contained in that Part [Directive Principles] are not enforceable by any court, but the principles therein laid down are, nevertheless, *fundamental in the governance of the country* and it shall be the duty of the State to apply these principles in making laws (Kerala Education case, 1959, para. 12).
>
> ...in determining the scope and ambit of the fundamental rights relied on by or on behalf of any person or body the court may not entirely ignore these directive principles of State policy laid down in Part IV of the Constitution but should adopt the principle of *harmonious construction* and should attempt to give effect to both as much as possible. (emphasis added) (Kerala Education case 1959, para. 14)

In the Sajjan Singh case, the Court noted:

> ...the second Article in Part IV which deals with 'Directive Principles of States Policy', imposes a duty on the State to apply those directive principles in mak-

1 Compared to India, there has been scant reference by courts in Ireland to its Directive Principles (De Villiers, 1992b, p. 430). Among the few examples, in the Ryan case, the Court, for the first time, suggested that some rights that may not be explicitly mentioned in the Constitution could derive from the Directive Principles (Ryan case, 1965). The Rodgers case saw one of the first judgements whereby the Court concluded that it was 'entitled' to investigate the aims of the Directive Principles in order to ascertain the nature and extent of the right to freedom of contract (Rodgers case, 1978). In the Landers case, meanwhile, the Court held that a fundamental right could be interpreted narrowly due to the provisions of the Directive Principles. In this case, the Court restricted the freedom of contract of a child on the basis of the protections envisaged in the Directive Principles for the rights of children (Landers case, 1982). Nonetheless, the courts in Ireland have not, by any comparison, applied the Directive Principles as actively as those in India. Some go as far as to label the Directive Principles in Ireland as a failed experiment (Kenny and McCann, 2022).

> ing laws. These principles are also fundamental in the governance of the country and the provisions of Part III of the Constitution must be interpreted harmoniously with those principles. (Sajjan Singh case, 1965)

In the Balwant Raj case, the Court relied on the Directive Principles to give content to a contractual clause concerning the phrase 'failing to resume duty'. It held that the clause, in its true meaning, applied only to individuals who voluntarily failed to report for duty. The Court emphasised that its interpretation had to align with the 'letter and spirit' of the Directive Principles (Balwant Raj case, 1968).

In the Chandra Bhawan case, the Court applied the Directive Principles to restrict the scope of freedom of contract by upholding a statute that sought to guarantee minimum wages, declaring:

> Freedom of contract does not mean freedom to exploit. The provisions of the Constitution are not erected as barriers of progress. They provide a plan for orderly progress towards the social order contemplated by the Preamble of the Constitution…While rights conferred under Part 3 [bill of rights] are fundamental, the directives given under part 4 [Directive Principles] are fundamental to the governance of the country. We see no conflict on the whole between them. They are complementary and supplementary to each other. (Sajjan Singh case, 1965)

In the Minerva Hills case, the Court found that an attempt to amend the Constitution in order to limit the scope of fundamental rights was in itself unconstitutional. It emphasised that fundamental rights and the Directive Principles must be interpreted harmoniously, as both form part of the 'broad spectrum of human rights'. The Court described the role of the Directive Principles in the Constitution as follows:

> Therefore the importance of Directive Principles in the scheme of our Constitution *cannot ever be over-emphasized.* Those principles project the high ideal which the Constitution aims to achieve. In fact, Directive Principles of State policy are fundamental in the governance of the country and the Attorney General is right that there is no sphere of public life where delay can defeat justice with more telling effect than the one in which the common man seeks the realisation of his aspirations… This harmony and balance between fundamental rights and directive principles is an essential feature of the basic structure of the Constitution… It is not possible to fit Fundamental Rights and Directive Principles in two distinct and strictly defined categories, but it may be

> stated broadly that Fundamental Rights represent civil and political rights while Directive Principles embody social and economic rights. Both are clearly part of the broad spectrum of human rights… *The Indian Constitution is first and foremost a social document.* The majority of its provisions are either directly aimed at furthering the goals of the socio-economic revolution or attempt to foster this revolution by establishing the conditions necessary for its achievement.… But it is in the Directive Principles that we find the clearest statement of the socioeconomic revolution. The Directive Principles aim at making the Indian masses free in the positive sense, free from the passivity engendered by centuries of coercion by society and by nature, free from the object physical conditions that had prevented them from fulfilling their best salves. (emphasis added) (Minerva Hills case, 1980)

In the Sanjiev Coke case, the legislation aimed at nationalising mines was found to be valid despite the limitations it placed on fundamental rights. The Court declared:

> What is necessary is that there must be a real and substantial connection and the dominant object of the law must be to give effect to the Directive Principle… If the law made to further the Directive Principle is necessarily non-discriminatory or is based on a reasonable classification, then such law does not need any protection such as that afforded by Art. 31C. Such law would be valid on its own strength, with no aid from Art 31A. … a law designed to promote a Directive Principles, even if it came into conflict with the formalistic and doctrinaire view of equality before the law, would most certainly advance the broader egalitarian principle and the desirable constitutional goal of social and economic justice for all. … A directive to the State with a deliberate design to dismantle feudal and capitalist citadels of property must be interpreted in that spirit and hostility to such a purpose alone can be hospitable to the meaning which excludes private means of production or goods produced from the instruments of production. (Sanjiev Coke case, 1983)

In the State of Tamil Nadu case, the Court emphasised its duty to harmonise the provisions of the Bill of Rights and the Directive Principles. It held that, in cases of apparent conflict between the two, a statute could be upheld if it had a direct nexus with a Directive Principle, was reasonable, and served the public interest – despite limiting a fundamental right. The Court declared:

> In recent decisions on the subject the view that has crystallised is that the courts should attempt to give a harmonious interpretation to the directive

> principles contained in part IV of the Constitution even though not enforceable. Attempt should, therefore, be made to reconcile the two important provisions rather than to arrive at conclusions which bring into collision these two provisions-one contained in part III and the other in part IV… On a careful consideration of the legal and historical aspects of the directive principles and the fundamental rights, there appears to be complete unanimity of judicial opinion of the various decisions of this Court on the point that although the directive principles are not enforceable yet the court should make a *real attempt at harmonising and reconciling* the directive principles and the fundamental rights and any collision between the two should be avoided as far as possible…. The only condition for application of Art. 31C is that there should be a direct and reasonable nexus between the law and the provisions of Art.39(b) and (c), and the reasonableness would be regarding the nexus rather than the law. (emphasis added) (State of Tamil Nadu case, 1984)

In the State of Gujarat case, the Court stated the following about reliance on the Directive Principles to justify a restrictive interpretation of a fundamental right:

> A restriction placed on any Fundamental Right, aimed at securing Directive Principles will be held as reasonable and hence intra vires [as long as] it does not run in clear conflict with the fundamental right… (State of Gujarat case, 2005)

Arising from the interaction between the Directive Principles and fundamental rights, the courts have upheld various pieces of legislation aimed at giving effect to the former, even when this has required a narrower interpretation of fundamental rights. Examples of legislation that has been upheld include laws concerning the imposition of minimum wages (Chandrabhavan case, 1970), arrangements to ensure workers' participation in company management (National Textile Workers' Union case, 1983), equal pay for equal work (Federation of AIC and CE Stenographers case, 1988), price fixing (Sonia Bhalai case, 1981), the right to education (Unnikrishnan case, 1993), and the distribution of free televisions to the poor (Subramaniam Balaji case, 2013).

This chapter on the Directive Principles does not seek to defend their legal status and operation, but rather to illustrate how the courts have used these non-enforceable principles to guide legislative and executive organs, justify restrictions on fundamental rights that may not have been otherwise possible, and shape judgements in a distinctive manner by referencing them. This chapter proposes that FPIC could play a similar role to that of the Directive Principles in India, by guiding internationally the dynamic development of consultation with Indigenous Peoples. Whilst UNDRIP is not a legally binding instrument, it could inform the way human rights treaties are interpreted (Fielitz and MacKay, 2025, p. 10). Under the framework of 'free, prior, and informed consent' and the prevailing international social recognition of the importance of consulting with indigenous communities, FPIC could assist to shape legal and policy approaches to Indigenous People in a meaningful way. For example, the provisions of the international instruments such as the ICCPR and the ICESCR can be given effect and guidance by reference to FPIC. In this respect the individual right to self-determination could, against the backdrop of FPIC, be interpreted as an individual and collective right according to which the rights and interests as a community are given effect. In similar way the rights to property and culture could be interpreted within the context of the collective native of right in FPIC.

4 Relevance of the Directive Principles to FPIC

The way India's Directive Principles have developed could offer insights for FPIC in several respects:

4.1 Constitutional Status

The Directive Principles' inclusion in the Indian Constitution confers on them the same constitutional status as fundamental rights. Courts are thus compelled, as far as possible, to harmonise interpretations of the fundamental rights and the Directive Principles. There is no hierarchical distinction between fundamental rights and the Directive Principles – only different functions. A constitutional presumption exists that the state, through its laws and policies, should attempt to give effect to the Directive Principles. As a result, legislation and policies must align, as closely as possible, with the obligations arising from these principles. While the Directive Principles are obligatory, they are not directly justiciable.

FPIC reflects global opinion, as seen in the broad support UNDRIP receives across UN bodies, through state actions, and in international organisations like the World Bank (Cambou, 2025) and the OECD (Chapter 8). Although the obligations under UNDRIP are not legally binding, there is a strong case for interpreting core human rights treaties such as the ICCR and ICESCR in a manner that accommodates FPIC as a directive principle of state policy. FPIC encompasses state obligations much like the Directive Principles, and while

UNDRIP does not have the same legal status as a treaty, its legitimacy is illustrated by its widespread support in the UN General Assembly along with various other international endorsements.

Furthermore, international courts, tribunals, and municipal courts can declare a presumption that a state's support for UNDRIP more broadly – as expressed in the General Assembly – and for FPIC, in particular, should be considered when adjudicating legislation and policies concerning Indigenous Peoples in a domestic setting. This proposition implies that despite FPIC's lack of formal legal status, its legal and constitutional relevance and significance are not diminished in municipal law. The focus should therefore not be on the justiciability of FPIC, but on how fundamental rights and government policies can be interpreted to give FPIC better effect.

4.2 Justiciability

The Directive Principles are by design and intent not justiciable. They do not give rise to any enforceable rights or legal entitlements against the state. The debates in the Indian Constituent Assembly made it clear that the Directive Principles reflect the state's general duty towards its people, without carrying legal or justiciable obligations. They are intended to inform fundamental rights and influence their interpretation in the governance process, encouraging an approach that facilitates social justice and fairness.

The same applies to FPIC. Despite ongoing academic debates, a plain reading of UNDRIP and the context of its adoption confirms that FPIC is neither a justiciable right in international law nor an emerging right in customary international law. Echoing the Indian Constituent Assembly's stance on the Directive Principles, the UN General Assembly has been clear that UNDRIP is not legally binding. FPIC is intended as an endeavour to reach consent – but the withholding of consent does not constitute a legal veto. However, this does not render FPIC irrelevant to the exercise of regulatory functions. FPIC has received overwhelming and undeniable international endorsement as a non-legal objective. FPIC is meant to guide the interpretation of fundamental rights and policies concerning Indigenous Peoples, facilitating their application in a way that promotes social justice and fairness, both globally and within individual states. FPIC is an essential 'safeguard' albeit not a legal entitlement (Fielitz and MacKay, 2025, p. 15).

FPIC, as a directive principle of state policy, can unlock itself from the proposition that it applies principally to indigenous customary lands. Instead, it can extend to other socio-economic policy areas affecting Indigenous Peoples only, ensuring that policies are shaped in line with its spirit as a directive principle of state policy. The potential value of FPIC lies not necessarily in its quasi-judicial nature, but in its ability to inform and direct social policy, as well as to assist in judicial dispute resolution.

4.3 State Obligations

The Directive Principles focus on the state's obligations towards the community, rather than the community's rights against the state or each other. The Directive Principles highlight the state's duty of care to actively address socio-economic disparities and inequalities. State actions are presumed to be motivated by a desire to fulfil the objectives of the principles. Legislation and policies must, therefore, be interpreted in the manner most conducive to and consistent with the fulfilment of the Directive Principles. This also implies that when state action appears to affect fundamental rights, courts may consider such a limitation lawful, provided it is proportionate, reasonable, and directly aimed at promoting the Directive Principles.

FPIC could serve a similar role as a directive principle of state policy. The UN General Assembly's support for UNDRIP reflects broad international consensus on the need to better protect and promote indigenous rights, address inequalities, and ensure consultation on traditional land issues and other matters directly impacting Indigenous Peoples. FPIC can help shape the interpretation of fundamental rights and guide administrative decisions affecting Indigenous Peoples. As such, international and domestic courts may consider FPIC, a state's support for UNDRIP, as well as broader international commitments to UNDRIP, in order to interpret fundamental rights in a way that advances FPIC's goals.

4.4 Harmonious Interpretation

The novel aspect of the Directive Principles is that, being part of the Indian Constitution, they hold the same legal status as fundamental rights, though not the same legal effect. Courts should thus be compelled to interpret the Constitution in a manner that recognises the equal standing of both parts, despite their differing purpose and effects. One cannot be given precedence over the other since each fulfils a unique function – the fundamental rights set out the rights of individuals, whereas the Directive Principles set out the state's obligations in respect of general governance. The Directive Principles and fundamental rights must, therefore, be interpreted in harmony, ensuring their implementation aligns as closely as possible with their respective objectives.

Adjudicators could accord FPIC a status similar to directive principles, recognising that while UNDRIP's legal status differs from that of human rights treaties, the widespread support for it and, more specifically, that FPIC have received from states support of equal measure to that associated with treaties. States can be expected to perform their duties consistent with their public positions adopted in the General Assembly, including their support for UNDRIP. Accordingly, their legislation and policies should be interpreted in a manner that aligns with both fundamental treaty rights and FPIC. International and domestic adjudicators may, therefore, consider FPIC when assessing government policies and programs within the broader context of UNDRIP. Such assessments are not strictly rights-based, but guided by the principles of fairness, reasonableness, proportionality, and morality.

4.5 FPIC to Expand or Restrict Fundamental Rights

India's Directive Principles can be relied on by courts to interpret fundamental rights in a manner that aligns with the country's socio-economic priorities and the state's obligations. This enables the courts to either expand or restrict the scope of fundamental rights based on the Directive Principles. Adjudicators could put FPIC to the same use by giving life and identity to fundamental rights in general, and indigenous rights in particular. When treaty rights are implemented, or fundamental rights in municipal law are interpreted, FPIC can help give practical effect to a state's commitment to promoting indigenous consultative rights in its domestic laws and policies. For example, the rights to self-determination, property, and culture could be interpreted in light of UNDRIP's objectives. This does not make FPIC a legal norm, but it sets the context for interpreting and applying fundamental rights.

4.6 Dynamic and Flexible

The inclusion of the Directive Principles in the Indian Constitution has lent it a dynamism, flexibility, adaptability, and a consciousness that otherwise may have been lacking. The adequately vague and non-specific wording of the Directive Principles allows them to remain timeless, while retaining very clear objectives for guiding government policies. As a result, the Directive Principles are as relevant today as they were when the Constitution was drafted.

FPIC provides a similar degree of dynamism, flexibility, and adaptability to the field of international human rights, especially as it pertains to Indigenous Peoples. The perceived weakness of FPIC as a legal norm – being vague and non-specific – can instead be viewed as a strength, offering a clear yet dynamic objective unshackled of the rigidity of legal definition and the controversy of veto power. FPIC envisages meaningful consultation with indigenous communities in the widest sense, informed by the objectives of UNDRIP. Adjudicating bodies could rely on these general objectives to ensure that, depending on the specific circumstances of a particular indigenous community, the principles of FPIC are upheld in fulfilling its role as a directive policy for state action.

5 Conclusion

The absence of legal enforceability should not diminish FPIC's utility as a source of inspiration, a guiding principle, and a philosophy for indigenous empowerment. Freed from the veto debate, FPIC can serve as a powerful tool for guiding policies that affect Indigenous Peoples and influencing jurisprudence concerning their rights. UNDRIP in general, and FPIC in particular, can help interpret fundamental rights such as the right to self-determination, culture, property, the environment, and family. The way India's Directive Principles of State Policy have been used by courts and governments to advance socio-economic justice offers a compelling model for expanding the role of FPIC in respect of Indigenous People.

The following guidelines, drawn from India's experience with the Directive Principles, may be relevant to the use and application of FPIC:

(a) Like the Directive Principles of State Policy, FPIC is not justiciable. It does not confer a right of veto but imposes an obligation on the state to ensure that Indigenous Peoples are given a reasonable and fair opportunity to effectively and meaningfully participate in measures and decisions affecting their identity, culture, traditions, and land.

(b) Like the Directive Principles, FPIC is open-ended and timeless. It can be given a dynamic interpretation depending on the circumstances and bundle of rights of a particular indigenous community.

(c) FPIC ought to be accorded substantial moral status alongside human rights treaties, due to the broad support for UNDRIP from both state and non-state actors in international forums, particularly the UN General Assembly. As a consequence, fundamental rights and FPIC would be interpreted harmoniously to achieve outcomes that align as closely as possible with the objectives of FPIC.

(d) FPIC can be adapted to reflect the specific bundle of rights of each indigenous community in a manner that best suits their circumstances.

(e) The manner of consultation under FPIC, the subjects of consultation, and the level of support required for a measure to proceed may vary depending on the specific circumstances of each country and indigenous community.

CHAPTER 6

Good Faith Negotiation: Case Law from Australia Demonstrating an Unlevel Playing Field

1 Introduction

The term 'good faith consultation' is often used in the context of FPIC to signify the sincerity with which consultation should occur between parties. Although FPIC has not made its way extensively into domestic legislation, the phrase 'good faith' is widely known in jurisprudence in respect of consultation and negotiation. Like FPIC, good faith consultation is not a term of art with a set meaning; it is, rather, a flexible term of which the meaning is ascertained according to the specific circumstances of a particular consultation or negotiation. Whether good faith was demonstrated in negotiations is determined by considering all the relevant facts, legal requirements, legislative objectives, and status of the parties, as well as their behaviour and conduct. The presence or absence of good faith may also be influenced by the relative power dynamics between the parties.

There is often a power imbalance between those seeking access to traditional lands and the affected local indigenous community. This is precisely why ILO 169 and UNDRIP, and more specifically FPIC, aim to bring greater equality and fairness to negotiations. The purpose is to level, at least to some extent, the playing field. For example, in Australia, following the Mabo case, Parliament enacted the standard of 'good faith' when access is sought to lands covered by Aboriginal native title. The Preamble of the Australian Native Title Act emphasises the objective of addressing inequality and the dispossession of Aboriginal people, particularly concerning their traditional lands:

> They [Aboriginal peoples and Torres Strait Islanders] have been progressively dispossessed of their lands. This dispossession occurred largely without compensation, and successive governments have failed to reach a lasting and equitable agreement with Aboriginal peoples and Torres Strait Islanders concerning the use of their lands. As a consequence, Aboriginal peoples and Torres Strait Islanders have become, as a group, the most disadvantaged in Australian society.

In Australian case law, 'good faith', as a general principle, has been defined as 'fairness in dealings between contracting parties' with a scope 'wider than that

 HTTPS://DOI.ORG/10.1163/9789004724792-007

of honesty' (Commonwealth Bank of Australia case, 2014). Good faith does not require a party to act against its own interests or for it to accept the position of another party, but it does require each party to

> act *honestly* and with a *fidelity* to the bargain; an obligation not to act dishonestly and *not to act to undermine* the bargain entered or the substance of the contractual benefit bargained for; and an obligation to act *reasonably* and with *fair* dealing having regard to the interests of the parties (which will, inevitably, at times conflict) and to the provisions, aims and purposes of the contract, objectively ascertained. (emphasis added) (Paciocco case, 2015)

This chapter examines Australian case law concerning native title (land rights) proceedings, where 'good faith' negotiations are required for activities that may affect the native title (traditional lands) of Aboriginal people. The Native Title Act of Australia does not explicitly mention FPIC, but it imposes the standard of good faith on land access negotiations, generally aligning with the principles underpinning FPIC.[1] While the Australian system may not be ideal, critics are slow to acknowledge that it is one of the few statutory frameworks to apply nationwide to all areas of native title, with extensive procedural rights and judicial oversight. Moreover, it includes a legal standard of 'good faith', and it provides for an adjudication system supported by federal government grants to determine whether negotiations with Aboriginal communities have met this standard. This chapter draws specifically on indicia of good faith negotiation from this imperfect system (Human Rights Commission 2009; Burnside 2009; Australia Inquiry into UNDRIP 2023) to gain insights into how Australian courts view the obligation to negotiate with Indigenous Peoples in good faith when seeking agreement to access their traditional lands, and how this compares to the non-justiciable principles underlying FPIC.

Like FPIC, the inherent meaning of good faith negotiation, as it appears in Australia's Native Title Act, cannot be encapsulated by legal definition. However, certain indicia can help assess the even-handedness and openness of negotiations within the context of good faith. These include acting with fairness, honesty, and reasonableness, keeping an open mind, avoiding arbitrary conduct, responding timeously to communications, sharing relevant information, meeting Indigenous Peoples on their own lands, communicating in a manner they understand, allowing them time for internal consultation, and

1 On 24 June 2024, the federal government announced a review of the Native Title Act to ascertain what improvements could be made to better protect the rights of traditional owners. The review had not been completed at the time of finalising this chapter.

considering the other party's position without necessarily having to adjust one's own stance.

That having been said, negotiations may be robust and driven by self-interest. Neither good faith nor FPIC imposes a legal obligation on a party to accommodate the other side at the expense of its own interests. Good faith permits a party to stand firm to protect and promote their interests and drive a hard bargain without have to change their stance. Furthermore, neither FPIC nor good faith is intended to empower courts to second-guess the merits of preferred negotiation outcomes or the reasons for failure of parties to reach agreement – the role of courts is not to act as a co-negotiator. Essentially, good faith places an obligation on all parties involved to behave reasonably in the process of attempting to reach agreement.

Importantly, the role of courts is not to rewrite a deal or ascertain the reasonableness of each party's negotiation position, but rather to evaluate the reasonableness of their conduct. The principle of good faith accepts that parties may fail to reach agreement even if they meet the required threshold of good faith. As to FPIC, good faith negotiation entails similar standards – notably, there is no obligation for a party to change its position, but it must keep an open mind and engage sincerely in the process with the aim of reaching agreement, even if not achieved. Moreover, the consultation must ensure that indigenous groups have a genuine opportunity to make a meaningful contribution to the negotiation process (Saugeen First Nation case 2017, paras 10–29). Significantly, as with FPIC, good faith does not imply the granting of a veto to indigenous communities (Poma Poma case 2002; CSF case 2016).

In the Australian Communications Services Union case, the Court elaborated on the inherent meaning of the obligation to consult:

> A key element of that content is that the party to be consulted be given *notice* of the subject upon which that party's views are being sought before any final decision is made or course of action embarked upon. Another is that while the word always carries with it a consequential requirement for the affording of a *meaningful opportunity* to that party to present those views. What will constitute such an opportunity will vary according to the nature and circumstances of the case. In other words, what will amount to "consultation" has about it an inherent *flexibility*. Finally, a right to be consulted, though a valuable right, is *not a right* of veto… (emphasis added) (Communications Services Union, 2010, para. 44)

2 Background to Good Faith and Native Title

The 'right to negotiate' in Australia is a statutory obligation imposed on developers (government and private entities) seeking to undertake a 'future act', such as mining, exploration, or infrastructure development on traditional lands of Aboriginal people, to negotiate in good faith with the relevant local community 'with a view to reaching an agreement' on the terms and conditions for the work to proceed (Native Title Act, 1993, sec. 25(2)). A future act refers to any proposed activity on land or waters that may affect native title rights and interests, including freehold creation, mining lease grants, land clearing, or infrastructure development (Native Title Act, 1993, secs. 227; 233). The Native Title Act does not mention FPIC or UNDRIP, but its objectives arguably align with those of FPIC in the sense that both call for efforts to be made to reach agreement for access to customary lands.

Under the native title regime, Aboriginal people's traditional lands are not comparable to the indigenous reserves in countries such as the USA or Canada where the ownership of land rests with the indigenous community. Traditional Aboriginal native title refers to those areas where Aboriginal ownership of land continues to exist together with other forms of land tenure[2] such as pastoral leases and nature reserves. It is estimated that approximately 52% of Australia's landmass is covered by some form of native title determination (Native Title Map, 2024). The right to negotiate thus provides a broad spectrum of Aboriginal people with consultation rights – and potentially self-determination rights – regarding their traditional lands across vast parts of the country (De Villiers, 2024a).

2.1 Bundles of Rights

The content of native title rights and interests is often likened to a bundle of rights whose elements may vary between Aboriginal communities. The bundle of rights of each community depends on the community's traditional laws and customs, and the extent to which those customs are still observed (Ward

2 Native title generally co-exists with other forms of tenure, such as pastoral leases, nature reserves, mining and exploration licenses, or water navigation and usage rights. Native title can also be exclusive in respect of certain uses but the underlying title of the Crown (state) to the land remains. The layered nature of native title requires that various interested groups must inevitably interact with each other in those areas where native title exists. If native title rights are taken away or infringed, then compensation may be payable under the Constitution of Australia (Timber Creek High Court appeal 2019; Yunupingu appeal case 2025).

case, 2002). The community must display an ongoing exercise of their traditional customs, practically or spiritually. Their bundle of rights is not frozen in history, but is assessed on the available facts of contemporary indigenous practices. A court may determine, for example, that a previous custom is no longer observed by the community and, therefore, no longer forms part of their contemporary bundle of rights. The connection to land can be physical or spiritual. This principle was noted in the Ward case:

> an order in which the Federal Court makes a determination of native title has an indefinite character which distinguishes it from a declaration of legal right as ordinarily understood in such authorities as *International General Electric Co of New York Ltd v Commissioners of Customs and Excise* ([1962] Ch 784 at 789). That indefinite character reflects the requirement for the continuing acknowledgment and observance of traditional laws and customs and *continuing connection* with land implicit in the definition of "native title" in s 223(1) of the Native Title Act. (emphasis added) (Ward case, 2002, para. 32)

In the Akiba case, the High Court of Australia emphasised that the content of native title rights is ascertained not by reference to the common law, but by reliance on the traditional laws and customs of the specific Aboriginal community (Akiba case 2013, para. 20).[3] Native title is, therefore, not fixed at a particular moment in time, as the community must continue to adhere to and practice its rights and interests as a society concerning its traditional lands, but their way of interaction with their land may change over time. The exact nature of each community's rights and the extent of good faith negotiation required depend on the bundle of rights held by the community at a given time.

Generally, native title includes rights such as the use of natural resources (excluding mineral rights), hunting, camping, practicing traditions, protecting sites of cultural importance, and controlling access, as well as deriving income from the use of rights (Pilki case, 2015). Given the potential for conflicts between the rights and interests of native title holders and those of those seeking access to their native title areas, international best practice encourages negotiated rather than litigated resolutions to regulate land access (Boydell and Baya, 2012). Notable, is that the Australian statutory regime safeguards the state's sovereignty as the final decision-maker on land use issues while ensuring, by means of the Native Title Act, that Aboriginal people are

3 This approach is consistent with South African case law where the content of traditional landholding and traditional customs is ascertained through the customary legal system of the indigenous or tribal community (De Villiers, 2025g, p. 578).

accorded a reasonable opportunity to participate in the approval process (Neate, 2006).

2.2 Good Faith Negotiation

A person who wants to undertake certain activities on land covered by native title is required to negotiate in good faith with the relevant Aboriginal community. The Native Title Act, which regulates the recognition of native title and matters associated with it, provides for the so-called right to negotiate (Native Title Act, 1993, secs. 25–44). In an international comparative sense, this right is potentially one of the most powerful, albeit not perfect, statutory tools granted to indigenous communities. It protects their interests, grants them procedural rights, enables them to look after their traditional lands, allows them to benefit from resource access for activities such as mineral exploration, mining, and fishing, and provides for compensation in cases of loss or diminution of native title (De Villiers 2022b; Yunupingu appeal case 2025). As elaborated on later in this chapter, the right to negotiate is subject to two important caveats: first, that Aboriginal people do not have a statutory veto over access to their land for future act purposes (which is consistent with the non-justiciability of FPIC in UNDRIP); and second, there is a statutory presumption that developments and approvals must be granted for the public benefit.

The Australian approach to the absence of Aboriginal veto-rights is not dissimilar to Canadian case law (Kebaowek First Nation case, 2025, para. 183) or efforts in the Americas to give effect to FPIC (Bear Creek Mining case, 2021, para. 412). Note, for example, the Tsilhqot'in Nation case, where the Supreme Court of Canada held that once it is established that land traditionally belonged to Indigenous People, their consent is required for any development on that land. However, the Court went on to acknowledge that consent is not an absolute entitlement and may be overridden if the state can demonstrate that it has discharged its consultation functions properly and that the objective being pursued is in the interests of the wider community (Tsilhqot'in Nation case, 2014). In this regard, the Forrest appeal in the state of Western Australia is also noteworthy. The Court in this case found that, in its recognition of indigenous interests to prevent the building of weirs in a river, the Tribunal had given inadequate consideration to the public interest that may arise from irrigation (Forrest appeal case, 2024).

At face value, the right to negotiate appears to grant Aboriginal people control over what happens on their lands, as well as the ability to impose reasonable terms and conditions for any adverse impact an activity may have on their rights and interests. However, this perception is incorrect. First, it must be understood from the outset that the right to negotiate does not amount to a veto over access to land, but is principally a procedural right to require good faith negotiations concerning proposed mining and infrastructure activities in particular. Second, in both law and practice, this right is weaker than it may initially seem. While it grants procedural entitlements, such as notification of mining and other development proposals as well as an opportunity to negotiate access conditions, the right to negotiate does not bestow on Aboriginal people a veto power or significant control over land use, and there is a time limit of six months before the proponent can seek a determination. In the case of mining specifically, there is a presumption that favours granting approval. Native title holders do have the right to claim compensation for the diminution of their title. This right to compensation helps restore some balance in the relationship between native title holders and those seeking access to their land (Timber Creek High Court appeal 2019; Yunupingu case 2023; Yunupingu appeal case 2025).

Both sides in the negotiation process face significant pressure when access to traditional land is sought. Native title holders have a short timeframe to strike a deal under a statutory framework that is ultimately skewed towards granting land access. Meanwhile, developers are under pressure due to time constraints, shareholder expectations to engage with local communities, potential conditions imposed by financiers and banks, and the risk of compensation claims if a mutually acceptable arrangement is not reached (O'Faircheallaigh, 2016, p. 92). The confirmation by the High Court in the Yunupingu appeal that native title rights are akin to property and hence reasonable compensation is required for its taking or diminution, has brought greater equality in the relationship between traditional owners of land and those seeking access to the land.[4] When the right to negotiate was introduced, the objective stated by the federal government was that the negotiations

> should be aimed at achieving mutually acceptable arrangements under which the interests of those wishing to use the land are reconciled with the interests of the native title holders. (Commonwealth of Australia, 1993, p. 61)

O'Faircheallaigh observes as follows about the practical effect the right to negotiate has had in facilitating different forms of access agreements:

---

4 It must be noted, without going into too much detail about Australian constitutional law, that the states do not have the same obligation when property is taken as the federal government (Yunupingu case 2023; Yunupingu appeal case 2025).

> A number of agreements strongly favourable to Aboriginal interests have been negotiated pursuant to the Native Title Act, while some groups that lack even the minimal legal rights offered by the Native Title Act have also been able to secure favourable outcomes. (O'Faircheallaigh, 2016, p. 202)

Despite its shortcomings, the right to negotiate has enabled many Aboriginal communities to become incorporated by way of legal entities[5] and to interact with developers by negotiating various types of benefits for their communities. These benefits include royalty (financial) payments, heritage protection agreements, consultative mechanisms, charitable funds, joint management of nature reserves, administrative support for communities, land parcel acquisitions, as well as employment, education, and contracting opportunities (De Villiers, 2020b).

2.3 Community Representatives

The right to negotiate is discharged by an Aboriginal community through its representatives.[6] This requires consultation with the community and its representatives in a manner consistent with the traditions and culture of the specific community and Australian law (Harrington-Smith case, 2007). Each community's bundle of rights determines the scope within which good faith negotiation should occur. A community usually nominate or elect their representatives and should an entity that seeks access to their lands circumvent their representatives, it may be held as not acting in good faith (Richman case, 2025).

The benefits that accrue from the right to negotiate must be used for the benefit of the traditional owners to whom the native title belongs. Many Aboriginal communities, especially those whose native title falls within active mining areas, have adopted internal policies to regulate the distribution of financial benefits, including determining the eligibility of families to speak for certain parcels of land (e.g. Esperance Heritage Agreement 2024). Other so-called non-native title agreements – such as land access, land ownership transfers, joint management of national parks, and employment and contracting opportunities – may also be entered into by the Aboriginal legal entity

5 The legal entities are called Aboriginal Corporations and are specifically designed to assist Aboriginal people to become incorporated for the conduct of their own affairs (De Villiers 2022, 17–120).

6 See, for example, Sections 24DB; 30A and 56 of the Native Title Act, 1993.

concerned to give practical effect to the community's self-administration and self-government aspirations.

An Aboriginal community may also agree to the extinguishment of their native title in exchange for a package of rights, which may include compensation, negotiation and consultation requirements. Arguably the best example of such an arrangement is the so-called Noongar Settlement, often described as a modern-day treaty agreement (Noongar Recognition Act 2016; Hobbs and Williams 2018; Barrie 2018; De Villiers 2020).

2.4 Limited Application of Native Title

While the recognition of native title has been an important milestone for Aboriginal people, not all Aboriginal communities are able to prove ongoing possession of native title. Even when native title is established, the content of their bundle of rights may be limited. Native title has been extinguished in cities, towns, and freehold farms, leaving many Aboriginal communities without recourse to a right to negotiate whose land had been usurped by other interests. In many other rural areas, the traditional and cultural lives of Aboriginal people have been so disrupted that they may be unable to prove ongoing connection to country. Even if they remain connected in mind and spirit, they may no longer constitute a 'society' that holds native title.[7] The High Court has, however, emphasised that even if a physical connection to land has not been maintained, an ongoing spiritual connection remains significant (Banjima case, 2015).

This raises a question that also underlies FPIC: what protections and recognition are offered to Indigenous Peoples outside the context of their traditional lands?

Although UNDRIP suggests that all aspects of policy affecting Indigenous Peoples should be subject to FPIC, countries have not adopted such a broad approach in their municipal laws concerning consultation rights of Indigenous People. While states may consult with Indigenous Peoples on certain policies in the normal course of public consultation, this cannot be regarded as arising from FPIC. FPIC generally applies restrictively to customary lands and not to broader socio-economic policies or administrative measures that may directly or indirectly affect Indigenous Peoples. This explains why, in Austra-

7 Reference can be made, for example, to the Yorta Yorta judgement which highlights how difficult it may be for claimants to establish native title, particularly over areas of land where there has been intensive European settlement. In many cases, claimants may find it difficult to adduce the oral and historic evidence necessary to meet the criteria of ongoing connection set down by the High Court (Yorta Yorta (HCA) case 2002; Ward case 2002).

lia, there are ongoing efforts to design consultation processes that engage Aboriginal people on socio-economic issues beyond the scope of native title processes (De Villiers, 2024a). Indigenous People in urban settings may feel particularly marginalised, as they are often excluded from rights over their ancestral lands while also not qualifying for FPIC or good faith negotiations about socio-economic issues that affect them in an urbanised milieu. Although some countries have established advisory and consultative bodies for Indigenous Peoples, these generally fall well short in terms of co-decision-making and do not comprehensively address broader socio-economic issues concerning urbanised Indigenous Peoples (De Villiers, 2024c).

In light of the foregoing, native title should not be seen as a general remedy for recognition or self-government of Aboriginal people and the restoration of sovereignty, as a legal recognition of the right to self-determination, or as a mechanism to address socio-economic marginalisation of Aboriginal people. The procedural rights of native title apply exclusively to the traditional lands of indigenous communities. However, native title can serve as a potential springboard for broader self-determination initiatives, given the large extent of land in Australia that is subject to native title.

In reality, the legal benchmark to prove the continued existence of native title is high (Native Title Act, 1993, sec. 223); not all Aboriginal communities benefit from native title; the content of native title differs between communities; the procedural rights favour those seeking access to land; and the Native Title Act is complex in its operation. On the other hand, the native title regime is not limited to so-called indigenous reserves; procedural rights are accorded even if native title has not yet been proven; while the legal scale in negotiations is tipped in favour of those seeking access, political and social pressure on developers to reach agreements is strong; the state and private entities face potential compensation claims; and native title has become a launch pad for Aboriginal people to promote their broader socio-economic interests.

Many Aboriginal people perceive the native title process as inherently unfair, discriminatory, a continued denial of historic sovereignty, and a perpetuation of dispossession and dominance by white society over indigenous society. Others view native title as a potential catalyst for negotiating more extensive consultative and participatory rights (Taylor, 2023), as a form of recognition of their customary role over traditional lands, and as a basis for local self-determination.

3 Practical Meaning and Effect of Good Faith Negotiation

An Aboriginal community may, pursuant to the Native Title Act, submit an application seeking a finding that native title exists over the specific land and waters covered by their claim. Native title only exists when it is so determined by the courts. The person/s making the claim must be authorised by their community to lodge the claim and to act on the community's behalf (Native Title Act, 1993, sec. 61(1); 251B). The wording of the claim must clearly specify who is claiming native title, the area being claimed, the specific rights and interests asserted (Native Title Act 1993, sec. 62; Ward case 2002), areas where native title has been extinguished, the apical ancestors to whom the community is linked, and who has authorised the applicant to submit the application (Harrington-Smith, 2007, paras. 1206–1217). The lodgement of a claim, therefore, identifies the indigenous community, the nature of their bundle of rights claimed, the area within which the rights are asserted, and the individuals representing the community. This information is consistent with the requirements of UNDRIP which aims to clearly demarcate indigenous lands and the context on rights.

3.1 Negotiations with a View to Obtaining Agreement

The National Native Title Tribunal (NNTT) is a special administrative tribunal created under the Native Title Act to adjudicate, among other matters, disputes over whether the requirement for good faith negotiations, pursuant to the right to negotiate, has been met (Native Title Act 1993, pt. 6; Perry and Lloyd 2018, 782–849).[8] Pursuant to the right to negotiate, the parties involved are obliged to 'negotiate in good faith *with a view to obtaining* the agreement' (emphasis added) (Native Title Act, 1993, sec. 31(1)(b)). Although the Native Title Act predates UNDRIP, the words 'with a view to obtaining the agreement' resemble those found in UNDRIP concerning FPIC: '*in order to obtain* their free, prior and informed consent before adopting and implementing legislative or administrative measures that may affect them' (emphasis added) (UNDRIP, 2007, art. 19). The right to negotiate, like FPIC, does not grant a veto or mandate consensus.

8 The National Native Title Tribunal is an administrative tribunal, not a court. The Tribunal is responsible for several functions regarding the native title regime. One of its key functions is to resolve disputes about whether negotiations concerning land access have been conducted in good faith (National Native Title Tribunal, 2020).

The right to negotiate provides parties with a potential opportunity to establish an 'amicable relationship' (North Ganalanja case, 1996, para. 617), but it does not mandate effective collaboration or joint decision-making. The Preamble to the Native Title Act sets the following standard for consultation:

> In future, acts that affect native title should only be able to be validly done if, typically, they can also be done to freehold and if, whenever appropriate, *every reasonable effort* has been made to secure the agreement of the native title holders through a special right to negotiate… (emphasis added) (Native Title Act, 1993 Preamble)

The parties do not pursuant to the Native Title Act have equal standing around the negotiation table for several reasons. First, the procedural rights in the Native Title Act operate under the assumption that land access should be granted to benefit the country's broader socio-economic development. Second, negotiations are limited to six months, after which a party may request that the NNTT grant approval. Third, the NNTT and courts lack jurisdiction to impose royalty or cash payment conditions, or to rule that negotiations were not held in good faith simply because a mining company refused to offer such payments. The rather conservative approach adopted by the courts is that good faith negotiations do not require a developer to 'make reasonable substantive offers or concessions to reach agreement' (Strickland case, 1998).[9]

When negotiating land access, it is essential to consider the special relationship Aboriginal people have with their traditional country, particularly the significance of the specific area affected by the proposed future act. Some areas of country may be culturally more sensitive than others, possibly requiring the establishment of exclusion zones or other mitigation measures. Even though the right to negotiate does not grant Aboriginal people a veto over land developments, it should nevertheless not be 'narrowly construed' (FMG case, 2009, para. 18).

9 It is notable, however, that even if land access approval has been granted against the wishes of an Aboriginal community, the community may in due course claim compensation for their loss of use and enjoyment of their native title (Timber Creek High Court appeal 2019; Yunupingu appeal case 2025). This compensation mechanism introduces some balance into negotiations, as developers – encouraged by their financiers – and the state which is ultimately responsible for the grating of approvals to access land, may attempt to mitigate any risks of future compensation claims through an agreement of some sort.

3.2 Details of Community Identity

Any application to undertake a future act is notified by the NNTT to the Aboriginal community holding native title over the area where the act is proposed (Native Title Act, 1993, sec. 29). The Aboriginal community, the proponent of the future act, and the relevant government department must then engage in good faith negotiations regarding possible conditions for granting access approval. The requirement for good faith negotiations is thus 'clearly important and central to the permissible act process' (North Ganalanja case, 1996). The Aboriginal community must negotiate as a collective entity, which requires internal processes within the community about the authorisation of negotiators and conditions for granting access (Placer case, 2000, pp. 3–6).

All parties are obliged to negotiate in good faith, even though the Native Title Act does not define good faith negotiations (Native Title Act, 1993, sec. 31(1)).[10] Negotiating in good faith requires the negotiating parties to act honestly and sincerely with the aim of reaching an agreement to do what is reasonable in the circumstances. The Native Title Act does, however, stipulate that negotiations must focus solely on the proposed future act and not on unrelated matters (Native Title Act, 1993, sec. 30(3); 31(2)). This limits the ability of Aboriginal people to use their native title rights and interests to raise wider cultural, heritage and social concerns regarding the potential impact of a proposed development on their land (Bartlett, 2020, p. 615).

3.3 Six Months for Negotiations (unless Extended)

The statutory period for good faith negotiations is limited to six months (Native Title Act, 1993, sec. 35). While the parties may mutually agree to extend negotiations, the proponent of a development can, after six months, request the NNTT to declare that good faith negotiations had taken place, no agreement was reached, and that access to the land should be granted. Any party may request a determination prior to the expiry of the six months if it becomes clear that the negotiation process is stalled and not progressing (Rita Dempster case, 1999, p. 5). If an Aboriginal community opposes the granting of land access, it may commence proceedings in the NNTT alleging that good faith negotiations have not taken place. However, any resulting delay could

10 Although some view the right to negotiate as having little practical value, Burnside contends that it should rather be seen as the 'least worst option', as it is an improvement on not having any statutory role, even if it is not as powerful as Aboriginal people would like (Burnside, 2009, p. 15).

be significant, potentially causing public embarrassment or funding delays for the proponent. Case law indicates that it is relatively rare for the NNTT or courts to uphold such complaints, because the threshold for demonstrating good faith is not particularly high, even if no agreement is ultimately reached.

The essential question, of course, remains: what is meant by 'good faith' negotiations? Since good faith forms an 'integral part' of the protection of native title, this right 'is not to be narrowly construed' (FMG case, 2009, para. 18). As with FPIC, it is worth reiterating that the absence of a veto associated with good faith negotiation does not imply that the procedural steps it entails lack significance. Non-compliance with these steps can still be subject to litigation and even payment of compensation, even if no veto is intended.

3.4 Indicia of Good Faith

The following are among the essential elements of good faith negotiations as determined by Australian courts:

- The parties must demonstrate though their conduct a genuine desire to reach agreement;
- The totality of the parties' conduct must be taken into account, including whether they display an open mind, show a willingness to adjust from their opening position, and engage the other side constructively (ABC case 1995, para. 421; Gomeroi People case 2024, para. 77);
- The subjective attitude of the parties is relevant, as a 'patently unreasonable offer' may indicate a certain state of mind – but even then, all conduct must be assessed, not just the content of the offer (Gomeroi People case 2024, para. 96);
- The merits of the respective proposals are not weighed, and there is no 'reasonable person' test regarding the merits of a position – but a grossly unreasonable position may reflect an absence of good faith;
- The parties must display 'an open mind, willingness to listen, and willingness to compromise, to reach an agreement…' (Brownley case, 1999, para. 25), but a party may maintain a firm position (Murphy case, 2021 par. 125);
- The parties must exchange communications and engage with each other (Strickland case 1998 para. 38);
- The parties must demonstrate that they have made proposals and responded to the proposals made by the other side, even if not agreeing to those proposals (Walley case, 1996, para. 576);
- The parties must act 'honestly, legitimately and fairly in negotiating towards an agreed outcome' (Gomeroi People case 2024, para. 78).

3.5 Indicia of a Lack of Good Faith

Other indicators may demonstrate that negotiations do not meet the threshold of good faith, such as:
- Delays in communication or a failure to respond adequately to communication;
- Failure to participate in mediation or consider heritage protection protocols, as well as a lack of honest intention (Mobile Concreting Solutions case, 2022);
- Failure to negotiate with the person/s appointed by the indigenous community (Richman case, 2025);
- Failure to make proposals or respond to proposals;
- Failure to provide relevant information on a timely basis (Pathfinder Exploration case, 2022);
- Failure to agree on trivial matters or showing unreasonable inflexibility;
- Failure to respond to reasonable requests for information;
- Failure to attend meetings (Taylor 1996, paras 224–225; Maduwongga 1997, paras 15–21);
- Disrespect toward the other party, mocking behaviour, misrepresentation of legal positions, and inflexible conduct (De Roma case, 2022);
- Use of public pressure and protests to secure a better deal, or any other unilateral process that harms the negotiation process.

3.6 Indicia of Good Faith Even without Agreement

The following are examples of conduct that does not indicate a lack of good faith negotiations:
- Failure by the parties to reach an agreement is not an indication of an absence of good faith in the negotiations. The party claiming there has not been good faith negotiations bears the burden of proving this (Strategic Minerals case, 2003, p. 7);
- The rejection of another party's report, or serious disagreement over a report's content, does not imply an absence of good faith (Gomeroi People case 2024, para. 89);
- The mere fact that six months has lapsed without an agreement reached is not accepted as an absence of good faith. The courts must be guided by the totality of the parties' conduct (Njamal case, 1996 par. 17–18);
- Parties may lose faith in each other, or become frustrated by a breakdown in relations, but this alone does not constitute a lack of good faith (Marine

Produce case, 2018, para. 66). Good faith is about the honesty of intention and sincerity to reach agreement (Gomeroi People case, 2024).

- The inability of parties to agree on the rules of negotiation before the main negotiations start does not indicate an absence of good faith;
- If parties fail to reach agreement on a preliminary issue, such as the conduct of negotiations or financial support for the Aboriginal community in preparing for negotiations, this does not imply an absence of good faith, even if the main agenda regarding the proposed future act has yet to be considered (FMG case, 2009, para. 29);
- A lack of resources for the Aboriginal people to effectively prepare for or participate in negotiations, or a lack of capacity to assess the merits of a proposal regarding royalty payments, does not in itself indicate an absence of good faith negotiations (Daniel case, 2002, para. 146);
- The reasonableness of offers, or lack thereof, made by the parties does not indicate the presence or absence of good faith in negotiations. The adjudicator does not consider the merits of the parties' respective negotiation positions, unless a proposal is obviously unreasonable;
- The protection accorded to Aboriginal people is procedural in nature and does not extend to the substance of the proposal presented to them or their response.[11] Essentially, the NNTT is not a court and its role is not to consider the reasonableness of a *proposal,* though the reasonableness of *conduct* can be considered; and (Strickland case, 1998, p. 9)
- The conduct of a party prior to the lodging of a future act notice has no material relevance in determining if it has negotiated reasonably (Santos case 2022; Tipakalippa case 2022).

3.7 Role of the National Native Title Tribunal

If no agreement is reached, any of the parties may ask the NNTT to determine whether the proposed act may proceed and, if approved, under what conditions, if any (Native Title Act, 1993, secs. 35; 38).[12] The NNTT must, among

11 Although the right to negotiate does not grant a veto, it does provide some procedural rights. In doing so, it allows communities to exert a degree of control over their lands and, as a consequence, places a moral and legal obligation on those seeking land access to develop a relationship with them. Shareholders may also require from their companies negotiated access to traditional land. The right to negotiate is, therefore, at best described as a 'minimal safeguard' (Burnside, 2009, p. 4) that can be supplemented through public, shareholder, and financing pressure.

12 It is noteworthy that, while the parties may – by way of negotiations – agree to some form of compensation to be paid by the developer to the native title group, the NNTT

other considerations, take into account the significance of the proposed future act for the state's economic interests, thereby indicating that the statutory preference is for the granting access to land (Native Title Act, 1993, sec. 39(1)(c)). The requirement for good faith is directed to the quality of a party's conduct, which is to be assessed by reference to what a party has done, or not done, in the course of negotiations (FMG case, 2009).

The foregoing demonstrates that, while the requirements for good faith negotiations may seem to give Aboriginal people a controlling position over projects affecting their native title rights and interests, the substance of the right is relatively weak in practice, as it emphasises the procedural rather than the substantive elements of negotiations. In this respect, the right to negotiate and FPIC share a similar weakness in that neither entails a veto. However, the right to negotiate in Australia is at least supported by an institutional framework, an extensive body of case law, government funding, a potential for compensation, and a general practice that, in many respects, leads other countries.

4 Conclusion

The right to negotiate offers useful insights into how Australian courts have approached the duty to negotiate in good faith with Aboriginal people. The right to negotiate itself is limited at law to customary lands subject to native title (covering more than 51% of Australia) and faces criticism for being a rather weak procedural right. Nonetheless, the substance and protocols arising from the right to negotiate enhance the participation of Aboriginal people in negotiations over access to their 'country'. There are few countries, if any, with a similarly vast body of case law concerning the practical requirements for good faith negotiation.

Although FPIC is not a term legally utilised in Australia, in substance both FPIC and good faith negotiation focus on the conduct of parties rather than establishing a legal right to a veto. The case law arising from the right to good faith negotiations is more extensive than any comparative case law in countries where FPIC is occasionally referenced.

Although the right to negotiate is a statutory right, and thus unique to Australia and specifically to Aboriginal people in respect of their traditional lands,

may not impose a condition for such a payment to be made (Native Title Act, 1993, sec. 38(2)(a)-(c)). Nonetheless, a claim for compensation may be brought to the Federal Court once a determination has been made that native title exists and its use and enjoyment has been diminished as a result of a development approval (Timber Creek appeal 2017; Yunupingu appeal case 2025).

the practices associated with the right to negotiate have a much wider impact on the self-determination of Aboriginal people (O'Faircheallaigh, 2016). Many Aboriginal communities have leveraged their native title rights as a springboard to promote their broader interests in society through advocacy, service agreements, and commercial undertakings (De Villiers, 2024a). Much remains to be done to give effect to Aboriginal people's right to self-determination, but the right to good faith negotiation and the institutional arrangements surrounding it represent a progressive step forward, especially when compared to other international jurisdictions. The approach adopted by the Australian courts may also provide guidance to other jurisdictions when assessing the reasonableness of consultation and FPIC.

The Australian approach to good faith negotiations within the context of the right to negotiate can be summarised as follows:

The right to negotiate and the obligation to negotiate in good faith arise from statute. As the Native Title Act does not define good faith, it is left to the courts to determine, within the context of a specific dispute, whether negotiations have met this common law standard.

Good faith is ascertained by assessing the conduct of the parties and the objectives of the statutory arrangements. There is no fixed list of criteria to adhere, but courts generally consider the reasonableness of conduct and sincerity of their engagement. Ultimately, the focus lies on the efforts made to reach agreement rather than the merits of the proposals or the reasonableness of any compensation offered.

Australian law does not refer to FPIC as a legal or normative standard. However, on proper analysis and compared to international case law referencing FPIC, the right to good faith negotiation has a similar legal substance (or lack thereof) to FPIC as it appears in UNDRIP.

The Native Title Act provides a legal basis for communities to become incorporated and thereby exercise collective rights on behalf of the entire community, both in relation to their native title and broader self-determination activities.

The content of each community's bundle of rights determines the scope of the good faith negotiations required when access to their traditional lands is sought. These bundles of rights may vary between communities and can change over time within a specific community.

The community holding native title is defined by apical ancestors, a specific territorial area, nominated representatives, and genealogical lists that assist in resolving community membership disputes. The rights and interests of the community are ultimately determined by an order of the Federal Court.

Aboriginal communities can become incorporated pursuant to their native title or the registration of a land use agreement. Substantial support from the federal government is available to assist communities in registering a corporation, obtaining legal and corporate governance advice, ensuring the corporation performs in accordance with its statute of incorporation, and delivering services to the corporation's members. The corporation provides the community with a legal identity, enabling it to sue and be sued, act on behalf of the entire community, be held accountable for its actions by its members, and, if necessary, be subject to judicial oversight.

The outcomes that arise are typically framed within a charitable context, focusing on improving members' well-being, alleviating poverty, and promoting the community's culture and identity. In many instances, the benefits derived from good faith negotiations have enabled local Aboriginal communities to give practical effect to their self-administration aspirations.

Like the sliding scale of activities established in the Americas, the scale and scope of a proposed activity may influence the standard courts apply in assessing the reasonableness of good faith negotiations.

To summarise, despite various shortcomings, native title in general and the right to negotiate in particular have enabled many Australian Aboriginal communities to participate in matters impacting their traditional lands. Substantial case law has arisen from the right to negotiate in general and more specifically what is meant by good faith negotiation. Like FPIC, the right to negotiate neither grants a veto nor implies co-decision-making, but it is an important procedural right that has benefited numerous Aboriginal communities. These benefits include incorporation, election of community representatives, autonomous decision-making, the pursuit of projects and other commercial ventures, negotiations with those seeking access to their country, roles in advocacy and advisory bodies, pursuing charitable objectives, and involvement in diverse forms of community self-determination and self-administration initiatives.

CHAPTER 7

Selected Case Law: Practical Meaning of the Phrase *in Order to Obtain* Their Free, Prior, and Informed Consent

1 Introduction

In previous chapters, the following essentials about FPIC have been established: FPIC is not a legal term of art arising from binding international law, nor is it a legal right arising from customary international law; it is not legally defined by international law or domestic law, though it is frequently referenced in soft law, advocacy and policy materials; UNDRIP sets an objective to seek FPIC rather than a mandatory requirement for agreement; 'consent' as used in FPIC does not equate to a legal veto or co-decision-making; states are required to give practical effect to UNDRIP in general and FPIC in particular through their domestic arrangements when engaging with Indigenous Peoples; FPIC is applied selectively based on a sliding scale, depending on the nature, scope and impact of the project; in a legal sense, courts do not differentiate substantively between good faith consultation and FPIC; state compliance with the normative aspects of FPIC is assessed based on the specific circumstances of consultation rather than in the abstract; and, in the event that agreement is not reached, courts interpret FPIC in the context of the process undertaken 'in order to obtain' consent, rather than by considering the merits of the proposals and positions involved.

If FPIC does not amount to a veto, then what is it? This chapter examines the meaning of the phrase '*in order to obtain their* free, prior, and informed consent' by referencing selected jurisprudence. Rather than relying on literature and advocacy interpretations of what FPIC is purported to mean, this chapter looks at selected case law to ascertain how courts and expert arbitration bodies have interpreted the phrase 'in order to obtain' FPIC and whether the same standard applies to good faith consultation.

The essential question here is: what practical measures do courts deem adequate to ensure Indigenous Peoples have a reasonable opportunity to participate effectively and meaningfully in good faith consultation, in compliance with natural justice and procedural fairness, in order to obtain their consent?

As previously explained, courts typically do not distinguish between good faith consultation and FPIC as if the terms constitute two different legal stand-

 | HTTPS://DOI.ORG/10.1163/9789004724792-008

ards of consultation. Non-judicial bodies seem more open to cite FPIC as if it is a distinct normative standard, whereas domestic courts tend to approach FPIC within the context of good faith consultation – an area familiar to them. Basically, courts require that the entirety of the parties' conduct be assessed. They consider, for example, whether the parties kept an open mind, showed a willingness to adjust from their opening position and engage constructively, and acted openly and honestly (ABC case 1995, para. 421; Gomeroi People case 2024, para. 77). In judicial forums where FPIC is cited, it is often used interchangeably with good faith consultation. Even in the few instances where FPIC is relied on by a court as if a distinct norm, in substance it amounts to no more than good faith consultation (Kebaowek First Nation case, 2025, para. 215).

Courts tend to focus on whether consultation obligations in a specific circumstance have been properly observed to ensure Indigenous Peoples have a reasonable and meaningful opportunity to express their views, influence a proposed development, withhold consent if they so choose, or propose alternative options or mitigating measures. In general, the approach adopted by courts regarding consultation with Indigenous Peoples is in effect an expansion of the well-known rules of procedural fairness and natural justice. The proposition in administrative law that a person who is affected by a measure is entitled to express their views on it is exemplified, enhanced, and expanded through FPIC.

Importantly, courts do not treat consultation or FPIC as an approval process that operates beyond state regulatory authority. This is consistent with the view that indigenous interests cannot enjoy 'automatic prevalence' over other national interests (Tomaselli and Cittadino, 2021, p. 166). FPIC does not imply that the state has relinquished its regulatory or approval processes. Regardless of a proponent's compliance with FPIC obligations, the state retains a regulatory duty and broader responsibility to serve the best interests of the wider public.

While the outcome of the FPIC process is relevant to the decision-making process of the state, it is not necessarily determinative of the regulatory authority's decision (Forrest appeal case, 2024). FPIC reflects public interest in the sense that the protection of indigenous rights is approached as a public good – but it does not encompass the totality of public interest. Other elements of public interest must also be considered, for example economic development, urbanisation, national security, and food security. The Tsilhqot'in Nation case is noteworthy in this respect; the Supreme Court of Canada held that once traditional indigenous ownership of land is established, the community's consent is required for any developments on the land. However, the

Court acknowledged that consent is not an absolute entitlement and may be overridden if the state can demonstrate that it has fulfilled its consultation obligations properly and that the pursued objective serves the broader public interest (Tsilhqot'in Nation case 2014). In the Kebaowek First Nation case the court emphasised that FPIC is, in effect, and interpretative aid through which conduct is assessed, but it does not grant a veto right (Kebaowek First Nation case, 2025, para. 215). A similar sentiment was expressed in the Australian Forrest case, where a tribunal's original decision – rejecting the proposed erection of weirs in a river for irrigation purposes – was set aside. While the tribunal panel had sought to protect Aboriginal heritage, it was found by the appeal court that the tribunal had inadequately considered the broader societal interests, potential benefits, and overall impact of the proposed agricultural development (Forrest appeal case 2024; Forrest case 2023).

This chapter proposes that useful insights can be drawn from: (a) the approaches adopted by various courts and expert bodies to ascertain whether consultation with Indigenous Peoples has been adequate and aligned with the standard of 'in order to obtain' FPIC; (b) the criteria used by courts and expert bodies to assess compliance with the 'in order to obtain' FPIC standard; and (c) most importantly, the reasonable steps required to fulfil the obligation of 'in order to obtain' FPIC.

2 Case Law

In this section, I use recurring themes identified in jurisprudence to demonstrate the standards that courts have applied to efforts made 'in order to obtain' FPIC:

2.1 A Sliding Scale When FPIC Is Required

FPIC is not a fixed standard or a rigid set of rules to which the same methodology can be applied in each case involving consultation with Indigenous Peoples. The nature, scope, scale, and duration of FPIC vary depending on factors such as the type of project, its timeframe, the extent of its impact on an indigenous community, its effect on the land, the bundle of rights of the particular community, the feasibility of land rehabilitation, its long-term impact, and any other relevant considerations. This does not necessarily mean that a project must be large in scale to necessitate FPIC, as even a potential minor impact on a highly valued site may require consultation (see Chapter 9 on the destruction of an Aboriginal site). That said, an indigenous communities whose customary land faces more severe impacts from a development may be entitled to greater involvement under FPIC compared to a community experiencing lesser or indirect effects.

A sliding scale is typically used to ascertain whether FPIC is required and, if so, with whom consultation should take place, the extent to which actual consent is sought, and the duration of the FPIC process. As a general guide, the more severe the direct impact of a measure on Indigenous Peoples and their customary land, the greater the effort required to consult 'in order to obtain' FPIC (Poma Poma case 2002; CSF case 2016). For example, in the Samsung case, the Roundtable on Sustainable Palm Oil (RSPO) found that a subsidiary of the company had failed to comply with basic FPIC requirements when clearing native forests by failing to provide the affected community with alternative land (Samsung case, 2024).

Meanwhile, in the Poma Poma case, an effort was made to draw a distinction between consultation and FPIC:

> In the Committee's view, the admissibility of measures which substantially compromise or interfere with the culturally significant economic activities of a minority or indigenous community depends on whether the members of the community in question have had the opportunity to participate in the decision-making process in relation to these measures and whether they will continue to benefit from their traditional economy. The Committee considers that participation in the decision-making process must be effective, which *requires not mere consultation but the free, prior and informed consent* of the members of the community. In addition, the measures must respect the *principle of proportionality* so as not to endanger the very survival of the community and its members. (emphasis added) (Poma Poma case, 2002, para. 7.6)

The consultation process must therefore take into account the impact, scale, and duration of a measure, which in turn determines the standards for information sharing, the time allocated for consultation, the parties to be consulted, the consideration of alternatives or mitigation options, engagement with sub-communities, potential compensation, conditions of approval, and possible ongoing involvement as the project progresses (Saramaka case 2007). In the Saramaka case, the following was declared:

> The State failed to consult the Saramaka people regarding development or investment plans in their territory and also failed to obtain their free, prior, and informed consent to *large-scale projects with a major impact.* (emphasis added) (Saramaka case, 2007, paras. 133–134)

In the Clyde River case, the Court, in its criticism of an inadequate consultation process, spoke about the need for 'deep consultation', given that there had been a lack of meetings, limited opportunities for the affected communities to express their views, and an absence of any funding to enable them to attend meetings and conduct intra-indigenous consultation (Clyde River case, 2017). The Court found that, considering the nature and scope of the project, such 'deep consultation' should have taken place with greater efforts made to ensure the indigenous communities' participation and possible approval.

However, the proposition of a sliding scale can also be a highly discretionary exercise, given that not all indigenous communities may be equally affected by a proposed measure and the difference, at law, between consultation and FPIC is at best vague and at worst fictional.

The nature and extent of a proposed project ought to determine the nature and extent of the required consultation. Good faith consultation encompasses a range of options that correspond to the scope and scale of a project and all the relevant facts surrounding it. In this respect, the Supreme Court of Canada observed as follows:

> The content of the duty [to consult], once triggered, *falls along a spectrum* ranging from limited to deep consultation, depending upon the strength of the Aboriginal claim, and the seriousness of the potential impact on the right. Each case must be considered individually. Flexibility is required, as the *depth of consultation* required may change as the process advances and new information comes to light. (emphasis added) (Clyde River case, 2017, para. 20)

In the Canadian Kebaowek case UNDRIP was described as a 'contextual factor' through which adequacy of domestic consultation should be assessed (Kebaowek First Nation case, 2025, para. 183). The court concluded that:

> While the FPIC standard is *not a veto*, it requires significant robust processes tailored to consider the impacted Indigenous Nations laws, knowledge, and practices and employs processes that are directed toward finding mutual agreement. In this case, the record demonstrates that the Commission and the CNSC were not prepared to modify or alter their processes to respond to Kebaowek's requests for accommodation. This was not reasonable and failed to consider the important added *contextual factors* of the UNDRIP, which must now be considered when assessing the adequacy of Crown consultation. (emphasis added) (Kebaowek First Nation case, 2025, para. 183)

In the Sustaining the Wild Coast case, the question arose of whether the local indigenous community had been adequately consulted before a decision was made pursuant to the Minerals and Petroleum Resources Development Act, for seismic testing to be conducted on their territory. The Court concluded that consultation had been insufficient, as the process had not been 'meaningful', stating:

> When administrative action *materially and adversely* affects the rights of any person, their right to procedural fairness is triggered. It can hardly be in dispute that Impact was required to *meaningfully consult* with the communities and individuals that would be affected by the seismic blasting. (emphasis added) (Sustaining the Wild Coast case, 2024, para. 19)

In short, the nature, extent, and duration of good faith consultation 'in order to obtain' FPIC are determined by the circumstances of the proposed measure. Courts do not generally distinguish between good faith consultation and FPIC as if they are distinct legal norms or different standards. Courts, along with expert bodies, occasionally cite FPIC, but do so in the context of what is ordinarily implied by good faith consultation. Courts do, however, require greater efforts to reach agreement when a measure is deemed likely to have a major impact on an indigenous community or if an important site may be affected. This amounts, in effect, to a sliding scale, where the extent of efforts 'in order to obtain' FPIC should match the level of the measure's impact.

2.2 General Guidelines to Satisfy FPIC Benchmarks

The vagueness surrounding the obligation to take steps 'in order to obtain' FPIC, combined with the lack of a legally definitive checklist, can leave those seeking access to land confused and frustrated. They may not know whether they are consulting with the appropriate individuals, whether the consultation process is adequate, and whether the approval granted by the state is legally secure and final.

As highlighted by the Juukan Gorge incident in Australia (Chapter 9), an approval process that appears legally secure may still result in actions (such as the destruction of an important Aboriginal heritage site) that later prove costly and humiliating to the developer (De Villiers, 2025b). Also in Australia, the Munkara case demonstrates how allegations of inadequate consultation with a sub-group of an indigenous community can cause significant delays. Even if the objections to the laying of an undersea pipeline were ultimately dismissed, such delays can still lead to substantial costs for the proponent (Munkara case, 2024).[1]

In the Kichwa case, the Court identified some of the essential steps required 'in order to obtain' FPIC: the consultation process must commence before the final decision is made; the process must be undertaken in good faith with the objective of reaching an agreement; information provided about the proposed project must be both adequate and accessible; the project and consultation must consider and environmental impact assessments; and any advice provided by the community must be informed (Kichwa case, 2012). The following are a few insightful excerpts from the Court's reasoning:

- the Court has observed that the consultation shall be performed *in conformity with the traditions* of the indigenous community and during the first stages of the development or investment plan, not only when the need to obtain the community's approval arises, if this were the case.
- Consultations shall be performed in *good faith* and in a manner that is adequate *under the circumstances*, with the objective of achieving agreement or consent to the proposed measures. In addition, consultation shall not be exhausted as a mere formality but shall be understood as a true *instrument of participation* which must respond to the goal of establishing dialogue between the parties, based on the principles of trust and mutual respect, and with the goal of reaching consensus between the parties. Good faith requires the absence of any type of coercion by the State or agents or third parties, and is incompatible with practices such as attempts at disintegrating the social cohesion of the communities affected.
- The consultation of indigenous communities shall be performed through *culturally adequate procedures*, meaning, in conformity with their own traditions. Even though there is no single adequate model of procedure, national circumstances and those of the indigenous communities must be taken into account, as well as the context of the nature of the measures under consultation.
- the consultation must be informed, in the sense that the indigenous communities must have *knowledge of the possible risks* of the proposed development or investment plan, which requires for the State to accept and provide information, and implies constant communication.

---

1 Some estimates put the costs caused by the delay at A$800 million (Macdonald-Smith, 2024). The presiding judge in the appeal described aspects of expert evidence as 'so lacking integrity that no weight can be placed on them'. The Court ultimately awarded A$9 million in legal costs against the Environmental Defenders Office which supported and financed the proceeding (Rauso 2024, Munkara consent orders cost 2024).

- The Court deems that the right to *cultural identity is a basic right* and of a collective nature for indigenous communities, which must be respected in a multicultural, pluralist and democratic society.

In the Bengwenyama Minerals case, it was held that the consultation with a community affected by a proposal must be *'fair'*, requiring that adequate information be provided to enable the community to make an informed decision about the application (Bengwenyama Minerals case 2011). The court explained as follows:

> One of the purposes of consultation with the landowner must surely be to see whether some *accommodation is possible* between the applicant for a prospecting right and the landowner insofar as the interference with the landowner's rights to use the property is concerned… Of course the Act *does not impose agreement* on these issues as a requirement for granting the prospecting right, but that does not mean that consultation under the Act's provisions does not require engaging in good faith to attempt to reach accommodation in that regard. Failure to reach agreement at this early consultation stage might result in the holder of the prospecting right having to pay *compensation* to the landowner at a later stage…
>
> Another more general purpose of the consultation is to provide landowners or occupiers with the *necessary information* on everything that is to be done so that they can make an *informed decision* in relation to the representations to be made, whether to use the internal procedures if the application goes against them and whether to take the administrative action concerned on review. The consultation process and its result is an integral part of the *fairness process* because the decision cannot be fair if the administrator did not have full regard to precisely what happened during the consultation process in order to determine whether the consultation was sufficient to render the grant of the application procedurally fair… (emphasis added) (Bengwenyama Minerals case, 2011, paras. 64–67)

In short, there are various indicia of measures required 'in order to obtain' FPIC, but they do not form a closed list. Ultimately, the adequacy of good faith consultation is assessed based on the facts of a proposed measure. Fairness, natural justice, and reasonable opportunity to make inputs and to be heard serve as key principles in evaluating the conduct of the parties.

2.3 Reasonable and Workable Consultation Benchmarks Required

The standard of good faith consultation must be tailored to the specific circumstances of the approval sought. There is no fixed checklist that can simply be followed to establish that adequate consultation 'in order to obtain' FPIC had taken place. FPIC is not a new legal standard, but rather an objective that underscores the importance of consulting with Indigenous Peoples in the context of their legal, political, social, and economic status. Even though FPIC does not legally imply co-decision-making, at least good faith, honest, and sincere efforts should be made to closely involve indigenous communities in the consultation and decision-making process – ideally, consent should be an objective even if it is not always achievable. As a general principle, consultation implies that parties engage each other in a 'proactive and honest endeavour to find mutually acceptable solutions' (Port Elizabeth Municipality case 2005, para. 39).

In the Tipakalippa case, the Court drew on the standards that have developed under Australia's native title regime concerning 'good faith negotiations' to inform itself on the benchmarks that could be applied to 'consultation' with Indigenous Peoples pursuant to other legislation (Tipakalippa case, 2022). This cross-fertilisation between good faith negotiation, good faith consultation, and FPIC highlights two aspects particularly relevant to this chapter: first, there is no clear legal distinction between efforts to achieve FPIC, good faith consultation, or good faith negotiation; and second, interjurisdictional lessons on good faith consultation can help shape FPIC standards, but those standards must be adapted to the specific circumstances of each dispute and the rights and interests of the Indigenous People involved. Importantly, the obligations arising from the duty to consult must be '*capable of practicable and reasonable discharge* by the person' upon whom the duty rests (emphasis added) (Tipakalippa case, 2022, para. 89).

An essential objective of consultation is to provide the proponent of a development an opportunity to receive information from the relevant indigenous community and hear their perspectives on the potential impact of the project. The key elements of a proposal must be adequately explained to the community concerned in a manner that allows them to understand these elements, seek advice, form an opinion, and respond. 'Effective' and 'fair' participation and the opportunity to make a 'meaningful' contribution thus serve as operating standards, particularly when different sub-communities may have to be consulted (Tipakalippa case 2022, para. 94). It is nevertheless important that seemingly rigid consultation criteria are approached with flexibility and pragmatism. For consultation to be effective and enforceable, it must be practical and 'workable' (Tipakalippa case 2022, para. 96).

In the Tsleil-Waututh Nation case, the Court emphasised that 'deep consultation' must take place if the impact of a proposed development has serious consequences for Indigenous Peoples (Tsleil-Waututh Nation case, 2019, para. 501). This reinforces the earlier observation that the practical requirements for good faith consultation 'in order to' achieve FPIC can be adjusted depending on the nature and scope of a project, its potential impact, and the overall interests at stake. Good faith consultation encompasses all potential interactions with an indigenous community, meaning there is no justification for imposing a different standard called FPIC for certain ventures.

The overarching objective – whether termed consultation, good faith negotiation, or FPIC – is to provide indigenous communities, and where applicable sub-indigenous groups, with a 'reasonable opportunity' to participate in the application process, but with no obligation to consult with everyone who claims to have an interest in the land or in a project (Tipakalippa case 2022, para. 96). In this respect consultation and FPIC have a collective nature whereby the community is consulted. Ultimately, it is essential to 'construe a consultation requirement in a *practical and pragmatic* way that makes a process *both reasonable and workable*' (emphasis added) (Tipakalippa case 2022, para. 109).

2.4 Who Is Entitled to Be Involved in FPIC: Indigenous People or Any Local Community?

FPIC has developed as a term reflecting the special consideration of Indigenous Peoples' rights when seeking approval for projects that may affect their interests. Three notable observations can be made in this respect: first, FPIC is specifically associated with the consultation of Indigenous Peoples particularly concerning their traditional lands; second, not all community consultations, such as environmental impact assessments, should be seen as meeting the standard of FPIC with Indigenous People; and third, not all Indigenous Peoples affected by a measure necessarily fall within the scope of FPIC, as the extent and scale of consultation depend on the nature of their interests. For instance, a large-scale project or one that affects a site of great significance may impact some indigenous communities more than others.

In the Project Sepik case, a dispute arose over who qualifies as an indigenous community entitled to FPIC. It was determined that the obligation to seek FPIC does not apply to every community identifying as indigenous – and even if a community is indigenous, the requirement for FPIC depends on the nature of their interests affected. FPIC applies when consideration is given to the indigenous community's cultural connection to the area, the potential impact of a project on cultural values in a broad sense, the views of the affected group, and whether the nature of the project and the rights asserted justify FPIC (Project Sepik case, 2023, para. 89). The Examiner cited international human rights approaches to FPIC, as follows:

> The human rights case guidance about how significant impacts need to be, to necessitate FPIC, includes: developments threatening the way of life and culture of an Indigenous group; impacts amounting to a denial of the right to enjoy cultural rights in that region; endangering the very survival of the community and its members; and substantially compromising or interfering with culturally significant activities. *These are, obviously, context specific.* (emphasis added) (Project Sepik case, 2023, para. 81.4)

As previously noted, the emphasis of FPIC is on the process and not just the outcome (Project Sepik case 2023, para. 82).

Generally FPIC has a collective element; however, an individual may, pursuant to their individual right to culture or property, or their interest in land, commence proceedings due to an alleged lack of adequate consultation (Fosen case, 2021). Note in this respect the Norwegian Fosen case, in which the Court emphasised that Article 27 of ICCPR, which addresses individual rights, 'must be viewed in context with Article 108 of the Constitution of Norway, which imposes a duty on the state authorities "to create conditions enabling the Sámi people to [collectively] preserve and develop its language, culture and way of life"' (Fosen case, 2021, para. 99).

The South African Baleni case is often cited in discussions on the right of Indigenous Peoples to FPIC, notwithstanding the fact that the dispute in that case did not concern the broad topic of indigenous rights, but rather on the communal rights of a tribal/indigenous community stemming from their long-term occupation of land pursuant to apartheid legislation.[2] The protection accorded by the relevant Act (Informal Land Rights Act, 1996) in that case related specifically to indigenous or tribal communities whose land rights had been affected as a result of the abolishment of the previous homeland system. However, the legislation does not extend the protection of a veto right to all other indigenous or tribal communities whose interests in land

2 The relevant Act (a1) defines community as follows: '"community" means any group or portion of a group of persons whose rights to land are derived from shared rules determining access to land held in common by such group'.

may be affected (Baleni case, 2019). The case illustrates how domestic legislation may grant special consultation rights to some communities but not to others.

From the perspective of case law, the proposition that FPIC is legally distinguishable from good faith consultation is weak. Nonetheless, case law demonstrates that good faith consultation has been enriched and inspired by the special recognition of indigenous interests embodied in the philosophy underpinning FPIC. The effort to achieve FPIC ought not to be viewed as creating a distinct right, but rather a reminder and directive that special consultation measures and procedures may be required when a proposed measure could affect the traditional lands of Indigenous Peoples.

2.5 Importance of Keeping an Open Mind

An essential requirement for good faith consultation 'in order to obtain' FPIC is that the proponent of a measure must commence consultation as soon as is possible in the process the conceptualisation of a proposed measure and before a final decision is made. FPIC is not merely a public relations process to inform indigenous communities of a decision that has already been made. While a proponent may hold strong views on the merits of a proposal, they are also expected to keep an open mind, actively listen to the indigenous community's position, and genuinely absorb and consider what is conveyed to them. Notably, good faith likewise applies to the indigenous community, which must also maintain an open mind, show a willingness to listen to and understand the case being put, and provide a coherent, informed, and credible response to a proposed measure. An indigenous community's refusal to engage in consultation, or its failure to agree on procedural issues may be perceived as close-mindedness and reluctance to engage in good faith (Rita Dempster case, 1999, p. 5). In the Gomeroi case, it was emphasised that good faith focuses on 'assessing the course of a negotiation, measuring it objectively against a standard of honesty, open mindedness and willingness to listen' (Gomeroi People case, 2024, para. 96).

However, indigenous communities face the risk that their participation in a consultation process may lend credibility to the state's eventual approval of a project even if they, as a community, had rejected it. In other words, indigenous participation may provide legitimacy to a process over which they have no control. This is exemplified by the Norwegian Sara case, where the Sámi's participation in deliberations was construed as an endorsement of the outcome – which was clearly not the case given they had objected to the approval

(Sara case, 2017).[3] The Court found as follows in its reasoning that self-determination does not equate to sovereign determination:

> Although the Sami Parliament has not succeeded with its view on all points, the rules implement a *substantial degree of self-determination*. Against this background, I have concluded that Sara's rights under ICCPR article 27 have not been violated. (emphasis added) (Sara case, 2017, para. 94)

In the Barngarla case, the dispute concerned the Australian government's decision to select a site for nuclear waste storage and whether, in the lead-up to the decision, adequate consultation had taken place with the local Aboriginal community. This community, the Barngarla people, regarded the land designated for the waste site as part of their traditional country. Although they did not possess native title over the specific site, their native title area was in close proximity to it. The Court found that despite not holding native title over the designated storage site, the Barngarla people's 'spiritual connection' to this land gave them sufficient interest to object to its development (Barngarla case, 2023, para. 16). Furthermore, the Court held that although the Barngarla people had been consulted on the site's use as a nuclear waste storage facility, the facts indicated 'apprehended bias' on the part of the government in that it had already decided on the site's location *before* consultation commenced (Barngarla case 2023, para. 187). Since the site selection was predetermined, the process was more accurately described as information sharing rather than genuine consultation. Moreover, the consultation was found to have been inadequate, as the public ballot conducted to ascertain local opinion worked to the detriment of the Barngarla people, many of whom were not ratepayers

3 Dunlap cautions against FPIC becoming a 'bureaucratic trap' that potentially undermines the interests of Indigenous Peoples (Dunlap, 2018). He refers to a Mexican case study of FPIC, concluding as follows: 'Instead, the FPIC consultation in Juchitán all but mimicked all the negative features mentioned in the literature review and suffered a conflict of interest between state and corporate collaboration, violated cultural norms, provided inadequate information and also *served as a marketing platform to sell the idea* of the project rather than adequately address the issues raised by participants such as income transparency or social and environmental impacts. Consequently, the FPIC has *served to entrench state power* and reinforce existing political and economic asymmetry between different actors' (emphasis added) (Dunlap, 2018, p. 105). Note also the observation by Cambou about the Norwegian case of Fosen (Fosen case, 2021) that 'in the context of the green transition, consultation is assuredly considered a necessary instrument for guaranteeing human rights, but as the Fosen case illustrates, it is a *double-edged sword* that can either support Indigenous self-determination or legitimise green colonialism when it perpetuates decisions that deprive Indigenous communities from the benefits of their lands and livelihoods' (Cambou, 2024, p. 65).

and thus effectively disenfranchised. Importantly, the Court did not consider the merits of the site's proposed location, but rather the inadequate process that led to its identification and acquisition. The Court also found that the relevant minister had acted dismissively towards the interests and concerns of the Barngarla people (Barngarla case 2023, para. 197).

The Barngarla case offers several relevant insights: First, the purpose of consultation is to ascertain and consider the views of Indigenous Peoples that may otherwise be unknown or unavailable to the proponent. Second, while a proponent may strongly support a proposed development, they must demonstrate an open mind, ensuring that objections and suggestions to mitigate impacts are heard and assessed on their merits. Third, if a community comprises different interest groups – for example, if one part of the wider community is indigenous – consultation practices may have to be adjusted to engage each sub-entity in a manner that reflects its distinct background and interest in the land. Fourth, consulting the broader community through measures like environmental impact assessments or opinion surveys may not satisfy the specific consultation obligations required towards Indigenous Peoples.

2.6 Relevance of Public Interest

The public interest is a relevant consideration when making decisions on measures that may affect indigenous communities. Reasonable steps undertaken to obtain the consent of Indigenous Peoples cannot be construed as an abdication by the state of its regulatory powers and broader obligation to consider the entirety of public interests. Similarly, Indigenous Peoples' participation in consultation cannot be construed as an automatic endorsement of a proposed project by the regulatory authority. Two realities encircle FPIC: first, the state is not bound by an indigenous community's refusal to consent to a proposal; and second, a proposal may be approved despite an indigenous community's opposition to it. If actual consent is not obtained, the state remains the regulatory authority with the power to make a final decision to either reject or approve the proposal and, if necessary, impose relevant conditions. This reinforces the fact that the obligation to make efforts 'in order to obtain' FPIC does not imply a veto but rather requires a good faith consultation process, where the outcome of consultation is relevant but not decisive for the final decision by the state as the regulator. If the state or a court treats an indigenous community's rejection of a proposal as a veto, such a decision may also be subject to review, as in the Forrest case, to determine whether the public interest had been adequately considered.

In the Forrest case in the state of Western Australia, a private entity sought approval to erect ten weirs in a river for the purposes of agricultural development (Forrest case, 2023). The river is protected as an Aboriginal site of importance under the Aboriginal Heritage Act of 1972 (WA). The Minister for Aboriginal Affairs refused approval due to the river's significance to the local Aboriginal people, including the impact the weirs may have on the mythological ancestral snake that created the river and, according to indigenous belief, continues to reside in it. The developer sought a review of the minister's decision with the State Administrative Tribunal. The Tribunal upheld the decision of the minister. The Tribunal concluded that the interests of the Aboriginal community should prevail, as they reflect the community's standards for protecting sites of importance (Forrest case, 2023, paras. 623–630). The developer then appealed to the Supreme Court. The Supreme Court acknowledged the river's importance as an Aboriginal site, but opined that the minister should also have considered the 'general interest' of the proposed development for the wider community.[4] The Court found that the Tribunal, in upholding the decision to reject the development, had not given adequate consideration to the broader community's interests (Forrest appeal case, 2024, para. 118). The Court emphasised the discretionary role of the decision-maker, requiring a balance between the Aboriginal community's interest in protecting a site of importance and the broader community's interest in developing infrastructure and agriculture. The court proceeded to note that while the protection of Aboriginal sites is a primary objective under the Aboriginal Heritage Act, the Act's scope is broader, encompassing not only indigenous interests but also those of the wider community (Forrest appeal case 2024, para. 189). It stated the following about the public interest:

> The statutory reference to the 'general interest of the community' is a *broad concept* which encompasses an evaluation of a range of social and economic factors. It is a concept akin to the identification of the public interest, which generally imports a *discretionary value judgment* to be made by reference to *undefined* factual matters, confined only in so far as the subject matter, scope and purpose of the legislation may enable given reasons to be pronounced

4 Section 18(3) of the Aboriginal Heritage Act provides as follows: 'Where the Committee submits a notice to the Minister under subsection (2) he shall consider its recommendation and *having regard to the general interest of the community* shall either – (a) consent to the use of the land the subject of the notice, or a specified part of the land, for the purpose required, subject to such conditions, if any, as he may specify; or (b) wholly decline to consent to the use of the land the subject of the notice for the purpose required, and shall forthwith inform the owner in writing of his decision' (emphasis added).

> definitely extraneous to any objects the legislature could have had in view. (emphasis added) (Forrest appeal case 2024, para. 190)

This approach reflects the Canadian Supreme Court' view of consultation and the intersection with the state's regulatory powers. In the Tsilhqot'in case, the Court noted that the absence of consent does not imply a legal veto; that, in some instances, the state may use a refusal to consent as an adequate basis for rejecting a proposal; but that if consent is withheld, the government has the discretion to ascertain if the 'proposed incursion on the land is justified' (Tsilhqot'in Nation case, 2014). The Court went on to state that, in exercising its regulatory function, the state must bear in mind its fiduciary obligations towards Indigenous Peoples; the objective pursued by granting access to land must be 'compelling and substantive'; and the goal aimed for by the proposed measure must be weighed against the 'adverse effect' on indigenous interests (Tsilhqot'in Nation case, 2014, para. 77).

The following conclusions of relevance to this chapter can be drawn: first, Indigenous Peoples' right to be consulted arises principally from domestic statute and not from international law, although domestic courts may draw inspiration from international hard and soft law; second, the protection of indigenous customary lands and historic sites is important not only to indigenous communities but also the general public; third, the obligation to take steps 'in order to obtain' FPIC does not create a veto for indigenous communities, as the ultimate regulatory discretion to determine the approval or rejection of a proposal remains with the state. However, the withholding of consent by an indigenous community is a relevant consideration in the state's decision-making process; and fourth, the state's decision to refuse or approve a development that may impact on traditional lands or sites must be based on all relevant considerations, including the wider public interest.

2.7 Language of Communication

The principle of good faith consultation requires that the individuals or communities being consulted must, as far as is practicable, be communicated with through accessible means using a language they understand. While this may not always be feasible for remote indigenous groups or in the case of highly technical subject matters, efforts should at least be made to present information in a way that is understandable and accessible, and for the community to hear submissions in a language in which they can comfortably express themselves.

Practical measures in this regard include on-site meetings, exploring the terrain in question, identifying project sites, visiting villages, using visual materials to explain the project, considering mitigation or compensation measures if the project proceeds, and involving experts such as anthropologists and linguists.

In the Project Sepik case, it was stressed that communication for obtaining FPIC must be conducted in a language the community understands, ensuring they fully comprehend what is being proposed and can respond in their best interests. This obligation extends to engaging with different communities in their own language as much as possible. The following was said:

> Informed consent requires engagement *in a manner and language* which the relevant community can understand. In both parties' material, there is information explaining that Tok Pisin language may not be understood in some areas. The enterprise's material acknowledged the project area involved different cultures and languages. That would suggest that FPIC would require effective engagement within *each of those cultures and languages*... Where FPIC is required from a group, and if English and Tok Pisin is not understood by that group, neither of these measures (volunteer interpreters and written materials in Tok Pisin / English) would be sufficient to enable FPIC. (Project Sepik case, 2023, para. 96)

In the Sustaining the Wild Coast case, the Court identified several practical steps as indicia of measures to ensure a fair good faith consultation process. While not an exhaustive list, these include: providing adequate and timely notifications; offering adequate details for the community to assess the impact of the measure; using a language and technical terms that are understandable to the community; communicating in a language familiar to the community; and publishing notices in media accessible to and used by the community (Sustaining the Wild Coast case, 2024, paras. 21–24). The Court found that in that dispute the consultation 'which was more illusory than real, was thus manifestly inadequate' (Sustaining the Wild Coast case, 2024, para. 24), noting the following about the inadequacy of the medium of communication in the case:

> As is the case with many communities along the Wild Coast, the people of Amadiba mostly get their news from the *radio*. They mainly listen to Ukhozi FM and Umhlobo Wenene. The respondents say that had there been notice or discussion of Shell's proposed seismic blasting on the radio, they would certainly have commented. The *adverts* in the four newspapers were intended to

> notify the public about the proposed project and provide details of the consultation process and information as to how members of the public could provide input in respect of the forthcoming survey. In the circumstances, the *choice of print media was plainly ill-advised.* This was exacerbated by the choice of English and Afrikaans language newspapers. The process, which was *more illusory than real,* was thus manifestly inadequate. (emphasis added) (Sustaining the Wild Coast case, 2024, para. 24)

2.8 The Ongoing Nature of FPIC

Meeting the objective of 'in order to obtain' FPIC can range from a one-off event to an ongoing process, depending on the bundle of rights of the community, the project's overall nature, including its scale, impact, and duration. While some literature attempts to distinguish between consultation as predominantly a single event and FPIC as a continuous process, this distinction is weak and not supported by case law. It is, in fact, the nature of the project and the bundle of rights which dictate whether and when good faith consultation has concluded, or whether there is an ongoing obligation to consult with the indigenous community into the future. The duration of indigenous involvement is determined by what is considered reasonable in the specific circumstances, as some projects may have intergenerational impacts, while others are more immediate and short term.

The ILO summarised the obligation to consult in an effort to achieve consent as follows:

> In keeping with paragraph 2 of Article 6, consultation must take place in accordance with procedures that are appropriate to the circumstances, through the Indigenous Peoples' representative institutions, in good faith and with the objective of achieving agreement or consent to the proposed measures. Appropriate procedures are those that create the conditions necessary to reach an agreement or consent concerning the proposed measures. This means that the expression appropriate procedures must be understood in relation to the aims of the consultation. There is *no single model of appropriate procedures*, which should take into account national circumstances, the circumstances of the Indigenous Peoples concerned and the nature of the measures which are the object of the consultation process. (emphasis added) (ILO Brazil 2009, para. 142)

The Project Sepik case raised the question of whether FPIC should be considered a one-off or an ongoing obligation. In this case, the development was of a long duration, possibly taking many years to materialise (Project Sepik case, 2023). The Examiner emphasised that it is not necessary for all FPIC processes to be completed before a development approval application is submitted to the state. Sometimes, continuous consultation is required such as when a development occurs in multiple phases or has ongoing impacts. In such a scenario, FPIC entails an ongoing obligation of good faith consultation throughout the project's implementation. The following was declared in this regard:

> It is not correct that FPIC must be obtained from everyone relevant before any application process for development can begin (see paragraph 85 above). The information and engagement necessary for FPIC may only become known as part of that application and assessment processes. Particularly where the proposal is for many decades (construction and mining here is expected for over 30 years and the hydro power facility for 100 years) *FPIC has ongoing relevance*, as the enterprise has noted. (emphasis added) (Project Sepik case, 2023, para. 105.2)

2.9 New Topics Possibly Requiring Consultation

The required topics of consultation with Indigenous Peoples vary depending on the nature of the proposed measure and its potential impact on indigenous rights and interests. It basically comes back to the bundle of each community in respect to its traditional laws and culture. For example, in the Gomeroi case, it was declared that the potential impacts of climate change on traditional lands are a relevant consideration in good faith negotiations (Gomeroi People case, 2024). Despite objections by the indigenous community that the project may affect and even contribute to climate change, the NNTT of Australia decided the project could proceed without any regard to the potential climate impact as a relevant consideration. On review, it was held that a wide range of public interests, including a project's impact on the environment, may – pursuant to the relevant legislation (Native Title Act, 1993 Section 39(1))[5] – form part of any objections raised against it (Gomeroi People case, 2024, para. 172). This aligns with the observation made in Canada, that it is 'well established that climate change is causing significant environmental, economic and human harm nationally and internationally, with especially high impacts … on Indigenous Peoples' (Greenhouse Gas Pollution case, 2021). An argument can therefore be made that FPIC should not only cover direct

5 Section 39 of the Native Title Act 1993 requires the NNTT to consider in making its determination (among other factors) 'any public interest in the doing of the act' and 'any other matter that the arbitral body considers relevant' (see s 39(1)(e); s 39(1)(f)).

impacts on indigenous lands but also secondary impacts such as those caused by major projects on the wider environment.

2.10 Interaction between FPIC and Domestic Law

States are, pursuant to UNDRIP, encouraged to enact FPIC within their domestic laws and policies. There is, however, no pre-established formula for operationalising FPIC, with each state free to decide how to give effect to the objectives of UNDRIP. Only a few nations explicitly include the term FPIC in their domestic legislation,[6] though many refer to consultation when engaging Indigenous Peoples.

For example, it is common for statutes to refer to consultation with Indigenous Peoples or local communities when their rights and interests may be affected, but without mention of FPIC. In Canada, it has been recognised that the state bears an 'obligation to consult and accommodate Indigenous groups' since the 'fundamental objective of the modern law of aboriginal and treaty rights is the reconciliation of aboriginal peoples and non-aboriginal peoples and their respective claims, interests and ambitions' (Anderson case, 2022, para. 25). Although state laws must be viewed through the prism of UNDRIP as a 'contextual factor', FPIC does not constitute a right of veto (Kebaowek First Nation case, 2025, para. 183).

In the State Forest case in Indonesia, an indigenous community objected to the classification of forests traditionally known as customary forests, as 'state' forests in legislation, implying state ownership (State Forest case, 2012). The Constitutional Court granted relief by ordering the removal of the word 'state' from the relevant statute. The Court cited the 1996 Rio Declaration on Environment and Development as an example of the importance placed by international law on the role of Indigenous Peoples in protecting the environment, a function that the government is duty-bound to support. This illustrates that although international instruments such as ILO 169 and UNDRIP are not legally binding in Indonesia, these developments have had a 'major impact on the development of indigenous rights' in the country (Arizona and Cohen, 2024, p. 189).

---

6 Note, for example, in the Philippines, The Indigenous Peoples Rights Act of 1997, Republic Act No. 8371 (1997) which establishes the following about FPIC: '[T]he consensus of all members of the ICCs/IPs [Indigenous Peoples] to be determined in accordance with their respective customary laws and practices, free from any external manipulation, interference and coercion, and obtained after fully disclosing the intent and scope of the activity, in a language and process understandable to the community.' However, see Magno for challenges arising from and shortcomings exhibited in the legislation (Magno, 2013).

In South Africa, measures were adopted to protect the rights of individuals whose informal residence was on land that formerly formed part of the apartheid-era homelands. The legislation was not enacted pursuant to FPIC, and is not directed at all Indigenous Peoples but rather at specific categories of tribal communities. The Interim Protection of Informal Land Rights Act 31 of 1996 addresses the acquisition of communal land, providing that land *may not* be acquired without consent and, if held communally, only in compliance with the community's customs and usage (s2(1) and (2)). The acquisition of communal land requires a process to be followed, as specified below:

> a decision to dispose of any such right may *only* be taken by a majority of the holders of such rights present or represented at a meeting convened for the purpose of considering such disposal and of which they have been given sufficient notice, and in which they have bad a reasonable opportunity to participate' (s 2(4)). As explained in greater detail below, actual consent is not required in international law under FPIC regardless of the word 'consent' being used. It is only when a statute specifically mandates consent, as in the case of the *Interim Protection of Informal Land Rights Act*, that actual consent of the land-owing community is required. (Baleni case 2019, para. 79)

Although the Baleni case is often cited in literature as an example of FPIC in action in South Africa, the international citations considered by Basson added little, if any, value to the outcome of the dispute.[7] In fact, her statement that 'granting special protection to these communities by requiring consent as opposed to mere consultation *is in accordance with international law*' (emphasis added) (Baleni case 2019, para. 78) is open to challenge, as there is no binding treaty in international law that mandates the consent of Indigenous Peoples when their interests in land are affected (De Villiers, 2023d, p. 80).

In a similar vein, the Supreme Court of Canada has established that consultation with Indigenous Peoples forms part of Canadian law (Kebaowek First Nation case, 2025, para. 183). Importantly, the nature of the duty to consult and the right, if any, of an indigenous community to veto a measure 'vary

7 Barrie argues that the Baleni case has 'far reaching implications' for the South African land reform process due to the standard of consent required pursuant to international law (Barrie, 2024a, p. 900). My proposition is that Justice Basson erred by stating that international law requires free, prior, and informed consent, as is understood by actual consent, instead of a striving towards consent. Barrie's conclusion is therefore also challenged, including his assertion that FPIC '*has evolved* into a norm of customary international law' (emphasis added) (Barrie, 2024a, p. 906).

with the circumstances'. In the Haida Nation case, the Court described the varying degree of responsibilities and rights as follows:

> from a minimum "duty to discuss important decisions" where the "breach is less serious or relatively minor"; through the "significantly deeper than mere consultation" that is required in "most cases"; to "full consent of [the] aboriginal nation" on very serious issues. (Haida Nation case, 2004, para. 24)

The collective right of an indigenous community within the context of consultation and FPIC reflects the dynamic interpretation of individual rights such as the right to culture, property, and self-determination, as found in international law instruments like the ICESCR and ICCPR. The Norwegian Fosen case is noteworthy in this respect: the Court emphasised that Article 27 of ICCPR 'must be viewed in context with Article 108 of the Constitution of Norway, which imposes a duty on the state authorities 'to create conditions enabling the Sámi people to preserve and develop its language, culture and way of life' (Fosen case, 2021, para. 99). The Court, in rejecting the argument that Article 27 only protects individual rights and not the rights of a community, declared:

> According to Article 27, the protection applies to "persons belonging to such minorities". This wording in the first part of the provision indicates that the protection is enjoyed by the individuals in a minority group. However, the provision further states that the individuals have the right to enjoy their own culture, etc. "in community with the other members of their group". This element was added to clarify the collective nature of the provision....Article 27 protects the individual, but adds that the protection has certain collective features...Against this background, I find that Article 27 at the outset protects individuals in a minority. However, the minorities' culture is practiced in community, *which gives the protection a collective nature.* (emphasis added) (Fosen case 2021, para. 104–106)

2.11 Discrimination Possibly Implied by a Failure to Consult

Failure to consult an indigenous community may not only breach the duty to obtain FPIC pursuant to UNDRIP, but may also constitute a violation of the constitutional right of indigenous individuals to equal treatment and protection against discrimination. As explained above, the rights to self-determination, property, and culture display both individual and collective elements. For example, failing to engage in consultation when property rights are affected may constitute discrimination not only against the individual but also against the community to which they belong. In a case involving the Sámi people of Sweden, the UN Committee on the Elimination of Racial Discrimination ruled that neglecting to consult with the local indigenous community about the impact of a mining project may constitute discriminatory conduct. The Committee noted that disregarding the territorial rights of the community and

> their right to offer free, prior and informed consent whenever their rights may be affected by projects carried out in their traditional territories constitutes a form of discrimination as it results in nullifying or impairing the recognition, enjoyment or exercise by Indigenous Peoples, on an equal footing, of their rights to their ancestral territories, natural resources and, as a result, their identity. (Lars-Anders Ågren case 2013, para. 6.7)

2.12 FPIC and the Challenges of Intra-community Dissent

Literature often presents the FPIC process as a straightforward interaction between the proponent of a measure and an indigenous community, assuming a unanimous position within the community. In reality, however, members of an indigenous community may hold diverse opinions on a proposed measure. Intra-community differences may complicate the determination of when efforts 'in order to obtain' FPIC have met the required threshold.[8] A simple majority vote by an indigenous community may not accurately reflect the whole community's interests, not to mention that such a voting mechanism may also be culturally inappropriate. At the same time, expecting unanimity is probably unrealistic, as internal factions may have differing views on a response to a measure for various reasons.[9] The nuances arising from commu-

8 Although commonly overlooked in the literature and jurisprudence regarding FPIC, it is vital that the body representing the indigenous community must also be subject to some form of internal scrutiny to ensure that it is indeed representative of the community; that the negotiators consult with the community; that they provide feedback and seek instructions from the community; and that the body fairly distributes whatever benefits may be received as a result of negotiations. In this regard, consider also the findings of Almanza and Salazar that the indigenous bodies they analysed were often exclusionary, stifled internal opposition and disagreement, and came to disempower the very communities they were supposed to empower (Almanza and Salazar, 2022).

9 During my time as a legal representative for indigenous communities in Australia, I had experienced of several native title negotiations where the majority of a community may support an initiative, while some Elders, though in the minority, would oppose a measure. In such cases, great sensitivity was needed to ascertain whether a majority decision is truly the culturally 'correct' approach, or whether a minority 'veto' by some Elders may in fact be justified.

nities highlight the challenges proponents face in taking reasonable steps 'in order to obtain' FPIC.

The Munkara case illustrates the potential complexity of the interplay between FPIC, state regulatory authority, and indigenous community sub-group opinions. In the case, the proponent had obtained the necessary approvals from the regulatory authority to proceed with a project after consulting with the indigenous community. However, the project became the subject of an injunction at the last minute due to an allegation that consultation had not taken place with a particular sub-group regarding the possible disturbance of important Aboriginal sites (Munkara case, 2024). Ultimately, the objectors' complaint was dismissed, but this came at a significant delay and cost to the proponent and left uncertainty about the extent to which third parties can rely on the finality of an approval process by the regulatory authority (Tipakalippa case 2022, para. 104; Munkara case 2024; Munkara consent orders cost 2024).

In New Zealand, the ICCPR made some pertinent observations concerning consultation with the Māori and the response to minority views within the community. In the Mahuika case, an agreement reached between the government and the Māori on fishing regulations was contested by some Māori individuals. They filed a complaint alleging that the state was violating their cultural rights (and its international obligations) under the ICCPR. The Committee dismissed the complaint, stating:

> In such circumstances, where the right of individuals to enjoy their own culture is in conflict with the exercise of parallel rights by other members of the minority group, or of the minority as a whole, the Committee may consider whether the limitation in issue is in the interests of all members of the minority and whether there is reasonable and objective justification for its application to the individuals who claim to be adversely affected. While it is a matter of concern that the settlement and its process *have contributed to divisions amongst Māori*, nevertheless, the Committee concludes that the State party has, by engaging itself in the process of broad consultation before proceeding to legislate, and by paying specific attention to the sustainability of Māori fishing activities, taken the necessary steps to ensure that the Fisheries Settlement and its enactment through legislation, including the Quota Management System, are compatible with article 27. (Mahuika case 2000, para. 9.6, 9.8)

In a 2022 judgement in Australia, the Court noted that while there is no statutory definition of 'consult', Australian courts have interpreted the concept as requiring that 'the underlying premise of the authorisation provisions is to give all group members a "reasonable opportunity" to participate in decision-making…' (Tipakalippa case, 2022, para. 104). In this case, the company seeking approval to lay an undersea pipeline failed to provide satisfactory evidence of having consulted with all the sub-groups of the indigenous community that could potentially be affected. The defence raised was that the development proponent had in fact consulted with the affected community through their legal corporation. Nonetheless, the Court held that the consultation with the applicant's clan as a sub-group within the community had been inadequate (Tipakalippa case, 2022).

These examples underscore the challenges faced by those seeking access to land to work out whom to consult, whether the consultation participants are adequately representative and authorised, and whether they will properly engage in internal consultation with other members of their community. Notably, the Court in the Munkara case did not suggest that all the community's sub-groups must be in agreement with a proposal. Rather, the Court held that the proponent should demonstrate that consultation with these sub-groups had been attempted. While approval was ultimately granted for the project to proceed after the company had provided additional evidence of its consultation, objections from a sub-group caused substantial delays. The Court dismissed the objections by the sub-group, criticising aspects of both the lay and expert evidence presented in an attempt to halt the project (Munkara case, 2024). The presiding judge described the parts of expert evidence as 'so lacking integrity that no weight can be placed on them'. The Court ultimately awarded A$9 million in legal costs against the Environmental Defenders Office which had, frivolously in view of the Court, supported and financed the proceeding.[10]

2.13 The Role of Government in the FPIC Process

The state's role in the steps taken 'in order to' achieve FPIC is multifaceted. First, the state has the regulatory authority to implement legislation and policies that give effect to its international commitments regarding consultation

10 In 2023, independent anthropologist Dr Brendan Corrigan compiled a report, finding that after extensive consultation with the affected indigenous communities, no cultural heritage sites that might be impacted by the proposed pipeline could be identified. Despite the local Aboriginal land council's rejection of this finding, the relevant regulating agency gave approval for the project to proceed based on the report's conclusions. After further consultation had taken place and approval granted for the project to proceed, a sub-group sought an injunction on the grounds that they had not been consulted. The application was ultimately dismissed, with the Court criticising both the lay and expert evidence presented – but only after a substantial delay was caused to the project and additional costs incurred (Munkara case, 2024).

with Indigenous Peoples. Second, the state is usually the final decision-maker on granting access to lands for development. Third, the state may itself have to engage in consultation, as it may be the entity seeking access to land. Finally, the state bears the responsibility of overseeing the process to ensure that FPIC is properly obtained. If indigenous land without a lawful process, is taken the state may be liable for compensation (Yunupingu appeal case, 2025). In the Saramaka case, the state's role was described as follows:

> First, the State must ensure the effective participation of the members of the Saramaka people, in conformity with their customs and traditions, regarding any development, investment, exploration or extraction plan (...). Second, the State must guarantee that [Indigenous Peoples] receive a reasonable benefit from any such plan within their territory. [Third], the State must ensure that no concession will be issued (...) unless and until independent and technically capable entities, with the State's supervision, perform a prior environmental and social impact assessment. (Saramaka case, 2007, para. 129)

2.14 Actual Consent Not the Required Standard

While 'actual consent' may be the ideal, international law does not mandate that agreement *must* be achieved, stipulating instead that serious consideration be given to the position put forward by the indigenous community. The ILO has commented as follows on the objective of reaching consent:

> The Committee considers that in the process of implementation of the law, all the representative organizations of peoples or communities should be able to participate and be consulted about legislative or administrative measures that may affect them directly, with the *objective of achieving agreement or consent.* The Committee points out, however, that Article 6 does not stipulate that consent must be obtained in order for the consultations to be valid but it does require pursuit of the objective of achieving consent, which means setting in *motion a process* of dialogue and genuine exchange between the parties to be carried *out in good faith.* (emphasis added) (ILO Argentina 2008, para. 81)

3 Conclusion

This chapter examined judgements to identify indicia regarding (a) the approaches adopted by various courts and expert bodies to ascertain whether consultation with Indigenous Peoples had been adequate and consistent with the standard of 'in order to obtain' FPIC, (b) the standards used by the courts and expert bodies to ascertain 'in order to obtain' FPIC, and (c) the reasonable steps required 'in order to obtain' FPIC.

The jurisprudence shows that courts and expert bodies focus on the process followed 'in order to obtain' FPIC, not the actual merits of an indigenous community's reasons for withholding consent – unless the position it adopts is blatantly unreasonable. It is acknowledged in jurisprudence that parties may hold strong views, disagree, or attempt to drive a hard bargain. It is also accepted that there is no legal obligation for a party to adjust its position against its own best interests, or solely to accommodate the other side. Consultation can be robust and even bruising. However, the participating parties must engage honestly, demonstrate a genuine willingness to listen, make serious efforts to accommodate each other, and adopt communication processes suited to the specific circumstances. Engagement must be sincere, not merely window-dressing designed to inform an indigenous community of a pre-determined outcome under the guise of consultation. On the other hand, an indigenous community cannot use the consultation process simply to object to a proposal in an arbitrary manner, without explaining the reasons, or providing proper evidence, to support its opposition.

Case law does not distinguish between good faith consultation and FPIC. While literature often portrays FPIC as a more lofty and prolonged form of consultation, this proposition has not been embraced by courts. Courts tend to be comfortable with the obligations associated with good faith consultation. Courts have been open to expanding and reinterpreting established understandings of consultation to fit the context of indigenous consultation. When FPIC is referenced in judgments, it is typically used in a generic sense, not as a legal term but rather as a substitute or equivalent for good faith consultation.

FPIC represents a fresh approach to consultation rather than a new and distinct legal norm. There are no rigid set of criteria that can be ticked off to prove the adequacy of the process followed 'in order to obtain' FPIC. Instead, the entirety of the parties' conduct is assessed and reviewed within the context of the specific project and the indigenous interests involved, rather than in the abstract. It is accepted in jurisprudence that the more severe the impact of a project on the interests of an indigenous community, the greater the effort should be to obtain FPIC from this community. Meanwhile, the greater the potential benefit to the general public, the more detailed the objections from the indigenous community must be in explaining why approval should not be granted. In essence, this is a logical extension of the rules of administrative review, the principles of procedural fairness, and the tenets of natural justice.

At the same time, there is also a recognition that indigenous communities may hold differing views, and that good faith consultation may, in practice, be very complex, potentially leading to confusing or even contradictory outcomes. Consultation processes must be structured in a way that allows for at least some degree of certainty and predictability to ensure their effectiveness. Courts are generally willing to uphold the legal norms associated with good faith consultation, and to apply and expand these as new circumstances emerge.

Ultimately, however, regardless of a consultation process' outcome, the state retains its regulatory authority to determine the approval or rejection of new projects.

CHAPTER 8

FPIC from a Non-Judicial Perspective: OECD National Contact Points

1 Introduction

The private sector often bears the burden of FPIC, as private enterprises must ensure compliance, both legal and practical, with local, municipal, and international requirements for consulting with Indigenous Peoples. Failure to comply with good faith consultation standards, even if only alleged failure, can be costly for a private enterprise since it may give rise to project delays, litigation, reputational damage, shareholder criticism, political instability, and financier concerns. Although, strictly speaking, a private enterprise only needs to adhere to the regulatory authority of the nation in which it operates, international social norms and standards – including conditions imposed by financiers, shareholder expectations, and public opinion – increasingly demand compliance with international soft legal norms concerning FPIC – even when a country's regulatory regime is not as stringent as soft international law. The notion of being a good international citizen imposes obligations on private enterprises that may exceed the municipal legal requirements of the country in which they operate. Should a private enterprise fall short in its FPIC obligations, the court of public opinion may ultimately turn out to be far harsher than a court of justice (Chapter 9).

The private sector faces multiple, and sometimes contradictory, regulatory regimes encompassing domestic laws, international standards, industry regulations, public opinions, and indigenous expectations. Adding to this complexity, third-party activists may pursue their own agendas under the banner of indigenous concerns. Navigating a pathway through approval processes can therefore be challenging, risky and complicated. It's important to recognise that the different processes can lead to inconsistent, even conflicting, outcomes. For example, a municipal regulatory authority may approve a project while shareholders remain dissatisfied; domestic legal and policy requirements may be met, yet an industry body expresses concern; or an indigenous community may appear to endorse a project, only for one of its sub-groups to object due to alleged inadequate consultation (Munkara case 2024, Mahuika case 2000, para. 9.6, 9.8).

 HTTPS://DOI.ORG/10.1163/9789004724792-009

In response to these challenges, some in the private sector has sought to claim the moral high ground by developing universal standards that require corporations to uphold human rights norms through industry self-regulation, regardless of the legal and policy regime of the country where they operate. As a result, industry self-regulation has taken on a supra-national character, whereby companies are held accountable by their peers irrespective of domestic regulatory regimes. Significant steps in this regard include: the 2011 endorsement by the UN Human Rights Council of the UN Guiding Principles on Business and Human Rights (UNGPs) (UNHRC Corporations 2011); the adoption of the OECD Guidelines for Multinational Enterprises by the OECD Investment Committee (OECD Guidelines 2011 & OECD Guidelines 2023); and the ILO's 2017 adoption of amended standards in the Tripartite Declaration of Principles concerning Multinational Enterprises and Social Policy (ILO MNE Declaration & ILO MNE Declaration 2017).[1]

These three instruments commit global private enterprises to respecting fundamental human rights in their conduct, regardless of the country in which they operate. While the instruments do not have formal legal status, they reflect social and industry norms based on self-regulation requiring businesses to uphold human rights, including indigenous rights, in their activities. The norms reflected by these instruments serve as a minimum standard, independent of municipal legal requirements. As soft law, the instruments are not legally enforceable, but nevertheless demand compliance in a social and moral sense.

An essential aspect of business self-regulation is meeting the obligation to take the necessary steps to seek FPIC when engaging with Indigenous Peoples. The OECD Guidelines elaborate as follows:

> Enterprises should pay special attention to any particular adverse impacts on individuals, for example human rights defenders, who may be at heightened risk due to marginalisation, vulnerability or other circumstances, individually or as members of certain groups or populations, *including Indigenous Peoples*. OECD due diligence guidance, including the OECD Due Diligence Guidance on Responsible Business Conduct, the OECD Due Diligence Guidance on Meaningful Stakeholder Engagement in the Extractive Sector, and the OECD-FAO Guidance for Responsible Agricultural Supply Chains provides further practical guidance in this regard, including in relation to *Free, Prior and Informed Consent* (FPIC). (OECD Guidelines, 2023, p. 26)

1 Curiously, the ILO MNE Declaration does not specifically reference FPIC despite ILO 169's leading role in promoting greater indigenous involvement and consultation.

Notably, private enterprises are not subject to compliance or direct regulation under international human rights protection treaties. They are, therefore, not directly bound by ILO 169, UNDRIP, or other human rights treaties. Instead, it is the state that is a party to treaties or a signatory to declarations, making the state accountable for any breaches of international norms within its territorial jurisdiction. States, in turn, must enact legislation and adopt policies that extend respect for and adherence to international norms to private entities operating within their borders. As explained below, the OECD Guidelines seek to provide a voice for individuals and communities whose views have been 'structurally locked out' by existing domestic consultation and judicial mechanisms (Bhatt and Erdem Turkelli, 2021, p. 447).

Importantly, even if state legislation or policies are deficient concerning FPIC, industry obligations may still be placed on enterprises to seek FPIC from indigenous communities on whose lands they operate. For example, the OECD-FAO Guidance for Responsible Agricultural Supply Chains of 2016 outlines the duty of private enterprises to seek FPIC, even in the absence of domestic legal mandates:

> In countries *where FPIC is not mandated,* enterprises should consider local expectations, the risks posed to Indigenous Peoples and to the operations as a result of local opposition… Agree with affected Indigenous Peoples on a consultation process for *working towards seeking FPIC.* This should identify the specific current and future activities where consent should be sought… Recognise the process of seeking FPIC as *iterative rather than a one-off discussion.* Continuous dialogue with the local community will lead to a trust relationship and a balanced agreement that will benefit the investment across all phases of the project. (emphasis added) (OECD Guidance for Responsible Agricultural Supply Chains 2016, 80)

An enterprise may therefore comply with a municipal norm, only to face criticism for non-compliance with an international norm, an industry self-regulatory norm, or an indigenous norm that requires efforts to achieve FPIC. In this respect the obligations placed on private enterprises can seem confusing or even contradictory. The Juukan Gorge debacle in Australia is a case in point (Chapter 9). Rio Tinto received governmental approval to destroy an Aboriginal site (rock caves) as part of its mining activities. However, due to the ensuing public outcry and a scathing review of procedures preceding the blasting, the company suffered extensive international humiliation and embarrassment (Chapter 9; Parliament Juukan Gorge 2020; Final Report Juukan 2021).

This raises some obvious questions: How do the different formal and informal regulatory norms concerning indigenous consultation intersect? When is consultation deemed adequate and concluded? If national laws and regulatory authorities are not the primary determinants of approval, then what is? Most importantly, how reliable and final is approval by a state regulatory body if non-state entities can challenge, delay, or even derail a project? There are no simple answers to these questions, and I do not propose to develop any responses. However, it is notable that the environments in which corporations operate often feature overlapping, competing, and even contradictory norms.

It is no surprise that private enterprises have identified the so-called social license to operate as one of the greatest risks and uncertainties they face in a world where environmental, indigenous, and social interests are receiving ever growing attention (Ernst Young, 2010, pp. 3–7). Ernst Young assessed the situation as follows:

> Even when miners operate *in accordance with the law and their formal license*, issues can arise, and executives will be held accountable. The importance of regular formal and informal reviews and ongoing discussions of LTO with local communities and traditional landowners is critical. (emphasis added) (Ernst Young 2010, 5)

The OECD's creation of country-based National Contact Points (NCPs) has become an interesting instrument of industry self-regulation. These conciliation and standard-setting bodies function like tribunals in a non-judicial capacity, unlike courts. NCPs can hear disputes concerning business practices and duly recommend actions. The following section focuses on the establishment of these National Contact Points under the OECD's auspices. As part of self-regulation, the NCPs provide a platform for addressing complaints against private enterprise conduct, particularly in relation to interactions with Indigenous Peoples, which aligns with the themes elaborated on in this book.

2 Self-Regulatory Framework for Corporations through NCPs

While the three business-led instruments mentioned above – the UNGPs, the OECD Guidelines, and the ILO MNE Declaration – do not have the force of law, both separately and collectively represent self-regulating norms for respecting human rights in terms of business practices. Although FPIC is not a right in itself, the concept underlying it includes an emphasis on private enterprise having to seek the consent of Indigenous Peoples both prior to and throughout the duration of a project. These instruments have been endorsed by UN agencies and reflect the corporate sector's recognition of the importance of the social license to operate in general, and more specifically how private enterprise should address indigenous rights.

The OECD's NCPs are an institutional arrangement designed to give effect to self-regulation. Essentially the NCPs are state-based grievance mechanisms that are aimed at ensuring responsible business conduct, the NCPs operate in a non-judicial manner in response to complaints about corporate activities, and their outcomes are voluntary adhered to. While any complaint can be brought to an NCP, this chapter specifically focuses on complaints made by Indigenous Peoples regarding land access issues.

NCPs are agencies established and funded by governments to promote the OECD Guidelines. They hear disputes about grievances in a non-judicial setting, aiming to resolve a dispute amicably or to provide advisory recommendations. Fifty-two governments have established NCPs to date (Annual Report NCP Activity, 2025). States are responsible for funding the operations of NCPs, providing information to the public about their existence, offering them administrative and logistical support, and explaining how a complaint can be submitted. In essence, NCPs should be legitimate, accessible, predictable, equitable, transparent, rights-compatible, and serve as a source of continuous learning (Pulver, 2022, p. 217). The functioning and operations of each NCP are, in turn, subject to peer review, typically conducted by 2–4 representatives from different NCPs. Peer review reports are published to encourage learning, transparency, and accountability among NCPs (OECD Peer Reviews, 2024).

The OECD describes the NCPs as follows:

> NCPs make up a network and a community of practitioners, dealing with a wide array of impacts involving companies either through their operations or their supply chains. To deliver on this broad mandate, governments have the flexibility to organise their NCP in the form and structure they deem most appropriate. While there is no prescribed model, NCPs must operate in accordance with a number of *'core criteria'*, namely visibility, accessibility, transparency and accountability. In addition, NCPs must handle cases in a way that is impartial, predictable, equitable and compatible with the Guidelines. (OECD NCPs Guidelines, 2024)

Ideally, NCPs do not operate in isolation from host-state policies, instead pursuing so-called policy coherence which seeks to harmonise the OECD

Guidelines with relevant prevailing state legislation and policies. The non-adversarial and non-judicial approach of NCPs is aimed at helping private enterprise to gain insight into the shortcomings of their approach to engagement with Indigenous Peoples, rather than adopting an adversarial stance. Since the inception of NCPs in 2000, around 700 complaints have been lodged with them, although relatively few (around 20) have dealt with indigenous issues.

The NCP process implies, in short, that any individual or corporate entity with a legitimate interest in a matter can commence a proceeding before the relevant NCP (Buhmann, 2018). Legal representation is not required. The NCP hearing process is flexible and can involve both written and oral submissions and evidence. The remedies on offer are non-judicial and non-binding; they may include dismissal of the complaint, mediation and reconciliation, recommendations, or a determination in the form of a final statement (OECD NCP Guidelines 2024). Parties may also withdraw from a proceeding if agreement is reached between them (Indigenous community case, 2023). An NCP may also decline to investigate or report on a matter if there are ongoing parallel court proceedings that involve overlapping issues (Olephiri Franklin Igoma of Uwema Aminigboko Community case, 2021). Furthermore, a NCP may suspend an investigation if a parallel review or reconsideration process is underway (Hart and Fox, 2024, p. 4). Since a complaint may be lodged either in the country where a company conducts business or in the country where it is registered, there is a risk of more than one NCP receiving the same complaint. In such cases, a 'lead NCP' may need to be agreed upon between the NCPs involved to handle the complaint (Hart and Fox 2024, 5).

There is an continuing debate about the effectiveness of the NCPs, with particular regard to their accessibility and the remedies they offer (Backer, 2018). Despite being described as 'one of the most important frameworks for responsible business conduct' (Gottlieb, 2023), NCPs risk having their credibility undermined due to their inability to make binding declarations. At the same time, however, their non-legal nature may make them more effective at joint problem solving – the soft law outcomes they produce, including recommendations, can still sometimes have 'bite' (Achtouk-Spivak and Garden, 2022). Sanchez suggests government support for NCPs enhances their status and potential impact (Sanchez, 2015, p. 20). An OECD study published in 2020 found that from 2011 to 2019, around 47% of complaints handled by NCPs led to companies adjusting their policies, while up to around 40% resulted in some form of agreement between the parties (OECD Report 2020).

While this chapter does not assess the effectiveness of the NCPs, it is useful to examine the outcomes of some proceedings where NCPs have considered the concepts of FPIC and good faith consultation regarding Indigenous Peoples. Although NCP findings and recommendations do not carry legal weight, the opinions can help clarify the practical steps required from private enterprises to comply with the obligation of good faith consultation in pursuit of FPIC.

The non-judicial nature of NCPs has advantages and drawbacks. On one hand, the absence of an adversarial approach may foster learning and self-reflection in an environment focused on improvement of relationships rather than blame for agreement not being reached. On the other hand, their lack of enforceability and real legal-teeth may erode the credibility of NCP findings and recommendations (Ruggie and Nelson, 2015). Furthermore, the option of resorting to an NCP may encourage forum-shopping, where parties choose to pursue a complaint through this avenue rather than a municipal court, believing it may offer them a better chance of a favourable outcome or at least to put the proponent under time and shareholder pressure.

NCP findings are not a source of rights, but they may serve as a 'source of insight' (Buhmann, 2018, p. 92). The growing case load on NCPs due to complaints by indigenous communities, underscores the increasing significance of corporate engagement with such communities (Pulver, 2022, p. 244). The outcomes of NCP processes regarding Indigenous Peoples display similar requirements for effective consultation as those identified through judicial processes. The advantage of NCP processes, however, is that they establish some level of universality in supra-national industry norms, whereas municipal judgements are often limited to local relevance and tied to the specifics of the local municipal regulatory regime. Although courts may be informed about relevant industry practices through NCP recommendations or outcomes, courts have not generally cited NCP decisions in municipal dispute resolution related to FPIC.

3 Selected NCP Findings Concerning FPIC

This section provides a brief overview of a few selected disputes brought before NCPs that involved issues related to indigenous consultation and FPIC. It is not an in-depth analysis of the findings and recommendations provided in each case, but it aims to complement the previous chapter which focused on decisions of a legal character. The non-judicial findings and observations of NCPs may, in due course, inform judicial processes, much like NCPs themselves can draw on municipal and international jurisprudence.

Comparisons of judicial and NCP outcomes reveal a common-sense approach to consultation, emphasising that indigenous communities affected by a measure should be given a reasonable opportunity to participate meaningfully in consultations regarding the merits of the proposed project, as well as potential alternatives to its scope, scale, and location, and the conditions for its approval.

3.1 Meaningful Participation

The principle that consultation should provide Indigenous Peoples with an opportunity to participate in meaningful deliberations affecting their traditional lands is a consistent theme in international law (Indigenous Federations from Peru case, 2025). There is no fixed definition of 'meaningful' in the context of FPIC, but the word conveys an objective: Indigenous communities should have the opportunity to influence outcomes, receive respect and a genuine hearing before any final decisions are made, be communicated with clearly and understandably, and engaged in ways that acknowledge their customs and traditions. While the requirement for 'meaningful' consultation does not imply the existence of a veto if unmet, it does signify a qualitative standard – less than co-decision-making but requiring a process in which indigenous views and positions are taken into consideration, and taken seriously, when striving to secure an agreement.

In the Survival International case, the NCP's final statement criticised the company concerned for failing to provide the indigenous community with adequate and timely information about the proposed project and for not sufficiently involving them in the process (Survival International case, 2009). The company only gave notice of its intended operations in English language newspapers and no special allowance was made to accommodate the high level of illiteracy within the indigenous community. Moreover, the project's emphasis was solely on its economic merit of the proposed project to the company, without adequate regard for India's international obligations under various human rights instruments or the potential impact on the affected indigenous community (Survival International case, 2009, paras. 13–16).

The NCP recommended that the company engage with the indigenous community in good faith, according it timely and meaningful participation by, inter alia, considering options to mitigate impacts, to identify alternative infrastructure locations, to consider possible relocation of some community members, and to devise other practical steps to ensure that the consultation outcomes were not a mere 'paper policy' but could translate into 'concrete procedures and actions on the ground' (Survival International 2009, paras 21–22). The report stated:

> As explained above, the UK NCP only found evidence of two consultations on the construction of the mine in February and March 2003. However, neither of these consultations can be considered adequate for the reasons also explained above. The UK NCP has not found any evidence, either in documentary form or video recordings, that confirms that the Dongria Kondh were consulted in an *adequate and timely* manner and that their views had been collected and taken into account. (emphasis added) (Survival International 2009, para. 49)

In the Indigenous Federations from Peru case, it was observed that although there is no set definition of 'meaningful participation', it is expected that enterprises 'apply practices that foster a relationship of confidence and mutual trust between enterprises and the societies in which they operate, and to engage in consultation with the communities directly affected by the environmental, health and safety policies of the enterprise and by their implementation. This means that enterprises are expected to enter into reliable, fair and reciprocal relationships with the local communities' (Indigenous Federations from Peru case, 2025, p. 19).

3.2 Weak or Ineffective Municipal Standards

Private enterprise may not use the absence of municipal standards on good faith consultation nor the poor implementation of domestic laws and policies concerning consultation with Indigenous Peoples as an excuse to evade meeting international OECD standards for good faith consultation. The OECD standards aim to establish minimum international norms for private enterprise, even in cases where municipal arrangements are weak or inadequate. The OECD recognises that not all states pay equal attention to the recognition of indigenous rights. The private sector, through self-regulation, is expected to universally apply OECD norms regardless of municipal regulatory shortcomings or the ineffective implementation of domestic standards.

In the Future In Our Hands case, an NCP identified deficiencies in the implementation of statutory and policy arrangements in the Philippines aimed at protecting the interests of Indigenous Peoples (Future In Our Hands case, 2011). The NCP commented: 'Although the Philippines have developed legislation and procedures for protecting the interests of Indigenous People, its implementation is often lacking' (Future In Our Hands case 2011, 18). The

NCP encouraged the company concerned to comply with the higher standard set by the OECD Guidelines, even if domestic standards were not properly enforced. Furthermore, since the company was registered in Norway, the NCP stated that obligations arising from Norway should also guide indigenous consultation, despite the company operating outside Norwegian borders. It further stressed that the government of Norway, as the regulating authority over the company, had a duty to ensure compliance with OECD standards, irrespective of any shortcomings in the Philippines' regulatory regime. The NCP declared:

> [w]here there is weak national implementation or legislation, or a discrepancy between national and international standards, the NCP encourages the company to base its business on the more stringent standard. (Future In Our Hands case 2011, paras. 12, 21)

Meanwhile, in the Indigenous People's representatives case, it was noted that while an environmental impact assessment had been conducted in accordance with Chilean law, the OECD Guidelines are intended to 'supplement' state requirements and call for 'further consideration' (Indigenous people's representatives case, 2024). Consequently, a company may be expected to perform an environmental impact assessment, including specific consultation with indigenous people, to a standard that exceeds the municipal requirements of the country in which it is operating.

3.3 When Is a Community 'Affected' by a Proposal?

FPIC requires that indigenous communities affected by a proposal should be consulted about its potential merits and impacts. Private enterprises often face the challenge of not knowing who to consult when disagreements arise between or within indigenous communities. A project may be located on land regarded as customary by more than one indigenous community, or the impact and associated infrastructure of a proposed project may indirectly affect other indigenous communities. Furthermore, internal disputes may occur within a community over who holds the authority to 'speak' for a particular area of land. These challenges arise not only due to competing interests among different indigenous communities, but potentially also from disagreements within the same community.

In the Future In Our Hands case, the 'frequent inaccuracy with which indigenous representatives are selected' was noted (Future In Our Hands case

2011, 22).[2] The Report cited an expert commenting on the divisions among indigenous communities:

> …the existence and proliferation of various IPOs [Indigenous Peoples Organisations] *promoting different objectives* within an Ancestral Domain *is often the cause of divisiveness* between and among community members. There arises the selection of many leaders/representatives, many of whom *may not be recognised* as such by other community members and the creation of positions or titles/designation that may be contrary or not within the indigenous leadership or political structure of the community. (emphasis added) (Future In Our Hands case 2011, 22)

With regard to whether Indigenous Peoples who do not reside on the affected land but can demonstrate a connection to it should be included in consultations, the NCP affirmed that they should and stated:

> The Indigenous Peoples understood as "affected" include not only those that inhabit the land, but also those who use it according to their tradition and culture. The NCP understands the term "affected" as referring to *all affected Indigenous Peoples*, and not only a fraction of the group or tribe, or those inhabiting the land who may be forced to relocate due to the project or related infrastructure. It would be contrary to the intention of instruments designed to protect Indigenous Peoples or tribes to allow a fraction of the group, without individually based property rights, to enter into agreements affecting the tribe without consulting the tribe in its entirety. The effect of this may be that members of the tribe become unable to use the land according to tribal customs. (Future In Our Hands case 2011, para. 23)

The term 'affected' is, therefore, given an expansive meaning to include not only communities directly impacted by a proposed project but also those which may be indirectly impacted, whether now or in the future, as a result of infrastructure development, increased traffic, pollution, rehabilitation, or

2 The Indigenous People I represented in the Goldfields of Australia developed a corporate process by nominating a negotiating team to represent a specific community when access is sought to their lands. The negotiating team would report back to the community periodically as required by the complexity of the project. However, even in these well-structured arrangements, there were often inter – and intra-indigenous disagreements about who should serve on the negotiating team, how representative the negotiators were of the area affected by the proposed development, and whether they had adequate knowledge of the local indigenous laws and customs applicable to that specific area.

other consequences of the project (Survival International 2009, para. 39). The NCP delivered the following rebuke:

> The company should have systematically investigated whether Indigenous Peoples other than those [which issued FPIC] could be impacted by project components (mine and infrastructure), and if the groups with which they consulted were the legitimate representatives of all the affected Indigenous Peoples. This should have been done at *an early stage in the project…* (emphasis added) (Future In Our Hands case 2011, paras. 25–27)

3.4 Who Qualifies for FPIC Consultation?

FPIC is a term primarily associated with the rights of Indigenous Peoples, but it may also have broader applications to any local community that feels efforts should be made to obtain its consent for a proposed development. Nonetheless, the OECD guidelines specifically use FPIC in the context of indigenous consultation, as Indigenous Peoples have a unique relationship with land, shaped by their long-standing and historical ties, custodial responsibilities, and pre-settlement rights.

In the Project Sepik case, a dispute arose over who was entitled to FPIC. The decision was made pursuant to the OECD Guidelines for Multinational Enterprises, which include, among other requirements, an obligation to consult with local communities and, in the case of Indigenous Peoples, to do so within the framework of FPIC (Project Sepik case, 2023). It was alleged that the developer seeking to establish a mine and associated infrastructure had not complied with these guidelines. Among the questions that arose in the dispute was who qualifies for FPIC. It was determined that the obligation of FPIC does not extend to any community that identifies as indigenous. Moreover, even if a community is indigenous, the scope and scale of the required consultation depend on the nature and extent of their affected interests.

FPIC applies when considering the indigenous community's cultural linkage to the area, the potential impact of the project on cultural values in a broad sense, the views of the affected group, and whether the nature of the project and the asserted rights justify it (Project Sepik case, 2023, para. 89). The Examiner cited international human rights approaches to FPIC in observing as follows:

> The human rights case guidance about how significant impacts need to be, to necessitate FPIC, includes: developments threatening the way of life and culture of an Indigenous group; impacts amounting to a denial of the right to enjoy

> cultural rights in that region; endangering the very survival of the community and its members; and substantially compromising or interfering with culturally significant activities. *These are, obviously, context specific.* (emphasis added) (Project Sepik case, 2023, para. 81.4)

In the Indigenous People's representatives case, the complexity of the issue about who should be consulted was highlighted when several indigenous communities claimed connection to the same land, resulting in inter-community disputes over which entity was best placed to speak for this land (Indigenous people's representatives case, 2024). In such a complex environment, the development proponent must take reasonable steps to consult with different indigenous interest groups based on the extent to which their interests may be affected. The inability of these groups to reach a common position does not imply a veto over a project, as it is the effort to achieve agreement that is assessed, not the actual attainment of agreement – the emphasis of FPIC is not just on the outcome, but also the process involved (Project Sepik case 2023, para. 82).

Parties may, at the conclusion of the FPIC process, disagree on the merits of the project or certain aspects of it. However, the key question for the NCP is whether the consultation process itself was inclusive and offered opportunities for meaningful participation to all indigenous communities affected.

3.5 Good Faith: An Obligation on Both Sides

The obligation to act in good faith during the consultation process rests with both parties. Each side must engage constructively and consistently, according with what is considered good faith, demonstrating a genuine willingness to listen to the other's views while freely expressing their own perspectives and preferences. Even if an indigenous community opposes a development, it is still expected to participate in consultation in good faith, just as a private company supporting the development must do the same. However, as previously mentioned, indigenous communities face the risk that by participating in consultation, they may inadvertently lend credibility and legitimacy to a process that ultimately conflicts with their own interests – given that approval may be granted by the regulating authority for a project to proceed despite objections raised by the community. Regardless of the risks involved, Indigenous Peoples are required to explain why they oppose a project, recommend mitigation measures, consider various forms of compensation, or suggest different locations. There must be an exchange of views, perspectives, and preferences in an effort to reach a mutually acceptable outcome. In the Fredemi Coalition case, the following observation was made:

> At the same time, community members *should be willing to engage* with the company. A lack of effort by either party can lead to erroneous perceptions and misunderstandings, lack of trust, opposition and grievances. (emphasis added) (Fredemi Coalition case, 2011, p. 14)

3.6 Language of Communication

As discussed above, the principle of good faith consultation is largely undefined, but it includes the requirement that the community being consulted must, as far as is practicable, be communicated with in a language they understand and through means accessible to them. While this may not always be possible with remote indigenous communities or when dealing with highly technical subject matters, there must at least be a genuine effort to present information in a comprehensible and accessible manner, and to hear submissions using a language in which the community can comfortably express themselves.

In the IAP and WDM case, it was found that although the quality of the information provided to the indigenous community met the required standard, the way the project was communicated to the community – along with the reliance on government agencies to facilitate the consultation – contributed to a process that was ultimately ineffective and inadequate. Although the state has an interest in ensuring effective consultation, a development proponent cannot delegate or relinquish their responsibility to consult with the indigenous community to the state (IAP and WDM case, 2014, paras. 13–14). The NCP offered three key observations concerning the adequacy of ongoing consultation and the need for the company to maintain and review the effectiveness of its engagement outcomes:

> The NCP considers that the company should have done three things. Firstly and most importantly it should have ensured that communication channels it had developed (including online written information and relationships with NGOs and other organisations operating in the area) *remained open* so that people potentially affected by the mine could access up to date information and receive answers to questions about the project's status, the company's current activities and its intentions. Secondly, it should have *re-appraised* its earlier communications plans to see whether these had contributed to community impressions that it exercised undue influence. Thirdly, it should have appraised the *new risks* to communities arising from political opposition to the project and updated its plans to address these. (emphasis added) (IAP and WDM case, 2014, para. 81)

In the Project Sepik case, it was emphasised that communications aimed at obtaining FPIC must be delivered in a language the indigenous community can understand, enabling them to grasp what is being proposed and respond in accordance with their best interests. This obligation extends, to the greatest extent possible, to engaging with different communities in their own languages. The following was stated:

> Informed consent requires engagement *in a manner and language* which the relevant community can understand. In both parties' material, there is information explaining that Tok Pisin language may not be understood in some areas. The enterprise's material acknowledged the project area involved different cultures and languages. That would suggest that FPIC would require effective engagement within *each of those cultures and languages*... Where FPIC is required from a group, and if English and Tok Pisin is not understood by that group, neither of these measures (volunteer interpreters and written materials in Tok Pisin / English) would be sufficient to enable FPIC. (Project Sepik case, 2023, para. 96)

In the CCFD case, the consultation process was criticised for being overly informal, thereby denying the community a structured opportunity to be properly informed about the nature of the project and of their right to formally respond to it (CCFD case, 2013, para. 14). In the CCFD Follow-up case, meanwhile, a recommendation was made for indigenous individuals to be included on the company's local board so that their views on the project's ongoing implementation could be heard (CCFD Follow-up case, 2016, para. 4).

3.7 Ongoing Consultation

Depending on the nature of a project, including its scale and impact, ongoing consultation after the initial approvals may be required due to the lifespan of a project. In the case of smaller projects, it may be easier to conclude the consultation process as soon as approval is given, whereas with larger projects it may be necessary to establish more enduring consultation mechanisms to cover not only the project's operational phase but also subsequent rehabilitation.

In the Southeast Alaska Conservation Council case, the NCP emphasised the importance of ongoing consultation for the life of the project. In addition to continuing consultation, the NCP recommended identifying stakeholders in a manner exceeding the relevant municipal statute's requirements (Southeast Alaska Conservation Council case 2020, para. 7). In the IAP and WDM case, it was emphasised that the company 'should have ensured that communication channels it had developed (including online written information and relationships with NGOs and other organisations operating in the area) *remained open* so that people potentially affected by the mine could access up to date information and receive answers to questions about the project's status, the company's current activities and its intentions' (emphasis added) (IAP and WDM case, 2014, para. 81).

4 Concluding Observations

An important outcome of the increasing focus on FPIC is the development of self-regulating norms and standards by the private sector for consulting with Indigenous Peoples. These standards have a supra-national reach, making them, in some respects, more relevant to the development of international soft-law standards than national standards and policies. While some disputes, such as the Juukan Gorge debacle (Chapter 9), make international headlines, thousands of agreements, both formal and informal, are reached every year by development proponents in their dealings with Indigenous Peoples. These agreements are often unrecorded, unreported, and unresearched. For example, in Australia, thousands of agreements have been entered into since 1993 by Aboriginal people pursuant to the right to negotiate under the Native Title Act. Some of these have been limited to the protection of important Aboriginal traditional and sacred sites, while others have included substantial royalty, employment and contract opportunities, trust funds, scholarships, and compensation. O'Faircheallaigh observes as follows:

> A number of agreements strongly favourable to Aboriginal interests have been negotiated pursuant to the Native Title Act, while some groups that lack even the minimal legal rights offered by the Native Title Act have also been able to secure favourable outcomes.' (O'Faircheallaigh, 2016, p. 202)

An essential element for the private sector of the social license to operate is consultation with Indigenous Peoples affected by proposed developments. The OECD's initiative to establish self-regulating NCPs to resolve disputes – through mediation, conciliation, and recommendations – highlights the progress made in addressing concerns over consultation adequacy through amicable means rather than litigation. Viewed in isolation, the effectiveness of NCPs is open to debate, but when assessed as part of the overall institutional response to the importance of consultation with Indigenous Peoples, the

NCPs play a crucial role in conflict resolution and shaping universal standards that encourage FPIC.

This chapter summarised the following key points regarding industry self-regulation under the OECD Guidelines:

The private sector often finds itself caught up between conflicting norms, expectations, policies, and legal requirements regarding the adequacy of consultation with Indigenous Peoples. This creates an uncertain and unpredictable approval landscape for private enterprises, as the simplicity of a single state-based regulatory authority has been replaced by multiple potential approval benchmarks, none of which, especially in complex cases, can absolutely guarantee the finality of an outcome. The complexity of consultation is heightened when multiple indigenous communities claim interest in the same land or when there is disagreement within an indigenous community about a response to a proposal. Inter- and intra-indigenous disputes potentially place any approval by the regulating authority at risk. Meanwhile, an approval granted through a state regulatory regime after consultations deemed to have been held in good faith may be undermined by the court of public opinion, industry self-regulation, legal challenges, financier concerns, or shareholder criticism, leaving a private enterprise in a conundrum. On the other hand, indigenous communities risk that their participation in consultation may lend credibility and legitimacy to a process that ultimately results in an outcome contrary to their interests.

Although the OECD Guidelines refer to the term FPIC, the reports and recommendations made by NCPs generally rely on the concept of good faith consultation, rather than becoming involved in the legal requirements for FPIC as if a distinct norm from consultation. As with municipal courts and international expert bodies, NCPs do not draw a distinction between consultation and FPIC, but instead assess the obligation of good faith consultation – including its scope – in light of the proposed project and its potential impacts. If consent cannot be obtained, a development proponent must at least demonstrate that it has duly considered the opinions and concerns of the indigenous community. As with FPIC, indigenous communities are not accorded the right of veto by the OECD standards, though, as previously discussed, some municipal arrangements may provide for a right of veto.

The consultation standards required by NCPs are guided by logic, good faith, and reasonableness as applied to the circumstances of the specific project, rather than by objective norms. On balance, the standards are not unduly onerous – they simply require a genuine effort to consult, a meaningful process, and a willingness from all parties to remain open to persuasion, even if consensus is not ultimately reached.

The nature of consultation – encompassing its scope, duration, and intensity – is shaped by the specifics of the project under consideration. While general indicia can guide the private sector when approaching consultation, its practical requirements depend on the unique circumstances of each project. In some cases, consultation may be straightforward and concluded within a short timeframe, whereas in others circumstances, consultation may need to continue throughout the project's life. A development proponent should therefore consider not only the immediate project location, but also other areas and communities that may be affected by future infrastructure development, expansion, environmental impacts such as pollution, and other related consequences.

The non-litigious procedures of NCPs are useful in encouraging dialogue, mutual accommodation, and the development of common standards, rather than becoming entangled in adversarial litigation with entrenched positions and high costs. There is a risk, however, that indigenous communities may not receive a fair hearing in NCP processes because of their non-legal nature. The NCPs may also not adhere to the same rules of natural justice and procedural fairness that apply in courts which may affect the fairness of the hearing.

CHAPTER 9

Juukan Gorge: How Can Right Turn Out to Be so Wrong?

1 Introduction

The mention of 'Juukan Gorge' evokes the deep complexities and nuances associated with FPIC.[1] The damage and destruction caused on 24 May 2020 of two Aboriginal sites – one with a dated history spanning around 46,000 years – highlight how much remains to be done to secure and protect indigenous sites and dreaming storylines of both national and international importance. Juukan Gorge and its rock shelters in particular are more than archaeological sites; they are evidence of the world's oldest continuous living culture, connecting human presence in Australia in the area to the Ice Age (Slack, Fillios, and Fullagar 2009; Slack, Law, and Gliganic 2020). And yet, mining company Rio Tinto lawfully destroyed one site and damaged another, despite expert reports describing the sites' unique status and regardless of the vehement objections of the land's traditional owners. It is unfathomable that so much was known about Juukan Gorge – scientifically, anthropologically, culturally, and even managerially – and that so many people had voiced concerns about the importance to preserve the sites – and yet the blasting went ahead anyway, unfolding like a Greek tragedy with a foreseeable, yet uncontrollable, outcome.[2]

What makes this action particularly poignant is that the company acted under the lawful authority of the state of Western Australia, and thus Rio faced no prosecution for the obliteration of an irreplaceable link to pre-ancient history.[3]

---

1 The Juukan Gorge is located in the Pilbara region of the state of Western Australia about 1100 km north of Perth. The Gorge is about 400m long and 70m wide and includes several rock shelters and a rock pool. These sites are regarded as sacred by the area's traditional Aboriginal custodians.

2 The parliamentary report arising from the investigation conducted after the destruction, explains in some detail the efforts made to prevent the blasts; the risks involved in removing pre-loaded explosives; and, ultimately, the inevitability of the blasts on 24 May 2020. (Juukan Inquiry Final Report 2021, 303–4).

3 It is said that an undisclosed sum was paid by Rio in the aftermath of the event into a trust fund management for the benefit of the indigenous community (Jackson, 2025).

The events leading to the Juukan Gorge incident reflect a culmination of all the facets of FPIC discussed in this book, including: the meaning and ongoing nature of FPIC; the legal status of UNDRIP; corporate culture; industry self-regulation; the social license to operate; country-based legislative and administrative standards; interactions between public and indigenous interests; intra-indigenous cooperation and information-sharing; the question of who speaks for country; the regulatory authority of the state; and, perhaps most crucially, what happens in the legal vacuum between consultation and consent – a gap with the potential to give rise to actions that are 'lawful but awful' (Passas, 2005).

This chapter reflects on the events at Juukan Gorge considering the various aspects of FPIC explored in previous chapters. The reports produced by the Australian parliamentary committee that investigated the incident provide a detailed account of the events leading up to and following the destruction (Parliament Juukan Gorge 2020; Final Report Juukan 2021).

The destruction of Juukan Gorge will be discussed under the following subheadings: essential facts; statutory framework; and elements of FPIC as they relate to the Juukan events.

The Juukan Gorge case study is perhaps *the* most relevant contemporary example (at least in Australia) of how what seems right can easily turn out to be wrong. When indigenous, public, and private interests intersect, achieving the ideal of a consent-based outcome is not always possible. The reality is that the public interest in economic development often directly conflicts with the protection of an indigenous site. Which interest prevails if this conflict is irreconcilable? And, very importantly, who carries the burden of a final decision? (De Villiers, 2025b).

FPIC, as it appears in UNDRIP, is often erroneously interpreted as granting Indigenous Peoples' final control over what happens on their ancestral lands. While FPIC strives to foster consensus, it does not mandate it, nor does it confer a legal right of veto. The final decision usually remains with the regulating authority, which may consider the indigenous community's withholding of consent without being bound by it. Serving as the final decision-maker is far from simple. The following legal position expressed by the Law Society of Western Australia in respect to Juukan Gorge is likely mirrored in other jurisdictions:

> There is no legislative regime at a State or Commonwealth level which is effective to *guarantee* the protection of culturally and historically significant sites such as the caves at Juukan Gorge. (emphasis added) (Juukan Law Society WA, 2020, p. 28)

Previous chapters emphasised the following:
- FPIC is not a justiciable legal right in either international law or customary international law;
- the 'consent' in FPIC does not constitute a legal veto;
- the withholding of consent does not imply the legal rejection of a proposal; courts consider the process rather than the outcome of consultation;
- the obligation of FPIC may be deemed to have been met even if a development goes ahead against the wishes of an indigenous community;
- the final regulatory and approval authority of the state is not displaced by the obligation seek to obtain FPIC;
- industry continues to pursue improvements in its engagement with Indigenous Peoples through self-regulation; and
- FPIC has infused good faith consultation with deeper significance and broader application.

Nonetheless, the Juukan Gorge fiasco shows how easily good intentions can be derailed, how weak domestic legal arrangements can be exploited by the private sector, how scientific knowledge can be buried under layers of bureaucracy and mismanagement, and how poor communication, along with the fallibility of human judgement, continues to pose a serious risk of flawed outcomes.

2 Essential Facts Surrounding the Juukan George Destruction

On 24 May 2020, mining company Rio Tinto damaged and destroyed two Aboriginal rock shelters (sites) in Juukan Gorge as part of an expansion of its Brockman iron ore mine in Western Australia.[4] The destruction was a permitted act under the Aboriginal Heritage Act of the state of Western Australia (Aboriginal Heritage Act, 1972, sec. 18(3)). Ministerial approval for the destruction of the sites had been granted some six years earlier,[5] despite it being known since 2003 that the sites held a 'moderate to high degree of archaeological significance' (Final Report Juukan, 2021, p. 293).

4 For a chronology of the events leading up to the destruction, refer to the summary of the parliamentary report (Final Report Juukan, 2021, pp. 293–303).

5 The approval granted to Rio Tinto permitted the destruction or damage of twelve rock shelters and twenty artefact scatters after the completion of salvage excavations. It was during those subsequent salvage excavations that additional evidence about the significance of the two sites was collated. Note that the discussion in this chapter and references to the Aboriginal Heritage Act reflect the provisions of the Act as they stood in 2020.

The sites contained evidence of Aboriginal occupation and use dating back at least 46,000 years (Slack, Law and Gliganic, 2020). The local Aboriginal people – the traditional owners of the land and custodians of the sites – the Puutu Kunti Kurrama and Pinikura peoples (PKKP people) held the sites in high regard for their cultural, ethnographic, and archaeological importance. Extensive scientific knowledge existed prior to the destruction of the sites, affirming their cultural, ethnographic, archaeological, and historical value. A 2014 report by archaeologist Dr Michael Slack for Rio Tinto noted that one of the sites contained artefacts 'of the highest archaeological significance in Australia' (Borschmann, 2020). This information about the high value of the sites was conveyed to Rio Tinto after it had received ministerial approval to destroy them, but still around six years prior to the actual destruction. A subsequent 2018 report by Scarp Archaeology reiterated that one of the sites held the 'highest archaeological significance in Australia' (Final Report Juukan, 2021, p. 297).

The authority under which Rio Tinto destroyed the sites was issued by the Minister for Aboriginal Affairs on 31 December 2013 pursuant to Section 18 of the Aboriginal Heritage Act of the state of Western Australia. None of the excavation findings produced *after* 2013, nor the PKKP people's opposition to any harm being done to the sites, were submitted to the minister. This was at least partly because neither Rio Tinto nor any researcher was legally obliged under the Act to inform the minister of any relevant new information. Ironically, even if the minister had been given the new information, he had no legal power to rescind an approval after it had been granted. Therefore, the approval granted in 2013 for the destruction of the sites remained valid, regardless of any subsequent discoveries of important Aboriginal sites or artefacts. Despite the public outcry, the actions taken by Rio Tinto were therefore technically lawful.

Following the ministerial approval issued in 2013, experts retained by Rio Tinto undertook, in cooperation with the PKKP people, further excavation of the sites. They catalogued and preserved around 7000 artefacts. A detailed report, including the ethnographic findings and importance of the sites, was provided to Rio Tinto. The company later conceded to the Parliamentary Committee that the additional information obtained after the 2013 approval provided sufficient grounds to voluntarily re-assess the importance of the sites (Final Report Juukan 2021, para. 2.62). However, such a reassessment was never done by Rio Tinto. According to the company, the failure was due to poor internal communication. Nonetheless, the events also reflect the broader 'power imbalance' between mining companies and Indigenous Peoples in respect of this and other companies (Kaur, Lodhia and Lesue, 2024, para. 6.1).

Prior to the destruction of the Juukan Gorge sites, Rio Tinto had engaged extensively with the PKKP people, maintaining a relationship that spanned at least eighteen years. This extended to awareness of the importance of their sacred sites, agreements with them concerning exploration and mining in their traditional areas, as well as other forms of cooperation including heritage protection and commercial arrangements.[6]

In the lead-up to the blasting of the sites, the quality of communication between Rio Tinto and the PKKP people declined. Rio Tinto, on reflection, acknowledged that both its internal and external communication the PKKP people had been poor, with internal communication lines becoming 'blurred' – a breakdown that ultimately affected its engagement with the PKKP people. Essential staff skills had been lost for a variety of reasons including personnel changes, which contributed to the deterioration in communication both within the company and with the PKKP people. For example, in the days prior to the destruction, Rio Tinto failed to inform the PKKP people of the planned blasts, including their scale. By the time the indigenous communities became aware of the impending blasts, it was too late to intervene. Nonetheless, having communicated to Rio Tinto that the sites must not be destroyed, they believed the company was taking appropriate steps to prevent the blasts or at least mitigate their impact (Final Report Juukan 2021, para. 2.80–2.81). An investigation into the days leading up to the blasts found, however, that it would be too risky for the explosives to be removed. Rio Tinto conceded that:

> In allowing the destruction of the Juukan Gorge rock shelters to occur, we fell far short of our values as a company and breached the trust placed in us by the Traditional Owners of the lands on which we operate. (Rio Tinto Juukan Gorge, 2025)

A pertinent question that arose in the aftermath of the destruction is whether the PKKP people had known about the intended blasts since 2013 and, if so, whether they had had adequate opportunity to prevent the damage from taking place. The Parliamentary Report heard detailed evidence about this issue (Final Report Juukan, 2021, para. 2.6–2.25). With the benefit of hindsight and

6 The investigation into the Juukan Gorge destruction brought attention to the agreement process between Rio Tinto and the PKKP people. In one example, a contract of around 740 pages had to be approved by the PKKP communities, yet plain English summaries were reportedly distributed only shortly before the meeting at which the approval was to be granted (Kemp, Kochan and Burton, 2023, p. 397). The parliamentary committee noted that it is difficult to see how 'free, prior and informed consent can be achieved in such circumstances' (Final Report Juukan, 2021).

in light of the actions taken by Rio Tinto since the destruction, it is not controversial to conclude that the PKKP people did not know about all the options available to Rio Tinto to prevent or mitigate damage to the sites;[7] that the PKKP communities were not aware of the intended destruction of the sites; and that there was inadequate opportunity for the blasting to be stopped. It is similarly uncontroversial to state that while the possible destruction of the sites had been on the agenda since the Minister for Aboriginal Affairs granted approval in December 2013, the PKKP people had no legal right to appeal that approval. Nevertheless, the actual destruction of the sites – given the additional evidence that had emerged since the approval, as well as the ongoing discussions between Rio Tinto and the PKKP people – came as a shock to the communities involved and the scientists who had been studying the sites.

Another relevant question for Rio Tinto is whether it could have taken alternative steps to either prevent or mitigate the damage to the sites. Although the company had ministerial approval authorising its actions, could self-regulation and internal checks and balances have prompted it to reconsider the extent of the blasting? Again, in retrospect, and considering the subsequent measures taken by Rio Tinto, the answer to that question is yes. More could and should have been done to prevent the destruction and damage of the sites or, at the very least, to mitigate the impact of the blasts. The Parliamentary Report found that as far back as 2013, when the approval was granted, Rio Tinto 'failed to properly adhere' to the letter and spirit of its agreements with the PKKP communities; failed to apply its own internal standards; and failed to disclose to the PKKP people alternative design options for the expansion of the mine that would prevent or mitigate damage to the sites (Final Report Juukan, 2021, para. 2.40). Additionally, Rio Tinto admitted that its internal management and communication systems as well as their community liaison had broken down. Furthermore, the 2013 notice in which the company explicitly acknowledged that the sites would be impacted by the blasts was not sent directly to the PKKP people, but to a different Aboriginal corporation which, in turn, failed to pass the notice on to the PKKP communities (Final Report Juukan 2021, para. 2.50, 2.105). Moreover, the initial approval granted by the minister in 2013 was based on incomplete and deficient information. For example, the material provided in support of the destruction failed to explain

7 In October 2012, Rio Tinto produced an internal memorandum in which possible design options for the mine were considered. Of the four options identified, three avoided or limited impacts to the sites. These options were not disclosed to the PKKP people and the only option given to them was presented as a *fait accompli* (Final Report Juukan, 2021, p. 294).

the ethnographic importance of the sites. In fact, an explicit expert recommendation that the sites be preserved was completely omitted from the application submitted to the minister. To make matters worse, Rio Tinto did not divulge to the PKKP people the availability of alternatives to the destruction. Notably, and despite these missteps, shortcomings and oversights, the Aboriginal Heritage Act did not make it an offence to present incomplete information to the minister or to Aboriginal people in general.

Although substantial additional ethnographic evidence pertaining to the importance of the sites had been obtained after the issuing of the 2013 notice, the new information was not submitted to the Minister for Aboriginal Affairs. Again, it is worth noting that the Aboriginal Heritage Act did not require any subsequently obtained research findings to be submitted to the minister. However, in the absence of a statutory requirement, the question arises whether Rio Tinto, pursuant to its corporate commitments, ethics, and self-regulation, should have voluntarily provided the information to the minister, or at least initiated an internal reassessment of the mine's expansion. Although the report detailing the significance of the sites was submitted to Rio Tinto, its content was not effectively communicated within the company. The flaws of self-regulation were thus clearly exposed.

The next section briefly examines the statutory arrangements in place when the destruction of the sites was approved.

3 Statutory Framework Giving Rise to the Juukan Gorge Destruction

The Aboriginal Heritage Act of the state of Western Australia was drafted at a time when there were essentially few, if any, legal, moral, or ethical obligations of any substance to consult with Indigenous Peoples about access to their traditional lands, sites, or interests. At the time, the conventional wisdom held that Australia was considered *terra nullius* at the time of settlement in 1788, and that no traditional native title rights or interests had survived colonisation (Milirrpum case, 1971). In the 1970s, advocates for indigenous rights in Australia, and elsewhere, received little international or national attention. ILO 169 and UNDRIP were still far on the horizon. Importantly, the 'living' aspects of indigenous law, culture, and customs – especially as they relate to the ongoing connection to land, expressed through storylines, interactions with country, and continued stewardship for it as a society governed by unique laws and traditions – had not yet been appreciated (Yorta Yorta

(HCA) case, 2002). Instead, the focus was on conserving indigenous artifacts and recorded stories within museums (Kaur, Lodhia and Lesue, 2024).

The Aboriginal Heritage Act predated the establishment of native title in Australia by around two decades, (Mabo case (2), 1992), but by 2020 it was arguably among the most outdated pieces of legislation on the country's statute books. Ironically, although by 2020 industry practices and self-regulation by the private sector in its interactions with Indigenous Peoples had advanced significantly compared to the 1970s (see Chapter 8), Rio Tinto chose to rely on legislation that was no longer fit for purpose rather than on contemporary standards and practices when proceeding with the destruction of the sites. The agreements Rio Tinto had with the PKKP people were advanced and set the industry standard in Australia. In addition, cultural awareness training for staff had become common practice, and the recognition of Aboriginal culture as a living system of law was well established.

The two key operative provisions of the then Aboriginal Heritage Act relevant to this chapter are Sections 17 and 18. The former establishes that it is an offence to damage or destroy an Aboriginal site without authorisation from the relevant minister pursuant to Section 18. Section 18, meanwhile, provides that the minister must consider the recommendations of the advisory Aboriginal Cultural Materials Committee (ACMC) (s 28), along with the general interests of the community, before deciding whether to grant or refuse approval for the destruction or damage of an Aboriginal site.[8]

There are five notable aspects of the Aboriginal Heritage Act relevant to the Juukan Gorge events:

First, there is no national or state register of all Aboriginal sites in Australia or Western Australia respectively,[9] meaning a person or entity could damage an Aboriginal site without knowing of its existence, and be prosecuted;

Second, any person or entity applying for approval to destroy or damage an Aboriginal site could appeal the decision of the minister not to grant approval,

8 In the Juukan Gorge case, the ACMC did not properly scrutinise the Section 18 application, failing to identify any shortcomings or inconsistencies associated with it. Importantly, the ACMC does not have powers to conduct its own investigations or hear evidence. It is therefore possible for it to recommend the destruction of a site without having detailed information about it. In the case of the Juukan Gorge application, the recommendations made by researchers Slack and Builth for the sites to be considered of high ethnographic importance were not included in the application before the ACMC. In fact, the application was so deficient that under the heading 'dealing with the ethnographic significance of the sites', Rio Tinto replied with "N/A" (not applicable).

9 There are various reasons why Aboriginal sites are not recorded, but one important consideration is that some sites are considered secret or sacred, meaning their location cannot be disclosed to uninitiated persons (Juukan Government Response, 2022, p. 9). Furthermore,

whereas Aboriginal people opposing a granted approval did not have a right of appeal; (s 18(5))

Third, there was no obligation on any person or entity to bring to the attention of the Minister for Aboriginal Affairs any new information obtained after the approval for a site's destruction had been granted;

Fourth, having made a decision to allow the damage to an Aboriginal site, the Minister had no power to revisit the decision. Consequently, even if Rio Tinto or the researchers had informed the minister of the importance of the sites, he did not have the authority to rescind or modify the approval granted. The only entity that could reconsider was Rio Tinto; and

Fifth, given the evidence that emerged, Rio Tinto could, or rather should, have taken the initiative of adjusting the location of the mine and blasting holes, or taken other steps to prevent or mitigate damage to the sites. However, despite its endorsement of the UNDRIP principles, the company had 'effectively neutralised these commitments in their front-line practices' (Kemp, Kochan and Burton, 2023, p. 382). Rio Tinto duly suffered the consequences of corporate reputational damage caused when legal compliance is fulfilled 'but in the absence of corporate ethics and community responsibilities' (Oliveri *et al.*, 2022). Rio Tinto has also paid an undisclosed sum to a PKKP Aboriginal Corporation-linked charity and in 2025 entered into a new heritage protection agreement with the PKKP people (Jackson, 2025).[10]

4 FPIC and Its Application and Shortcomings in Juukan Gorge

The Juukan Gorge incident highlights several aspects of FPIC discussed in the foregoing chapters, of which the following are most pertinent:

4.1 Limitations of International Law

Although Australia subscribes to UNDRIP as well as several other international instruments aimed at protecting and promoting the rights of Indi-

---

the relevant minister can also deregister Aboriginal sites, a decision that cannot be appealed by the affected Aboriginal community (Traditional Owners – Nyiyaparli People case, 2009).

10 At the signing of the agreement Rio Tinto Iron Ore Chief Executive Simon Trott said: 'Our actions were wrong. We failed to uphold our company values, and our systems and processes were inadequate. Simply put, it should never have happened, and for that we will forever be sorry' (Rio/PKKP Agreement, 2025).

genous Peoples, the international norms underlying these instruments must be incorporated into domestic legislation to have legal effect. The gaps between the promises made by international instruments and the protections on offer within domestic legislation are often confusing and frustrating to indigenous communities. Despite the undoubted importance of international legal and ethical developments, domestic regulatory arrangements are often slow to respond to them. In some cases, such as the Juukan Gorge incident, the domestic arrangements are substantially below the benchmark sought to be established by international hard and soft law for the protection of indigenous rights. States consistently reject a right of veto, insisting that ultimate decision-making power over development projects rests with the state.

4.2 Domestic Legislative Frameworks

The shortcomings in Western Australia's domestic legislation were mainly to blame for the Juukan Gorge events. Among the most glaring gaps in the legislation were: the absence of any requirement for applications to damage or destroy sites to disclose detailed and current information about the site and its scientific, cultural and historical importance; the absence of any requirement to submit new information about a site to the relevant minister; Aboriginal people's inability to appeal an approval given for a site to be damaged or destroyed; the minister's inability to revoke or amend a previously issued approval; a lack of ongoing responsibility on the developer to share information and engage in continuing consultation with the affected Indigenous People; and a lack of oversight by the regulating authority to ensure compliance with the Aboriginal Heritage Act's provisions.

Despite Rio Tinto's commitments to protecting and promoting Aboriginal culture, a lack of clearly defined and enforceable legal responsibilities exposed the weaknesses of both the legislative regime and corporate self-regulatory protocols.

4.3 Meaning of 'Free' in FPIC

The meaning of 'free' is to be ascertained in the context of its use, but in the case of Juukan Gorge, the lack of a genuinely freely made decision was obvious. For example, some of the legal material provided to the PKKP people for their approval was so voluminous and complex and the time to review it so limited, that it would be unreasonable to suggest they had adequate opportunity to consider it and give informed consent to the provisions. Furthermore, Rio Tinto's failure to disclose to the PKKP communities the four possible options for the mine's location – instead presenting only one option as though it were final and non-negotiable – clearly fell short of enabling the communities to make a free and informed decision. Finally, the absence of an appeals mechanism allowing the PKKP people to challenge the approval granted by the minister, as well as the company's failure to share with them the blasting schedule, were at odds with even the most basic elements of procedural fairness and natural justice.

4.4 Meaning of 'Prior' in FPIC

The meaning of 'prior' is likewise to be determined in the context of its use, but the most straightforward plain English interpretation is that Indigenous Peoples should be consulted before any development takes place or before approval for a development is granted. Moreover, the scope and scale of a project may require ongoing FPIC.

In the Juukan Gorge case, the standards associated with the term 'prior' were breached in several respects, but most notably: the application for the destruction of the sites was not submitted to the PKKP people for comment; the legal arrangements entered into with Rio Tinto precluded the PKKP people from pursuing legal options outside the terms of the contract; the PKKP people had no right to appeal the ministerial approval to destroy the sites; the new ethnographic information gathered by the researchers after the approval had been granted could not be used by the PKKP people to seek mitigation of damage or a redesign; and the minister's approval remained valid regardless of new research findings about the significance of the sites. As a result, the ongoing nature of FPIC was denied, and the blasts proceeded without the adequate prior involvement or consent of the PKKP communities.

4.5 Meaning of 'Informed' in FPIC

The meaning of 'informed' is to be ascertained in the context of its use, but in plain English it implies that all relevant information pertaining to the proposal under consideration must be made available to the indigenous community concerned to enable it to make a reasoned and logical decision, seek advice, and propose mitigation measures. This obligation does not necessarily extend to the provision of commercially confidential or sensitive information, but it does include supplying information concerning the nature and extent of the access sought to traditional land; the timing and duration of such access; the overall duration of the project; the anticipated impacts on land, the environment, and communities; mitigation measures available to limit these impacts;

and arrangements for ongoing consultation as the project progresses. The Juukan Gorge project exemplified failures in this obligation in several material respects.

4.6 Meaning of 'Consent' in FPIC

The term 'consent' does not imply a legal veto, but it does require a sincere and good faith effort to obtain the approval of the affected indigenous community. While the community has the right to withhold consent, this does not equate to a veto, as the final decision-making authority remains with the regulatory authority. That said, the process adopted by Rio Tinto in seeking consent was seriously deficient, and it is therefore reasonable to conclude that the company failed in its obligations.

Some of the major shortcomings that undermined a good faith effort to secure consent include the following: insufficient information was provided to the PKKP communities; legal arrangements restricted their ability to seek alternative legal remedies; Rio Tinto's failure to disclose to the PKKP communities essential information; inadequate time was given for the PKKP communities to review and consider complex legal documents; there was a lack of consistent communication between Rio Tinto and the PKKP communities; the submission of an incomplete application to the Minister for Aboriginal Affairs for approval to destroy the sites; Rio Tinto's failure to undertake an internal reassessment based on expert-verified additional material; and Rio Tinto's neglect in not informing the PKKP people of the time and place of the blasts.

4.7 Disclosure of New and Additional Material

The Juukan Gorge incident highlights the importance of recognising that FPIC may, depending on the nature of the project, be an ongoing process. As a project progresses, new information about indigenous sites may emerge, previously unforeseen impacts on the indigenous community or environment may arise, or the project's scope, footprint and scale may shift. Accordingly, some allowance should exist for approvals to be amended – for example, by requiring mitigatory measures in areas previously deemed suitable for operations. The Juukan Gorge experience, in which ministerial approval was granted unconditionally and could not be rescinded or amended, is obviously untenable. The Juukan Gorge destruction could have been prevented, and the mine's footprint could have been adjusted, if Rio Tinto had conducted an internal reassessment based on the evidence it received after 2013. Although self-regulation alone cannot fulfil the requirements of FPIC, Juukan Gorge highlights the importance of self-reflection and internal review in upholding a company's social license to operate.

4.8 Carrots and Sticks

FPIC contains elements of both carrot and stick. On one hand, strong relationships with indigenous communities can enhance a company's social profile, attract investor support, reinforce its social license to operate, and facilitate access to traditional lands. On the other, poor relationships can result in consequences, including penalties, sanctions, breakdown of relationships, and negative media coverage. Rio Tinto also failed to comply with acceptable industry practices, further tipping the statutory balance in the company's favour.

4.9 Who Makes the Final Decision?

A final decision must inevitably be made in the absence of agreement. Legally, FPIC as articulated in UNDRIP does not empower indigenous communities to become the ultimate decision-maker. The obligation is to seek consent – not to guarantee it. Similarly, the right to withhold consent under UNDRIP cannot be construed as a right of veto. Government agencies are unlikely to relinquish their decision-making authority over development projects in favour of indigenous groups. The question is not who makes the final decision – as that clearly remains the responsibility of the state – but rather what checks and balances are in place to govern the exercise of that power. The Juukan Gorge debacle illustrates the serious limitations of the Aboriginal Heritage Act: the Section 18 notice was not open to legal challenge; the ministerial approval was immune to legal review, had lasting effect, and could not be reconsidered despite the emergence of critical new information about the sites' cultural significance. However, addressing such shortcomings by transferring decision-making power to indigenous communities is not the answer, considering that they too may act unreasonably and improperly. Instead, the best course of action is to ensure that due process in courts is available to all parties before a state's decision is implemented.

CHAPTER 10

A Legal Guide to FPIC

1 Introduction

The concept 'free, prior and informed consent' has come to symbolise the shared aspiration of Indigenous Peoples to be genuinely consulted, meaningfully involved, and decision-makers having regard to their lives, lands, and communities. FPIC is used in the context of indigenous communities seeking a participatory role in decision-making impacting them, including the ability to veto developments that impact on their traditional lands. However, the term FPIC has no precise legal meaning and many of its proposed definitional aspects require additional clarification. This lack of clarity stems from FPIC's simultaneous embodiment of a desire, an objective, a legal demand, a purported right, a doctrine, a philosophy, a code of conduct, a rallying cry, and at times even a quasi-ideology. It is not a term that can be easily confined by legal definition, reflecting a broader value system rather than a legal entitlement.

There is an advocacy dimension to FPIC that has not been adopted as a justiciable legal entitlement in international or municipal jurisprudence. While FPIC appears in various international instruments, it does not confer a veto under municipal law – unless such a veto is explicitly established within that domestic legal system. Domestic courts do not typically distinguish between good faith consultation and FPIC, unless the applicable domestic law specifically refers to FPIC as a distinct normative standard. Even in such cases where FPIC is cited in municipal laws and policies, the content of FPIC generally aligns with the principles underpinning good faith consultation (Kebaowek First Nation case, 2025, para. 183). It is rare for FPIC to be regarded in domestic law as implying a right of veto, though a legislature may, as in the South African Baleni case, grant final decision-making authority over specific land-related issues to an indigenous community (Baleni case, 2019).

Although FPIC implies that an indigenous community may withhold consent, the final decision usually rests with the state, subject to judicial review of the state's decision. Courts must ultimately weigh both indigenous and public interests – which are not necessarily mutually exclusive – to determine whether alleged inadequate consultation warrants refusing approval or whether an objection against a proposed development should be overruled (Forrest appeal case, 2024, para. 190). In literature, indigenous interests are

HTTPS://DOI.ORG/10.1163/9789004724792-011

often depicted as unidimensional, but this does not necessarily reflect reality – in practice, there may be differing perspectives within an indigenous community, with some voices supporting and others opposing a proposed development.

FPIC is often caught up in an implementation conundrum due to its highly ambiguous interpretation of protections in theory and soft law, its limited domestication through legislation, its ambivalent status in soft law, and the practical challenges associated with applying it domestically. The gap – both legal and practical – between FPIC as articulated in UNDRIP, and FPIC as found in domestic legislative arrangements, is substantial. This conceptual and implementation gap is further compounded by the lack of agreement on what FPIC actually entails – whether it is a justiciable right distinct from the right of consultation, when it applies, to whom it applies, what the mechanism for its implementation is, and what form sanctions for its breach should take.

In short, as a purported legal norm, FPIC is weighed down by the lack of definitional clarity regarding its legal object, legal subject, and legal remedy.

Nonetheless, FPIC represents a new philosophy and normative standard for indigenous engagement. It offers a dynamic approach to working with and respecting the rights of Indigenous Peoples. FPIC may, in fact, be even more powerful, broader in scope, and more enduring than a legal entitlement. The case law concerning consultation standards discussed in this book would have been improbable just a few decades ago. In this book I show that FPIC is more than a purported right – it is an evolving code of conduct carrying legal, social, environmental, economic, policy, humanitarian, and political implications.

In this final chapter, the essential elements of FPIC are outlined to provide a legal framework for its application in both international and municipal law.

2 Legal Application of FPIC

The following questions and discussion points serve as legal guidelines for the application of FPIC:

2.1 Who Are Indigenous People?

Like the concept of 'minority', the question of who are Indigenous Peoples is best answered by reference to the history and circumstances of a particular country and its peoples, rather than in the abstract or through universal definition (Delgamuukw case 1997; Mabo case (2) 1992; Alexkor case 2003). Broadly, the word indigenous refers to a community of people united by common ancestry who inhabited and used land according to their own system of traditional laws and customs prior to the arrival of settler or colonial societies. Indigenous Peoples typically share a distinct culture, customs, traditions, language, and religion, as well as a continued adherence as a society to ancestral laws and practices (Ward case, 2002; Yorta Yorta (HCA) case, 2002). They do not necessarily constitute a numerical minority within the broader population, but often do. This description is both simple in concept and complex in application.

2.2 Differences between Indigenous Peoples and Ethnocultural Minority Groups

The protective regimes, in both hard and soft international law, for upholding the rights of Indigenous Peoples and minority groups differ. International law tends to encourage the assimilation of ethnocultural minorities by protecting the individual rights of their members without granting them separate collective rights as a community. In contrast, international (soft) law typically accommodates the rights of Indigenous Peoples separately, acknowledging their collective rights as a society alongside the individual rights of their members (Mahuika case 2000, para. 8.2). These distinctions are more pragmatic and arising from effective advocacy, than legally principled.

Both concepts – Indigenous Peoples and ethnocultural minorities – are vaguely described rather than defined, and the legal rationale for why one group is entitled to collective rights while the other is not, remains unconvincing. The groups may have different histories but that is not adequate to sustain the difference in proposition that Indigenous People having collective rights while ethnocultural minorities do not have collective rights.

Courts have been reluctant to engage in the search for definitional clarity, avoiding efforts to generically define 'indigenous' or distinguish between 'indigenous' and 'minority' in the abstract. Ultimately, communities – whether indigenous or ethnocultural – define themselves through the right to freedom of association of their members (Matson case 2022, para. 18.4; PCIJ-Greco-Bulgarian case 1930, para. 17). Meanwhile, human rights treaties must also be seen as dynamic instruments, capable of evolving and being adapted to new circumstances (Kichwa case, 2012, para. 161).

The essential distinction said to separate the rights of Indigenous Peoples and ethnocultural minorities is that the former are regarded as pre-settlement societies that share a common ancestry; they are organised as a society in accordance with indigenous laws and customs; they previously exercised sovereignty over their traditional lands; and they continue to exhibit these characteristics in contemporary society (Yorta Yorta (HCA) case 2002; Alexkor case 2003; Delgamuukw case 1997; Sawhoyamaxa Community case 2006, para. 118). Ethnocultural minorities, on the other hand, are not considered pre-settlement traditional societies even if they have had a long presence in a country, and they are not regarded as a distinct society with its own rules of governance. These purported grounds for a distinction are contestable, weak in legal principle, and not agreed to in international treaties.

2.3 Indigenous Rights: Collective or Individual?

Indigenous rights feature both an individual and a collective element (Awas Tingni case, 2001, para. 148). While international law principally recognises cultural, language, religious, and other identity rights as individual in nature, the existence of a society with its own legal system and collectively observed customs which are still practiced allows Indigenous Peoples to also exercise their rights collectively as a community (Tiina Sanila-Aikio case, 2018, para. 6.9). It is particularly in respect of their relationship to their traditional lands that the collective nature of indigenous rights is evidenced (Alexkor case 2003, paras. 62–64; Mabo case (2), 1992).

It is important for indigenous legal systems to be understood on their own terms, and by reference to the traditional collective rights of the community, rather than from the perspective of another legal system (Forrest case 2023; Kashela case 2018, para. 81; Akiba case 2013, para. 20). In Kenya, for example, an indigenous community's relationship with their traditional land was recognised as the basis for a collective claim under the right to property (Endorois Welfare Council case, 2003). The elevated status of Indigenous Peoples as distinct groups deserving consultation stems from their ongoing observance and practice of customary legal systems, primarily in relation to their traditionally held lands and associated activities like hunting and fishing, looking after land, and resource management (Fosen case 2021; Kalina and Lokono case, 2015, para. 172; Sawhoyamaxa Community case 2006, para. 118).

However, this also raises the question: what is the status of an indigenous community, or part of one, that no longer maintains a connection to traditional lands, no longer adheres to traditional customs, becomes urbanised, or ceases to function as a traditional society? Do they then become an ethnocultural minority and forfeit their collective rights as Indigenous People? (Ward case 2002, para. 32; Tiina Sanila-Aikio case 2018). Courts have steered away from this question. The question underscores the challenges and contentiousness of distinguishing between indigenous rights and ethnocultural minority rights as if they can be divided into watertight compartments.

2.4 What Is Meant by FPIC?

The term FPIC remains legally undefined. Its meaning is often derived from description and factual events rather than abstract definition as if a legal norm. Southalan correctly observes that 'there is no universal agreement on exactly what FPIC entails' (Southalan and Fardin, 2019, p. 373). By including the word 'consent', the phrase 'free, prior, and informed consent' seems to suggest a right of veto. However, a closer reading of UNDRIP – the most generous international instrument in referencing FPIC – does not support interpretations that include joint decision-making, power-sharing, or an actual veto. While UNDRIP seeks to promote, clarify, and enhance the rights of Indigenous Peoples, in fact, 'the lack of conceptual clarity surrounding the notion of Indigenous consent is rightly considered an obstacle to its institutionalisation' (Papillon, Leclair and Leydet, 2020, p. 224).

Municipal law courts tend to focus on whether proper consultation processes have been followed when Indigenous People are engaged, rather than considering the reasonableness or appropriateness of a proposal's merits, or the reasons for failing to reach agreement (Communications Services Union, 2010, para. 44). FPIC can be fulfilled without an agreement having been reached. In short, the phrase '*in order* to obtain their free, prior and informed consent' in UNDRIP is not construed at law as implying a veto, legally requiring that agreement *must* be reached, or establishing a form of co-decision-making with legal force (Kebaowek First Nation case, 2025, para. 183). Courts in domestic settings may, depending on their legal tradition, take note of developments related to FPIC in international law, but ultimately the responsibility to enact arrangements aimed at protecting indigenous rights lies with the state (Dann case 1985; Consultation case 2023; Baleni case, 2019).

FPIC signifies that a bona fide effort must be made to reach agreement, rather than imposing an enforceable requirement to agree. In this respect, the regulatory authority of the state remains intact (Tsilhqot'in Nation case 2014). It is, therefore, the attempt made by parties to achieve agreement that may be judicially evaluated, rather than the outcome of the consultation, the reasons for disagreement, or the merits of the respective proposals (Barngarla case, 2023).

Consent, in its ordinary sense, implies agreement; however, in the context of UNDRIP, it is the effort to seek or obtain consent that is embraced as the normative standard, rather than consent in the conventional sense of actual agreement. As such, the terms 'consultation' and 'consent' are notoriously misunderstood and frequently used interchangeably, despite carrying distinct meanings in legal contexts.

2.5 Legal Obligations Arising from FPIC

International law does not impose a legally enforceable obligation for co-decision-making with Indigenous People, nor does FPIC grant a veto to Indigenous Peoples over a proposed measure. This does not mean that state municipal arrangements cannot grant a veto, as happened in the Baleni case, but such a right of veto is not enlivened pursuant to international law intrinsic in FPIC (Baleni case, 2019). In Canada, where legal recognition is given to FPIC within the context of UNDRIP, the statutory obligation is short of a right of veto (Kebaowek First Nation case, 2025, para. 183). The same applies to recent legislative amendments in Finland in respect of negotiation rights of the Sami.

UNDRIP identifies some areas where a right to veto is proposed – such as protection against removal from traditional lands or the storage of hazardous materials on those lands (UNDRIP, 2007, arts. 10 and 29) – but even in these cases, it does not create legally enforceable rights. Ultimately, there is no single model for appropriate consultation procedures, as these depend on the specific circumstances of a particular indigenous community within domestic law (ILO Brazil 2009, para. 142; Strickland case 1998). In relatively few instances, domestic courts have sought guidance from international soft law to assist with resolving domestic disputes concerning the adequacy of consultation within municipal law (Girjas case 2020; Nesseby case 2018, para. 97; Kebaowek First Nation case, 2025, para. 183).

2.6 When Is FPIC Applied?

International law does not provide a closed list of topics or policy areas that require FPIC. FPIC is particularly applicable when Indigenous Peoples' interests in land are affected (Milirrpum case 1971, para. 167; Tsilhqot'in Nation case 2014, para. 211), but its application is not necessarily limited to land. Article 18 of UNDRIP states: 'Indigenous Peoples have the right to participate in decision-making in *matters which would affect their rights*, through representatives chosen by themselves in accordance with their own procedures, as well as to maintain and develop their own indigenous decision-making institutions' (emphasis added).

FPIC is, however, not mandated for general socio-economic matters, public policies, administrative measures, or legislation that also affects other communities and individuals (Law Society case, 2019, paras 86–88; Pabai case, 2025). Ultimately the duty to consult arises principally from domestic law in respect to traditional lands (Demarcation of territories case, 2022). As such, it is municipal legal, administrative and policy standards that determine the subject areas of consultation (Tiina Sanila-Aikio case, 2018). Courts have not been drawn into applying FPIC or good faith consultation to policy areas that are totally unrelated to indigenous lands, although some have acknowledged that the right to culture may include rights to health and a clean environment (Lhaka Honhat Association case, 2020). Courts do not, however, recognise a general duty of care to consult towards Indigenous People in respect of general policies that may impact on them (Pabai case, 2025).

2.7 Differences between FPIC and Good Faith Consultation

There is arguably no difference in the legal obligations arising from consultation and those from FPIC. Neither entails a right of veto (McJannet case, 2016, para. 60; Kebaowek First Nation case, 2025, para. 183). In the Kichwa case, it was observed that there is an 'obligation to consult' based on international law (Kichwa case, 2012, para. 164). In the Kebaowek First Nation case it was made clear that the emphasis is on consult, not on consent as a legal entitlement (Kebaowek First Nation case 2025). Courts sometimes even use consultation and FPIC interchangeably (Kalina and Lokono case, 2015). FPIC is a term specifically intended to enhance the consultation rights of Indigenous Peoples, but the emphasis lies not on an actual veto or co-decision-making, but on the effort to reach agreement (Barngarla case 2023; FMG case 2009).

FPIC relates more to advocacy than to being a term of law. Legally, FPIC is not dissimilar to good faith consultation (Kichwa case 2012, para. 165). Courts focus on the conduct of the parties involved to ascertain the presence or absence of good faith rather than on the merits of their respective positions or the right of veto of an indigenous community (WMC case 1999; Observatory Civic Association case 2023, para. 585). A blatantly unreasonable proposal or response to a proposal may thus be seen as indicating a lack of good faith in the way a party conducts itself.

The normative elements within which FPIC must occur can generally be outlined as follows: (Wild Coast appeal case 2024; Isolated Indigenous People case 2023) (a) material information about a proposed event, measure, or action must be provided to the Indigenous Peoples affected or those with an interest in the matter; (b) the information must be provided promptly and as soon as possible (Saramaka case, 2007); (c) the information must be sufficiently detailed – covering the entire scope of the project, including rehabilitation plans – to enable affected communities to seek advice, including expert advice, and to formulate an intra-community position; (d) consultation must be genuinely aimed at reaching some form of agreement, though there is no legal obligation to agree; (e) the position adopted by the community must be developed freely, without external pressure or undue influence; (f) both sides are required to engage in consultation in good faith; and (g) depending on the project's nature, including its scale and scope, the obligations arising from good faith consultation may extend throughout the life of the project (Kalina and Lokono case 2015; Poma Poma case 2002; CSF case 2016; Communities of the Sipakapense case 2014).

2.8 Is FPIC a Customary International Legal Norm?

Although consultative processes with Indigenous Peoples are widely endorsed as best practice in international law, as well as adopted as a requirement of the social license to operate, FPIC cannot be regarded as a justiciable legal norm of customary international law. For a customary norm to exist, two essential elements must be present: a general practice by states and its acceptance as law by states (UN International Law Commission 2018, 123; Icelandic Fisheries case 1973; North Sea Continental Shelf cases 1969). FPIC satisfies neither requirement.

UNDRIP, although the most widely cited instrument articulating the standard for FPIC, is not a treaty. It cannot be legally enforced and has not been widely incorporated into municipal law. ILO Convention 169, while binding as a treaty, has only limited scope. Isolated instances of adherence to FPIC or sporadic references to it in municipal judgements do not amount to a consistent and general practice accepted as law, and therefore cannot establish FPIC as a binding norm of customary international law (Jurisdictional Immunities of the State case, 2012).

UNDRIP may best be seen as the prism through which content is given to indigenous rights (Kebaowek First Nation case 2025). The legal content of indigenous consultation rights arises principally from domestic laws, not from international soft law declarations or expert opinions. While the individual rights of persons belonging to indigenous communities are recognised and protected under international law, the collective rights of Indigenous Peoples – particularly the requirement of 'consent' as envisaged in UNDRIP – are aspirational in nature. Those soft rights cannot be considered sufficiently endorsed by widespread international legal practice to meet the threshold of a justiciable legal principle under customary international law.

Since customary international law is derived from widespread state practice accepted as law (Yong Vui Kong case, 2010), it cannot be asserted that the notion of 'consent' in FPIC is widely or universally acknowledged as a binding legal norm arising from customary international law. While FPIC may, in the context of good faith consultation, have become to symbolise a standard of best practice from a policy perspective, as a distinct term of law it is too vague and inconsistently applied to be deemed a binding legal norm pursuant to customary international law.

2.9 FPIC as a Transformative, Directive Principle

Its absence of legal enforceability does not diminish FPIC's utility as a source of inspiration, a guide for direction, and a philosophy for indigenous empowerment. UNDRIP in general, and FPIC specifically, can inform the way in which fundamental rights, such as rights to self-determination, culture, property, environment, and family, are interpreted. FPIC can serve as a directive principle that inspires the broader recognition of indigenous rights (Balsara case, 1959). Government support for UNDRIP in international forums may be a factor that courts consider when relief is sought under municipal law.

While FPIC does not imply a relinquishment of government regulatory authority, it may operate as a constraint on how that authority is exercised in practice in similar way as a directive principle of state policy (State of Tamil Nadu case, 1984). FPIC does not amount to a right of veto, but it does place an obligation on the state to ensure that Indigenous Peoples are given a reasonable and fair opportunity to participate effectively and meaningfully in decisions and measures that affect their identity, culture, traditions, and lands (Saugeen First Nation case 2017, paras 10–29; Poma Poma case 2002, para. 7.6). FPIC can be interpreted dynamically depending on the specific circumstances of a particular indigenous community.

Fundamental rights and FPIC ought to be read together in a harmonious manner to achieve outcomes that approximate the social objectives of FPIC as closely as possible (Chandra Bhawan case, 1970). FPIC, as a directive principle, can therefore assist to imply new meanings of fundamental rights.

FPIC reflects each indigenous community's bundle of rights in a way that best suits their lived reality. Human rights treaties are living instruments that evolve in response to the practices and customs of the communities they aim to protect (Sámi mining case, 2024, paras. 13–14). The way consultation is conducted pursuant to FPIC may vary depending on the history and circumstances of each country and the relevant indigenous community.

2.10 Meaning of 'Good Faith'

Good faith is ascertained based on the fairness of each party's conduct and the objectives underlying domestic statutory arrangements (Commonwealth Bank of Australia case, 2014). The duty to act in good faith applies equally to both sides of the negotiating table (Munkara case 2024; Munkara consent orders cost 2024). Literature often underplays the importance of Indigenous People also bearing an obligation to act in good faith. The Munkara case in Australia illustrates the costs that can arise if it is found that an indigenous-objection to a project and subsequent delays caused, seriously lacked merit (Munkara consent orders cost, 2024). While there is no finite list of indicia used to determine good faith, courts generally look to the reasonableness of conduct, fairness of responses, the openness displayed by both sides, and sincerity of engagement (Communications Services Union, 2010, para. 44; Richman case, 2025; Indigenous Federations from Peru case, 2025).

Good faith implies providing a genuine opportunity for meaningful input and a reasonable chance to participate in and to influence the decision-making process (Tipakalippa case 2022, para. 104; Saugeen First Nation case 2017). Ultimately, what matters when consultation is assessed is the effort made to reach agreement, not the merits of the respective proposals, or the reasons for disagreement. Good faith does not permit a court to judge the merits of a party's position, unless that position is 'patently unreasonable' (Gomeroi People case, 2024, para. 77). Parties are entitled to negotiate hard, to adopt a firm position, and to pursue their own interests. The court does not in its review function become a co-negotiator. However, indicia of sincerity of intention and honesty can be considered (Strickland case, 1998). Rather, they assess – within the context of a specific dispute – whether the consultation process was conducted in good faith and whether the decision-maker had adequate 'regard' to the interests of Indigenous People (Murray Rivers Indigenous People case, 2025). A court must ultimately be satisfied that the measure is both necessary and proportionate for it to proceed (Mahuika case, 2000, para. 8.1).

2.11 Consultation in Respect of the Bundle of Rights

The content and scope of rights exercised by indigenous communities may differ. In the Ward case, this was described as the 'bundle of rights' held by each indigenous community (Ward case, 2002). The nature of the bundle of rights determines the extent and scope of the good faith consultation required when access to traditional lands is sought or for other related matters. The content of the bundle of right of a community depends on its traditional laws, customs, and the continued adherence thereto. Not only do these bundles of rights vary between indigenous communities, but the content of any given community's bundle may change over time (Poma Poma case 2002; CSF case 2016).

There is no legally secure list of topics to which FPIC applies. Generally, a bundle of rights originates from the customary lands of Indigenous Peoples and the customary rights associated with those lands. Courts have been wary of expanding these bundles of rights to encompass contemporary socio-economic policies that may not be directly related to traditional lands or customs, but courts have sometimes applied the FPIC to land that strictly speaking does not fall within traditional lands (Murray Rivers Indigenous People case, 2025). The interests of Indigenous People in land should not be restricted to highly technical definition based on an exact demarcation of their traditional lands, since an indigenous community may have an interest in a measure even if, technically, it affects land outside of their customary land (Barngarla case 2023; Murray Rivers Indigenous People case, 2025). The special interest Indigenous People may have in social policies and land-related policies such as water management, do not, however, imply that those policy areas become the subject of FPIC unless so determined by municipal law. The state does not have a general legal duty of care towards Indigenous People that grants then distinct collective rights to separate consultation in all societal policies that may affect them (Murray Rivers Indigenous People case, 2025).

2.12 Meaning of 'Consult'

While the word 'consult' is not a term of art with a clearly settled meaning, courts and expert bodies have developed indicia outlining the practical steps that ought to be taken to discharge obligations arising from the duty to consult (Kichwa case, 2012).

These indicia do not form an exhaustive list, but they include, for example, the following benchmarks applied within the context of a specific factual situation: voluntary participation by the community in the consultation process; negotiation through their own chosen or nominated representatives; provision of relevant, timely, and complete information about a proposed measure (Bengwenyama Minerals case 2011; Orissa Mining case 2013); openness from all parties to adjust their positions, though without a legal obligation to do so; meaningful participation and engagement; regular communication; ongoing consultation where the scope of the project requires it; and a genuine desire to reach agreement (Saramaka case 2007, paras. 133–134).

Importantly, the consultation undertaken must take into account the circumstances of the indigenous community, for example by being conducted in a language they understand, through media accessible to them, and by way of meetings held on site and in villages if that is appropriate (Paradise Park case,

2023; Sustaining the Wild Coast case, 2024). Essentially, as highlighted by the Juukan Gorge incident, Indigenous Peoples should be provided with ongoing information about the impact of a measure, including and especially about newly available evidence, and revised plans, as well as informed of relevant changes in circumstances. At the same time, however, the consultation process must remain practical and 'workable' (Tipakalippa case, 2022, para. 96).

2.13 Meaning of 'Good Faith'

Although international law does not provide a justiciable definition of FPIC, the obligation to consult in good faith applies to all parties. Nonetheless, even in those jurisdictions where good faith consultation with Indigenous Peoples is a normative requirement, how that good faith is given legal and practical effect depends on the specific circumstances of each case.

There is no international normative standard or checklist that conclusively proves whether the consultation that occurred was conducted in good faith – it depends on the facts of each dispute (Sesana case 2006). The impact of some measures may require 'deep consultation' (Clyde River case, 2017, para. 20), others less so. Courts tend not to focus on the merits of a proposal, considering instead the consultation process – how the proposal was presented, discussed, addressed, and adjusted (Observatory Civic Association case, 2023, p. 585). The same approach applies when a decision-maker 'must have regard' to the interests of Indigenous People (Murray Rivers Indigenous People case, 2025). Although in a statutory context the phrase 'having regard' is used, the meaning is derived from what can generally be described as FPIC-obligations.

General good practice guidelines on how to comply with FPIC have been developed internationally, but these do not constitute binding legal norms, as adherence to good faith consultation for compliance with FPIC ultimately depends on the circumstances of the indigenous community, their bundle of rights, and the prevailing municipal law (Project Sepik case, 2023, para. 97). The Bear Creek case highlights how a private entity can rely on a state's approval process to demonstrate that consultation with an indigenous community met legal and social license obligations (Bear Creek Mining case, 2021). On the other hand, the Juukan Gorge debacle underscores the risks a company faces when acting solely based on government approval, only to be confronted later by a maelstrom of negative public opinion for its actions due to inadequate community consultation.

2.14 What Information Should Be Shared?

A threshold requirement to meet consultation obligations is for the proponent of a development to share all relevant information with the affected indigenous community as soon as possible as part of the FPIC process (Mahuika case, 2000). The sharing of information is subject to considerations of the degree and reasonableness necessary to enable the indigenous community to make such an informed decision, but considering the non-disclosure of commercial in confidence (Human Rights Council-FPIC, 2018, para. 22).

Sharing of relevant information is also an obligation that rests on the indigenous community. If access to land is opposed by an indigenous community, they are obligated to explain the reasons for their opposition to allow the developer an opportunity to propose mitigation steps, measures to protect artefacts, or consider another location. Importantly, both sides are responsible for information-sharing as part of efforts to reach a mutually acceptable outcome (Sustaining the Wild Coast case, 2024, para. 19).

If a decision-maker uses consultation merely as a cloak to inform an indigenous community of a pre-determined decision, the requirements for good faith consultation, including keeping an open mind and transparent sharing of information, have not been met (Barngarla case 2023). On the other hand, if an indigenous community procrastinates during consultation, fails to participate or engage in FPIC-related processes, opposes a measure without providing relevant reasons, or initiates litigation without adequate evidence, a court may find that the community did not act in good faith (FMG case, 2009, para. 29), and may even award costs against it (Munkara consent orders cost, 2024).

2.15 Consultation with Whom?

All indigenous communities affected by a proposed measure must form part of the FPIC process to the extent that their interests are impacted. FPIC may involve different layers, with some indigenous communities participating more extensively in consultation than others. FPIC also applies to sub-communities, although courts acknowledge that there are limits to how far consultation can reasonably extend to every splinter group (Khoin case, 2022, para. 28).

The underlying premise of the authorisation provisions is to give all group members a 'reasonable opportunity' to participate in the decision-making process (Tipakalippa case, 2022, para. 104). The indigenous community is entitled to determine the mechanism through which its leaders or elders represent it in consultation (Richman case, 2025). It cannot be presumed that the community will reach consensus on every issue presented to them – the possibility of internal dissent is part of the reality of the process. The regulatory authority may, in its final deliberation and decision-making, take into account the differences of opinion that may exist in an indigenous community.

2.16 Dealing with Dissent

It is important for third parties to have confidence in the preferred negotiating mechanism of an indigenous community, including how the community manages internal dissent and how decisions are made by the community. The credibility of the consultation process may be undermined if a community does not speak coherently through a unified negotiation process, or if dissenting opinions cause unnecessary or vexatious delays. Dealing with various subgroups or factions may complicate FPIC, but proponents should at least make a reasonable effort to provide sub-groups with an opportunity to participate meaningfully in the consultation process (Tipakalippa case, 2022). That said, neither international law nor municipal law mandates consultation with or agreement by all community sub-groups (Munkara case, 2024). The consultation process must ultimately be 'both reasonable and workable' (Tipakalippa case, 2022, para. 109). It is acknowledged by courts that FPIC processes are limited by time and resources, and that at some point the processes concludes. If an indigenous community fails to participate in consultation as a cohesive unit or if the community is splintered into feuding groups, the community may be deemed to have fallen short in its obligation to engage in good faith consultation.

2.17 What Is Meant by 'Meaningful' in FPIC?

'Meaningful' is an ambit word of which the meaning is ascertained by the specific circumstances of consultation. It is, for example, the conduct, interaction, responses, behaviour, and mannerisms of the proponent that may establish whether consultation was meaningful. Importantly, however, the assertion by an affected community that consultation was not meaningful cannot, in itself, be used as a veto against a proposed measure – unless domestic legislation accords such a right (Maledu case 2018, paras 16, 78, 80, 97). Meaningful is ultimately determined by a court taking account of all relevant evidence. It is not the phrase that matters, being consult, consent, meaningful, or having regard, but the process whereby the decision-maker comes to a decision (Murray Rivers Indigenous People case, 2025).

Examples of essential principles underlying meaningful participation include: provision of adequate information to enable Indigenous Peoples to make informed decisions; recognition of their right to determine what happens on their land; consideration of the potential deprivation of customary and usage rights as relevant factors in assessing the right to meaningful participation; allowing the community time for internal consultations, organising meetings in a culturally appropriate way, using interpreters, and accommodation of the statutory regime under which the FPIC process occurs. Consultation may be required in relation to cultural aspects of the community (Fosen case, 2021); the impact of a proposal on the rights of children within the community (African Climate Alliance case, 2024); the potential effects of the proposal on climate change and how this might affect the community (Gomeroi People case, 2024); and issues concerning the ownership and management of forests (State Forest case, 2012).

2.18 Lack of Agreement

FPIC does not legally imply that the state has abdicated its regulatory responsibilities in respect of the measure under consideration. Neither UNDRIP nor ILO 169 suggests that, in policy areas where FPIC applies, the state ceases to hold the final regulatory role. Moreover, a lack of community consensus does not in itself indicate inadequate consultation (Mahuika case, 2000, para. 9.6) (ILO Argentina, 2008, para. 81). FPIC can comply with all legal requirements without an agreement being reached.

The final decision-making authority usually remains with the state, and in exercising its discretion, the state must take into account both the outcome of the FPIC process and the public interest (Bear Creek Mining case 2021; Forrest appeal case 2024). The extent of consultation may vary depending on the circumstances of each case, with 'full consent' required in some rare instances, but mostly not (Haida Nation case, 2004, para. 24). The failure to sufficiently consult in good faith can lead to litigation, potentially resulting in the setting aside of legislation, administrative measures, or approvals. Additionally, compensation may be awarded if an action occurred or damage to customary land was caused without good faith consultation having taken place (Timber Creek High Court appeal 2019; Yunupingu appeal case 2025). In practice, however, the award of compensation for a lack of good faith consultation is rare. The converse may also apply: an indigenous community which does not engage in good faith consultation, unnecessarily prolongs negotiations, or engages in litigation without good reason thereby causing an unreasonable delay to a project, may be held liable for compensation (Munkara case 2024; Munkara consent orders cost 2024).

2.19 Self-Regulation by the Private Sector

One of the most important outcomes of the increasing international attention on the FPIC process is the private sector's development of self-regulating norms and standards for consultation with Indigenous Peoples (Indigenous Federations from Peru case, 2025). These standards are intended as minimum, voluntary benchmarks and may not be relied on to undermine or override national norms (Project Sepik case 2023; Future In Our Hands case 2011, para. 18). On the other hand, if the industry standard is higher than a national norm, the expectation is that the industry standard would be adhered to.

The industry norms have a supra-national application that, in some respects, makes them more relevant to the development of international legal norms than national standards and policies. While high-profile disputes like Juukan Gorge attract international attention, thousands of agreements – both formal and informal – are reached each year between development proponents and Indigenous Peoples. These agreements are often unrecorded, unreported, and unresearched.

The nature of FPIC, including its scope, duration, and intensity, is determined by the specifics of the project under consideration (Project Sepik case, 2023, para. 81.4). Although general indicia can be identified as a guide for industry, the practical requirements for FPIC depend on the unique facts and circumstances of the proposed project (Survival International case, 2009, paras. 13–16). In some instances, consultation may be straightforward and conducted as a one-time process, while in other cases it may need to continue throughout the project's life. An environmental impact study that engages the general public about the impact of a measure, may not be adequate to meet the requirement of consultation with a specifically affected indigenous community if their lands or interests are uniquely affected (Indigenous people's representatives case, 2024).

2.20 Self-Regulation by Individual Companies

Developers may find themselves caught between conflicting norms, expectations, policy considerations, regulatory systems, and legal requirements regarding the adequacy of their FPIC processes with Indigenous Peoples. These overlapping and even competing norms may create an uncertain and unpredictable approval environment, as the simplicity and clarity of a single state-based regulatory authority granting final approval for a measure may be replaced by a myriad of potential approval benchmarks – none of which, especially in some complex cases, may provide an absolute guarantee of a non-litigated outcome.

The complexity of consultation is also heightened when multiple indigenous communities assert interests in the same land or when disagreements emerge within a community over how to respond to a proposal. Such inter- and intra-indigenous disputes can jeopardise the certainty sought to be given by an approval process. An approval granted under a state regulatory regime may later be undermined by the court of public opinion, industry self-regulation, legal challenges, financier concerns, or shareholder activism. In this sense, FPIC acts as an additional regulatory layer, but one that reflects the broader public interest in upholding and respecting indigenous rights.

2.21 Risk of Unintended Legitimacy and Credibility

Indigenous Peoples face the risk that their participation in the FPIC process may lend credibility and legitimacy to an approval of a measure which is contrary to their interests (Sara case, 2017, para. 94). Participation in consultation does not equate to co-decision-making. FPIC is only one part of a consideration process. While efforts to obtain FPIC have strengthened the participatory rights of Indigenous Peoples, FPIC does not imply Indigenous People are the final decision-makers. Therefore, the regulator may approve a measure against the wishes of an indigenous community, with the decision-maker relying on indigenous participation in the FPIC process to give the approval legitimacy and credibility. This may leave an indigenous community disillusioned. On the other hand, an indigenous community's refusal to engage in the FPIC process, possibly to avoid lending legitimacy to an anticipated and unwanted outcome, may be considered as conduct inconsistent with the concept of good faith (Fredemi Coalition case, 2011).

2.22 Summary

In summary, the following conclusions can be drawn about FPIC as a potential legal entitlement:

- FPIC is not a legal term in binding international law;
- FPIC is akin to a non-justiciable directive principle of state policy that inspires and influences the interpretation of rights of Indigenous People;
- FPIC is not a legally recognised right in customary international law;

- FPIC is not legally defined in international law or domestic law, though the term is often used in soft law, advocacy, and non-legal policy materials;
- UNDRIP outlines the objective of an obligation to seek FPIC rather than a mandate that legally obliges agreement;
- The word 'consent' in the context of FPIC in international materials is not construed as conferring a legal veto or co-decision-making power to Indigenous People;
- States are required to give practical effect to UNDRIP in general, and FPIC in particular, through their domestic legal arrangements when dealing with Indigenous Peoples;
- FPIC does not apply to every measure or policy that may affect Indigenous Peoples, but it is applied on a sliding scale depending on the nature of the project, including its scope, duration, and the specific bundle of traditional rights and interests held by the community;
- Legally, courts in domestic settings do not draw a distinction of substance between good faith consultation and FPIC;
- Courts assess compliance with the normative aspects of FPIC based on the specific circumstances of consultation within domestic law, rather than what FPIC may mean in the abstract;
- Courts interpret FPIC in the context of the process followed 'in order to obtain' consent, without assessing the reasons why agreement was not reached – unless a position adopted by either party is so unreasonable that it may signal an absence of good faith during the consultation process; and
- FPIC has reshaped the recognition of and engagement with indigenous rights, as it reflects an aspiration for fairness, a philosophy of justice, and a desire to address historical injustices by protecting Indigenous Peoples and their cultures, customs and traditions, while recognising their uniqueness, their love and responsibility for their land, their marginalised status, and, ultimately, their right to self-determination.

Bibliography

ABC case (1995) *Public Sector Union v Australian Broadcasting Commission (1995) 36 AILR 372.*

Aboriginal Heritage Act (1972) *Aboriginal Heritage Act 1972 (WA).*

Achtouk-Spivak, L. and Garden, R. (2022) "OECD National Contact Point Specific Instances: When 'Soft Law' Bites?," *Journal of International Dispute Resolution*, 13, pp. 608–642.

African Advisory Opinion (2007) "Advisory Opinion of the African Commission on Human and Peoples' Rights on the United Nations Declaration on the Rights of Indigenous Peoples."

African Charter (1981) "African Charter on Human and Peoples' Rights (Adopted 27 June 1981, OAU Doc. CAB/LEG/67/3 rev. 5, 21 I.L.M. 58 (1982), entered into force 21 October 1986)." Available at: https://www.achpr.org/public/Document/file/English/banjul_charter.pdf (Accessed: September 1, 2020).

African Climate Alliance case (2024) *African Climate Alliance and others v Minister of Mineral Resources and Energy and others 56901/2021 High Court Gauteng 4 December 2024.*

African Commission on Human Rights and Peoples' Rights case (2017) *African Commission on Human Rights and Peoples' Rights v Republic of Kenya Application No. 006/2012(Judgment) of 26* May *2017.*

Ago, R. (1957) "Positive Law and International Law," *AJIL*, 51, pp. 691–725.

Ahmed, T. (2011) *The impact of EU Law on minority rights*. Oxford: Hart Publishing.

Ahren, M. (2023) "An unsettled liberal democratic order and indigenous peoples' rights," in A. Biro and D. Newman (eds.) *Minority rights and liberal democratic insecurities*. Oxon: Routledge, pp. 171–188.

Akiba case (2013) *Akiba v Commonwealth (2013) 250 CLR 209, [55] citing Western Australia v Ward (2002) 213 CLR 1, [20] (Gleeson CJ, Gaudron, Gummow and Hayne JJ).*

Albania case (1935) *Minority Schools in Albania, Advisory Opinion*. Available at: http://www.worldcourts.com/pcij/eng/decisions/1935.04.06_albania.htm (Accessed: February 17, 2023).

Alexkor case (2003) *Alexkor Ltd v The Richtersveld Community (2003 (5) SA 460 (CC)).*

Almanza, M.C. and Salazar, J.C. (2022) "Limitations on Democracy in Multilateral Policies to Regulate the Political Participation of Indigenous and Tribal Peoples," *Colombia Internacional*, September, pp. 111–133.

Alva-Arevalo, A. (2021) "A critical evaluation of the domestic standards of the right to prior consultation under the UNDRIP: lessons from the Peruvian case," in D. Short

HTTPS://DOI.ORG/10.1163/9789004724792-012

et al. (eds.) *The United Nations Declaration on the Rights of Indigenous Peoples: A Contemporary Evaluation*. London: Routledge, pp. 233–247.

American Convention (1969) "American Convention on Human Rights, 'Pact of San Jose', Costa Rica." Organization of American States. Available at: https://www.refworld.org/docid/3ae6b36510.html (Accessed: May 1, 2022).

Anaya, J. (2009) *International human rights and indigenous peoples*. New York: Aspen.

Anaya, S.J. (1996) *Indigenous Peoples in International Law*. Oxford: Oxford University Press.

Anaya, S.J. (2009) *Report of the Special Rapporteur on the Situation of Human Rights and Fundamental Freedoms of Indigenous People*. A/HRC/12/34. Geneva: UNHRC.

Anderson case (2022) *Anderson v. Alberta, 2022 SCC 6.*

Annual Report NCP Activity (2025) "Annual Report on the OECD Guidelines for Multinational Enterprises 2020: Update on National Contact Point Activity." Available at: https://www.oecd.org/content/dam/oecd/en/networks/national-contact-points/OECD-2024-Annual-Report-on-NCP-Activity.pdf (Accessed: January 8, 2026).

Arajarvi, N. (2022) "Misinterpreting Customary International Law: Corrupt Pedigree or Self-Fulfilling Prophecy?," in P. Merkouris, J. Kammerhofer, and N. Arajarvi (eds.) *The Theory, Practice, and Interpretation of Customary International Law*. Cambridge: Cambridge University Press, pp. 40–61.

Arizona, Y. and Cohen, M. (2024) "The recognition of customary land rights at the Constitutional Court of Indonesia: a critical assessment of the jurisprudence," in B. De Villiers, S. Isra, and P. Faiz (eds.) *Courts and Diversity: Twenty Years of the Constitutional Court of Indonesia*. Leiden: Brill, pp. 173–194.

Asylum case (1950) *Colombian-Peruvian asylum case, Judgement of 20 November 1950, I.C.J Reports, 266.*

Australia Inquiry into UNDRIP (2023) *Inquiry into the application of the United Nations Declaration on the Rights of Indigenous Peoples in Australia*. Joint Standing Committee on Aboriginal and Torrs Strait Islander Affairs. Canberra: Parliament of Australia.

Australian Law Reform Commission (2010) "Consent." Australian Government. Available at: https://www.alrc.gov.au/publication/family-violence-improving-legal-frameworks-alrc-cps-1/16-sexual-offences/consent/ (Accessed: August 15, 2024).

Awas Tingni case (2001) *The Mayagna Awas Tingni v. Nicaragua, Inter-American Court of Human Rights, (2001).*

Backer, L.C. (2018) "The Arc of Triumph and Transformation of the OECD Guidelines: Quo Vadis Triumph? Into a Era of Transformation! Triumphi Quo Vadis? Temporibus Transmutatio Parere," in OECD (ed.) *OECD Guidelines for Multinational Enter prises – A Glass Half Full: A Liber Amicorum for Dr. Roel Nieuwenkamp, Chair of the OECD Working Party on Responsible Business Conduct 2013-2018*. OECD, pp. 45–62.

Baka, A.I. (2022) "The Logic of Absence in Customary International Law: An Open-System Approach," in P. Merkouris, J. Kammerhofer, and N. Arajarvi (eds.) *The Theory, Practice, and Interpretation of Customary International Law.* Cambridge: Cambridge University Press, pp. 62–86.

Baker, R.B. (2010) "Customary International Law in the 21st Century: Old Challenges and New Debates," *European Journal of International Law*, 21, pp. 173–204.

Bakirdzi case (2022) *Bakirdzi and E.C. v. Hungary – 49636/14 and 65678/14, Judgment 10.11.2022.*

Baleni case (2019) *Baleni v Minister of Mineral Resources 2019 (2) SA 453 (GP).*

Balsara case (1959) *F.N. Balsara v Bombay 1959 Bom 17*

Balwant Raj case (1968) *Balwant Raj v Union of India AIR 1968 All, 14.*

Banjima case (2015) *Banjima People v State of Western Australia (2015) 231 FCR 456.*

Barclays Bank case (1994) *Barclays Bank plc v O'Brien [1994] 1 AC 180 at 189–190.*

Barkey, K. and Gavrilis, G. (2017) "The Ottoman Millet System: Non-Territorial Autonomy and its Contemporary Legacy," in J. Coakley (ed.) *Non-territorial autonomy in divided societies – comparative perspectives.* London: Routledge, pp. 25–42.

Barngarla case (2023) *Barngarla Determination Aboriginal Corporation RNTBC v Minister for Resources [2023] FCA 809.*

Barrie, G.N. (2011) "The quest for indigenous land rights intensifies," *South African Public Law*, (26), pp. 497–512.

Barrie, G.N. (2013) "The United Nations Declaration on the Rights of Indigenous People: Implications for Land Rights and Self-Determination," *Journal of South African Law*, 22, pp. 292–305.

Barrie, G.N. (2021) "The concept of 'indigenous land tenure' surfaces in Namibia: a comparative overview of Agnes Kahimbi Kashela v Katima Mulilo Town Council (SA 15/2017) [2018] NASC 409 (16 November 2018)," *Obiter*, pp. 175–185.

Barrie, G.N. (2024a) "The introduction of "free, prior and informed consent' to the land reform legal lexicon," *Obiter*, pp. 900–912.

Barrie, G.N. (2024b) "The 'Right' to Free, Prior and Informed Consent: Evolving Customary International Law," in B. De Villiers, S. Isra, and P. Faiz (eds.) *Courts and Diversity: Twenty Years of the Constitutional Court of Indonesia.* Leiden: Brill, pp. 195–227.

Barten, U. (2015) "Article 27 ICCPR – a first point of reference," in U. Caruso and R. Hofmann (eds.) *The United Nations Declaration on Minorities: An Academic Account on the Occasion of its 20th Anniversary (1992–2012).* Leiden: Brill, pp. 46–65.

Bartlett, R. (2020) *Native Title in Australia.* Australia: LexisNexis Butterworths.

Bear Creek Mining case (2021) *Bear Creek Mining Corporation v. Republic of Peru, ICSID Case No. ARB/14/21.*

Becher, V. (1988) "The Informed Consent for the Sur gical Procedure: An Introduction," *Contemporary Orthopaedics*, 17, pp. 15–32.

Beham, M.P. (2022) "Schrödinger's Custom: Implications of Identification on the Interpretation of Customary International Law," in P. Merkouris, J. Kammerhofer, and N. Arajarvi (eds.) *The Theory, Practice, and Interpretation of Customary International Law*. Cambridge: Cambridge University Press, pp. 87–101.

Bellinger, J.B. and Haynes, W.J. (2007) "A US government response to the International Committee of the Red Cross study Customary International Humanitarian Law," *International Review of the Red Cross*, 89, pp. 443–461.

Bengwenyama Minerals case (2011) *Bengwenyama Minerals (Pty) Ltd and Genorah Resources (pty) Ltd (CCT 39/10) [2010] ZACC 26; 2011 (4) SA 113 (CC)*.

Bhatt, K. and Erdem Turkelli, G. (2021) "OECD National Contact Points as Sites of Effective Remedy: New Expressions of the Role and Rule of Law within Market Globalization?," *Business and Human Rights Journal*, 6, pp. 423–448.

Bhe case (2005) *Bhe v Khayelitsha Magistrate (Commission for Gender Equality as Amicus Curiae); Shibi v Sithole; South African Human Rights Commission v President of the Republic of South Africa [2004] ZACC 17; 2005 (1) SA 580 (CC); 2005 (1) BCLR 1 (CC)*.

Bloch, A. (2001) "Minorities and indigenous peoples," in A. Eide (ed.) *Economic, social and cultural rights*. Leiden: Kluwer, pp. 373–388.

Boirin-Farguess, Z. and Theriault, S. (2024) "Mining and Indigenous Livelihoods Rights, Revenues, and Resistance," in T. Rodon et al. (eds.) *Mining and Indigenous Livelihoods: Rights, Revenues, and Resistance*. London: Routledge, pp. 23–41.

Borschmann, G. (2020) "Report reveals Rio Tinto knew the significance of 46,000-year -old rock caves six years before it blasted them," *ABC News*, 5 June. Available at: https://www.abc.net.au/news/2020-06-05/rio-tinto-knew-6-years-ago-about -46000yo-rock-caves-it-blasted/12319334.

Boydell, S. and Baya, U. (2012) "Resource Development on Customary Land – Managing rhe Complexity Through a Pro-Development Compensation Solution," in. *Annual World Bank Confrence Land and Poverty*, Washington D.C.

Brown case (1954) *Brown v. Board of Education, 347 U.S. 483 (1954)*.

Brownley case (1999) *Brownley v Western Australia (no 1) [1999] FCA 1139*.

Büchler, A. (2016) *Islamic law in Europe? legal pluralism and its limits in Europoean family laws*. Routledge.

Buhmann, K. (2018) "Analysing OECD National Contact Point Statements for Guidance on Human Rights Due Diligence: Method, Findings and Outlook," *Nordic Journal of Human Rights*, 36, pp. 390–419.

Burmester, H. and Reye, S. (2000) "The Place of Customary International Law in Australian Law: Unfinished Business," *AUYrBkIntLaw*, 3. Available at: https://www5.austlii.edu.au/au/journals/AUYrBkIntLaw/2000/3.html (Accessed: December 2, 2024).

Burnside, S. (2009) "Negotiations in Good Faith under the Native Titlte Act: A Critical Analysis," *Land, Rights, Laws: Issues of Native Ttitle*, 4, pp. 1–16.

Cambou, D. (2024) "The significance of the Fosen decision for protecting the cultural rights of the Sámi indigenous people in the green transition," in D. Cambou and O. Ravna (eds.) *The significance of Sámi Rights*. Oxon: Routledge, pp. 52–70.

Cambou, D. (2025) "To reform Indigenou's Peoples' worlds: the methamorphis of free prior and informed consent at the World Bank," in M. Ahren, C. Charters, and J. Hohmann (eds.) *Oxford Handbook of Indigenous Peoples and International Law*. Oxford: Oxford University Press.

Canada UNDRIP Act (2021) *United Nations Declaration on the Rights of Indigenous Peoples Act S.C. 2021, c. 14, Assented to 2021-06-21.*

Canterbury case (1972) *Canterbury v. Spence, 464 F2d 772, Washington, D.C., 1972.*

Capotorti, F. (1979) *Study on the rights of persons belonging to ethnic, religious and linguistic communities.* E_CN.4_Sub.2_384_Rev.1. New York: Sub-commission on prevention of discrimination and protection of minorities.

Cardoret and Le Bihan case (1991) *Cadoret and Le Bihan v. France (Communication No. 323/1988: France. 11/04/91. CCPR/C/41/D/323/1988).*

Cassese, A. (1995) *Self-determination of peoples: A legal reappraisal.* New York: Cambridge University Press.

Castellino, J. (2010) "The Protection of Minorities and Indigenous Peoples in International Law: A Comparative Temporal Analysis," *International Journal on Minority and Group Rights*, 17, pp. 393–422.

CATSI/NTRB (2010) "Interaction between the Corporations (Aboriginal and Torres Strait Islander) Act 2006 and the Native Title Act 1993." ORIC. Available at: https://www.oric.gov.au/sites/default/files/documents/06_2013/ORIC_Interaction CATSI-NTA_2010-01.pdf (Accessed: June 6, 2020).

CCFD case (2013) *CCFD et al v Michelin, NCP France (Final Statement, 27 September 2013).*

CCFD Follow-up case (2016) *CCFD et al v Michelin, NCP France (Follow-Up Statement II, 29 February 2016.*

CERD General Recommendation (1997) "CERD, General Recommendation 23, Rights of Indigenous Peoples (Fifty-fisrt session, 1997), UN Doc A/52/18, annex V at 122 (1997) Para 4(d), 5." CERD.

Certification case (1996) *In re: Certification of the Constitution of the RSA, 1996 1996 10 BCLR 1253 (CC), 1996 4 SA 744 (CC).*

Chan, L. (2016) "The Dominance of the International Court of Justice in the Creation of Customary International Law," *Southampton Student Law Review*, 6, pp. 44–71.

Chandra Bhawan case (1970) *Chandra Bhawan Boarding and Lodging Bangalore v The State of Mysore 1970 SCR 600.*

Chandrabhavan case (1970) *Chandrabhavan v. State of Mysore 1970 SCR (2) 600.*

Chaundri, A.S. (1955) *Constitutional rights and limitations*. New Delhi: Wadhwa.

Clyde River case (2017) *Clyde River (Hamlet) v. Petroleum Geo-Services Inc., 2017 SCC 40 (CanLII), [2017] 1 SCR 1069*. Available at: https://www.canlii.org/en/ca/scc/doc/2017/2017scc40/2017scc40.html (Accessed: April 15, 1921).

Cobo, J.R.M. (1986) *Study on the Problem of Discrimination against Indigenous Populations E/CN.4/Sub.2/1986/Add.4*. E/CN.4/Sub.2/1986/Add.4. Geneva: UN Human Rights Committee.

Cocanour, C.S. (2017) "Informed consent – It's more than a signature on a piece of paper," *The American Journal of Surgery*, 214, pp. 993–997.

Commonwealth Bank of Australia case (2014) *Commonwealth Bank of Australia v Barker [2014] HCA 32*.

Commonwealth of Australia (1993) "Mabo: The High Court Decision on Native Ttitle."

Communications Services Union (2010) *Communications, Electrical, Electronic, Energy, Information, Postal, Plumbing and Allied Services Union of Australia v QR Limited [2010] FCA 591; (2010) 198 IR 382*.

Communities of the Sipakepense case (2014) *Communities of the Sipakepense and Mam Mayan People of the Municipalities of Sipacapa and San Miguel Ixtahuacán-Guatemala April 3, 2014 Report no. 20/14 Petition* 1566-07.

Community Garifuna of San Juan case (2023) *Community Garifuna of San Juan and its members v. Honduras. Preliminary Objections, Merits, Reparations and Costs. Judgment of August 29, 2023. Series C No. 496*.

Constitution of Brazil (2010) "Constitution of the Federative Republic of Brazil." Available at: https://www.globalhealthrights.org/wp-content/uploads/2013/09/Brazil-constitution-English.pdf (Accessed: July 29, 2024).

Constitutional Assembly (1947) "Constituent Assembly Debates (CAD) vol. 5." Available at: https://www.constitutionofindia.net/constitution_assembly_debates/volume/5 (Accessed: September 2, 2022).

Constitutional Assembly Debates (1937) "Constitutional Assembly Debates."

Consultation case (2023) *Costa Rica CRC-2023-3-005*.

Corn case (1955) *Corn v. French, 71 Nev. 280,289 P. 2d 173, Nevada, 1955*.

Cristescu, A. (1981) *The right to self-determination: Historical and current development on the basis of United Nations instruments*. E/CN.4/Sub.2/404/Rev. 1. New York: United Nations.

CSF case (2016) *CSF de la C-B v British Columbia 2016 BCSC 1764*.

D'Amato, A. (1965) "The Neo-Positivist Concept of International Law," *AJIL*, 59, pp. 321–345.

Daniel case (2002) *Western Australia v Daniel [2002] NNTTA 230*.

Dann case (1985) *United States v. Dann, 470 U.S. 39, 43 (1985)*.

Darrah case (1969) *Darrah v. Kite, 32 A2d 108, New York, 1969*.

D'Aspremont, J. (2022) "The Custom-Making Moment in ustomary International Law," in P. Merkouris, J. Kammerhofer, and N. Arajarvi (eds.) *The Theory, Practice, and Interpretation of Customary International Law*. Cambridge: Cambridge University Press, pp. 29–39.

De Roma case (2022) *Kevin Alfred de Roma v Western Yalanji Aboriginal Corporation RNTBC* [2022] *NNTTA 40*.

De Villiers, B. (1992a) "Directive principles of state policy and fundamental rights: the Indian experience," *South African Journal on Human Rights*, 8, pp. 29–49.

De Villiers, B. (1992b) "Socio-economic rights in a new constitution: critical evaluation of the recommendations of the South African law commission," *Journal of South African Law*, pp. 421–436.

De Villiers, B. (1994) "Social and economic rights," in D. Van Wyk et al. (eds.) *Rights and constitutionalism: the new South African legal order*. Cape Town: Juta, pp. 599–628.

De Villiers, B. (1998) "The San and the new South Africa: The right to land restitution," in G. Carpenter (ed.) *Suprema Lex: essays on the Constitution presented to Marinus Wiechers*. Cape Town: Juta, pp. 195–216.

De Villiers, B. (1999) *Land claims in national parks – the Makuleke experience*. Pretoria: HSRC Press.

De Villiers, B. (2004) "Native title Down Under: From hot tub to preservation of evidence – mediation in complex land claims," *South African Public Law*, pp. 440–448.

De Villiers, B. (2008) *People and Parks – Sharing the benefits*. Johannesburg: Konrad Adenauer Foundation.

De Villiers, B. (2012) "Language, Cultural and Religious Minorities: What and Who are they?," *University of Western Australia Law Review*, 36, pp. 67–89.

De Villiers, B. (2020a) "Chasing the Dream – Self-determination on a Non-Territorial basis for the Noongar Traditional Owners in the South West of Australia," *International Journal on Minority and Group Rights*, 27, pp. 171–193.

De Villiers, B. (2020b) "Privatised autonomy for the Noongar people of Australia – a sui generis Model for Indigenous Non-Territorial Self-Government," *Verfassungs Und Recht Ubersee*, 53, pp. 171–189.

De Villiers, B. (2021) "The elephant in the room – resolving disputes about membership of a minority or indigenous community," in B. De Villiers et al. (eds.) *Litigating the Rights of Minorities and Indigenous Peoples in Domestic and International Courts*. Leiden: Brill, pp. 52–80.

De Villiers, B. (2022a) "Does a constitution have a soul? The role of Bundestreue in Germany and Ubuntu in South Africa to give life and identity to a constitutional text," in *Navigating the Unknown – essays on selected case studies about the rights of minorities*. Leiden: Brill, pp. 163–214.

De Villiers, B. (2022b) "Using control over access to land to achieve self-government (of some sort): Reflecting on the experiences of Aboriginal people with the right to negotiate in Australia," in *Navigating the Unknown – essays on selected case studies about the rights of minorities*. Leiden: Brill, pp. 104–137.

De Villiers, B. (2023a) "Breathing life into the Constitution: The transformative role of courts to give a unique identity to a constitution," *Constitutional Review*, 9, pp. 109–141.

De Villiers, B. (2023b) "Dithering between consultation and consensus – whereto with advisory bodies for Indigenous Peoples?," *Journal of Ethnopolitics and Minority Issues in Europe*, 22, pp. 32–63. Available at: https://doi.org/10.53779/HBKA3992.

De Villiers, B. (2023c) "Our Land, Our Life Linking Self- determination to Land Restoration in the Case of the Makuleke Joint Management Agreement in the Kruger National Park," in *Indigenous rights in the modern era: Regaining what has been lost*. Leiden: Brill, pp. 241–296.

De Villiers, B. (2023d) "Right to be consulted, but the frustration of being ignored: The ongoing efforts in international law to give practical meaning to free, prior, and informed consent," in *Indigenous rights in the modern era: Regaining what has been lost*. Leiden: Brill, pp. 68–130.

De Villiers, B. (2024a) "Life after the failed Voice: Options for Aboriginal self-determination and consultation in Australia," *International Journal on Minority and Group Rights*, pp. 1–32.

De Villiers, B. (2024b) "The rejection of the Voice for Aboriginal people in Australia – a postmortem of causes of failure," *Constitutional Review*, pp. 266–306.

De Villiers, B. (2024c) "The rejection of the Voice for Aboriginal people in Australia – do indigenous advisory bodies have a place in modern society?," *Verfassungs Und Recht Ubersee* [Preprint].

De Villiers, B. (2025a) "Diversity: A Beautiful Difficulty," in *The South African Bill of Rights and Pluralism: A comparative Perspective of Judicial Responses to Diversity*. Cape Town: Juta, pp. 1–14.

De Villiers, B. (2025b) "Free, prior, and informed Consent in Indigenous rights: The Juukan Gorge Debacle," *Constitutional Review*, 11, pp. 340–362.

De Villiers, B. (2025c) "Impact of Ubuntu on South African Jurisprudence: From a source of Rights to a Customary Way to explain Complex Judgments," in *The South African Bill of Rights and Pluralism: A comparative Perspective of Judicial Responses to Diversity*. Cape Town: Juta, pp. 215–264.

De Villiers, B. (2025d) "Pluralism In Law: Pathway to the Rainbow Nation," in *The South African Bill of Rights and Pluralism: A comparative Perspective of Judicial Responses to Diversity*. Cape Town: Juta, pp. 15–58.

De Villiers, B. (2025e) "Recognition and Restoration of Indigenous Peoples' Rights to Land: Free, Prior and Informed Consent – Theory and Practice," in *The South*

African Bill of Rights and Pluralism: A comparative Perspective of Judicial Responses to Diversity. Cape Town: Juta, pp. 265–354.

De Villiers, B. (2025f) "Recognition of Customary Law: Harmonising Tradition with Modernity (or the Other Way Around?)," in *The South African Bill of Rights and Pluralism: A comparative Perspective of Judicial Responses to Diversity*. Cape Town: Juta, pp. 483–531.

De Villiers, B. (2025g) "The Bill of Rights and Pluralism: Reflection on South African Jurisprudence," in *The South African Bill of Rights and Pluralism: A comparative Perspective of Judicial Responses to Diversity*. Cape Town: Juta, pp. 532–580.

Delgamuukw case (1997) *Delgamuukw v British Columbia, 3 S.C.R. 1010 (1997)*.

Demarcation of territories case (2022) *Arguição de descumprimento de preceito fundamental ADPF 709*.

Denmark: UNDRIP (2018) "Response from the Kingdom of Denmark to the questionnaire regarding the study of the Expert Mechanism on the Rights of Indigenous Peoples on free, prior and informed consent." Government of Denmark. Available at: https://www.ohchr.org/sites/default/files/Documents/Issues/IPeoples/EMRIP/FPIC/Denmark.pdf (Accessed: October 15, 2024).

Diala, A. (2019) "Our Laws Are Better Than Yours: The Future of Legal Pluralism in South Africa," *Revista General de Derecho Público Comparado*, 26, pp. 1–23.

Dinstein, Y. and Tabory, M. (eds.) (2023) *The Protection of Minorities and Human Rights*. London: Marthinus Nijjhof.

Doyle, C. (2014) *Indigenous Peoples, Title to Territory, Rights and Resources The Transformative Role of Free Prior and Informed Consent*. London: Routledge. Available at: https://www.taylorfrancis.com/books/mono/10.4324/9781315780665/indigenous-peoples-title-territory-rights-resources-cathal-doyle (Accessed: May 16, 2022).

Doyle, C. (2022) "Free prior and informed consent and Indigenous rights: a bulwark against discrimination and platform for self-determination," in D. Newman (ed.) *Research Handbook on the International Law of Indigenous Rights*. Cheltenham: Edward Elgar Publishing Limited, pp. 96–128.

Dugard, J. (2018) *International law*. Cape Town: Juta.

Dunlap, A. (2018) "'A Bureaucratic Trap:' Free, Prior and Informed Consent (FPIC) and Wind Energy Development in Juchitán, Mexico," *Capitalism Nature Socialism*, 29, pp. 88–108.

ECOSOC: Guidelines FPIC (2005) *Report of the International Workshop on Methodologies regarding Free, Prior and Informed Consent and Indigenous Peoples: E/C.19/2005/3*. UN Economic and Social Council (ECOSOC). Available at: https://digitallibrary.un.org/record/544406?v=pdf (Accessed: July 2, 2025).

Eichler, J. (2019) *Reconciling Indigenous Peoples' Individual and Collective Rights Participation, Prior Consultation and Self-Determination in Latin America*. London: Routledge.

Eide, A. and Daes, E. (2000) *Working Paper on the Relationship and Distinction between the Rights of Persons Belonging to Minorities and Those of Indigenous Peoples*. E/CN.4/Sub.2/2000/10. Geneva: United Nations.

Endorois Welfare Council case (2003) *Centre for Minority Rights Development (Kenya) and Minority Rights Group (on behalf of the Endorois Welfare Council), 273 of 2003.*

Ermacora, F. (1983) *The Protection of Minorities before the United Nations*. Leiden: Brill.

Ernst Young (2010) *Global Mining and Metals Top 10 Business Risks and Opportunities – 2021' (EYGM Limited, 2020).*

Esperance heritage agreement (2024) "Esperance Nyungar Agreement – Aboriginal Heritage information." WA Government. Available at: https://www.wa.gov.au/government/document-collections/esperance-nyungar-agreement-aboriginal-heritage-information#:~:text=The%20agreement%20was%20executed%20following,square%20kilometres%20of%20this%20area. (Accessed: October 8, 2024).

European Framework Convention (1998) *European Framework Convention for the Protection of National Minorities, 1998*. Strasbourg: Council of Eurppe (H (95) 10). Available at: https://www.refworld.org/docid/3ae6b36210.html (Accessed: March 1, 2023).

Eveready case (1962) *Eveready Flashlight v Labour Court AIR 1962 All 497.*

Explanatory Report on FCNM (1995) "Explanatory Report to the Framework Convention for the Protection of National Minorities." Council of Europe.

Federation of AIC and CE Stenographers case (1988) *Federation of AIC and CE Stenographers v Union of India AIR 1988 SC 1291.*

Fedotova case (2023) *Case of Fedotova and Others v. Russia, Applications nos. 40792/10, 30538/14 and 43439/14, 2023.*

Fielitz, P. and MacKay, F. (2025) "Envisioning Self-Determination through the UNDRIP: more steps necessary towards advancing the rights of Indigenous peoples." Berlin.

Final Report Juukan (2021) *A Way Forward: Final report into the destruction of Indigenous heritage sites at Juukan Gorge*. Canberra: Joint Standing Committee on Northern Australia. Available at: https://nativetitle.org.au/sites/default/files/2021-10/AWayForward.pdf (Accessed: January 20, 2025).

Fink, C. (1998) "The Minorities Question at the Paris Peace Conference: The Polish Minority Treaty, June 28, 1919," in G. Boemeke, G. Feldman, and E. Glaser (eds.) *The Treaty of Versailles: A Reassessment after 75 Years*. London: Cambridge University Press, pp. 249–274.

Flemmer, R. (2022) "The Implementation Paradox Ambiguities of Prior Consultation and Free, Prior, and Informed Consent (FPIC) for Indigenous Peoples' Agency in Resource Extraction in Latin America," in K. Ruckstuhl et al. (eds.) *The Routledge Handbook of Indigenous Development*. London: Routledge, pp. 126–142.

FMG case (2009) *FMG Pilbara Pty Ltd v Cox [2009] FCAFC 49.*

Forrest appeal case (2024) *Forrest and Forrest Pty Ltd -v- Minister of Aboriginal Affairs [2024] WASCA 96.*

Forrest case (2023) *Forrest and Forrest Pty Ltd v Minister for Aboriginal Affairs 2023 [WASAT] 28.*

Fortescue Metals case (2019) *Fortescue Metals Group v Warrie on behalf of the Yindjibarndi People [2019] FCAFC 177; 273 FCR 350.*

Fosen case (2021) *Supreme Court of Norway, HR-2021-1975-S.*

FPIC & Rights Forum (2020) *Free, Prior and Informed Consent Protocol.* Nepal: FPIC & Rights Forum. Available at: https://www.iwgia.org/images/publications/new-publications/2020/FPIC_protocol_Nepal.pdf (Accessed: April 22, 2021).

Fredemi Coalition case (2011) *Fredemi Coalition v Goldcorp Inc., NCP Canada (Final Statement, 3* May *2011.*

Fredericks, C.F. (2016) "Operationalizing free, prior, and informed consent," *Albany Law Review*, 80, pp. 429–482.

Future In Our Hands case (2011) *Future In Our Hands (FIOH) v Intex Resources ASA, NCP Norway (Final Statement, 30 November 2011).*

Gaspardus, R. (2025) "Complementarity of National and International Courts on Protection of Indigenous Peoples' Right to Ancestral Lands in the Contemporary World," *International Journal of Law and Society*, 8, pp. 207–217.

Gaum case (2019) *Gaum and others v Van Rensburg NO and others (Commission for Gender Equality and another as amici curiae) [2019] 2 All SA 722 (GP).*

Ginsburg, T. (2004) "Bounded Discretion in International Judicial Lawmaking," *Va. J. Int'l L*, 45, pp. 631–652.

Girjas case (2020) *Girjas v. the State (Swedish Supreme Court), 2020. (No. T 853–918).*

Giupponi, B.O. (2018) "Free, Prior and Informed Consent (fpic) of Indigenous Peoples before Human Rights Courts and International Investment Tribunals: Two Sides of the Same Coin?," *international journal on minority and group rights*, 25, pp. 485–529.

Gomeroi People case (2024) *Gomeroi People v Santos NSW Pty Ltd and Santos NSW (Narrabri Gas) Pty Ltd [2024] FCAFC 26.*

Goodland, R. (2004) "Free, Prior and Informed Consent and the World Bank Group," *Sustainable Development Law and Policy*, 4, pp. 66–74.

Gottlieb, C. (2023) "OECD Publishes Update to Its Guidelines for Multinational Enterprises," 22 June. Available at: https://www.clearygottlieb.com/news-and-insights/publication-listing/oecd-publishes-update-to-its-guidelines-for-multinational-enterprises#_ftn7 (Accessed: November 5, 2024).

Gradoni, L. (2015) "The International Court of Justice and the international customary law game of cards," in M. Andenas and E. Bjorge (eds.) *A Farewell to Fragmentation: Reassertion and Convergence in International Law. Studies on International Courts and Tribunals.* Cambridge: Cambridge University Press, pp. 371–406.

Greenhouse Gas Pollution case (2021) *References re Greenhouse Gas Pollution Pricing Act 2021 SCC 11.*

Griffiths, J. (1986) "What Is Legal Pluralism?," *The Journal of Legal Pluralism and Unofficial Law*, 18, pp. 1–55. Available at: https://doi.org/10.1080/07329113.1986.10756387.

Grootboom case (2000) *Government of the Republic of South Africa and Others v Grootboom and Others (CCT11/00) [2000] ZACC 19; 2001 (1) SA 46; 2000 (11) BCLR 1169 (4 October 2000).*

Gulf of Maine case (1984) *Delimitation of the Maritime Boundary in the Gulf of Maine Area (Can. v. U.S.), 1984 I.C.J. 246.*

Haida Nation case (2004) *Haida Nation v British Columbia (Minister of Forests) [2004] 3 SCR 511.*

Hall, N. (2023) "New Zealand Abandons Indigenous Rights and Pacific Priorities in Foreign Policy," *The Diplomat*, 21 December.

Handbook ILO (2013) *Understanding the Indigenous and Tribal Peoples Convention, 1989 (No. 169).* Geneva: ILO Office. Available at: https://www.ilo.org/wcmsp5/groups/public/–ed_norm/–normes/documents/publication/wcms_205225.pdf (Accessed: May 2, 1921).

Hannum, H. (2023) *Documents on Autonomy and Minority Rights.* Leiden: Martinus Nijhoff Publishers.

Harrington-Smith (2007) *Harrington-Smith on behalf of the Wongatha People v Western Australia (no 9) [2007] FCA 31.*

Harrington-Smith case (2007) *Harrington-Smith on behalf of the Wongatha People v Western Australia (no 9) [2007] FCA 31.*

Hart, N. and Fox, D. (2024) "Environmental harm and the OECD NCP complaints process: the road increasingly travelled," 16 January. Available at: https://essexcourt.com/publication/environmental-harm-and-the-oecd-ncp-complaints-process-the-road-increasingly-travelled-week-4-series-3/ (Accessed: February 22, 1925).

Hassan, M.S., Nordin, R. and Wook, I. (2025) "Free, Prior, and Informed Consent (FPIC) and the Right to Self-Determination: A Case Study of Indigenous Peoples in ASEAN Member States," in R.B. Swain and P. Dobers (eds.) *Routledge Handbook of UN Sustainable Development Goals Research and Policy.* London: Routledge.

Healey, R. (2019) "From Individual to Collective Consent: The Case of Indigenous Peoples and undrip," *International Journal on Minority and Group Rights*, 27, pp. 251–269.

Henrard, K. (2010) "'The EU, Double Standards and Minority Protection': A Double Redefinition and Future Prospects," in K. Henrard (ed.) *Double Standards Pertaining to Minority Protection.* Leiden: Brill, pp. 21–70.

Hobbs, H. and Williams, G. (2018) "The Noongar Settlement: Australia's First Treaty," *Sydney Law Review*, 40, pp. 1–24.

Hofmann, R., Malloy, T.H. and Rein, D. (2018a) "Introduction," in R. Hofmann, T. H. Malloy, and D. Rein (eds.) *The Framework Convention for the Protection of National Minorities: A Commentary*. Leiden: Brill, pp. 1–21.

Hofmann, R., Malloy, T.H. and Rein, D. (eds.) (2018b) *The Framework Convention for the Protection of National Minorities*. Leiden: Brill.

Horowitz, D.L. (1993) "Democracy in divided societies," *Journal of Democracy*, (4), pp. 18–38.

Hoskot case (1978) *Hayawauadanrao Hoskot v Maharashtra AIR 1978 SC 1548.*

Human Rights Commission (2009) *Native Title Payments Discussion Paper – Optimising Benefits from Native Title Agreements*. Australian Human Rights Commission. Available at: https://humanrights.gov.au/our-work/legal/native-title-payments-discussion-paper-optimising-benefits-native-title-agreements (Accessed: July 1, 2020).

Human Rights Council-FPIC (2018) *Free, prior and informed consent: a human rights-based approach – Study of the Expert Mechanism on the Rights of Indigenous Peoples*. A/HRC/39/62. Geneva: Human Rights Council.

IAP and WDM case (2014) *IAP and WDM v GCM Resources Plc NCP UK (Final Statement, 20 November 2014).*

ICCPR (1966) "The International Covenant on Civil and Political Rights." United Nations office of the High Commissioner for Human Rights. Available at: https://www.ohchr.org/en/professionalinterest/pages/ccpr.aspx (Accessed: August 10, 2020).

ICCPR Comment Minorities (1994) *ICCPR General Comment No. 23: Article 27 (Rights of Minorities)*. Adopted at the Fiftieth Session of the Human Rights Committee, on 8 April 1994 CCPR/C/21/Rev.1/Add.5, General Comment No. 23. (General Comments). Geneva: UN Human Rights Committee. Available at: https://www.refworld.org/docid/453883fc0.html (Accessed: May 1, 2022).

Icelandic Fisheries case (1973) *Fisheries Jurisdiction (United Kingdom of Great Britain and Northern Ireland v. Iceland) I.C.J., 1973 I.C.J. 3.*

ICESCR (1966) "International Covenant on Economic, Social and Cultural Rights, Adopted and opened for signature, ratification and accession by General Assembly resolution 2200A (XXI) of 16 December 1966 entry into force 3 January 1976, in accordance with article 27." Available at: https://www.ohchr.org/en/professionalinterest/pages/cescr.aspx (Accessed: August 20, 2020).

ILO 169 (1989) "Indigenous and Tribal Peoples Convention, 1989 (No. 169)." Available at: https://www.ilo.org/dyn/normlex/en/f?p=NORMLEXPUB:12100:0::NO::P12100_ILO_CODE:C169.

ILO Argentina (2008) *Report of the Committee set up to examine the representation alleging non-observance by Argentina of the Indigenous and Tribal Peoples Conven-*

tion, 1989 (No. 169), made under article 24 of the ILO Constitution by the Education Workers Union of Río Negro (UNTER), local section affiliated to the Confederation of Education Workers of Argentina (CTERA). ILO. Available at: https://www.ilo.org/dyn/normlex/en/f?p=1000:50012:0::NO:50012:P50012_COMPLAINT_PROCEDURE_ID,P50012_LANG_CODE:2507187,en:NO (Accessed: March 9, 2022).

ILO Brazil (2009) *Report of the Committee set up to examine the representation alleging non-observance by Brazil of the Indigenous and Tribal Peoples Convention, 1989 (No. 169), made under article 24 of the ILO Constitution by the Union of Engineers of the Federal District (SENGE/DF)*. ILO. Available at: http://www.ilo.org/dyn/normlex/en/f?p=1000:50012:0::NO:50012:P50012_COMPLAINT_PROCEDURE_ID, P50012_LANG_CODE:2507317,en:NO (Accessed: April 22, 2022).

ILO Case Book (2009) *Application of Convention No. 169 by domestic and international courts in Latin America*. ILO. Available at: https://www.ilo.org/wcmsp5/groups/public/–ed_norm/–normes/documents/publication/wcms_123946.pdf (Accessed: May 18, 2022).

ILO Experts (1988) "Report of the Meeting of Experts, para. 46, reprinted in part in Partial Revision of the Indigenous and Tribal Populations Convention, 1957 (No. 107), Report 6(1), International Labour Conference, 75th Sess. at 100-18 (1988)." ILO.

In Re Melideo case (1976) *In re Melideo, 390 N.Y.S. 2d 523, New York, 1976.*

Indigenous and Tribunal Convention 107 (1957) "Indigenous and Tribal Populations Convention, 1957 (No. 107)." Available at: https://normlex.ilo.org/dyn/normlex/en/f?p=NORMLEXPUB:12100:0::NO::P12100_ILO_CODE:C107#:~:text=The%20populations%20concerned%20shall%20not,health%20of%20the%20said%20populations. (Accessed: July 12, 2024).

Indigenous community case (2023) *Indigenous community and foreign mining company NCP Chile 27 June 2023.*

Indigenous Federations from Peru case (2025) *Indigenous Federations from Peru et al. vs Pluspetrol Resources Corporation B.V. 3 September 2025 NCP Netherlands.*

Indigenous people's representatives case (2024) *Indigenous people's representatives and Statkraft AS NCP Chile Initial Assessment 19 September 2024.*

Informal Land Rights Act (1996) *Interim Protection of Informal Land Rights Act 31 of 1996*. Available at: chrome-extension://efaidnbmnnnibpcajpcglclefindmkaj/https://www.gov.za/sites/default/files/gcis_document/201409/act31of1996.pdf (Accessed: June 22, 2023).

Institute for Human Rights and Business (2022) "What Is Free, Prior and Informed Consent (FPIC)?" IHRB. Available at: https://www.ihrb.org/explainers/what-is-free-prior-and-informed-consent-fpic (Accessed: January 12, 1925).

International Law Commission (1950) "Report of the International Law Commission to the General Assembly (Part II): Ways and Means of Making the Evidence of

Customary International Law More Readily Available] 2 Y.B. Int'l L. Comm'n 367, ILC Doc. A/1316."

Iseli, C. (2020) "The operationalisation of the principle of free, prior and informed consent: a duty to obtain consent or simply a duty to consult," *Journal of Environmental Law*, 38, pp. 259–271.

Isolated Indigenous People case (2023) *Allegation of Non-Compliance with a Fundamental Precept ADPF 991.*

Jackson, B. (2025) "Historic deal following sacred site destruction," *MSN News*, 2 June. Available at: https://www.msn.com/en-au/news/australia/historic-deal-following-sacred-site-destruction/ar-AA1FTPIz?ocid=msedgntp&pc=LCTS&cvid=6d8513324 5d74a809e10870obeecf9d8&ei=39 (Accessed: June 10, 2025).

Jain, M.P. (1978) *Indian constitutional law*. New Delhi: LexisNexis Butterworths.

Jennings, R. and Watts, A. (2008) *Oppenheim's International Law*. Oxford: Oxford University Press.

Jennings, R.Y. (1982) "The Identification of International Law," in B. Cheng (ed.) *International Law: Teaching and Practice*. Stevens: London, pp. 3–24.

Jimenez, E. (2024) "Ownership of the deep seas: an old dilemma in deep seabed mining: free, prior and informed consent of indigenous peoples in areas beyond territorial jurisdiction," *AJIL*, 118, pp. 83–87.

Jiménez, M.J.O. (2022) "Indigenous peoples' normative orders and restitution:Latin American private international law and humanrights," *Legal Pluralism and Critical Social Analysis*, pp. 176–192.

Jurisdictional Immunities of the State case (2012) *Jurisdictional Immunities of the State (Germany v Italy: Greece intervening) (Judgment) [2012] ICJ Rep 99, 122.*

Juukan Government Response (2022) "Australian Government response to the Joint Standing Committee on Northern Australia's A Way Forward: Final Report into the destruction of Indigenous Heritage Sites at Juukan Gorge." Australian Government.

Juukan Law Society WA (2020) "Submission to the Inquiry into the Destruciton of 46,000 year old Caves – Juukan Gorge Western Australia."

Kalina and Lokono case (2015) *Kalina and Lokono Peoples v Suriname (Merits, Reparation, Costs) IACHR No. 309 (25 November 2015).*

Kammerhofer, J. (2022) "Between Pragmatism and Disenchantment," in P. Merkouris, J. Kammerhofer, and N. Arajarvi (eds.) *The Theory, Practice, and Interpretation of Customary International Law*. Cambridge: Cambridge University Press, pp. 3–28.

Kashela case (2018) *Agnes Kahimbi Kashela v Katima Mulilo Town Council (SA 15/2017) [2018] NASC 409 (16 November 2018).*

Kaur, A., Lodhia, S. and Lesue, A. (2024) "Being left behind: disclosure strategies to manage the Juukan Gorge cave blast," *Accounting, Auditing and Accountability Journal* [Preprint].

Kebaowek First Nation case (2025) *Kebaowek First Nation v Canadian Nuclear Laboratories 2025 FC 319.*

Kemp, D., Kochan, K. and Burton, J. (2023) "Critical reflections on the Juukan Gorge parliamentary inquiry and prospects for industry change," *Journal of Energy and Natural Resoruces Law*, 41, pp. 379–402.

Kenny, D. and McCann, L.M. (2022) "Directive Principles, Political Constitutionalism, and Constitutional Culture: the Case of Ireland's failed Directive Principles of Social Policy," *European Constitutional Law Review*, 18, pp. 207–238.

Kerala Education case (1959) *The Kerala Education Bill 1959 1 S.C.R. 995.*

Khoin case (2022) *Khoin v Jenkins in Re: Observatory Civic Association v Trustees for the Time Being of the Liesbeek Leisure Properties Trust*[2023] *1 All SA 110* (*WCC*)).

Khoisan Act appeal (2023) *Mogale and Others v Speaker of the National Assembly and Others* [2023] *ZACC 14.*

Kichwa case (2012) *Kichwa Indigenous People of Sarayaku v Ecuador, Merits and Preparations, Judgment, Inter-Am. Ct.H.H.* (*ser.C*) *No. 245,* (*June 27, 2012*).

Kokkinakis case (1993) *Kokkinakisv Greece, ECtHR Appl. No. 14308/88, judgement of 25* May *1993.*

Kolb (2013) *The International Court of Justice.* Oxford: Hart Publishing.

Kolb, R. (2014) *The Elgar Companion to the International Court of Justice.* Elgar Online.

Kosovo case (2010) *Accordance with International Law of the Unilateral Declaration of Independence in Respect of Kosovo* (*Advisory Opinion*) [*2010*] *ICJ Rep 403* (*Kosovo Opinion*) [*79*].

Kryazhkov, V.A. and Garipov, R.S. (2021) "ILO 169 convention as a vector for the aboriginal legislation development in Russia," *The International Journal of Human Rights*, 25, pp. 1007–1031.

Kuc, O. (2022) *The International Court of Justice and Municipal Courts: An Inter-Judicial Dialogue.* London: Routledge.

Kunz, J.L. (1954) "The present status of the international law in the protection of minorities," *American Journal of International Law*, 48, pp. 275–292.

Kusniati, R. (2024) "Free, Prior, and Informed Consent Principles as Indigenous Peoples' Right: Soft Law or Hard Law?," *Jambe Law Journal*, 7, pp. 169–193. Available at: 10.22437/jlj.7.1.169-193.

Kymlicka, W. (1999) "Theorizing Indigenous Rights," *University of Toronto Law Journal*, 49, pp. 281–294.

Kymlicka, W. (2008) "The internationalization of minority rights," *ICON*, 6, pp. 1–32.

Kymlicka, W. (2012) *Multiculturalism: Success, Failure, and the Future.* Washington D.C.: Migration Policy Institute.

Landers case (1982) *Landers v Attrney General IR* (*1982*) *109.*

Large case (1986) *Large v. Superior Court of Arizona, 714 P.2d 399,1986.*

Lars-Anders Ågren case (2013) *Lars-Anders Ågren et al. vs. Sweden, CERD/C/102/D/54/2013.*

Larsen, P.B. (2020) "Contextualising Ratification and Implementation: A Critical Appraisal of ILO Convention 169 from a Social Justice Perspective," *The International Journal of Human Rights*, 24, pp. 94–111.

Law Society case (2019) *Law Society of South Afriuca and Others v President of the Republic of South Africa and Others 2019 (3) BCLR 329 (CC).*

Lhaka Honhat Association case (2020) *Indigenous Communities of the Lhaka Honhat (Our Land) Association v. Argentina. Merits, reparations and costs. Judgment of February 6, 2020. Series C No. 400.*

Lijphart, A. (1969) "Consociational Democracy," *World Politics*, 21, pp. 207–225.

Lizarazo-Rodriguez, L. and De Lombaerde, P. (2025) "Free, Prior, and Informed Consultation," in A. Marciano and R. Ramello (eds.) *Encyclopedia of Law and Economics*. New York: Springer, pp. 1–9.

Ljubljana Guidelines (2012) "The Ljubljana Guidelines on Integration of Diverse Societies." OSCE.

Lorca, A.B. and Marin, A.A. (2024) "Turning International Law against Indigenous Peoples." EUI Department of Law.

Lund Recommendations (1999) *The Lund Recommendations on the Effective Participation of National Minorities in Public Life*. The Hague: Organization for Security and Co-operation in Europe. Available at: https://www.osce.org/files/f/documents/0/9/32240.pdf (Accessed: November 21, 2022).

Mabo case (2) (1992) *Mabo v Queensland (No 2) [1992] HCA 23, (1992) 175 CLR 1.*

Macdonald-Smith, A. (2024) "'Damage has been done': Broader hit from Santos' Barossa gas case," *Financial Review*, 16 January.

Mackay, F. (2018) "The Case of the Kaliña and Lokono Peoples v. Suriname and the UN Declaration on the Rights of Indigenous Peoples: Convergence, Divergence and Mutual Reinforcement," *Erasmus Law Review*, April.

Mackay, F. (2022) *A Compilation of UN Treaty Body Jurisprudence, Special Procedures of the Human Rights Council, and the Advice of the Expert Mechanism on the Rights of Indigenous Peoples Volume IX*. Indigenous Peoples Rights International.

Macnab, A. (2020) "Indigenous Law Expert Explains how UNDRIP Advances the Law of Consultation and Consent," *Canadian Lawyer* [Preprint]. Available at: https://www.canadianlawyermag.com/practice-areas/indigenous/indigenous-law-expert-explains-how-undrip-advances-the-law-of-consultation-and-consent/330496 (Accessed: March 22, 2021).

Madras case (1951) *Madras v Champakam Dorairajan 1951 AIR SC 226.*

Maduwongga case (1997) *Maduwongga People [1997] NNTTA 31.*

Magazzini, T. (2024) "When ethnicity is 'national': mapping ethnic minorities in Europe's framework convention for the protection of national minorities," *Ethnic and Racial Studies*, 47, pp. 1812–1833.

Magno, C. (2013) "Free Prior and Informed Consent in the Philippines: Regulations and Realities," *OXFAM*. Available at: https://s3.amazonaws.com/oxfam-us/www/static/media/files/fpic-in-the-philippines-september-2013.pdf (Accessed: February 22, 1925).

Mahuika case (2000) *Mahuika v NZL (Human Rights Committee, UN doc CCPR/C/70/D/547/1993, 16 November 2000).*

Makonen, T. (2000) *Identity, difference and otherness: the concepts of "people", "indigenous people" and "minority" in international law*. Helsinki: Eric Castren Institute.

Makwanyane case (1995) *S v Makwanyane 1995 3 SA 391 (CC).*

Maledu case (2018) *Maledu v Itereleng Bakgatla Mineral Resources (Pty) Limited (CCT265/17) [2018] ZACC 41; 2019 (1) BCLR 53 (CC); 2019 (2) SA 1 (CC) (25 October 2018).*

Mallonee, L.D. (2015) "The growth of custom into law," *Virginia Law Register*, pp. 1–13.

Malloy, T.H. (2020) "Non-territorial Autonomy: Traditional and Alternative Practices," in W. Romans, I. Ulasiuk, and A.P. Thomsen (eds.) *Effective Participation of National Minorities and Conflict Prevention*. Leiden: Brill, pp. 105–122.

Malloy, T.H. and Caruso, U. (eds.) (2013) *Minorities, Their Rights, and the Monitoring of the European Framework Convention for the Protection of National Minorities: Essays in Honour of Rainer Hofmann*. Leiden: Marthinus Nijjhof.

Marine Produce case (2018) *Marine Produce Australia Ltd and Wester Australia v Mayala People [2018] NNTTA 28.*

Markandan, K.C. (1987) *Directive principles of state policy in the Indian Constitution*. Jalandhar: ABS Publications.

Martin, E. (2025) "Expectations for meaningful free, prior, and informed consent: an exploration by the Little Salmon/Carmacks First Nation," *The Extractive Industries and Society*, 23.

Mathiba, G. (2024) "The Incorporation of the FPIC Principle in South African Policy on Mining-Induced Displacements: Bottlenecks and Opportunities," *International Journal on Minority and Group Rights*, 31, pp. 327–349.

Matson case (2022) *Matson et al v Canada CEDAW/C/81/D/68/2014/ (2022).*

Maya IACHR case (2004) *Maya Indigenous Community of the Toledo District v Belize (Merits) (Inter-American Commission on Human Rights, Report No 40/04, Case No 12.053, 12 October 2004).*

Maya Peoples case (2021) *Indigenous Maya Kaqchikel Peoples of Sumpango vs. Guatemala*. Available at: https://www.corteidh.or.cr/docs/casos/articulos/seriec_440_esp.pdf (Accessed: June 15, 2022).

Mayelane case (2013) *Mayelane v Ngwenyama 2013 4 SA 415 (CC).*

Mazur, G. (2012) *Informed consent, proxy consent, and Catholic bioethics.* Heidelberg: Springer.

McCormack, D.J., Gulati, A. and Mangwani, J. (2018) "Informed consent: a global perspective," *Bone Joint Journal*, 100-B, pp. 687–692.

McCreery, R. (2012) "Promoting Indigenous-Led Economic Development: Why Parties should Concult the UNDRIP," *Indigenous Law Bulletin*, 8, pp. 16–19.

McCulloch, A. (2021) "Free, Prior, and Informed Consent: A Struggling International Principle," *Public Land and Resources Law Review*, 44, pp. 241–264.

McGarry, J., O'Leary, B. and Simeon, R. (2008) "Integration or Accommodation? The Enduring Debate in Conflict Regulation," in S. Choudhry (ed.) *Constitutional Design for Divided Societies.* Oxford: Oxford University Press, pp. 41–88.

McJannet case (2016) *McJannet v Special Broadcasting Services (2016) FCCA 2937.*

McNeil, L. (2021) "Has Constitutionalizing Aboriginal and Treaty Rights Made a Difference?," *British Columbia Studies*, pp. 56–83.

M.E.V., S.E.V., and B.I.V. case (2024) *M.E.V., S.E.V., and B.I.V. v Finland CRC No. 172/ 2022, 13 September 2024.*

Mileva, N. (2022) "The Role of Domestic Courts in the Interpretation of Customary International Law: How Can We Learn from Domestic Interpretive Practices?," in P. Merkouris, J. Kammerhofer, and N. Arajarvi (eds.) *The Theory, Practice, and Interpretation of Customary International Law.* Cambridge: Cambridge University Press, pp. 453–480.

Milirrpum case (1971) *Milirrpum v. Nabalco Pty Ltd (1971) 17 FLR 141 (27 April 1971) Supreme Court (NT).*

Minerva Hills case (1980) *Minerva Mills Ltd v Union of India AIR 1980 SC 1843.*

Mobile Concreting Solutions case (2022) *Mobile Concreting Solutions Pty Ltd & Another v Wintawari Guruma Aboriginal Corporation RNTBC [2022] NNTTA 56.*

Morales, M. and Pérez-Cosgaya, T. (2025) "The Impact of Socio-Political Cleavages on Constitutional Referendums: The Case of Chile 2022," *Politics and Governance*, 13, pp. 1–22.

Moriarty case (2024) *Moriarty v Nye [2024] NSWCCA 116.*

Motoc, A. (2005) "Standard Setting: Legal commentary on the concept free, prior and informed consent E/CN.4/Sub.2/AC.4/2005/WP.1." UN Commissioner on Human Rights.

Mukaddam, F. (2024) *Muslim women between community and individual rights : legal pluralism and marriage in South Africa.* Cham: Springer.

Mukwevho, N. (2022) "The evolution and development of the principle of free, prior and informed consent in South Africa," *South African Journal on Human Rights*, 38, pp. 144–162.

Munkara case (2024) *Munkara v Santos NA Barossa Pty Ltd (No 3) [2024] FCA 9*. Available at: https://www.judgments.fedcourt.gov.au/judgments/Judgments/fca/single/2024/2024fca0009 (Accessed: January 16, 2024).

Munkara consent orders cost (2024) *SIMON MUNKARA and others v SANTOS NA BAROSSA PTY LTD VID907/2023(28 November 2024)*. Available at: https://www.comcourts.gov.au/file/Federal/P/VID907/2023/3967603/event/32048018/document/2398391 (Accessed: December 2, 2024).

Murphy case (2021) *Australian Potash Limited and Another v Kalman Murphy & Ors on behalf of Waturta [2021] NNTTA 24*. Available at: http://www.nntt.gov.au/searchRegApps/FutureActs/FA%20Determination%20Documents/WA/FutureActsDeterminations/2021/June/WF2021_0002-0004%2002062021.pdf (Accessed: July 2, 2021).

Murray, P.M. (1990) "The history of informed consent," *The Iowa Orthopaedic Journal*, 10, pp. 104–109.

Murray Rivers Indigenous People case (2025) *Murray Lower Darling Rivers Indigenous Nations v Commonwealth [2025] FCA 1029*.

Nandini, K. (2013) "Informed consent: Past and present," *Perspectives in Clinical Research*, 4, pp. 21–25.

Natanson case (1960) *Natanson v. Kline, 350 P2d 1093, Kansas, 1960*.

National Native Title Tribunal (2020) "What is the right to negotiate?" NNTT. Available at: http://www.nntt.gov.au/futureacts/Pages/Negotiation.aspx#:~:text=The%20right%20to%20negotiate%20is,future%20acts%20are%20lawfully%20done.&text=The%20right%20to%20negotiate%20gives,reaching%20agreement%20about%20the%20act.

National Textile Workers' Union case (1983) *National Textile Workers' Union v PR Ramakrishan AIR 1983 SC 75*.

Native Title Act (1993) *National Native Title Act, 1993*. Available at: https://www.legislation.gov.au/Details/C2019C00054 (Accessed: May 23, 1921).

Native Title Map (2024) "Native title determinations and claimant applications." NNTT. Available at: https://digital-classroom.nma.gov.au/images/national-native-title-tribunal-map-australia (Accessed: October 3, 2024).

Neate, G. (2006) "Native Title Agreement-Making: Law and Practice and Learning from Experience," in *AMPLA Yearbook 2006: Incorporating Papers Presented at the Thirtieth Annual AMPLA Conference*. Melbourne: AMPLA, pp. 142–179.

Neo, J.L. (2020) "State legal pluralism and religious courts," in P.S. Berman (ed.) *The Oxford handbook of global legal pluralism*. Oxford: Oxford University Press, pp. 879–900.

Nesseby case (2018) *Nesseby Regional Society v Finnmark Estate Agency HR-2018-456-P, (case no. 2017/860)*.

Newman, D. (2020) "Interpreting FPIC in UNDRIP," *International Journal on Minority and Group Rights*, 27, pp. 233–250.

Newman, D. (2025) "Implications of International Indigenous Rights Law for State Power in the Artic," in C. Holroyd and K. Coates (eds.) *The Palgrave Handbook of Arctic Policy and Politics*. Springer, pp. 463–476.

Nicaragua case (1986) *Nicaragua v USA ICJ Rep 14, 98 (1986)*.

Njamal case (1996) *Western Australia/Johnson Taylor on behalf of the Njamal people/ Garry Ernest Mullan [1996] NNTTA 34*.

Noongar Recognition Act (2016) *Noongar (Koorah, Nitja, Boordahwan) (Past, Present, Future) Recognition Act 2016*. Available at: https://www.legislation.wa.gov.au/legislation/statutes.nsf/main_mrtitle_13755_homepage.html (Accessed: July 4, 2020).

North Ganalanja case (1996) *North Ganalanja Aboriginal Corporation v Queensland (1996) 185 CLR 595 at 617*.

North Sea Continental Shelf cases (1969) *North Sea Continental Shelf cases (Federal Republic of Germany v Denmark; Federal Republic of Germany v Netherlands) (Judgment) [1969] ICJ Rep 3*.

Nuclear Weapons case (1996) *Legality of the Threat or Use of Nuclear Weapons, Advisory Opinion, I.C.J. Reports 1996, p. 226, 18*.

Nut, R. (2015) "Indigenous Rights vs Minority Rights: The Case of the Norwegian Sami," *Research and Science Today*, pp. 99–105.

Observatory Civic Association case (2023) *Observatory Civic Association and another v Trustees, Liesbeek Leisure Properties Trust and others 2023 (1) SA (WCC)*.

OECD Guidance for Agriculture (2016) "OECD-FAO Guidance for Responsible Agricultural Supply Chains of 2016." Available at: https://mneguidelines.oecd.org/oecd-fao-guidance.pdf (Accessed: February 15, 1925).

OECD Guidelines (2023) "OECD Guidelines for Multinational Enterprises on Responsible Business Conduct (2023, OECD Publishing)." Available at: https://api.research-repository.uwa.edu.au/ws/portalfiles/portal/336910632/southalan_2023_increasing.pdf.

OECD NCPs Guidelines (2024) "What are National Contact Points for Responsible Business Conduct?" Available at: https://mneguidelines.oecd.org/ncps/what-are-ncps-for-rbc.htm (Accessed: October 23, 2024).

OECD Peer Reviews (2024) "National Contact Point Peer Reviews." Available at: https://mneguidelines.oecd.org/ncppeerreviews.htm (Accessed: December 12, 2024).

O'Faircheallaigh, C. (2016) *Negotiations in the Indigenous World, Aboriginal Peoples and the Extractive Industry in Australia and Canada*. London: Routledge.

Ogoni case (2001) *Serac and CESR v Nigeria Communication No. 155/96 (2001); 10 HRR 287 (2003)*.

Olephiri Franklin Igoma of Uwema Aminigboko Community case (2021) *Olephiri Franklin Igoma of Uwema Aminigboko Community v. Daewoo E&C, Dawoo Nigeria Korea NCP 28 Seprember 2021.*

Oliveri, V. *et al* (2022) "The Juukan Gorge destruction: a case study in stakeholder-driven and shared values approach to cultural heritage protection," *Journal of Cultural Heritage Management and Development* [Preprint].

Orissa Mining case (2013) *Orissa Mining Corporation v. Ministry of Environment and Forest and Others.* Available at: https://indiankanoon.org/doc/109648742/ (Accessed: August 2, 2022).

Osman case (2025) *Osman and 164 Others v Northern Rangelands Trust and Others 2025 KEELC 99.*

Pabai case (2025) *Pabai v Commonwealth of Australia (No 2) [2025] FCA 796.*

Paciocco case (2015) *Paciocco v Australia and New Zealand Banking Group Limited [2015] FCAFC 50.*

Papillon, M., Leclair, J. and Leydet, D. (2020) "Free, Prior and Informed Consent: Between Legal Ambiguity and Political Agency," *International Journal on Minority and Group Rights*, 20, pp. 223–232.

Paradise Park case (2023) *Residents of Paradise Park v Magna Business Services (Pty) Ltd and another 2024 JDR 0141 (WCC).*

Parliament Juukan Gorge (2020) *Juukan Gorge Inquiry to Question Rio Tinto.* Canberra. Available at: https://www.aph.gov.au/About_Parliament/House_of_Representatives/About_the_House_News/Media_Releases/Juukan_Gorge_inquiry_to_question_BHP (Accessed: March 28, 2021).

Passas, N. (2005) "Lawful but awful: 'legal corporate crimes,'" *Journal of Behavioural and Experimental Economics*, 34, pp. 771–786.

Pathfinder Exploration case (2022) *Pathfinder Exploration Pty Ltd v Malarngowem Aboriginal Corporation RNTBC [2022] NNTTA 52.*

Pavel, C.E. (2021) *Law beyond the state.* Oxford: Oxford University Press.

PCIJ-Greco-Bulgarian case (1930) *Greco-Bulgarian "Communities."* Available at: https://jusmundi.com/en/document/decision/en-greco-bulgarian-communities-advisory-opinion#decision_1874 (Accessed: February 17, 2023).

Perry, M. and Lloyd, S. (eds.) (2018) *Australian Native Title Law.* Sydney: LawBook Co.

Petane case (1988) *State v Petane, Supreme Court decision, 1988 3 SA 51 (C), ILDC 1348 (ZA 1987), 3rd November 1987, South Africa; Supreme Court of Appeal [SCA].*

Petersen, N. (2017) "The International Court of Justice and the Judicial Politics of Identifying Customary International Law," *European Journal of International Law*, 28, pp. 357–386.

Petkar, I. (2017) *Conceptualizing Free, Prior and Informed Consent: Interpreting Interpretations of FPIC.* Master of Arts. Columbia University.

Phillips, A. (2015) "Historical Background on the Declaration," in U. Caruso and R. Hofmann (eds.) *The United Nations Declaration on Minorities: An Academic Account on the Occasion of its 20th Anniversary* (*1992–2012*). Leiden: Brill, pp. 3–18.

Pilki case (2015) *Western Australia v Pilki* [*2015*] *FCAFC 186*.

Pirie, F. (2023) "Beyond pluralism: a descriptive approach to non-state law," *Jurisprudence*, 14, pp. 1–21.

Placer case (2000) *Placer* (*Granny Smith*) *v Western Australia* [*2000*] *NNTT 75*.

Poma Poma case (2002) *Ángela Poma Poma v. Peru, CCPR/C/95/D/1457/2006*.

Port Elizabeth Municipality case (2005) *Port Elizabeth Municipality v Various Occupiers 2005 1 SA 217* (*CC*).

Posner, E.A. and de Figueiredo, M.F.P. (2005) "Is the International Court of Justice Biased," *Journal of Legal Studies*, 34, pp. 599–630.

Praet, P. (2018) "From legal pluralism towards plural (il)legalities," in M. Luts-Sootak et al. (eds.) *Legal pluralism – Cui Bono?* Tartu: University of Tartu Press, pp. 30–53.

Prince case (1944) *Prince v. Massachusetts, 321 US 158, 1944*.

Prince case (2002) *Prince v President of the Law Society of the Cape of Good Hope* (*CCT36/00*) [*2002*] *ZACC 1; 2002* (*2*) *SA 794; 2002* (*3*) *BCLR 231* (*25 January 2002*).

Project Sepik case (2023) *Independent Examiner Complaint submitted by Project Sepik and Jubilee Australia Research Centre on behalf of affected Sepik River communities against PanAust Limited* (*Final Statetment, 3 October 2023*) *Australian National Contact Point for Responsible Business Conduct, Department of Treasury*. Available at: https://ausncp.gov.au/sites/default/files/2023-09/29-ausncp-final-statement.pdf (Accessed: October 9, 2024).

Promotion of Administrative Justice (2000) *Promotion of Administrative Justice Act No 3 2000*. Available at: https://www.justice.gov.za/legislation/acts/2000-003.pdf (Accessed: June 5, 2024).

Protection against invasion case (2021) *Articulação dos Povos Indígenas do Brasil* (*APIB*) *ADPF 709 TPI-REF*.

Public Works case (1959) *Secretary Government Public Works v Adoni Ginning Factory AIR 1959 AP 838*.

Pulp Mill case (2006) *Pulp Mills on the River Uruguay* (*Argentina v. Uruguay*) (*Order on the Request for the Indication of Provision Measures* [*2006*] *ICJ Rep 135* (*2006*).

Pulver, F. (2022) *The implementation of free, prior and informed consent and Indigenous People's Rights under the OECD Guidelines for Multinational Enterprises*. Zurich: EIZ Publishing.

Quera Aboriginal Community case (2001) *Quera Aboriginal Community and Aguas Calientes – Cochinoca People v. Jujuy province, Judgment of September 14, 2001*.

Rauso, A. (2024) "$9 million green wipeout," *West Australian*, 29 November.

Rautenbach, C. (2021) "The phenomenon of legal pluralism," in C. Rautenbach (ed.) *Introduction to Legal Pluralism in South Africa*. 6th ed. Durban: LexisNexis, pp. 3–18.

Rautenbach, C. (2024) "State intervention in the customary law of succession in South Africa: what remains of customary norms in the 'Rainbow Nation'?," in A. Diala and C. Rautenbach (eds.) *Reimagining Legal Pluralism in Africa: Balancing Indigenous, State, and Religious Laws*. Leiden: Brill, pp. 21–61.

Ravna, O. (2020) "The Duty to Consult the Sámi in Norwegian Law," *Artic Review on Law and Politics* [Preprint].

Re T case (1992) *Re T (Adult: Refusal of Treatment) [1992] 4 All ER 649 at 669.*

Ready, K.J. (1980) "Fundamentalness of fundamental rights and directive pricinples of state policy in the Indian Constitution," *Journal of the Indian Law Institute*, 22, pp. 399–407.

Refah Partisi case (2003) *Refah Partisi (the Welfare Party) and Others v. Turkey [GC] – 41340/98, 41342/98, 41343/98 Judgment 13.2.2003 [GC].*

Reus-Smit, C. (2013) *Individual Rights and the Making of the International System*. London: Cambridge University Press.

Richman case (2025) *William Robert Richman v Kalman Murphy and Ors on behalf of the Waturta Native Title Claim Group [2025] NNTTA 4.*

Right of Passage case (1960) *Case concerning the Right of Passage over Indian Territory (Merits), Judgement of 12 April 1960, I.C.J. reports 1960, 6.*

Rio Tinto Juukan Gorge (2025) *Juukan Gorge*. Available at: https://www.riotinto.com/en/news/trending-topics/juukan-gorge (Accessed: January 28, 2025).

Rio/PKKP Agreement (2025) "PKKP and Rio Tinto sign Landmark Agreement." Available at: https://www.pkkp.org.au/pkkp-and-rio-tinto-sign-landmark-agreement/ (Accessed: June 3, 2025).

Rita Dempster case (1999) *Rita Dempster on behalf of the Southern Noongar People v Western Australia [1999] NNTTA 235.*

Rodgers case (1978) *Rodgers v. Irish Transport and General Workers Union 1978 WJSC-HC 922, [1978] ILRM 51, [1978] 3 JIC 1501.*

Rogers case (1993) *Rogers v Whitaker [1993] 16 BMLR 148 (High Court of Australia).*

Rolfe, J. (2024) "Aboriginal and Torres Strait Heritage Protection Act applicaitons mainly target resources projects and not renewables," *Daily Telegraph*, 19 December.

Rombouts, S.J. (2014) *Having a Say: Indigenous Peoples, International Law and Free, Prior and Informed Consent*. New York: Wolf Legal Publishers.

Rombouts, S.J. (2017) "The Evolution of Indigenous Peoples' Consultation Rights under the ILO and U.N. Regimes," *Stanford Journal of International Law*, 53, pp. 167–192.

Rombouts, S.J. (2018) "Consultation and Consent Norms under ILO Convention No. 169 and the UN Declaration on the Rights of Indigenous Peoples Compared."

EMRIP expert seminar on free, prior and informed consent, Tilburg. Available at: https://www.ohchr.org/Documents/Issues/IPeoples/EMRIP/FPIC/RomboutsSJ.pdf (Accessed: April 2, 1921).

Roucek, J.S. (1929) *The Working of the Minorities System under the League of Nations.* PhD. New York University.

Ruggie, J. and Nelson, T. (2015) "Human Rights and the OECD Guidelines for Multinational Enterprises: Normative Innovations and Implementation Challenges: Corporate Social Responsibility Initiative Working Paper 66."

Ryan case (1965) *Ryan v Attorney General IR (1965) 294.*

Ryngaert, C.M.J. and Hora Siccama, D.W. (2018) "Ascertaining Customary International Law: An Inquiry into the Methods Used by Domestic Courts," *Neth Int Law Rev,* 65, pp. 1–25.

Sachs, A. (2024) "Epilogue," in A. Diala and C. Rautenbach (eds.) *Reimagining Legal Pluralism in Africa: Balancing Indigenous, State, and Religious Laws.* Leiden: Brill, pp. 474–494.

Sajjan Singh case (1965) *Sajjan Singh v State of Rajasthan AIR 1965 SC 845.*

Sámi mining case (2024) *E/C.12/76/D/289/2022: Views adopted by the Committee under the Optional Protocol to the International Covenant on Economic, Social and Cultural Rights, concerning communications Nos. 251/2022 and 289/2022.* Available at: https://um.fi/documents/35732/0/TSS%20251-2022%20and%20289-2022.pdf/b3794529-3b02-769b-955e-34227cdd9f04?t=1728548574250 (Accessed: November 8, 2024).

Sámi Parliament as amended (2025) *The Act amending the Act on the Sámi Parliament (414/2025).*

Samsung case (2024) *Suipressed v PT Inecda (a subsidiary of S&G Biofuel Pte. Ltd) RSPO/2021/06/SW.*

Sanchez, J.C.O. (2015) "The Roles and Powers of the oecd National Contact Points Regarding Complaints on an Alleged Breach of the oecd Guidelines for Multinational Enterprises by a Transnational Corporation," *Nordic Journal of International Law,* 84, pp. 89–126.

Sanjiev Coke case (1983) *Sanjiev Coke Mfg Co v M/S Bharat Coking Coal Ltd AIR 1983 SC 239.*

Santos case (2022) *Santos NSW Pty Ltd and Another v Gomeroi People and Another* [2022] *NNTTA 74.*

Sara case (2017) *Norway v. Jovsset Ánte Iversen Sara HR-2017-2428-A (case no. 2017/981).*

Saramaka case (2007) *Saramaka, Preliminary Objections, Merits, Reparations and Costs, Judgement, Inter-Am. Ct. H.R. (ser.C) No 172,* (Nov. *28, 2007*).

Sarela, A.I. (2024) "Consent for Medical Treatment: What is 'Reasonable'?," *Health Care Analysis,* 32, pp. 47–62.

Sarivaara, E., Määttä, K. and Uusiautti, S. (2013) "Who is indigenous? : definitions of indigeneity," *Eurasian Multidisciplinary Forum*, pp. 369–378.

Saugeen First Nation case (2017) *Saugeen First Nation v. Ontario (MNRF), 2017 ONSC 3456.*

Sawhoyamaxa Community case (2006) *Sawhoyamaxa Indigenous Community vs. Paraguay, Judgment of March 29, 2006.*

Schoendorff case (1914) *Schoendorff v. Society of New York Hospital, 211 N.Y. 215,105 N.E. 92,1914.*

Seinecke, R. (2018) "What is legal pluralism and what is it good for?," in M. Luts-Sootak et al. (eds.) *Legal pluralism – Cui Bono?* Tartu: University of Tartu Press, pp. 13–29.

Sengadi case (2019) *Sengadi v Tsambo 2019 (4) SA 50 (GJ) and Tsambo v Sengadi* [*2020*] *ZASCA 46.*

Sesana case (2006) *Sesana and Others v Attorney General (52/2002)* [*2006*] *BWHC 1.*

Sharma, S.K. (1984) *Justice and social order in India.* New Delhi: Intellectual Pub. House.

Shilubana case (2008) *Shilubana and Others v Nwamitwa (CCT 03/07)* [*2008*] *ZACC 9; 2008 (9) BCLR 914 (CC); 2009 (2) SA 66 (CC) (4 June 2008).*

Sibisi, S. (2024) "Problems with Waiving the Handing-Over of the Bride in Customary Marriages," *Obiter*, pp. 921–935.

Sidaway case (1985) *Sidaway v Bethlem Royal Hospital* [*1985*] *1 AC 871 (HL).*

Slack, M., Fillios, M. and Fullagar, R. (2009) "Aboriginal Settlement during the LGM at Brockman, Pilbara Region, Western Australia," *Archaeology in Oceania*, 44, pp. 32–39.

Slack, M., Law, W. and Gliganic, L. (2020) "The early occupation of the Eastern Pilbara revisited: New radiometric chronologies and archaeological results from Newman Rockshelter and Newman Orebody XXIX," *Quaternary Science Reviews*, 236. Available at: https://doi.org/10.1016/j.quascirev.2020.106240.

Sonia Bhalai case (1981) *Sonia Bhalai v State of Andra Pradesh AIR 1981 SC 1274.*

South West Africa cases (1966) *Ethiopia v South Africa: Liberia v South Africa Second Phase 1966 ICJ Rep 169*

Southalan, J. and Fardin, J. (2019) "Free, prior and informed consent: how and from whom? An Australian analogue," *Journal of Energy & Natural Resources Law*, 37, pp. 365–388.

Southeast Alaska Conservation Council case (2020) *Southeast Alaska Conservation Council v Imperial Metals NCP Canada (Final Statement, 8* May 2020).

State Forest case (2012) *State Forest case No. 35/PUU-X/2012.*

State of Bombay case (1951) *State of Bombay v Balsara AIR 1951 SC 318.*

State of Gujarat case (2005) *State of Gujarat v. Mirzapur Moti Kasab Jamat 2005 (8) SCC 534.*

State of Tamil Nadu case (1984) *State of Tamil Nadu v Abu Kavier Bai AIR 1984 SC 725.*

Statute of ICJ (1945) *Statute of the International Court of Justice.*

Stavenhagen Report, R. (2003) "Report of the Special Rapporteur on the Situation of Human Rights and Fundamental Freedoms of Indigenous Peoples. (2003). UN Doc. E/CN/4/ 2003/90." UN Commission on Human Rights. Available at: https://www.refworld.org/reference/themreport/unchr/2003/en/31422 (Accessed: November 22, 2024).

Steward, C. and Lynch, A. (2003) "Undue influence, consent and medical treatment," *Journal of the Royal Society of Medicine*, 98, pp. 598–601.

Strategic Minerals case (2003) *Strategic Minirals Corporation NL/Allan Kyuna and Ors on behalf of Woolgar Group/Queensland* [2003] *NNTTA 83.*

Strickland case (1998) *Strickland v Minister of Lands (WA) (1998) 85 FCR 303.*

Strydom, H.A. (2021) "International treaty-based protection of minorities: selected cases of the UN Human Rights Committee," in B. De Villiers et al. (eds.) *Litigating the Rights of Minorities and Indigenous Peoples in Domestic and International Courts*. Leiden: Brill, pp. 219–238.

Subramaniam Balaji case (2013) *S. Subramaniam Balaji v. State of T.N., (2013) 9 SCC 659.*

Survival International case (2009) *Survival International v Vedanta Resources Plc., NCP UK (Final Statement, 25 September 2009.*

Sustaining the Wild Coast case (2024) *Minister of Mineral Resources and Energy and Others v Sustaining the Wild Coast NPC and Others (Case no 58/2023; 71/2023; 351/ 2023)* [2024] *ZASCA 84 (3 June 2024).*

Sutherland, N.M. (1987) "The Huguenots and the Edict of Nantes 1598–1629.," in I. Scouloudi (ed.) *Huguenots in Britain and their French Background, 1550–1800*. London: Palgrave Macmillan, pp. 158–174.

Talmon, S. (2005) "Determining Customary International Law: The ICJ's Methodology between Induction, Deduction and Assertion," *EJIL*, 26, pp. 417–428.

Tamanaha, B. (1993) "The folly of the 'social scientific' concept of legal plurality," *Journal of law and society*, 20, pp. 192–215.

Tamil Nadu case (1984) *State of Tamil Nadu v L Abu Kavier Bai AIR 1984 SC 725.*

Tan, N.Q., Truong, L.T. and Van K'Tip, N.T. (2010) *Evaluation and Verification of the Free, Prior and Informed Consent Process under the UN-REDD Programme in Lam Dong Province, Vietnam*. Hanoi: Centre for People and Forests.

Taromenane case (2024) *Pueblos Indigenas Tagairi y Taromenane v Equador IACHR, 4 September 2024, Series No. 537.*

Tas, L. (2013) "One state, plural options: Kurds in the UK," *Journal of Legal Pluralism and unofficial law*, 45, pp. 167–189.

Tauli-Corpuz, V. (2019) *Autonomy Report of the Special Rapporteur on the rights of indigenous peoples*. A/74/149. New York: United Nations. Available at: https://www.undocs.org/A/74/149 (Accessed: May 2, 2022).

Taylor case (1996) *Minister of Mines (WA) v Taylor (1996) 134 FLR 211.*

Taylor, L. (2023) "Paul Keating says voice referendum was 'wrong fight' and has 'ruined the game' for a treaty," *Guardian*, 27 October. Available at: https://www.theguardian.com/australia-news/2023/oct/27/paul-keating-says-voice-referendum-was-wrong-fight-and-has-ruined-the-game-for-a-treaty (Accessed: April 10, 2024).

Taylor, P.M. (2020) *A Commentary on the International Covenant on Civil and Political Rights The UN Human Rights Committee's Monitoring of ICCPR Rights*. London: Cambridge University Press.

Teubner, G. (2012) *Constitutional fragments, societal constitutionalism and globalization*. Oxford: Oxford University Press.

Teubner, G. and Bukovina, G. (1997) "Legal pluralism in the world-society," in G. Teubner (ed.) *Global law without a state*. Dartsmouth: Aldershot, pp. 3–28.

Thirlway, H. (2005) "The Law and Procedure of the International Court of Justice 1960-1989," *British Yearbook of International Law*, 76, pp. 116–237.

Thornberry, P. (1991) *International Law and the Rights of Minorities*. Oxford: Clarendon Press.

Tiina Sanila-Aikio case (2018) *Tiina Sanila-Aikio vs. Finland, CCPR/C/124/D/2668/2015.*

Timber Creek appeal (2017) *Timber Creek Appeal (2017) 256 FCR 478.*

Timber Creek High Court appeal (2019) *Northern Territory v Mr A. Griffiths (deceased) and Lorraine Jones on behalf of the Ngaliwurru and Nungali Peoples [2019] HCA 7, 13 March 2019.*

Tipakalippa case (2022) *Santos NA Barossa Pty Ltd v Tipakalippa [2022] FCAFC 193.*

Toki, V. and Raman, D. (2024) "Indigenous and minority activism under the United Nations," *International Journal on Minority and Group Rights*, pp. 1–19.

Tomaselli, A. (2016) *Indigenous Peoples and Their Right to Political Participation: : International Law Standards and their Application in Latin America*. Baden-Baden: Nomos.

Tomaselli, A. (2017) "The Right to Political Participation of Indigenous Peoples: A Holistic Approach," *International Journal on Minority and Group Rights*, 24, pp. 390–427.

Tomaselli, A. (2019) *Indigenous Peoples and Their Right to Political Participation*. Baden-Baden: Nomos.

Tomaselli, A. and Cittadino, F. (2021) "Land, Consultation and Participation Rights of Indigenous Peoples in the Recent Jurisdictions of the Inter-American Court of Human Rights: The Cases of Sarayaku v. Ecuador and Kalina and Lokono v. Suriname," in B. De Villiers et al. (eds.) *Litigating the Rights of Minorities and Indigenous Peoples in Domestic and International Courts*. Leiden: Brill, pp. 149–179.

Tomlinson, K. (2019) "Indigenous rights and extractive resource projects: negotiations over policy and implementation," *The International Journal of Human Rights*, 23, pp. 882–896.

Traditional Owners – Nyiyaparli People case (2009) *Traditional Owners – Nyiyaparli People and Minister of Health, Indigeous Affairs* [2009] *WASAT 71.*

Tripathi, S.M. (2016) *Fundamental Rights and Directive Principles in India.* Hamburg: Anchor Acedemic Publishing.

Tsilhqot'in Nation case (2014a) *Tsilhqot'in Nation v. British Columbia 2014 SCC 44.*

Tsilhqot'in Nation case (2014b) *Tsilhqot'in Nation v. British Columbia 2014 SCC 44.*

Tsleil-Waututh Nation case (2019) *Tsleil-Waututh Nation v Canada (Attorney General), 2019 CanLIIDocs 4635.*

Tusseau, G. (2020) "Debating legal pluralism and constitutionalism: new trajectories for legal theory in the global age," in G. Tusseau (ed.) *Debating legal pluralism and constitutionalism.* Cham: Springer, pp. 1–92.

UN Declaration on Minorities (1992) "United Nations Declaration on the Rights of Persons Belonging to National or Ethnic, Religious and Linguistic Minorities General Assembly resolution 47/135." United Nations. Available at: https://www.ohchr.org/EN/ProfessionalInterest/Pages/Minorities.aspx (Accessed: June 16, 2020).

UN Declaration on Minorities (1993) "Declaration on the Rights of Persons belonging to National or Ethnic, Religious and Linguistic Minorities :: resolution /: adopted by the General Assembly." UN. Available at: https://digitallibrary.un.org/record/158458 (Accessed: March 1, 2023).

UN Food and Agricultural Organisation (2016) "Free Prior and Informed Consent: An indigenous peoples' right and a good practice for local communities: Manual for Project Practitioners." United Nations. Available at: https://openknowledge.fao.org/server/api/core/bitstreams/8a4bc655-3cf6-44b5-b6bb-ad2aeede5863/content#:~:text=FPIC%20is%20a%20principle%20protected,%2C%20social%20and%20cultural%20development%27. (Accessed: September 2, 2025).

UN Human Rights Committee (2019) *Right to Vote in Elections to the Sami Parliament.* CCPR/C/124/D/2668/2015. Geneva: Human Rights Committee.

UN International Law Commission (2018) "Draft conclusions on the identification of customary international law, with commentaries." United Nations. Available at: https://legal.un.org/ilc/texts/instruments/english/commentaries/1_13_2018.pdf (Accessed: July 12, 2022).

UN Resolution (2004) "Resolution adopted by the General Assembly on 22 December 2003 A/Res/58/182." United Nations General Assembly.

UN: UNDRIP after 14 years (2021) "Adoption of the United Nations Declaration on the Rights of Indigenous Peoples: 14 years later," *United Nations: Department of Economic and Social Affairs Indigenous People*, 13 September. Available at: https://www.un.org/development/desa/indigenouspeoples/news/2021/09/adoption-of-the-united-nations-declaration-on-the-rights-of-indigenous-peoples-14-years-later / (Accessed: November 12, 2024).

UNDRIP (2007) "United Nations Declaration on the Rights of Indigenous People." Available at: https://www.un.org/development/desa/indigenouspeoples/declaration-on-the-rights-of-indigenous-peoples.html. (Accessed: September 7, 2020).

UN-Experts (2022) *Comprehensive anti-discrimination legislation must be a priority, say UN experts ahead of Universal Declaration anniversary*. UNHRC. Available at: https://www.ohchr.org/en/statements/2022/12/comprehensive-anti-discrimination-legislation-must-be-priority-say-un-experts (Accessed: February 21, 2022).

UNHCR (no date) *Minorities and Indigenous Peoples*. UNHCR. Available at: https://www.unhcr.org/en-au/minorities-and-indigenous-peoples.html (Accessed: May 15, 2022).

UNHRC – Minority Rights (2010) *Minority Rights: International Standards and Guidance for Implementation*. HR/PUB/10/3. New York: UNHRC. Available at: https://www.ohchr.org/documents/publications/minorityrights_en.pdf (Accessed: May 12, 2022).

United Nations Implementing UNDRIP (2019) *United Nations, State of the World's Indigenous Peoples: Implementing the United Nations Declaration on the Rights of Indigenous Peoples*. New York: United Nations.

United States nations in Morocco case (1952) *Case concerning rights of nationals of the United States of America in Morocco, Judgement of 27 August 1952, I.L.J. Reports 1952, 176.*

Unnikrishnan case (1993) *Unnikrishnan v. State of AP (1993) SCR (1) 594.*

Ure case (2016) *Ure v Commonwealth (2016) 236 FCR 458.*

Venice Commission (1994) *The Protection of Minorities*. CDL-STD(1994)009. Strasbourg: Venice Commission.

Vicufia, F. (2005) "Customary International Law in a Global Community: Tailor Made?," *Estudios Internacionales*, 148, pp. 21–39.

Vienna Convention (1969) *Vienna Convention on the Law of Treaties.*

Walley case (1996) *Walley v Western Australia (1996) 137 ALR 561.*

Ward case (2002) *Western Australia v Ward (2002) 213 CLR 1; 191 ALR 2.*

Weis, L.K. (2017) "Constitutional Directive Principles," *Oxford Journal of Legal Studies*, 37, pp. 916–945.

Weller, M. (ed.) (2005) *The Rights of Minorities: A Commentary on the European Framework Convention for the Protection of National Minorities*. Oxford, New York: Oxford University Press (Oxford Commentaries on International Law).

Western Sahara case (1975) *Advisory Opinion on Western Sahara (62) (1975) ICJR*

WGIP Principles (1984) "World Council of Indigenous Peoples Declaration of Principles." General Assembly of the WCIP. Available at: https://www.hawaiianperspec

tives.org/2016/09/13/world-council-indigenous-peoples-declaration-principles-circa-1984/ (Accessed: December 12, 2024).

Wiessner, S. (2008) "Indigenous sovereignty: a reassessment in light of the UN declration on the rights of indigenous peoples," *Vanderbilt Journal of Transnational Law*, pp. 1141–1176.

Wild Coast appeal case (2024) *Minister of Mineral Resources and Energy and Others v Sustaining the Wild Coast NPC and Others (Case no 58/2023; 71/2023; 351/2023) [2024] ZASCA 84 (3 June 2024).*

WMC case (1999) *WMC Resources v Western Australia [1999] NNTTA 230.*

Wohlberg, M. (2016) "Fully Adopting UNDRIP: Minister Bennett's Speech at the United Nations." United Nations, 11 May.

Woodman, G.R. (1999) "The idea of legal pluralism," in B. Dupret, M. Berger, and L. al-Zwaini (eds.) *Legal pluralism in the Arab world.* Amsterdam: Kluwer.

World Bank (2016) "Review and Update of the World Bank Safeguard Policies." World Bank. Available at: https://consultations.worldbank.org/consultation/review-and-update-world-bank-safeguard-policies (Accessed: May 7, 2021).

Wright, C. and Tomaselli, A. (eds.) (2019) *The Prior Consultation of Indigenous Peoples in Latin America: Inside the Implementation Gap.* London: Routledge.

Yafee, N. (2018) "Indigenous consent: a self-determination perspective," *Melbourne Journal of International Law*, 19, pp. 1–47.

Yakovleva, N., Gavrilyeva, T.N. and Makarov, A.I. (2023) "Free prior informed consent in the extractive industry: Approaches to involving Indigenous peoples in decision-making in Russia," *Journal of Environmental Management*, 344.

Yanner case (1999) *Yanner v Eaton (1999) 201 CLR 351; 166 ALR 258.*

Yong Vui Kong case (2010) *Yong Vui Kong v. Public Prosecutor*, [2010] *3 S.L.R. 489* [2010] *SGCA 20 (Supreme Court of Singapore – Court of Appeal, 14* May *2010*).

Yorta Yorta (HCA) case (2002) *Yorta Yorta v Victoria* [2002] *HCA 58;* (2002) *214 CLR 422.*

Yunupingu case (2023) *Yunupingu on behalf of the Gumatj Clan or Estate Group v Commonwealth of Australia* [2023] *FCAFC 75* (22 May *2023*).

Yunupingu appeal case (2025) *Commonwealth of Australia v Yunupingu* [2025] *HCA 6.*

Yupsanis, A. (2011) "The International Labour Organisation and its Contribution to the Protection of the Rights of Indigenous Peoples," *Canadian Yearbook of International Law*, 49, pp. 117–176.

Zillmann, B. and Moffatt, A. (2025) "FPIC in focus: implications of a recent Canadian Federal Court decision for Australian stakeholders," 10 April. Available at: https://www.allens.com.au/insights-news/insights/2025/04/fpic-in-focus-implications-of-a-recent-canadian-federal-court-decision-for-australian-stakeholders/ (Accesse d: June 21, 2025).

Index

 | HTTPS://DOI.ORG/10.1163/9789004724792-013

www.ingramcontent.com/pod-product-compliance
Lightning Source LLC
LaVergne TN
LVHW011216150926
848065LV00003B/27
* 9 7 8 9 0 0 4 7 2 4 7 8 5 *